THE
EXECUTIVE
COURSE

THE EXECUTIVE COURSE

Eleven Business Experts Tell The Corporate Leaders of Tomorrow What They Need to Know Today

Edited by **Gayton E. Germane**

Stanford University
Graduate School of Business

 Addison-Wesley Publishing Company, Inc.

Reading, Massachusetts • Menlo Park, California • New York
Don Mills, Ontario • Wokingham, England • Amsterdam • Bonn
Sydney • Singapore • Tokyo • Madrid • Bogotá
Santiago • San Juan

Library of Congress Cataloging-in-Publication Data
Main entry under title:

The Executive course.

   Includes index.
Contents: Step one: connect / John B. Fery — Marketing
management / Richard P. Bagozzi — Financial management /
James C. Van Horne — [etc.]
   1. Industrial management — Addresses, essays,
lectures.   I. Germane, Gayton E.
HD31.E863   1986   658.4   85-13453
ISBN 0–201–11553–0
ISBN 0-201-11557-3 (pbk.)

Cover design by Copenhaver Cumpston
Text design by Kenneth J. Wilson
Set in 10 point Century Schoolbook by Compset, Inc., Beverly, MA.

BCDEFGHIJ–DO–8987
Second Printing, December 1987

*In memory of John Hendry, whose editorial
contributions made this book possible.*

ABOUT THE CONTRIBUTORS

Richard P. Bagozzi holds undergraduate and advanced degrees in engineering and mathematics and an M.B.A. in general business. His Ph.D. is from Northwestern University where he specialized in behavioral science and statistics in management. Prior to coming to Stanford he was on the faculties of the University of California, Berkeley, and the Massachusetts Institute of Technology.

Professor Bagozzi has worked as a project engineer for Pontiac Motors of General Motors, where he was engaged in the design, development, and testing of new automobiles. He has continued his contact with industry through executive teaching and has occasionally advised companies, non-profit organizations, and government agencies on management practices.

Dr. Bagozzi has done extensive research into customer behavior, sales force behavior, marketing communication, and research methodology. He is the author of *Causal Models in Marketing* (Wiley) and has authored or coauthored more than 75 articles in professional and scholarly journals. Among other honors, Dr. Bagozzi has received the American Marketing Association's first place award for his doctoral dissertation, and a Senior Fulbright Research Grant to do research in Europe. At the University of California (Berkeley) he received the School of Business Administration Outstanding Teaching Prize, and the Campus-wide Distinguished Teaching Award. He serves or has served on the editorial boards of eight journals.

William H. Beaver holds a B.B.A. from the University of Notre Dame and a M.B.A. and Ph.D. from the University of Chicago. He is a Certified Public Accountant, has served on the faculty of the University of Chicago, and has been on the faculty of the Graduate School of Business of Stanford University since 1969. He has authored over forty articles in several journals and currently is on the editorial board of several journals.

Professor Beaver has served the Financial Accounting Standards Board in a variety of capacities and is currently a member of its Advisory Council. He has also been a member of the SEC's Advisory Committee on Corporate Disclosure. He has served the American Accounting Association in several positions including Chairman of the Financial Standards Committee, the Distinguished International Lecturer in Europe, and Vice President. His previous book is entitled *Financial Reporting: An Accounting Revolution*.

Professor Beaver's work has received several awards including the *Journal of Accountancy* Literary Award, the Graham and Dodd Award, and the Alpha Kappa Psi National Accounting Award. He is a three-time winner of the AICPA's Notable Contribution to Accounting Literature Award.

Charles P. Bonini is a Professor of Management Science at Stanford's Graduate School of Business. During his 25 years at Stanford, he has applied quantitative and statistical techniques to business problems and contributed to the use of computers in business. He is the author (or co-author) of *Quantitative Analysis for Business Decisions, Statistical Analysis for Business Decisions,* and *Computer Models for Decision Analysis,* as well as many articles in professional journals.

Professor Bonini received his M.S. and Ph.D. from Carnegie Mellon University. His thesis was one of the first applications of computer simulation to business information systems. In recent years, he has been actively involved in Stanford Business School's senior executive programs and has taught in programs both in the United States and overseas. Currently he serves as co-director of the Stanford/National University of Singapore Executive program.

Professor Bonini is a consultant to several companies and organizations on the applications of quantitative techniques and the use of computers. His professional activities include past president of the American Institute for Decision Sciences, of which he has been elected Fellow. He has also served as associate editor for several professional journals.

L. J. Bourgeois received his M.B.A. in marketing from Tulane University in 1970 and later was employed as a financial analyst in the corporate planning department of Castle & Cooke Foods. He then held several assignments in the firm's Latin American operations, including new product project manager, residential subdivision development, labor negotiations, and manager of industrial engineering (for the Honduras division).

Professor Bourgeois received his Ph.D. in strategic management and international business from the University of Washington. Prior to joining the Stanford faculty, he taught in the M.B.A. and Ph.D. programs at the University of Pittsburgh and in the M.B.A. program at McGill University. At Stanford, he is director of the Strategic Management Program and teaches strategic management and related electives in strategy implementation.

Professor Bourgeois has consulted for a variety of *Fortune* 500, Australian, and European corporations on strategic planning, strategy implementation, and corporate culture, and has designed and conducted various in-house seminars in strategic management. A frequent speaker, Dr. Bourgeois has published articles in various management journals, including *Strategic Management Journal, California Management Review, Strategic Planning Management, Academy of Management Review,* and *Academy of Management Journal,* and is currently authoring a book on strategy implementation.

Joel S. Demski has been Milton Steinbach Professor of Information and Accounting Systems since September 1985 at Yale University's School of Organization and Management. Prior to moving to Yale, Professor Demski was Joan E. Horngren Professor of Information and Accounting Systems at the Stanford Graduate School of Business and, prior to that, a faculty member at Columbia University. He has also served as a visiting professor at the University of Chicago and at the University of Michigan.

Professor Demski is the author of *Information Analysis* (Addison-Wesley) and a co-author of *Cost Accounting* (Harcourt), and *Cost Determination* (Iowa State University Press).

A specialist in the theoretical aspects of accounting, Professor Demski has published numerous articles in *Accounting Review, Journal of Accounting and Public Policy, Journal of Accounting Research, Journal of Economic Theory, Management Accounting,* and *Management Science.*

John B. Fery is chairman of the board and chief executive officer of Boise Cascade Corporation, a position he has held since May of 1978. He joined Boise Cascade at its inception in 1957 and was given the responsibility of establishing paper operations for the then small regional lumber company. He was elected a vice president in 1960; in 1967 he was named executive vice president and a director; and in 1972 he became president and chief executive officer of Boise Cascade.

Mr. Fery is a graduate of the University of Washington and holds an M.B.A. from the Stanford University Graduate School of Business.

Mr. Fery is also a director of the Union Pacific Corporation, Albertson's Inc., Hewlett-Packard Company, and The Moore Financial Group. In addition, he is immediate past chairman of the Board of Trustees of St. Alphonsus Regional Medical Center in Boise, Idaho. He is a member of the Stanford Business School Advisory Council, the American Paper Institute, The Business Council, and the Chase International Advisory Council.

Gayton E. Germane is the 1907 Foundation Professor of Logistics, Graduate School of Business, and by courtesy, Professor of Industrial Engineering, School of Engineering, Stanford University. He received an A.B. in Economics, University of Missouri (Columbia), an M.B.A. from the Harvard Graduate School of Business Administration, and an A.M. and Ph.D. in Economics from the Harvard Graduate School of Arts and Sciences.

For three years, Professor Germane was the Director of Transportation Planning and Research, U.S. Steel Corporation. He served as a consultant to numerous companies in industry, as well as air, barge, ocean, highway, and railroad transportation, and is currently Faculty Principal of Management Analysis Center, Inc., a consulting firm. Other positions include Director of Transportation Policy, U.S. Department of Defense, and Consultant on National Transportation Policy to the U.S. Secretary of Commerce. He has been an expert witness before the Committees of Congress, U.S. Bankruptcy Court, the ICC, and the FMC.

Professor Germane is the author or co-author of six previous books on transportation, logistics, and management, and has contributed to several other published volumes. He has led executive programs in the U.S. and in five foreign countries.

William F. Miller is the President and Chief Executive Officer of SRI International, an independent, non-profit institution whose activities range from management consulting to scientific research. As president of SRI and as an international lecturer, Dr. Miller has focused attention on the need for stimulating innovation and revitalizing industry by building on the nation's technological and entrepreneurial strengths. He makes a special point of emphasizing that our entrepreneurial strengths need to be blended with organization and discipline to create a fully competitive industrial society.

Dr. Miller was educated as a physicist at Purdue University where he received his Ph.D. in 1956. His career history includes experience in high-energy physics, computer science, university administration and as a business consultant and venture capitalist. He joined Stanford University in 1965 as head of the Computation Group at the Stanford Linear Accelerator Center. In 1970 he was appointed Vice President for Research and in 1971 became Vice President and Provost. He became the first Herbert Hoover Professor of Public and Private Management in Stanford's Graduate School of Business in 1979. He is currently professor of Public and Private Management, and of Computer Science, at Stanford.

Dr. Miller is a Fellow of the Institute of Electrical and Electronics Engineers, and the American Academy of Arts and Sciences. He was recently appointed as a member of the National Science Board of the National Science Foundation.

Dr. Miller currently serves as a Director of Varian Associates, Pacific Gas and Electric Company, Fireman's Fund Insurance Company, First Interstate Bancorp, and First Interstate Bank of California. He was founding partner of the Mayfield Fund.

Jeffrey H. Moore, Assistant Dean for computer and information systems at Stanford University Graduate School of Business, has developed and taught graduate courses in computers and management information systems in the M.B.A., Ph.D., and Sloan programs, as well as in several Stanford executive programs since 1972.

From 1968 to 1972, he was with the Center for Research in Management Science at the University of California at Berkeley, where he began as a systems analyst and in 1971 became principal administrative analyst.

Dr. Moore received a doctorate in business with emphasis in information systems, management science, and economics from the University of California at Berkeley in 1973 and a joint master's degree in business administration and computer science from Texas A&M University in 1968. With more than 30 professional papers and 24 seminars to his credit, Dr. Moore sits on the editorial review boards of *Management Science, Association for Computer Machinery,* and *American Institute of Decision Sciences.* In addition, he has served as advisory board member and associate member of the faculty council, Center for Research in Management Science; director, Morrow Designs, Inc.; and board of regents member, Institute for Information Management.

Professor Moore's research interests center on office automation and decision support systems. He is currently principal investigator on a grant researching computer use by senior executives.

Jerry I. Porras received a B.S. in Electrical Engineering from Texas Western College in 1960, an M.B.A. from Cornell University in 1968, and a Ph.D. in Management from UCLA in 1974. He served in the U.S. Army for three years and was employed at the Lockheed Missiles and Space Company and the General Electric Company prior to returning to graduate school.

Dr. Porras, currently an Associate Professor of Organizational Behavior in the Graduate School of Business, Stanford University, has published widely in both academic and management journals focusing his work on planned organizational change and Organizational Development processes. He has consulted with a variety of business and government organizations such as Hewlett-Packard Laboratories, Bell Laboratories, Pro-Log, and TRW Components International.

James C. Van Horne is presently the A. P. Giannini Professor of Banking and Finance at Stanford University Graduate School of Business. Previously he has worked at a commercial bank and as Deputy Assistant Secretary of the Treasury. He is the author of *Financial Management and Policy,* 7th ed.; *Financial Market Rates and Flows,* 2nd ed.; as well as three other books and over 50 articles in academic journals.

A graduate of DePauw University with a Ph.D. from Northwestern University, Van Horne is the past president of the American Finance Association and of the Western Finance Association. He currently serves on the boards of directors of a bank and of an international investment fund. His teaching and research interests embrace corporate finance, interest rate theory and behavior, monetary policy, and the theory of finance. In 1982, he was the first recipient of the M.B.A. distinguished teaching award at Stanford.

Steven C. Wheelwright received both an M.B.A. and Ph.D. in Business from Stanford University in 1970. Later he taught at INSEAD in Fontainebleau, France, and the Harvard Business School before joining the faculty at Stanford. He also worked for a year as Vice President of Marketing and Sales in a family-owned firm. His current teaching assignments are in the areas of business policy and strategy, manufacturing policy, and production/operations management. Previously he taught Managerial Economics, and Forecasting and Planning.

Professor Wheelwright's most recent book is *Restoring Our Competitive Edge: Competing through Manufacturing,* co-authored with Professor Robert Hayes of Harvard University (Wiley). He is also the co-author of several books on forecasting, including one in the PIMS/North Holland series of studies in the management sciences. His other publications include articles in the *Harvard Business Review* and several other journals.

Professor Wheelwright's current research interests deal with issues that relate a manufacturing functional strategy to the business and corporate strategies. Of particular interest are the adoption of advanced manufacturing technologies and the interface between R&D/Engineering and Manufacturing required for new product introduction. Professor Wheelwright and his family live in Palo Alto, California, and enjoy traveling, especially in the Far East and Europe.

David B. Zenoff specializes in international business management and the management of large international banks. His formal education (Stanford, B.A.; Harvard, M.B.A. and D.B.A.) focused on international management, and his career as an academician and management consultant has furthered that interest.

He has been a full- or part-time faculty member at the Columbia Graduate School of Business, IMEDE (Switzerland) and the Stanford Graduate School of Business. Since 1972 he has been President of David B. Zenoff & Associates, Inc., which provides consulting services to large corporations and banks on strategy, management style, financial management, structure, joint ventures, and the role for headquarters in international operations. Clients include numerous top 100 banks and companies headquartered in the United States, Canada, Western Europe, and Australia.

Dr. Zenoff has written several management articles and five books: *International Banking, Management Principles for Finance in the Multinational, International Financial Management, International Business Management,* and *Private Enterprise in the Developing Countries.*

CONTENTS

Introduction
Step One: Connect

John B. Fery
Chairman and Chief Executive Officer
Boise Cascade Corporation

By the late 1960s, ten years after I joined Boise Cascade, the company had gained a reputation for its "free-form" management style. It was described as a place for ambitious young executives who wanted to "do their own thing." That description was not entirely accurate, however.

To be sure, Boise Cascade had its free-form managers, and they were very visible. But there were also many in the company who practiced a more traditional style of management. These traditionalists ran Boise Cascade's basic forest products operations, while their more avant-garde colleagues concerned themselves with expanding the company's portfolio to include other businesses that seemed to offer greater growth potential.

By 1972, these attempts to diversify beyond forest products were in deep trouble, and I became the chief executive of a company whose future was very much in doubt — despite the fact that its underlying forest products business was solid. I had spent my career in that business, and I resolved to refocus the company on it. I also resolved to reemphasize the management style I was comfortable with. I had come to have great respect for it in the process of witnessing the free form approach close-up.

What is that style? Let me illustrate it by describing a meeting I'll participate in tomorrow. At 8:00 A.M. sharp, Boise Cascade's twenty-nine senior managers will gather in a Boise hotel conference room to discuss one thing: the implications of a survey of these managers, by the company's human resources staff, to learn their views on a variety of corporate policies, practices, and programs including senior management compensation. The session will probably take most of the day. Everyone will speak frankly and listen carefully, and we will all connect as a result. Our feeling of being teammates will be strengthened.

The cost of this get-together will be considerable. The participants will come from all over the United States. By the time they return to their desks, they might well have invested fifteen hours preparing for, traveling to and from, and participating in the meeting. That's 435 top management hours devoted exclusively to nurturing top management's team spirit. Sessions similar to this one, although with different agendas, take place at least twice a year at Boise Cascade, so we're talking about big chunks of high-priced time. And time, unlike trees, is a nonrenewable resource.

Some of my associates wonder whether these time investments are necessary. They think I might be overreacting to what I experienced fifteen years ago. Not surprisingly, I disagree. I am convinced that such investments are vital, and I'd like to explain why in some detail because I think the explanation will provide a useful framework for the ensuing chapters of this book.

My story is a personal one. I do not mean for it to suggest that I think it's necessarily applicable across the board. But I do think it provides a context for what my alma mater's distinguished professors have to say to you.

Remember the old 3-D movies, where the price of admission included a pair of throw-away glasses that you had to wear to see the third dimension? Well, consider what I say here as comparable to those glasses. I aim to help you see this book's third dimension, a chief executive's perspective.

THE OBJECTIVE: CONNECTEDNESS

Like most people, I'm a captive of my experiences. I started working when I was eleven and haven't taken too many days off since. I like what I do. I joined Boise Cascade in 1957, when it was a fledgling forest products company, and I'm still with the company today. I guided the growth of its pulp, paper, and packaging business and steered it back to those businesses after becoming its CEO. I participated in Boise Cascade's initial growth and lived through its time of diversification and decline. I guided its return to health: Boise Cascade today is a solid, successful forest products company, with 1984 revenues of $3.8 billion and some 27,000 employees. And I have become a particular kind of chief executive as a result.

I've had years of line management experience. I've developed organizations, built and run new facilities, manufactured and sold products, run divisions, and finally run a company. And my experience has convinced me that the way to build a solid, responsive, responsible, productive forest products company is to create an environment that fosters what I call *connectedness:* an environment in which people feel connected to each other and to the goals and objectives of the organization. I think "doing your own thing" is an anachronism in today's business world and a prescription for failure in tomorrow's — if only because almost all business problems and opportunities are now multifunctional. Creating value for shareholders has become a cooperative endeavor. There is still plenty of room for entrepreneurship; in fact, it's more essential than ever. But it has to be coordinated — connected, if you will.

So how does an executive go about creating an environment that fosters connectedness? The first step is to define and communicate the organization's philosophy, its values, what it stands for. Second is to define and communicate to everyone the organization's ground rules. And third is to monitor regularly to make sure that no one has forgotten steps one and two.

Getting these three steps accomplished is the executive's direct responsibility, in my view. He or she may consult widely — and I encourage this — but the responsibility cannot be delegated.

Once these steps have been taken, the real work starts. Creating an environment is a whole lot easier than maintaining one. At Boise Cascade, we maintain connectedness by managing for consensus. Our objective is an environment that fosters connectedness; consensus management is the process we employ to attain and maintain it.

The Process: Consensus Management

Some say that one of the lesser legacies of the Johnson administration was a distortion of the idea of consensus. As practiced by the Johnson people, consensus supposedly came to mean "Support the boss or get off the team; dissent is unpatriotic." And yet, as an approach to management, the notion of consensus has great value. It just needs to be redefined.

According to Webster, consensus means "collective opinion or concord, general agreement or accord." At Boise Cascade, consensus management means wrestling with issues until a clear majority view emerges and all dissenters believe they've been fully heard. It derives from the hypothesis that a thorough search for and airing of information will result in a right answer. It places great value on investigation and debate, even at the expense of time.

Consensus management is energy-intensive; digging and debating exhaustively are exhausting. It is messy; people who pursue consensus do so in fits and starts and zigs and zags, noisily. (A consultant once remarked, after participating in a Boise Cascade meeting that featured a number of exuberant exchanges, "I've just seen corporate democracy in action!")

And it is inherently temporary; it's supposed to break down. I spend a lot of my time trying to poke holes in yesterday's consensus, and I get nervous when I fail. As far as my associates and I are concerned, no case is ever closed, because there is always new information. I'm an infernal second-guesser, I admit. I rarely have trouble sleeping, but when I do, it's usually because I'm second guessing that afternoon's consensus. Like Dickens's Fagin, I'm "reviewing the situation."

What Consensus Is Not

First, consensus — as practiced at Boise Cascade, at least — is not unanimity. To gain consensus, one need only dig and debate, consider and reconsider, until a solid majority of the participants agree on a resolution and the entire minority agree that their views were heard and fully considered. (At Boise Cascade, given sufficient time, we almost always achieve such a consensus.)

Second, consensus is not compromise. In fact, it is the antithesis of compromise; by definition, compromise is a failure to achieve consensus. Third, consensus is not infallible; achieving it simply improves your odds. Fourth, consensus cannot be achieved without leadership. Managers who aim for consensus must do more than moderate or facilitate; they must lead — actively.

Finally, consensus is not always appropriate. At Boise Cascade, for example, we do not seek consensus when defining corporate values and philosophies. That's my job. I'll reach out for advice and counsel. I'll listen to anyone who cares enough to bring me an opinion, observation, or criticism. But I will not pursue consensus when defining what the company stands for.

The Cost of Consensus

Make no mistake, consensus doesn't come cheap. It demands time, discipline, and effort. And people give time and effort generously only when they're especially committed, when they care very much, when they're very disciplined — willing to dig and dig, listen and listen, even though it's Saturday afternoon and the sun is out, and, oh my, would it be nice to take a nice long walk.

How does an executive go about obtaining that special commitment from his or her people? What do you give in return? What's the medium of exchange? It can't only be money, because what you're asking of the recipient will leave him or her with little time or energy to enjoy it. So what should it be?

While I agree that you can't buy commitment entirely with money, I do think money is an important incentive. It promises security, and it is one measure of a person's value (there are, of course, many others). However, I also believe there are two other ways to win people's commitment: Challenge them fairly, and give them a stake in their work and an opportunity to take credit for it.

I push my people hard, question them pointedly, pick and probe for gaps. Have you considered this? Did you check that? Did you talk to legal? How will that affect the contract negotiations? Why can't you get this project finished by tomorrow morning? At the same time, I try hard to be accessible, to "be there." And I find that the harder I push, the more committed I become and the more commitment I receive in return.

AT THE CORE: THE MULTIFUNCTIONAL PROBLEM

Let's pause long enough to let me make sure I've made myself clear. To review: creating value for shareholders today is a cooperative endeavor, because today almost all business issues are multifunctional. Cooperation grows out of connectedness. Connectedness grows out of consensus. Consensus grows out of commitment. (Sounds like the old song about bones, doesn't it?)

The core of this line of reasoning is the statement that almost all business issues are multifunctional. If that's true, you can't read the rest of this book as eleven discrete chapters. You have to read it as one multifunctional chapter. For it to reflect an actual business situation, its pages would have to be shuffled like a deck of cards so that finance and marketing and production and transportation were all mixed up — because that's the way they really are, at least at Boise Cascade. Take our Wallula, Washington, paper mill, for example.

Digester Indigestion

As you may know, Boise Cascade supplies paper to publishers, printers, forms manufacturers, and many other paper consumers: the company is the world's fifth largest papermaker. What you may not know is that we also supply other paper producers around the world with a key papermaking ingredient, pulp. When you get a letter from Japan, the stationery might well have been made from Boise Cascade pulp.

We currently make pulp at three mills — two in Canada and one in Wallula, Washington. The process is straightforward: we buy wood chips from neighboring sawmills and plywood plants (our own and independents), or we bring in logs and convert them to wood chips; we cook and squeeze these chips into pulp; then we ship this pulp to papermakers throughout the Americas and the Far East. What's tricky is maintaining quality and profit margins, as we learned the hard way at Wallula.

We installed an expensive new piece of pulp-making equipment there not long ago (a continuous digester), promised our customers and agents that it would produce lots of top-quality pulp, and then failed to deliver. Both throughput and quality were way below specifications. At the same time, pulp's market price was falling; our shipping and manufacturing costs (for chips, natural gas, and electricity) were climbing; and our profit margins were disappearing. The company faced a nasty problem that was inherently multifunctional.

The solution: attack it on all fronts simultaneously. Shut down a portion of the pulp mill, then muster everyone who possessed a relevant expertise; to wit:

Foresters, researchers, and chip procurement people from the company's Timber and Wood Products Group

Engineering, manufacturing, marketing, strategic planning, transportation, R&D, and financial people from the company's Paper Group

Technical and production people from the Wallula mill and from the manufacturer of the continuous digester

Transportation and energy conservation people from the company's corporate headquarters

What did this group do? First and foremost, they discovered that the continuous digester was being improperly fed. The wood chips were coming from too many different kinds of trees. The western slope of a nearby mountain yielded Douglas fir; its eastern side yielded larch, lodgepole pine, jack pine, and ponderosa pine; and the mixture yielded inconsistent quality.

This discovery led to a new chip procurement system (fewer suppliers, tighter specs); new screening systems fore and aft of the digester, to cull off-size chips and too-coarse pulp; and lower raw materials costs.

Second, the group located and repaired a small but significant imperfection deep inside the digester. (Coping with this machine, which is 122 feet 6 inches tall and 20 feet 6 inches wide and weighs 250 tons, was itself a multifunctional problem. All sorts of technical and managerial people were involved in its care and treatment.) Third, they figured out how to reduce energy costs by 15 percent. Fourth, they came up with a shipping alternative that cut freight rates 33 percent. And fifth, they set up agreements with agents and customers that increased the stability of volumes and prices.

It's worth noting here that what began as one multifunctional problem turned out to be an interrelated collection of problems. As a result, the group kept splitting itself into ad hoc subgroups. Engineering, manufacturing, and finance dealt with energy conservation, for example, while transportation, strategic planning, and marketing tackled shipping alternatives.

It's also worth noting the role top management played in what was for Boise Cascade a major problem with significant financial implications: My colleagues and I stood on the sidelines, watched carefully, questioned insistently, and cheered. These activities — watching, questioning, and cheering — take up a good part of my time, because I think they're a big part of a chief executive's job.

Finally, I should note that the solution to this multifunctional problem created multifunctional opportunities. It led us to better integrate the company's manufacturing, marketing, and transportation functions, for example. And it prompted us to transfer the chip procurement function from our Timber and Wood Products Group to our Paper Group, which resulted in good-sized cost savings.

EARNING THE COST OF CAPITAL: THE ULTIMATE MULTIFUNCTIONAL ISSUE?

We all tend to label things; it's a convenient sort of shorthand. But sometimes our labels can be misleading because they oversimplify. Take the "forest products company" label someone long ago gave Boise Cascade and its competitors. It suggests a functional commonality that simply does not exist.

To be a "forest products company" today is to be involved in a collection of business activities that, for the most part, have only the tree in common. Boise Cascade, for example, manages forests (seven million acres of them); manufactures first- and second-generation paper and wood products (scores of them — including computer printout paper, plywood, corrugated containers, and composite cans); distributes office products (thousands of them); and operates wholesale and retail building materials centers.

The fact is, Boise Cascade is multifunctional in its businesses as well as in the disciplines within those businesses; and this fact makes the allocation of capital critically important and potentially very complicated. How does top management go about deciding who gets what in a way that yields maximum benefit to the company over time — factoring in the interests of all concerned, from divisional managers to shareholders? This may be the ultimate multifunctional issue. It certainly consumes a great amount of this chief executive's time and energy.

The challenge has two parts: first, you have to find a way to compare apples and oranges; second, you have to get everybody to use it. That is, you have to create a yardstick that measures the potentials of unrelated businesses, and then you have to convince the managers of these businesses that it's in their interest to use it.

At Boise Cascade, our response to this challenge was to work together to design a strategic planning process that was comprehensive, easy to apply, and future-oriented. Everybody who would be required to use the process participated in its creation. The company first published it in 1975, and it has become a routine in the years since. Although we keep fine-tuning, it's ingrained in the organization now, a procedure that's accepted and understood and almost reflexive.

Creating it was a classic multifunctional task: Everybody had an ax to grind, so everybody had to agree it was fair; and that required operating managers, financial staffers, and planners to accept a universal unit of measurement — one that could be applied to businesses as diverse as newsprint manufacturing (capital-intensive) and office products distribution (labor-intensive), and to projects whose returns would accrue over a decade or more (a new paper mill boiler) or whose payback would be almost immediate (an energy-producing turbine generator).

The unit of measurement that gained consensus was "cost of capital" because it is a common value. When a factor for risk is added to the cost of capital, it becomes a "hurdle rate," or the minimum after tax return an investment must earn to gain approval. At Boise Cascade, the first question managers now ask themselves is, "Will this investment earn its hurdle rate?" The second question, is "How fast?," and their answers have to pass muster with their superiors, their superiors' staff people, and sometimes — depending on the size of the expenditure — with their superiors' peers.

Managers also must develop long-term strategic plans that forecast the impact that these investments will have on the performance of their overall business in light of past or present performance and current or anticipated competitive situations. The analyses yield for each business an estimate of the business's annual pretax return on total capital, or PROTC. If each investment made by a business meets or beats its hurdle rate, over time the business will operate at an acceptable level of PROTC. Top management pays a great deal of attention to hurdle rates and payback periods for individual investments — and to PROTC goals for the business entities overall.

Top management also pays a great deal of attention to the entire strategic planning process. We review the plan of each business and staff group, and then we incorporate it into our overall corporate strategy. Managing the development of that corporate strategy is my primary responsibility to the company. As captain of the ship, it falls to me to chart its course.

Incidentally, I find that this responsibility creates a personal sort of multifunctional problem for me, and I suspect it does for many other executives too. Given the multifunctional nature of our jobs, where do we find the time to get the information we need to carry out our planning responsibility? I've coped with this problem in three ways over the years: by engaging in extracurricular activities that provide such information directly — serving on outside boards, for example; by asking my staff to pay close attention to the news media and brief me during spare moments in elevators and taxis; and by filtering the information I'm exposed to very carefully. I absorb only what concerns me directly.

This last tactic has produced its embarrassing moments. On one occasion, I was introduced to an attractive woman at a party, chatted with her for ten or fifteen minutes, and didn't realize, until my wife told me on the way home, that I'd been talking to Diana Ross.

CHECKING THE DIRECTION

You've probably gathered from what I've said so far that we at Boise Cascade pay a lot of attention to our company's direction. Perhaps because we work with a natural resource that takes three to eight decades to renew itself, we tend to think long-term. In the mid-1970s, that perspective prompted us to establish a single long-term strategic goal ("Optimize the company's long-term value to our shareholders and to society") and six strategic objectives. Nine years later, we decided to take another look at both the goal and the objectives.

We regarded this reexamination as a multifunctional issue that demanded consensus, and we decided therefore to retain an independent consultant to help us design and manage the process. We also decided not to set a deadline, but rather to let the process run at its own speed. Finally, we decided that the objective of this exercise was a written statement of corporate strategy.

Step one involved a series of six meetings attended by the nine senior corporate officers who reported directly to our president or to me. These meetings were held a month apart. Each lasted all day; each was led by the outside consultant; and each had as its objective the sharing of all relevant facts, feelings, opinions, rumors, biases, hunches, guesses, and so on. Hence, there were no agendas or proscriptions. The whole idea was to dig deep, probe, kick tires, look under rocks, to test the established corporate gospel.

I've never run a marathon, but I'm told one of the things that happens to people who do is that they gain fresh insights into themselves and their relationships with families, friends, and co-workers. I think that happened to the Boise Cascade officers who participated in the six meetings. We cut through a lot of conventional wisdom and arrived at solid consensus. Result: a written statement titled "Directions for Boise Cascade" that, by the way, incorporated an earlier "Working at Boise Cascade" statement, defining the relationship we hope to achieve between the company and our employees.

In step two, "Directions" was presented to a larger group consisting of the company's twenty-nine officers. They took it completely apart, checked it for unintended nuances, then endorsed it unanimously. That's no mean feat, as you know if you've ever tried to get twenty-nine people to agree on a written statement about anything.

The twenty-nine-person group, by the way, included people from every discipline covered in the subsequent chapters of this book. It was a thoroughly multifunctional collection of business executives tackling a thoroughly multifunctional issue — and achieving consensus, starting with the fine-tuning of our goal, which is now "to optimize the company's long-term value to our shareholders, to our employees, to our customers and to society."

As a result of that consensus, "Directions" was published and mailed to every Boise Cascade employee's home. Thereafter, all employees were invited to discuss the statement in small groups where they worked. Their feedback is percolating through the company as I write and will no doubt influence the next reconsideration a few years from now.

Incidentally, as you might expect, given the importance I attach to charting Boise Cascade's course, I participated in all of the top management meetings devoted to "Directions." And my vision improved as a result.

IF YOU WANT TO BE A CEO . . .

The cliché is correct: the view from the bridge (or the top floor) *is* different, and the difference goes beyond anything I've mentioned so far. Certainly, a chief executive has to be concerned with the things I've discussed here: solving multifunctional operating problems; setting up multifunctional strategic planning processes; charting a successful course, and winning support for it by achieving connectedness.

But the job has another dimension, one that is often overlooked in discussions about management practices. This dimension requires connecting with people who have nothing directly to do with Boise Cascade but upon whose support the company depends. They aren't employees, shareholders, customers, suppliers, investment analysts, reporters, regulators, or public officials. They may use the company's products, but they probably don't know it, because most of our products are used to manufacture or package other products with other companies' names on them. As far as these people are concerned, Boise Cascade is simply a fellow citizen, a corporate citizen that ought to meet their standards of corporate citizenship.

Essentially, they *expect* Boise Cascade to protect forests, air quality, and water quality while providing affordable wood and paper products, satisfying jobs, and generous contributions to social and cultural activities. In other words, they expect what you and I do, except . . .

Except some of them take these expectations to extremes, which creates conflicts, by definition. You have to cut down trees to produce wood and paper, and the fewer you cut down, the more expensive that wood and paper will be. And I, as Boise Cascade's CEO, have to explain that. That makes me a bearer of bad news. None of us likes to be told that our expectations conflict. In fact, we'll make every effort to disprove it. (And insofar as we're successful, we intensify the conflicts and the emotions surrounding them.)

A big part of my job today — and yours tomorrow, if you're your company's CEO — is dealing with an array of rising and therefore potentially conflicting expectations regarding product quality relative to price, environmental protection relative to cost, employee compensation, training, and benefits relative to the company's immediate profitability, and so on.

I find that dealing with these expectations requires even more patience, stamina, and commitment than achieving a consensus solution to a multifunctional problem, and that the skill required is far more difficult to master. That skill is the ability to communicate persuasively, to speak in a way that prompts a wide variety of dissimilar people with diverse and sometimes opposing points of view to listen, understand, and agree . . . to build connections. That's an art, an art tomorrow's CEO must master. So if you aim to become a CEO, I suggest that you study and practice the techniques of communication along with those described in the rest of this book. They're tools you will use in tackling every multifunctional problem.

CHAPTER 1

Marketing Management: Strategies, Tactics, New Horizons

Richard P. Bagozzi
Stanford University
Graduate School of Business

MARKETING: AN INTEGRATIVE FUNCTION

Marketing is a management function whose popularity seems to ebb and flow with the times. In the 1970s, every firm of course did its share of marketing, but as inflation raged or shortages became the rule, financial considerations, procurement, and production took center stage. Today, and for the rest of the 1980s, it is forecast that marketing will be the "new priority" that no organization can afford to ignore.[1] What are we to make of the up-and-down emphasis of marketing? Is it as important as contemporary observers make it out to be?

Actually, one should not pay too much attention to the apparent rise and fall of the marketing function, at least not in the short run. For beneath the surface of its swings in popularity lies a fundamental trend that is transforming the role of marketing dramatically. Marketing is moving from a separate, parallel function among production, finance, personnel, R&D, and other areas to an *integrative function* that not only binds the separate areas of the firm together but serves as the

---

I am indebted to my friend and colleague, Professor Lynn W. Phillips of Stanford University, who has unselfishly shared his wealth of knowledge with me and whose ideas can be seen throughout this chapter. Special thanks go to John C. Boyle for his critical comments on an earlier draft and John Hendry for his many substantive and editorial suggestions.

primary means for responding to and influencing the environment to advantage. Indeed, marketing is no longer synonymous with advertising or selling but consists of a variety of tasks, each attuned to the constraints within the firm and the opportunities and vicissitudes of the marketplace. Marketing is no longer solely a task for specialists but is shared also by managers traditionally concerned with other operating and planning tasks in the firm. Overall, marketing concepts and methods pervade the organization from boardroom to assembly line.

Before describing the emerging role of marketing and the new forms it is taking, let me briefly sketch the forces producing the changes. The forces are phenomena of which you are well aware, but you have probably not realized how far reaching their effects have been.

The most important changes concern the *consumer*. At the microlevel, individual tastes are becoming more varied, more refined, and more fickle. The result has been a proliferation of distinct market segments that demand unique products and services to reach them. At the same time, there has been a continual shift in aggregate markets. Some emerge overnight. Some persist for a long time and either experience a rebirth or die. Others grow slowly. Still others expand by leaps and bounds. Obviously, if it is to satisfy market segments and profitably reap the rewards of volatile markets, the firm must adjust and readjust its marketing programs on an ever more frequent basis.

Adjustment also becomes a new imperative because of a second factor: the *competitor*. In recent years, more aggressive, more sophisticated rivals have been vying for the same markets as those served by our brands. Advances in product and production technologies, market monitoring techniques, and strategic managerial know-how have raised the level of competition to a new plane. To compound matters, legal and regulatory bodies, which have always been procompetition, now seem to push free enterprise with an evangelistic fervor. Although this is most evident in the deregulation of the airline, trucking, banking, and telecommunications industries, it has been felt throughout the business community in forms ranging from antitrust and deceptive advertising regulations by the FTC to confrontation in the courts. Increased competition puts new burdens on marketing, since it is primarily through product design, pricing, promotion, advertising, and distribution that competitive effects are mitigated or overcome.

A third force influencing the nature and importance of marketing is the *economy*. Except during deep recessions or depressions that tended to be few and far between, heretofore managers could count on a growing population, ever-increasing disposable incomes, low credit terms, tax incentives, and in general a favorable business climate. But mild recessions have occurred more frequently, thus increasing competitive pressures and putting new strains on marketing. Even in inflationary times, marketing must be pursued with a new urgency as people feel the impulse to spend in new ways and marketers scramble to uncover the budding market segments. No longer can managers expect prosperity to continue unabated. Rather, we seem to face a never-ending alternation of turmoil and calm for indeterminate periods of time. Marketing tools are an essential means to adapt to these fluctuations.

As the consumer, the competitor, and the economic environment change, marketers increasingly realize that it is not enough merely to respond to the forces around them. New advances in marketing strategy and tactics make it possible to influence consumer choices, the competitive climate, and economic conditions to a certain extent.

This chapter introduces the most important concepts and methods of marketing management. It begins with a discussion of two broad objectives that guide any marketing effort: satisfying buyer needs and achieving a competitive advantage. It then turns to planning and implementing the marketing effort. Overall marketing strategy and market selection comprise the planning topics. Implementation is concerned with such tactical issues as product management and new product development, marketing communication (advertising, promotion, publicity, and personal selling), pricing, and channels of distribution. Finally, the chapter closes with some thoughts for the future.

TWO GUIDING PRINCIPLES

In much the same way that individual behavior is driven by one's fundamental values and social behavior is governed by norms and laws, marketing efforts are — or should be — motivated by two principles. Specifically, they are to (1) meet customer needs and (2) provide a product or service superior to that offered by the competition.

As simple as these principles might seem, they are difficult to sustain in practice, and each year the failures regularly outnumber the successes. Let us examine some of these failures and successes before we turn to an examination of the key functional areas of marketing.

Customer Analysis

To meet customer needs, firms spend a lot of time and money on research. A common strategy is to concentrate one's efforts on new product development. The rationale is that consumers are satisfied through products, so it behooves one to begin here.

Consider the case of Frost 8/80, a "dry white" whiskey introduced by Brown-Forman Distillers in the early 1970s.[2] After much fanfare and a reported $6.5 million investment, Brown-Forman withdrew the brand from the market, less than two years after its introduction. The reason given was that sales were simply too low. Estimates of the losses extend beyond the $2 million mark.

The Frost 8/80 case is noteworthy because Brown-Forman appeared to have done all the right things prior to launch. The brand was targeted at a unique niche in the market. Management thought that a large enough segment of consumers would welcome a clear whiskey, just as many buyers had earlier accepted the concept of a light whiskey. Unlike the latter, which was amber in color and considered a less strong-tasting whiskey intended to be drunken straight or with water, Frost 8/80 was positioned as a versatile mixer. The product seemed destined for success, given industry statistics showing a shift in drinking preferences from the harsher bourbons and whiskeys toward the softer liquors such as vodka, gin, and scotch. Moreover, women and young people increasingly were turning to the latter, preferring sweeter, less alcoholic mixed drinks. Since Frost 8/80 was basically a filtered whiskey, Brown-Forman hoped that sufficient sales here would forestall the effects of slow growth and eventual decline in the demand for its traditional whiskey brands.

Before deciding to market Frost 8/80, Brown-Forman performed a series of activities quite typical of modern companies. First, a concept study was conducted to get an idea of people's receptivity to a dry white whiskey. Favorable reactions to the study led to interviews and surveys to discover how people might consume the product and what their feelings were toward it. A third step was a taste test, which tended to show that people liked the product. Fourth, outside experts were consulted in the choosing of a name, bottle, and label. Consumer panels were utilized to obtain still more information in a fifth step. The final stage consisted of heavy advertising to inform the public of the brand and its uses.

With such a textbook program, why did Frost 8/80 fail? Industry watchers offered many reasons, including an insufficient market base, a neglect of test-marketing, and a reluctance of management to stick it out until a customer franchise could be built. The most likely explanations, however, lay in Brown-Forman's failure to perform a proper customer analysis. Essentially, the company did not carry its research deep enough into how consumers make choices and how they would respond to Frost 8/80.

As we will explore in more depth later in the chapter, one objective of customer research is first to discover which product attributes are important to consumers and only then design a product to meet the consumer's needs. Following a more or less armchair approach, Brown-

Forman turned the process on its head by assuming that a white whiskey would meet needs similar to those filled by the traditional clear liquors. They began with a product and then hoped to prove that a need existed.

More important, the research performed by Brown-Forman did not get to the heart of customer decision-making but rather only revealed surface symptoms of consumer behavior. Contemporary research over a wide range of products and services shows that key activities in the decision process concern how consumers make inferences as to product attributes, how they then organize the information so gleaned, and how finally the structure of information in memory influences consumer choices. The process proceeds something like the following:

Physical Cues ⟶ Subjective → Attitudes → Purchase Decision
(e.g., product   Judgments   and
features,   Preferences
ad appeals)

That is, information communicated through physical product attributes or ads is perceived by the consumer who, in turn, makes abstractions from the "hard" information to form subjective judgments. The inferred data need not be directly related to the physical cues but can be connected to other thoughts and feelings that may even be at odds with the intended communication. Next, the subjective information is integrated into an attitude, which then influences one's decision to make a purchase or not.

Consider how the process works for a hypothetical consumer, Tom R. Tom R. bought a bottle of Frost 8/80 at the suggestion of the retail clerk at his local liquor store. A dealer promotion made the purchase attractive in that it was a full dollar below the regular price and the price of existing liquors. Later at home, Tom R. poured a small amount of Frost 8/80 in a glass, just to see how it tasted. But Tom R. could not decide whether he liked or disliked Frost 8/80. The physical cues — the clear liquid, the lack of a strong odor, the advertising — suggested to him that the product would be tasteless. But once he tried it, he found something quite different: a strong whiskey taste. In effect, his expectations were violated, and the dissonance produced confusion. Had he tried first to mix Frost 8/80 with Seven-Up or Coke, say, he may never have had the ambivalent reaction. But the initial undiluted taste created a first impression that remained with him and generated uncertainties. His doubts were raised as to the purity of Frost 8/80 as well. After all, vodka is colorless and supposedly made of "pure" potatoes.

But Tom R. wondered what exactly the new taste was. Perhaps artificial ingredients were added to make the drink a synthetic concoction. Equally disconcerting was the thought that other people would have a similar reaction. The safe decision would be not to risk social embarrassment and to forgo serving it to guests. As a consequence of such reactions, repeat sales never reached desirable levels in the market.

It is easy to see how such negative inferences, both conscious and unconscious, could arise in response to the physical cues. In addition, such negative attributions could easily lead to unfavorable attitudes and a decision not to buy the brand again. If decision-making is construed as an attempt to gain knowledge and confidence about the world around us, then the uncertainty engendered by Frost 8/80 was an impediment to the process of consumer choice. It is interesting to note, too, that Brown-Forman compounded the uncertainty by switching ad agencies during the first year. The resulting change in themes only led to more confusion. This would be expected to affect the rate of first-time as well as repeat purchasing. What consumers needed was a way to "learn" about the product under favorable circumstances. Free tastings of mixed drinks in stores (where legal) or taverns where the seller could control the consumer's initial introduction to the product, advertising that prepared prospective customers for what they would experience when they tried the product, and other tactics might have been more fruitful. But even more basic than this, Brown-Forman never demonstrated that Frost 8/80 satisfied a genuine need and that a sufficiently large market existed.

The point of the Frost 8/80 example is to stress the importance of performing a sound customer analysis. This means discovering what consumers' needs are; which product attributes satisfy these needs; how customers will search for, evaluate, and consume the product; and how the tools under the control of the marketer can be used to facilitate the customer decision process.

Competitive Analysis

Even if one has developed a product that meets consumers' needs, success may not be forthcoming if competitors get the upper hand. Therefore, analysis of the competition is as important as study of the consumer. The goal is to meet customer needs with a product or service that achieves a differential advantage over the competition. The differential advantage might be superior product quality, a lower price, greater availability, more favorable credit terms, better service, a unique brand image, and so on.

Typically, to overcome competitive threats, one of three broad approaches can be taken: product differentiation, overall cost leadership, or special market focus.[3] Let us consider each through an illustration.

Product differentiation: The case of Seven-Up. Seven-Up was introduced in 1929 and quickly established itself as a popular drink, despite the presence of literally hundreds of competitors that tasted much the same. Nevertheless, its market share was small, and most people purchased it as either a good mixer (especially with bootleg whiskey in those Prohibition years) or a remedy for headache and other minor ills. Indeed, a key promotion advocated Seven-Up "for home and hospital use." In 1942, the J. Walter Thompson ad agency took over the account and stressed the product's fresh taste along with the old image of "you like it, it likes you." Although it eventually became the third leading soft drink behind Coca-Cola and Pepsi, it lagged far behind the two leaders. Moreover, sales growth in the mid-1960s was considerably below the industry average, and four new competitors were threatening Seven-Up: Coca-Cola's Sprite, Pepsi-Cola's Teem, Canada Dry's Wink, and Royal Crown's Upper-10.

Something had to be done, and the first step was consumer research. The findings were surprising. Management had believed that consumers thought of Seven-Up as one of a number of soft drinks. Therefore they had also believed that the brand would at least enter the set of possible thirst-quenching alternatives when consumers needed to choose a drink. But what they found was quite something else. When asked to list what they thought of when the words "soft drink" came to mind, most people listed Coke, Pepsi, Dr. Pepper, or another cola. In the minds of consumers, "soft drink" was equated with "cola." Seven-Up either never entered their thoughts or tended to be considered only as a mixer or health aid. So when consumers made up a shopping list, went to a restaurant, or were offered a soft drink at the home of a friend, most of them never really considered Seven-Up.

The problem can thus be seen to be one of brand image, consumer knowledge, and the strength and entrenchment of the competition. Yet the solution was not straightforward. One might think that the expenditure of more money on advertising or promotion was called for; but, nevertheless, examination of the competition suggested a caution. In 1967, Pepsi spent approximately $55 million on advertising and Coke about $44 million. This was about four times as much as Seven-Up's $12 million. To make matters worse, Sprite and Teem spent $10 million and $9 million, respectively, on advertising. Clearly, more advertising dollars would be expensive and problematic in effect. Seven-Up had to get many consumers who happened to be cola drinkers to try Seven-Up — and it had to do so without raising costs excessively or initiating a price/advertising/promotion war with the leaders, who had greater resources.

The solution pursued was the now famous "Uncola" campaign by the J. Walter Thompson agency. Seven-Up changed its advertising to introduce Seven-Up as an alternative to cola drinks. Some ads emphasized that Seven-Up has a "fresh, clean taste," and is "wet ... wild, never too sweet" with "no aftertaste." Other ads called attention to the occasions on which one might want a Seven-Up: at a restaurant, with a hamburger, on a picnic, with snacks, and so forth. Still other ads made direct comparisons to colas, stressing, for example, the "fresh, clean" and "alive" ingredients of Seven-Up (lemons and limes) versus the dark, shriveled, dead-looking contents of colas (cola nuts). Promotions included free Seven-Up glasses in the shape of the famous Coca-Cola glass, but upside down. In short, consumers were forced to consider Seven-Up uniquely and in a new comparative light.

The campaign worked. In the three years following the introduction of the Uncola campaign, Seven-Up's sales increased an average of nearly 20 percent per year compared with only about 14 percent for the industry. (The three prior years had shown a 3 percent per year average gain for Seven-Up, but a 10 percent yearly average for the industry.)[4]

The Seven-Up case is a classic example of a (pure) *product differentiation* competitive strategy. The firm's brand was positioned relative to the competition, and consumers perceived it in a unique way. This was done on a market-wide basis, in contrast to the alternative strategy of product differentiation for specific segments, which is a special case of the market focus strategy that we will consider shortly. Product differentiation creates a distinctive image for a brand and, if done properly, meets a genuine need and increases the loyalty of customers. It can make consumers less price-sensitive and vulnerable to the offerings of competitors. Although Seven-Up created differentiation primarily through its new advertising and secondarily through its product formulation, product differentiation can also be achieved by pricing, distribution, packaging, auxiliary services, or other marketing tactics. Product differentiation must be based on things perceived by the consumer as real benefits, or else repeat sales will not materialize. Also, it can be expensive to create, and it can be imitated by the competitors in the long run. Therefore, more than other strategies, it demands constant injections of new ideas. And money.

Overall cost leadership: From computers to chain saws. The goal in overall cost leadership is to keep manufacturing, material, and other costs to a minimum and in so doing to increase demand through the expected effect that a relatively low industry price will have. The increased volume, in turn, leads to absolute economies of scale and experience curve effects (discussed below), which then feed back lowering costs still further. The hoped-for ultimate effect, as with product differentiation, is a large market share. Indeed, cost leadership seems to work best for firms that already have a high relative market share. Furthermore, overall cost leadership entails a never-ending vigil of stringent cost and overhead control and the weeding out of marginal customers and product variations. Like the (pure) product differentiation strategy, overall cost leadership is a marketwide competitive strategy.

A number of firms follow an overall cost leadership approach. This is perhaps most obvious in the home computer industry. Let us briefly focus on Texas Instruments. Its president, J. Fred Bucy, has identified four strategic components as central to Texas Instruments' success.[5] The first is the *experience curve* concept.[6] As shown in Figure 1.1, the average cost per unit of an item typically decreases as cumulative output increases. In fact, the Boston Consulting Group asserts that the costs of most items will decline about 20 to 30 percent for each doubling of cumulative production. Why? Because with the passage of time, labor becomes more efficient, innovations arise in manufacturing, products are redesigned to take advantage of material and other savings, and other learning occurs. This is especially so within the solid-state electronics industry, where it is not uncommon to experience a doubling and even redoubling of cumulative production in the first two or three years. Obviously, firms that ride the trend of the experience curve phenomenon, such as Texas Instruments, can charge relatively lower prices and capture larger market shares. Notice, too, that experience curve effects are not limited to production costs but may apply to marketing costs as well.

A second component of Texas Instruments' overall cost leadership approach is the *importance of being first* to develop a new market. Although not a necessary component for success, being first typically permits an early capitalization on the experience curve, leads to a favorable brand image and the building of a customer base, and results in higher profit margins. Being first can be risky, however, if market acceptance is slower than expected and competitors wait in the wings to take advantage of the learning and primary demand investment of the market pioneer. In Texas Instruments' case, being first was a decided advantage.

Accumulated units of production with products related to a focal product is a third component of Texas Instruments' strategy and is termed *shared experience*. Thus, Texas Instruments finds similar uses

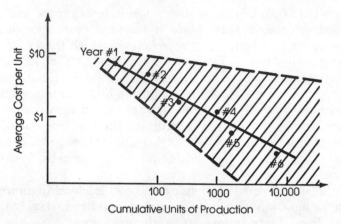

Figure 1.1 The Experience Curve Phenomenon:
A Hypothetical Example

The curve plotted through the datum points is typical;
shaded area indicates that the slopes of actual experience curves vary considerably depending on the nature
of the product and other variables.

for its semiconductors in hand calculators, minicomputers, digital
watches, and computer terminals. This permits a reduction in costs by
parceling them out among products, and the shared experience then
enhances the overall cost leadership of individual products still
further.

Finally, Texas Instruments follows a philosophy of *design to cost.* In
the words of its president, this involves "deciding today what the selling price and performance of a given product must be years in the future and designing the product and the equipment for producing it to
meet both cost and performance goals."[7] Primary emphasis is thus
placed on cost; the secondary objective is "to avoid designing into a
product more performance than the market is willing to buy."[8]

Overall cost leaderhip is thus at odds with the product differentiation strategy. It is not so much that firms such as Texas Instruments
do not differentiate their products. Indeed, they do this to some extent
through product design, advertising, market segmentation, and distribution policies. Nevertheless, low costs are given the highest priority,
and product differentiation is emphasized to a lesser extent than it is
by firms that pursue a (pure) product differentiation posture. Similarly, the product differentiator is not unconcerned with costs. It is just
that goals for superior product quality, brand image, or other factors
are met first. This generally entails spending more; hence the inherent

trade-off. In rare instances (for example the components businesses), it is in fact possible to find both high product quality and overall cost leadership.[9] But this is the exception rather than the rule.

Overall cost leadership is a powerful strategy, but it can be dangerous in the long run. I have already mentioned the possibility of slow consumer adoption of the product. Another potential problem is that price competition, the primary tool for stimulating demand, is easily copied by others. Still another threat is the possibility that competitors will develop new technologies and modify the product significantly to advantage or even create a substitute. Then, too, even if consumers are initially enthusiastic, tastes may change, and the firm will be left with an unfulfilled recovery of its investment.

For Texas Instruments, the home computer market proved damaging in the long run. The introduction of its Model 99/4A in 1979 led to a market share of 26 percent by 1982. However, competition based primarily on price by Commodore, Radio Shack, Atari, and Timex forced Texas Instruments to lower its price from a high of $1,000 in 1979 to less than $250 in 1982. Further intensification of competition in 1983 saw the price of Model 99/4A plummet to less than $89 with a rebate. Market share slipped to 19 percent in 1983 as well. Although the overall size of the market doubled between 1982 and 1983, Texas Instruments could not profitably compete in the home computer market and therefore withdrew. Not only the price wars but also consumer shifts in tastes took their toll as buyers became more sophisticated and demanded value and certain benefits as the primary product attributes. Price became relatively less important. Such is the pitfall of relying too heavily on an overall cost leadership strategy over time.

Each industry typically witnesses a variety of strategies, and one or more firms frequently find overall cost leadership viable. In the chain saw industry, for example, we see that one market leader in 1973, McCulloch (with 27 percent of the market), pursued an overall cost leadership approach, whereas the other market leader, Homelite (with 28 percent of the market), followed a product differentiation strategy based on high quality and a network of servicing dealers.[10] These firms and the industry as a whole tended to sell large, high-priced chain saws, most of which were bought by professional woodsmen and farmers. Then, beginning about 1973, Beaird-Poulan began marketing very low-priced, smaller chain saws for casual users. Its market share then was about 8 percent. With other firms soon following suit, the market exploded as a consequence of the new mass market appeal of chain saws. By 1977, the market shares of Homelite, Beaird-Poulan, and McCulloch were approximately 23 percent, 22 percent, and 20 percent, respectively, and the market for casual users increased from about 430,000 units in 1972 to 1,750,000 in 1977. The casual-user segment was now about 70 percent of a $1.15 billion market.

Notice that the market leaders employed the two generic strategies we have discussed so far. Notice also that, contrary to Texas Instruments' experience, price rivalry had not harmed the position of the original overall cost leader, McCulloch. And further, notice the dramatic rise of Beaird-Poulan, the other practitioner of overall cost leadership. The chain saw industry also illustrates the possibility of other strategic approaches. For example, the German company Stihl uses a product differentiation strategy but directs its brand to a particular market segment: professional users. Its product is of even higher quality (and price) than Homelite's, and it finds that a place exists for it in the market, too. In fact, it had maintained a market share of 7 or 8 percent from 1972 until 1980. Other firms in the industry with no or ill-defined competitive strategies (for example, Remington or Roper) have fared less well. Later in the chapter we will discuss other strategic concepts that help to explain why different approaches flourish in some cases but fail in others. Now we introduce the third generic strategy.

Special market focus: Lipton herbal teas. Whereas the product differentiation and overall cost leadership strategies strive to dominate — or at least survive in — entire markets, the market focus strategy aims for a particular segment or small number of segments of a larger market. Once such a segment is found, the firm employs either a product differentiation or overall cost leadership approach to attack it. In this sense, the special market focus strategy can be considered a subset of the previous two.

A good example of a market focus strategy is the case of Lipton Herbal Teas. Prior to 1978, the market for herb teas in the United States was minuscule, perhaps only 2 or 3 percent of the entire black tea market. In Germany and other parts of Europe, in contrast, herb teas were thought to account for 40 to 45 percent of the entire market for tea. Therefore, it was thought the United States might well represent a large, untapped market. (Note that herb teas are strictly not teas at all and are caffeine-free.)

In 1979–1980, Lipton launched its entries into the herb tea market, which at that time was pursued primarily by Celestial Seasonings and Bigelow. Its alleged goal was sales of at least 5 percent of the black tea market in the first year or so. Lipton hoped also to achieve economies of scale in production and reduce overhead, since it was already making regular tea. This should give Lipton a cost advantage over its smaller competitors, including Celestial Seasonings. Nevertheless, its principal strategy was one of product differentiation, for reasons to be mentioned shortly.

The target audience was defined as women aged 25–49, with middle to upper incomes, and who were average to heavy black tea drinkers. Herbal tea drinkers were of course also sought. In addition, the psychographic profile of the target consumer was "an independent woman, with strong convictions, and who feels comfortable making decisions."[11] As a consequence, a very specific and relatively small market segment was sought.

Differentiation from regular tea was accomplished through a variety of tactics. The product was made with high-quality, natural ingredients and, as noted, no caffeine. Originally, five flavors were offered: orange, spice, chamomile, hibiscus, and almond. Later a sixth was added: Citrus Sunset, which contains the davana herb from India. Print ads stressed "naturally delicious" and "no caffeine." They contained colorful pictures of the tea boxes and very little copy. A cents-off coupon worth as much as twenty-five cents on a box of sixteen bags was often part of the ad. One TV ad emphasized the quality of life, another natural settings. The theme of romance was discernible in most ads as well. Dealer promotions such as "two free with ten" and "no payment for six months" were tried to gain retail acceptance. Finally, although the familiar rectangular box was used, the package was made more exotic and flowery than traditional styles. Further, the rectangular box was designed so that the largest side caught the eye of the consumer, rather than the end as is usually the case. This not only provided a larger shelf facing, but also minimized overhead, since more boxes could be stacked advantageously to reduce space.

Lipton thus pursued a small segment of the market and used a product differentiation strategy. It explicitly strove to create "maximum differentiation" from its regular and flavored teas. This was done in order not to cannibalize sales. Also, Lipton was concerned that a "no caffeine" selling point might backfire on its other products, which, with sales in the hundreds of millions of dollars and heavy in caffeine, could be hurt if the same consumers were pursued. Finally, Lipton's marketing people believed that many American consumers would find the cost of herbal tea excessive (about ten cents more per box), the idea of drinking "flowers" repugnant, the image of an herb tea drinker too hip or exotic and not in keeping with the regular tea-drinker's self-image, or drinking herb tea dangerous (some people believe that herbs are upsetting or potentially toxic). Hence, product differentiation was called for to protect Lipton's existing products and to reach the proper market segment.

The market focus strategy is not applied only by giants such as Lipton. As a matter of fact, many small and medium-sized firms find the strategy the only way to survive against their larger rivals. In other words, they find it essential to go after market niches. We see the market focus strategy being applied with increasing frequency, too, as a consequence of the ever-greater splintering of consumer markets. In certain ways, a market focus orientation even requires more marketing than other strategies. Segments are difficult to find and reach. They must be of a sufficient size, and/or the product and a marketing campaign must be altered to make a profit. And they are more sensitive to competition and changes in consumer tastes, thereby requiring closer monitoring and more frequent changes in marketing programs.

Implicit in a discussion of customer analysis and competitive analysis is a third activity: *analysis of the constraints, power, and liabilities of the firm.* This takes into account the goals of the firm, its financial and human resources, its production capabilities, its organization structure, the economic environment, the social-political-legal environment, and other factors. Each of these must be considered from a marketing perspective. However, because each is covered in the remaining chapters of the book, nothing more will be said about them here. We turn now to the marketing tools managers have at their disposal to respond to or influence their markets.

PLANNING THE MARKETING EFFORT

Industry Analysis

Nowhere is the integrative function of marketing more evident than in its role as the lever regulating a firm's place in its industry. An industry may be viewed as having two attributes or consequences for the firm. The first is called a *shirttail effect.* To a certain extent, as the industry goes, so goes the firm. There are forces underlying every industry that more or less affect all firms equally. Thus all firms face, among other forces, an actual and a potential market; a particular economic, technological, and human environment with common assets and liabilities; and a set of competitive and legal rules governing conduct. Although these forces constrain or facilitate a firm's operations, they do not, by themselves, determine its performance. Rather, it is through the *bootstrap effect* that a firm controls its destiny. By this is meant the actions taken by a firm to respond to or influence the competitive pressures it feels as a member of an industry. Obviously, some firms are better able to do this than others. Let us describe the competitive threats and ways to combat them, for these serve as one basis for marketing strategy.

Any firm will face five classes of competitive threats in an industry.[12] These are (1) threats of new entrants, (2) rivalry among existing firms, (3) threats of substitute products, (4) bargaining power of suppliers, and (5) bargaining power of customers. The essence of marketing strategy with respect to these threats is to maximize the relative power of the firm vis-à-vis the sources of each threat.

Threats of new entrants. Firms within an industry often resist the entry of new firms. The rationale is that there is only so much business to go around and a new seller simply means less for all. In general, entrance to an industry is controlled by two factors. One consists of the specific actions taken by existing firms.

A case in point is the experience of Southwest Airlines. Claiming that the Texas market could not support another airline, Braniff, Trans Texas, and Continental Airlines asked for a restraining order prohibiting issuance of a license to Southwest in 1968. Only after Southwest appealed to the state supreme court was it allowed to fly in 1970. However, the company had no planes, pilots, or supporting staff. To raise capital, Southwest decided to sell stock. But just as the stock was to go public, Braniff and Trans Texas (now Texas International) again attempted to block the venture on the grounds that Southwest's proposal would violate certain intrastate exclusivity requirements. This claim, too, was found later to be groundless. Finally, Southwest began to fly in 1971, four years after incorporation. In the ensuing years, however, three more major lawsuits, two going all the way to the U.S. Supreme Court, nearly broke the back of Southwest.

But these were not the only roadblocks faced by Southwest. Braniff, in particular, allegedly tried to block the entrance of Southwest through numerous price cutting, scheduling, and other competitive marketing moves. Throughout the turmoil, Southwest persevered by following an overall cost leadership strategy aimed at a special market segment: people flying between large cities over short to medium hauls. Today Southwest has revenues approaching $400 million and regularly attains the highest profit margins among all domestic carriers.

The other force controlling entry to a market consists of natural barriers. These include high capital requirements, inherent economies of scale, special product differentiation (e.g., high advertising needed to build a brand image), impediments to distribution, established cost disadvantages, and certain government policies.[13]

From a marketing perspective, any firm must consider how strong the threat of another's potential entry is, what effects it would have on the firm and market, and what actions to take, if any. Barriers to entry, either natural or initiated by competing firms, tend to promote industry concentration over time. Some firms may want to increase the barriers and resist the entry of newcomers; the market leader invariably finds itself in this position. On occasion, firms may wish to reduce entry barriers or at least not resist a newcomer. For example, a firm that has a small share of the market and uses a market focus strategy based on product differentiation may welcome the entry of a firm that would compete with the low-cost market leader on the basis of price. Such battles tend to lower the quality of the low-cost firms' products or at least allow the high-quality marketer a chance to siphon off disenchanted buyers from the price-oriented combatants. In any case, the threat of a new entrant in an industry should cause the existing firms to reassess their pricing, product quality, advertising, and other marketing tactics, as well as their capital requirements, economies of scale, and government policies.

Rivalry among existing firms.   This is the classic notion of competition. The strategic alternatives include product differentiation, cost leadership, and market focus. The means to compete reside in product, price, communication, and/or distribution tactics. Specific choices of strategy and implementation are governed, in part, by market share, growth, and the nature of overlap of strategies among firms within the industry. We will discuss the managerial guidelines in these respects later when we consider portfolio and strategic group analysis.

For now, the only rivalry-based concept we'll discuss is that of *exit barriers* to firms in an industry. Firms find it difficult to leave an industry when their investments in land, labor, and capital are great within the industry or when government regulations forbid them to do so. In addition, entangling relationships with other products and departments within the firm, intangible commitments to employees and communities, and inertia and outright fear sometimes play a role. Exit barriers thwart the movement of excess capacity, intensify intra-industry competition, and in the extreme damage the profitability of an industry. Firms are forced into head-to-head confrontations and respond in kind (for example, by imitative price cutting) or are even forced to injure competitors. This is especially so when market growth slows or when competitors are numerous. While the ideal situation for a competitor often is where exit barriers are low and entry barriers are high, firms have little influence over their situation in this regard. Product differentiation and market segmentation may be key marketing options in the effort to reduce the harmful effects of high exit barriers (see discussion of tactics below).

Threats of substitutes. Competition occurs at many levels even when we limit consideration to the needs of consumers. People buy products because of the needs that the products satisfy. But needs are not always the obvious entities we sometimes believe them to be.

Imagine that you are the brand manager for Pringle's potato chips. What need does Pringle's satisfy and with what does it compete? Obviously, Pringle's satisfies a general hunger need or a specific craving for starch, salt, and bulk. And it competes with Frito-Lay, among other brands of potato chips. But behind the obvious we can see that the competition here is among similar firms and for a relatively circumscribed need. Competition among regular, ruffled, low-calorie, cheese, or barbecue-flavored potato chips — all of which address similar needs — involves basically the same class of competitors. However, this is only part of the picture.

At the same time, Pringle's competes with other snack foods — peanuts, pretzels, crackers, candy, hors d'oeuvres, even fresh cauliflower. To be sure, such competition is further removed from the Pringle's–Frito-Lay encounter. But a similar need is involved, and at least some of the time Pringle's competes with each of these or some other snack food. Actually, consumer needs may even be more complex than this. Pringle's may be consumed, not because of an urge for salt or bulk, but out of habit, or on an impulse, in a quest for variety, or as a social gesture so as to please a guest or not offend a host.

Then, too, we sometimes view consumption too narrowly. The decision to buy Pringle's is seldom an isolated choice. Rather, it fits within a larger pattern of consumption or expresses a part of the buyer's personality or life-style: the elderly buy Pringle's because of its long shelf life, the wealthy because of its novelty. Construed in this sense, Pringle's competes with other ideas (dieting, health consciousness) and activities (saving for a special gift), as well as in the traditional senses. We thus begin to see that any product competes in a generic sense with a wide spectrum of brands, products, and "things" that threaten to become substitutes.

What this means for a firm is that it must not view its offerings parochially. Competition from substitutes places constraints on price, product and package design, distribution, and even advertising. A firm must identify and take into account the larger competitive network. The study of competition in a generic sense also opens up new opportunities if a firm can discover new uses for its products. Thus, Arm and Hammer markets baking soda not only for traditional uses but for odor absorption in the refrigerator or in cat litter boxes, and for cleaning teeth. Chex is now promoted as a party snack as well as a crunchy cereal. And reflecting the changing times, as well as a very competitive gift-giving market, the diamond industry has progressed from an undifferentiated selling approach to specific emphasis of engagements and weddings in its ads ("Diamonds are forever") and most recently to highlighting anniversaries of all sorts as appropriate occasions for giving a diamond throughout one's life.

The threat of competition from substitutes again points up the crucial role of customer analysis. A firm must do research to look deeply into the consumer's psyche as well as to explore the larger life-space that surrounds the act of consumption. Of equal importance, the firm must view itself not as a producer of a specific product but as the provider of the means to satisfy particular needs. This forces the firm to open up its operations and compete at both deeper and broader levels. The National Cash Register Company for a long time perceived its mission too narrowly: it saw itself a seller of cash registers (and rather slow and unadaptable ones at that). When competitors offered new electronic systems that satisfied a wide spectrum of needs, including information storage and processing, NCR belatedly followed suit. The IBM corporation is not so much in the computer business as it is in the business of satisfying the information-processing needs of firms. Canon does not sell copy machines per se, but rather is concerned with helping firms improve office productivity. The firm that purposefully considers threats of substitutes builds its programs around the broader functions that its products satisfy and in the process enhances its chances for success in the long run.

Bargaining power of suppliers. The firms in an industry receive their resources from suppliers (the sellers of materials, service, and other things needed to produce one's offerings). Because suppliers to a certain extent control the prices and quality of their goods and services, they indirectly influence the performance of firms that are their customers. Although companies can pass along cost increases to the ultimate customer, the market can bear only so much, and excessive costs at the supply end can damage the profitability and growth of an entire industry.

The exact terms of trade depend on the relative power between suppliers and firms in the industry. Power lies in the bargaining abilities of the parties, the availability of alternatives, and the importance of the things exchanged. Five factors have been identified in this regard. A supplier group will be more powerful, vis-à-vis an industry customer, to the extent that (1) it is dominated by a few companies and is more concentrated than the industry it sells to, (2) it is not obliged to contend with other substitute products for sale to the industry, (3) the industry is not an important customer of the supplier group, (4) the supplier group's products are differentiated or it has built up *switching costs* (the costs that any one of its customers would incur in switching to another supplier), and (5) the supplier group poses a credible threat of forward integration (e.g., expansion into manufacturing in direct competition with its customers).[14]

To ensure success, a firm must overcome any dependence on its suppliers. Often its options may be limited, however, because many of the imbalances are external to the firm. Nevertheless, to the extent that a firm can purchase a large portion of a seller's goods (yet retain alternative sources in the wings), confine purchases to standardized items, threaten to backward-integrate, and/or reduce its switching costs in some way, it can lessen its dependence on the supplier. From a marketing standpoint, control over suppliers is essential to maintain product quality, pricing, and distribution programs. Moreover, as Coleco's experience shows with its introduction of the Cabbage Patch Kids dolls, a bottleneck at the supplier end can result in enormous numbers of missed sales, the loss of goodwill with retailer and consumer alike, and the opportunity for rivals to enter the still unsaturated market.

Bargaining power of customers. A parallel competitive threat to a firm lies in the relative power of its customers. A powerful buyer can command lower prices, more service, special product features, and other concessions: witness the clout that Sears and other giant retailers have in their dealings with some manufacturers of appliances, furniture, and housewares. A buyer group will be powerful in relation to a seller if (1) it is concentrated or purchases large volumes relative to the seller's sales, (2) the products it purchases from the industry represent a significant fraction of the customer's costs or purchases, (3) the products it purchases from the industry are standard or undifferentiated, (4) it faces few switching costs, (5) it earns low profits and therefore places special emphasis on paying a low price, (6) buyers pose a credible threat of backward integration, and (7) the industry's product is unimportant to the quality of the buyers' products or services.[15]

A nice illustration of the bargaining power of customers and what it means for marketing can be seen in the example of the U.S. apparel industry. With annual sales in the $20 billion range as of the mid-1980s, U.S. apparel makers face a life-and-death threat from importers. Whereas imports were a relatively minor consideration in the 1960s, when they represented only 10 to 12 percent of domestic production, today 50 percent or more of all clothing sales in the United

States originates overseas. The squeeze on domestic firms has forced them to compete on product differentiation terms, since the cheaper wages of manufacturers overseas make overall cost leadership impossible. As a consequence, domestic producers have been pushing so-called designer goods at an unheard-of pace. But anyone can play the designer-goods game, and imitators quickly joined in. This in turn has forced large retailers to demand that they, too, carry designer clothes so as not to be outdone by boutique shops, and even discount stores have managed to procure some designer brands. The result has been a decline in sales for many clothing manufacturers and retailers.

To compound matters, large retailers have been flexing their muscles in still another way, to the consternation of producers: they now market their own private-label clothing along with name brands. In this way, chains such as Neiman-Marcus, Saks Fifth Avenue, Lord & Taylor, and even J. C. Penney can offer "exclusive" merchandise and charge the prices necessary to make a profit. Given their buying power and the fact that private-label brands do not carry the overhead of a designer brand, retailers can demand favorable terms from the manufacturer. Indeed, the retailer can threaten to purchase more goods from importers, as its merchandise is made to its own specifications and U.S. makers offer no special expertise. In short, the power of retail buyers constitutes a threat to U.S. clothing manufacturers that is matched only by the threat of foreign rivalry. With labor costs higher here, U.S. clothing makers are caught in the middle, and their future looks bleak.

Generally, however, a firm faced by a powerful buyer has a number of marketing remedies. Perhaps the most far-ranging and fundamental lie in the product(s) the firm has to offer. Through product design, a brand image, service, exclusive or selective distribution, or other marketing tactics, sellers must create a distinctive offering. However, because this edge is typically short-lived, the firm must put considerable investment into the monitoring of consumer tastes and new product development, topics we will turn to shortly. Moreover, the firm must give special emphasis to market selection, for survival may well hinge on finding the right niches in the marketplace. Finally, either through outright vertical integration or through closer cooperation with intermediaries, the firm can seek to extend its power over consumer pricing, selling, consumer monitoring, and other marketing decisions. In Italy, a renaissance of sorts in the clothing industry has begun where "vertical disintegration" and the formation of "constellations" of firms has replaced both vertically integrated and totally independent enterprises.[16]

Successful marketing requires that a firm understand its position in an industry so that it can make choices that not only meet consumer needs but also overcome the five competitive threats noted earlier. This means taking special care to position a firm in relation to its customers, suppliers, and rivals, and its own internal capabilities. It means also an ability to plan, monitor, and forecast changes in the environment. All of this takes place, of course, within a legal and ethical environment that constrains choices still further.

Portfolio and Strategic Group Analysis

The product portfolio. Nearly every business markets a number of product classes or brands within a product class. However, seldom do all these products or brands perform equally well, and different strategies may be required for each to accomplish the larger goals of the organization. One way to manage the strategy of all products is to view them together (i.e., as the product portfolio) according to a small number of fundamental criteria. We will scrutinize one such scheme developed by the Boston Consulting Group (BCG).[17] However, it should be noted that other frameworks exist such as General Electric's strategic business screen,[18] Shell's directional policy matrix,[19] or McKinsey's integrated method.

The BCG product portfolio approach to corporate strategy is illustrated in Figure 1.2. Market growth and relative market share (the ratio of a firm's sales to that of the largest competitor) are used to classify a firm's products or brands. The choice of these two criteria is based on the supposition that market growth reflects both the vitality of the market and the stage a product is in in its life cycle, whereas relative market share reveals the competitive position of a firm. Because market growth is only indirectly and partially influenceable by a firm, the primary strategic decision is thought to reside in choices to improve market share. This, in turn, requires application of specific marketing tactics such as advertising or price changes. Moreover, it is believed that high market share will lead to profitability.[20] However, every firm must decide for itself the strength of the relationship and whether it is truly causal or not.

Notice in Figure 1.2 that the division of market growth and relative market share into high and low categories results in a fourfold classification. A 10 percent market growth rate and a 1.0 relative market share are used as arbitrary divisions of the two dimensions. A firm's products might then be plotted and appear anywhere in the matrix. So plotted, a product will be labeled either a cash cow, star, question mark, or dog. These are defined as follows:

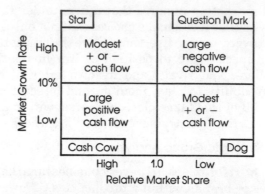

Figure 1.2   Summary of the Boston Consulting Group Approach to Corporate Strategy

- A *cash cow* is a product with low growth but high market share. It generates high amounts of cash and a profit. But because of poor prospects for growth and relative ease in maintaining share, not all the cash can or should be reinvested in the cash cow. (Investment means spending on product development, advertising, promotion, distribution, or other marketing tactics.) Rather, BCG maintains that the generated cash should optimally be used to invest in a question-mark product.

- *Stars* are high-growth and high-market-share products. To maintain share will require relatively more investment than for a cash cow. Although handsome profits typically occur for stars, the cash flow will be small and may even be negative (requiring support from a cash cow or outside help). Eventually, as market growth slows, stars become cash cows.

- High growth and low market share define a *question mark*. Not only does a question mark fail to generate a cash flow, but it draws cash from other products or sources (ideally from a cash cow). The cash is needed to maintain or gain share. Generally, profits will be low or nonexistent here. With no cash infusion, a question mark may become a dog. But with the proper investment, it can become a star. A strategic choice must be made with a question-mark product one way or the other.

- A *dog* consists of a low-growth and low-market-share product. It either does not generate much cash or does not require much. To extricate a dog from the category is either impossible or formidably expensive. The options open to a firm here typically involve harvesting (milking the product until it fails completely), sale of the product, or outright abandonment. Dogs, of course, are losing propositions and, given the cash drain, are often disposed of quickly.

The BCG product portfolio is designed to help a firm manage its products over time. A "success sequence" would be an investment from a cash cow to a question mark, in order to move the latter to star status and eventually to a cash cow. "Disaster sequences" include the star → question mark → dog ordering (or a subset of the progression) and the cash cow → dog sequence. At the same time, a firm must maintain a mixture and balance between products so as to ensure that some will generate cash and others will use it to advantage. The product portfolio is designed for long-run decisions of about five years or more.

To take the example of Texas Instruments again, we see that its home computer business was a question mark by 1983. To make it a star, considerable investment would have been necessary, especially given the very high market growth rate, the intensity of competition, and the much greater share by Commodore. Further, the rapidly declining price of home computers meant that less cash would be generated. All in all, Texas Instruments made the decision to disinvest its home computer business before it became a dog.

The Boston Consulting Group asserts that any firm should strive to create an internal balance of products based on the following "ideal" distribution in the product portfolio:

> Products with the largest sales ... should appear either as "stars" or "cash cows." Few products should appear in the "question marks" quadrant: they require heavy cash commitment to transform them into "stars" and can be major losers if something goes wrong. The majority of products should be positioned as "cash cows" ... since these underwrite the remaining products. ... Few products should appear as "dogs" since these are "cash traps." ...[21]

Further, as a competitive tool, the BCG product portfolio can be used in a number of ways. First, estimates of product portfolios for competitors should be made. These can be studied and compared among themselves and with the focal firm's to anticipate the effects of attempts to gain share or to divest, and to forecast possible moves by the competitors.

As an example, consider again the chain saw industry, especially the position of McCulloch. McCulloch's market share dropped from about 27 percent in 1973 to 20 percent in 1977. Worse, from a position where it and Homelite shared roles as the market leaders in 1973, it saw its ranking drop to third as Beaird-Poulan skyrocketed from relative obscurity to more than match the leaders. In terms of the BCG matrix, McCulloch was a question mark in 1973 but near the threshold of star status. What might have McCulloch, or rather its parent firm, Black and Decker, done to preserve McCulloch's market share? Well, Black and Decker had two cash cows at this time: its U.S. Power Tools and International Power Tools divisions, which together accounted for about 85 percent of its total business. Given the mushrooming casual-user segment of the chain saw market, Black and Decker might have invested in McCulloch to make it a star. It might also have pursued more aggressively the high-profit professional-user market. Instead, partly in response to an antitrust challenge of Black and Decker's acquisition of McCulloch by the Justice Department in early 1974, Black and Decker kept its businesses separate. By the time the case was settled in Black and Decker's favor in November 1976, it had missed its opportunity to become the market leader. Indeed, earnings for McCulloch dropped sharply in the late 1970s and into the 1980s as the chain saw market matured. Black and Decker then divested itself of McCulloch. Whether investment could have made it a star in the casual-user and pro markets is difficult to say. But it might well have enhanced its earnings in the short run and reaped more revenue from the sale of a stronger McCulloch. Although still in third place, McCulloch's market share is now below 20 percent.

The BCG matrix can also be used to forecast trends. Portfolios of the focal firm and competitors can be prepared for the previous five-year period, the present, and an anticipated future period to gain insight into changing market, product life cycle, and competitive conditions. In fact, analyses over time are essential, because a static application of the portfolio matrix can be misleading. For example, a small-share company in a low-growth market may do well over time if it succeeds in increasing its share significantly at the expense of its rivals.

It is important to realize that portfolio analysis, or any other such framework, provides only a partial picture of the health of a firm's products. Any particular firm may find that market growth and market share considerations are less important than other factors, given its unique situation. For example, government regulations, the nature of technology, or any one of the many threats to competition in industries that we mentioned earlier might be the dominant factor. Then, too, care must be taken to fashion a program to implement any strategy chosen. The soundest strategy may fall flat if the wrong marketing tactics are pursued. We turn now to the final strategic tool, one that is intermediate between industry analysis and the product portfolio approach.

Strategic group analysis. A vast array of marketing tactics is available to firms for implementing their strategic choices. The product can vary in features, quality, and packaging. Price can vary by quantity bought or time period. Service, credit, and warranties can be added as enticements. Different advertising messages can be employed along with varied media and scheduling alternatives. Dealer and customer promotions can augment the marketing effort. Sales forces permit forceful, face-to-face selling. Options in physical distribution and in retailing and wholesaling permit a tailoring of availability and selling at the grass roots level. And so on.

Despite the many possible combinations of tactics that might be chosen, in practice an industry is usually characterized by a small number of fundamental tactics common to all or most participants. The particular combination of tactics chosen constitutes the firm's strategy, and firms' strategies differ in their relative emphasis on the various tactics. Typically, two or three tactics are sufficient to define an industry. Moreover, a cross-classification of tactics generally finds well-defined clusters of emphasis whereby firms within a cluster can be seen to compete among themselves, each firm using a combination of options common to its cluster but different than combinations found in other clusters.

In one study of sixty-four companies in eight different industries, it was discovered that the following two goals described the strategic groups:

1. Achieve the lowest delivered cost position relative to competition, coupled with both an acceptable delivered quality and a pricing policy to gain profitable volume and market share growth.

2. Achieve the highest product/service/quality differentiation position relative to competition, coupled with both an acceptable delivered cost structure and a pricing policy to gain margins sufficient to fund reinvestment in product/service differentiation.[22]

The most successful companies scored high on one of these two dimensions *and* moderately high on the other. To score low on one dimension (for example, achieving a high delivered cost) or moderately high on both generally meant inferior performances. Success thus entails making a commitment to one of the dimensions while maintaining secondary emphasis on the other. Apparently only three of these firms were able to pursue both dimensions at a high level: Caterpillar in the heavy equipment industry, Philip Morris in cigarettes, and Daimler Benz in truck manufacturing. It was also found that in each of the eight industries the firm that offered the lowest delivered cost tended to grow slowly and have a lower sales turnover, whereas the differentiated position leader grew faster and had a higher sales turnover. In addition, contrary to the Boston Consulting Group's advice, cash cows were used more for internal reinvestment than for support of question marks. And overall cost leadership was practiced successfully by lower, as well as higher, market share firms, contrary to earlier conventional wisdom. Overall, companies succeeded best when they strove for a leadership position in either low delivered cost or product differentiation.

Strategic group analyses are important planning aids and can explain why some firms in an industry are more profitable than others.[23] In practice, every industry will have its own unique dimensions that define the groups. Typical dimensions include product differentiation, degree of vertical integration, overall cost leadership, type of distribution channel, and mix of communication strategies. Figure 1.3 presents an example of a strategic group analysis applied to the chain saw industry in the early 1970s. Notice that quality brand image and mix of distribution channels define three primary strategic groups: the professional, branded mass market, and private label groups (Skil, a small producer, is off by itself, though close to two groups). Notice, too, that Homelite and McCulloch, the market leaders, offer moderately high-quality brands that are distributed through hardware, farm, and department stores. Beaird-Poulan sells primarily under private labels to specialty and department stores and as a consequence has a lower-quality brand image. With its subsequent marketing of small, low-priced saws in the middle to late 1970s, however, it had begun to sell both branded and private label saws through nearly all channel options. In the process, it was able to function in two strategic groups. Finally, Stihl and the other members of the pro group market high-quality products through dealers. Of special note is the fact that the three groups permit relatively independent marketing strategies without much competition between groups.

To return to the case of McCulloch, we see that it failed to differentiate itself sufficiently from Homelite and at the same time was joined in the branded mass market group by Beaird-Poulan. One option for McCulloch might have been sale of a higher-quality saw created for the professional market (and for the casual users who might trade up) but sold through certain strategically located chain stores. Alternatively, it could have used regional servicing dealers with free

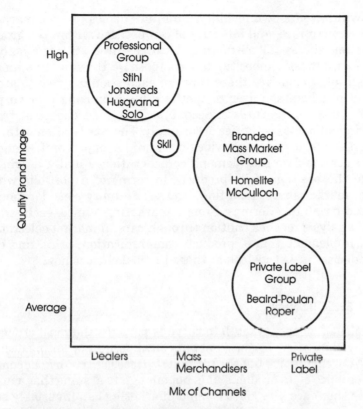

Figure 1.3 Example of a Stategic Group Map Applied to
the Chain Saw Industry

SOURCE: Michael E. Porter, *Competitive Strategy: Techniques for
Analyzing Industries and Competitors* (New York: Free Press,
1980), p. 153.

pickup and delivery. As it was, McCulloch chose to fight in both the
branded and the private label groups with lower- and moderately
priced saws. This worked fairly well as long as the casual-user market
was growing. But once this growth slowed, McCulloch was left with a
depressed, narrow position and increased competition.

A firm must decide which strategic group(s) to compete in and how
to achieve a leadership position within it. Profitability of a particular
firm will depend on the strategic group it functions in as well as its
ability to implement its strategy in that group. Strategic groups can
compete with each other, but they generally isolate competitors across
groups. Membership in a group will differentially affect a firm's ability
to resist entry into the industry, bargain with customers and suppliers,
and combat inroads from substitute products. Then, too, each strategic

group will have its own mobility inhibitors across groups, market potential, growth rate, and intensity of competition within the group.

In sum, successful marketing requires three strategic activities. First, a firm must combat the five competitive threats in its industry. Although all rivals face these threats, each should strive to attain a differential advantage over competitors by enhancing its own power position vis-à-vis the threats. Second, a firm must choose a strategic group and adjust its activities accordingly. The competition within and between strategic groups provides both unique opportunities and constraints for the firm that demand consideration. Finally, a firm must analyze the position of its products in terms of a portfolio wherein growth, market share, cash flow, and profitability considerations are managed for all its offerings. From a marketing stance, each strategic level of analysis reaches fruition through careful market selection and careful implementation of product, communication, price, and distribution decisions. Let us look at these tactical choices now.

MARKET SELECTION

The choice of what market(s) to serve is perhaps the most crucial decision faced by a firm because not only do all other marketing decisions follow from this choice but the ultimate success of the firm depends on the acceptance of its products. It is not enough to assume that a market exists or that once a product is made marketing can invariably sell it. Rather, one must begin with assessment of customer needs. Given that the product fills a need and (it is hoped) a competitive advantage, one can then evaluate the size of the market and begin to plan and carry through the tactical activities needed to reach it.

Consumer Behavior

A key activity in market selection is the analysis of customer behavior. Earlier I presented a simplified model and said that the consumer decision process begins by exposure to physical cues. The consumer then perceives these as subjective attributes, benefits, and so forth, and somehow organizes them in memory to form an attitude toward the product offering. Finally, attitude is thought to influence the decision process one way or the other.

In reality, of course, the decision process is much more complex than this. As a matter of fact, marketers have developed a number of theories that break down the process into many psychological and psychosocial components. It is beyond the scope of this chapter to consider these (references to some leading treatments appear at the end). I will, however, briefly describe the central elements that cut across many of the theories and indicate how these are used in practice.

Thinking processes. The dominant consideration in virtually all theories of consumer choice is how consumers process information. One way to represent information processing is in terms of the beliefs consumers have and the organization of these beliefs in their memory. Beliefs are subjective judgments as to which attributes a product has (for instance, its weight, durability, or cost) and how much of each attribute the product possesses (for instance, heavy, highly durable, or moderately expensive). A belief might consist also of a judgment about the consequences of purchase or product use (for example, "Brand X will keep my floors clean for two weeks"). Beliefs are used by consumers to make choices among alternative brands or among broad consumption options.

Marketers have developed many models to depict how beliefs are formed, grouped, and used in decision-making. Obviously, from a managerial perspective, if we know what beliefs a consumer has toward our brand, we can better decide how to communicate its attributes; change, add, or remove attributes; influence beliefs and decision-making; and so on. In addition, we can see how consumers view our brand and the competitors' brands in order to discover our relative advantage or disadvantage and help determine what, if anything, we must do to improve the situation. Thinking processes constitute the more or less rational side of consumption decisions. They dominate industrial buying, and they play an important role in everyday consumer choice as well.

Feeling processes. It is also important to understand the emotional reactions of consumers to our products. These reactions harbor needs and motives for buying, as well as evaluations of the utility or importance of specific product attributes. Together with beliefs, our feelings determine our attitudes and thus indirectly influence choice. A firm's knowledge of the feelings of consumers about its products (and the products of its competitors) contributes to the design of its products, packages, persuasive communications, promotions, and deals; to its pricing; and even to its distribution decisions. Like beliefs, feelings toward our brand and rival brands need to be considered in order to assess the strength of our competitive position. Emotional considerations obviously pervade everyday consumer decision-making, yet they can be salient factors in industrial buying, too, despite efforts to focus on economic and other supposedly rational criteria.

Social processes. Buying is not strictly a psychological process. Social processes shape consumption, too. This takes many forms, such as the influence of norms, peer pressure, family decision-making activities, organizational buying processes, and bargaining and negotiation, among others. Knowledge of the role of social factors in choice is especially helpful in the design of advertising and other marketing communications.

A model. In order to gain insight into how consumers make choices, marketers have developed representations, or models, of the processes. These imperfect models represent the causes of decisions or of actual choice outcomes. Sometimes this modeling is done in laboratory experiments; at other times naturalistic surveys are employed. One model that has proved useful in forecasting as well as in product design and advertising is the attitude model. In simplified form, this model can be written as

$$P \text{ or } I = f(B, F, S)$$

That is, actual purchase behaviors (P) or intentions to buy (I) are hypothesized to be a function of one's beliefs (B), feelings (F), and social pressure (S). More complicated models are used to represent choices among alternative brands and to account for the full range of psychological and social determinants. The literature is filled with specific examples. Although most of these models employ quantitative methods, qualitative research serves as an essential complement in most real-world applications.

Market Segmentation

Customer analysis is primarily an activity directed at the study of consumers as individuals. It thus focuses on micro phenomena. Although this helps in product design and other tactical decisions, it does not provide information on the size and composition of markets or how groups of consumers will respond to product offerings. Knowledge of the macro side of consumption is essential because for most firms it is impossible to make and deliver a unique product to each and every consumer. Trade-offs must be made between the ideal of fully satisfying everyone's needs and the capabilities of firms to meet these needs. In practice, well-defined markets or market segments must be identified so that some standardization and accompanying efficiencies can be taken advantage of. The process for doing so has come to be known as market segmentation.

Market segmentation is the activity of identifying subgroups of the population as potential customers. Segmentation should yield a group of people with favorable attitudes toward one's product — and, it is to be hoped, intentions to buy it. In addition, the segment should be of a sufficient size to warrant pursuit, reachable, and not overly competitive. The following criteria represent typical bases for market segmentation in that tastes of people classified into each category vary and represent differential opportunities for marketing that must be assessed:

Demographic. Age, sex, income, occupation, family size, education, religious affiliation, marital status, race

Geographic. Section of country; urban, rural, or suburban

Psychological. Personality, attitudes, life-style

Social. Social class, group affiliation

Behavioral. Benefits sought, typical consumption amount, end use, consumption status (e.g., nonuser, first time, repeat)

One of the most fruitful means of segmentation is known as *benefit segmentation.* Consumers are grouped according to the product attributes they desire most or the consequences of product use they value most highly. Notice that this procedure begins with criteria that are clearly related to consumer needs. Indeed, the objective is to discover relatively homogeneous clusters of buyers with similar needs. After consumers have been grouped in this way, correlates of people within segments are sought. For instance, key demographic and psychological attributes of people are often recorded, as are actual behaviors (previous purchases, statements of preferences, activities, and so on). This gives management a picture of the key benefits people seek in the product it offers, how many people prefer each benefit, and what characteristics describe the people in each benefit segment. Such information can be used in decisions about product design, advertising, pricing, and distribution. Table 1.1 provides an example applied to the market for bank services. Notice that five distinct groups of consumers emerge, each varying in size and benefit sought. Notice further how the consumers differ by segment and how they perceive the various banks. A particular bank could use these data to see if it is serving whom it thinks it is and determine whether an untapped market exists. The picture thus provided could also help the bank in tailoring services and communicating with customers.

Market segmentation can be a useful strategic tool. Consider the case of the copy machine business.[24] For years, Xerox owned the copy

Table 1.1 An Example of Benefit Segmentation

Segment	1	2	3	4	5
Name	Front Runners	Loan Seekers	Representative Subgroup	Value Seekers	One-Stop Bankers
Principal benefits sought	Large Bank for all Good advertising	Good reputation Loans easily available Low loan interest	No differences (about average on all benefits sought)	High savings interest Quick service Low loan interest Plenty of parking	Wide variety of services Convenient hours Quick service Encourage financial responsibility Convenient branch

Banks favored	Commercial Bank A	Commercial B Savings X	Commercial A Commercial B	Savings Y Savings Z	Commercial A Commercial B
Demographic	Young Rent home	More transient More blue collar		Tend to save more	Older
Life-style Characteristics*	High ability to manage money	Liberal about use of credit Positive about bank loans		Conservative overall life-style Conservative about use of credit Low propensity toward risk taking	Conservative about use of credit Positive toward checking account
Size (n)	8 (2%)	51 (15%)	118 (34%)	89 (26%)	78 (23%)

*Dimensions represent factor scores of all 196 general and banking-specific life-style items.

SOURCE: Roger J. Calantone and Alan G. Sawyer, "The Stability of Benefit Segments," *Journal of Marketing Research* 15 (August 1978); 400.

machine market. Its marketing was based on products that used a dry toner and parts unique to each model of machine. Xerox manufactured and assembled most of its components. This permitted the manufacture of a high-quality, durable machine suitable for customers who wanted high-quality or high-volume production, or both. Of course, the price of the machine was high, too. The company had its own sales force and service personnel. During this period, customers had to lease the machines from Xerox. Its high-quality machines regularly captured 70 percent or more of the market.

Enter the competition. Savin saw an opportunity to go after the low-price, infrequent-user market. To do this, it used the cheaper liquid toner technology and employed interchangeable parts across its line of machines. Although the speed and quality of its copies could not match Xerox's, the target market accepted this trade-off to get a much lower price. A side benefit was somewhat better reliability. To reach the more fragmented market, Savin used a dealer system and sold its machines rather than leasing them. This was not only necessary but cheaper. Service was provided by the dealers; a simpler machine made this possible, and Savin provided support to the dealer. Finally, Savin purchased all its parts and assembled them in Japan; this gave it a further cost advantage. The result was that Savin succeeded in finding an unfulfilled market segment and providing a product that would satisfy consumers in that segment. Today, many competitors pursue the low and high end of the copy machine market, and Xerox has been forced to more actively segment and alter its marketing tactics to meet this competition.

Market Monitoring and Decision Support Systems

A key factor in market selection, as well as in the management of the entire marketing program, is the collection, analysis, and use of information. Modern marketing organizations are increasingly establishing separate departments for this function, which goes by such names as *management information systems* or *decision support systems*. Just as frequently, firms perform the information function through closer coordination of their many separate departments. (A later chapter in this book discusses this important topic.) I'll simply note here that special attention must be given to consumer research, data analysis and storage (for example, statistical modeling, establishment of an archive), normative support systems (such as mathematical models and interactive computer support programs), and new ways of disseminating and using the information.

PRODUCT DECISIONS

New Product Development

Changing consumer tastes and evolving economic and competitive conditions make product innovation a necessity for maintenance of a healthy business. Today's leading companies no longer leave things to chance or the inventive genius of a founder; they rely on a purposeful program of new product development. To be sure, the program is part art and part science. But the large expenditures involved, together with the sobering realization that failure rates are high, make it imperative that efforts be made to meld art and science and do so well before the product is launched. It is estimated that the cost of designing, developing, and introducing a new industrial product averages more than $2 million, while expenditures for a new consumer product average about $6 million. The chance for success at the design stage is given as about 30 percent for industrial and 20 percent for consumer goods.[25]

Many activities must be coordinated to bring a product successfully to market. The most important fall within the following five stages:

Creative Phase → Design and Development Phase → Testing Phase → Launch → Ongoing Management

In the *creative phase,* new ideas are generated. These may arise from secondary sources, consumer research (for example, interviews), the R&D department, feedback from salespeople, consumer suggestions or complaints, employee contributions, and even the competition. Some firms use separate creative groups or executive brainstorming sessions. Brand managers generally provide important input here. Occasionally, outside agencies or individuals are consulted. Once a new idea is generated, its utility must be assessed. This is usually done through subjective judgments, perhaps aided by rules of thumb and ranking or rating methods. Criteria considered at this early stage include estimates of the cost of development, potential receptivity of consumers, ease and cost of manufacture and marketing, profitability, degree of probable competition, and likelihood of success at each of the remaining four stages of the new product development process.

The *design and development* stage is in many ways the most crucial. It is here that the product takes shape conceptually and physically, that marketing plans are first formulated, and that a realistic assessment of costs and expected sales and profits is made. A particularly critical activity is customer analysis and market segmentation. This is done, in part, through a technique termed *perceptual mapping,* which I will describe in a moment. At the same time, the new product must be analyzed vis-à-vis the competition. This also can be done, in part, through perceptual mapping in a process termed *product positioning.* Finally, in the case of most consumer goods, the design will be given its toughest evaluation through mock pretests in which consumers evaluate the product and ads and express their preferences in simulated purchase environments. Various models and rules of thumb have been developed to aid in the interpretation of the data thus obtained. The Assessor model or BBDO's NEWS model are two leading examples.[26] The goal is to get feedback on the attractiveness of product attributes and communication tactics and to estimate trial and repeat purchasing. The design and development phase is a particularly sensitive one, as managers have vested interests and the firm wants to avoid rejecting potentially fruitful products or approving losers. Yet considerable uncertainty persists at this stage.

The third stage, *testing,* is designed to reduce uncertainty and provide more feedback. Typically, the product is given to one or a few users if it is an industrial product, or introduced into one or a handful of cities if it is a consumer good. Test marketing is expensive, generally $1 to $1.5 million. However, the information it provides for the fine-tuning of the entire marketing effort is more valid than that supplied by most pretests. This is because testing is done under more naturalistic conditions and with larger, more representative samples. The information sought includes awareness of the brand, knowledge of product attributes, attitudes and preferences, intentions to try the product, and actual trial and repeat purchase rates. In addition, panel diaries of consumers are sometimes used, as are store audits, consumer intercepts at the time of purchase, and posttrial interviews. Demographic, psychographic, life-style, and media exposure data may also be monitored. As with pretest data, the information gained from test marketing may be used in formal models to forecast trial and repeat purchasing behaviors after the product is put on the market. The drawbacks of test marketing, in addition to high cost, are that roll-out and national introduction may be delayed. This permits the competition to learn at the firm's expense and to catch up. Some companies even sabotage the test marketing of their competitors by changing their own pricing, advertising, and promotion programs in the public test market. For these reasons, many firms bypass test marketing, despite the loss in information that entails. Some companies, such as manufacturers of durable goods or industrial goods, find it impractical to test-market in any event.

Product launch is the fourth step. Here the product is introduced to the public, either nationwide or on a market-by-market basis to coordinate with production or other constraints. Special care is given to the monitoring of consumer adoptions, reactions by competitors, and problems in distribution. Invariably there are bugs in the coordination of the entire marketing effort, and these require immediate attention. Planning, monitoring, and a resilient, fast-acting management control system are essential at this stage.

Finally, the new product development process "ends" with *ongoing management*. We will discuss this activity shortly when we consider managing the product through its life cycle.

Perceptual Maps and Product Positioning

Most products and services have many physical and intangible attributes, with varied consequences for a would-be purchaser. An automobile is not merely "an automobile." Rather, for a consumer, it is a bundle of objective and subjective characteristics (size, color, ease of handling, roominess, comfort, price, etc.) and consequences (such as feelings of pride, power, or prestige). The marketer's task is a difficult one, for he or she must decide how many attributes to build into the product, how much quality to include in each attribute, and how to put the attributes together to gain a competitive advantage. Fortunately, largely owing to implicit coping strategies employed by consumers in everyday decision-making, only a few product attributes are important in any actual choice process. Indeed, two or three key attributes are often sufficient to predict consumer choices. As products become more complex and consumers become more sophisticated, however, more attributes need to be taken into account.

The conjunction of key product attributes and consumer perceptions (or beliefs) can be fruitfully represented in a *perceptual map*. Figure 1.4 presents one consumer's perception of beers for sale in Northern California. Perceptual maps can also be prepared for groups of consumers and market segments. The dots show the perceived positions of different beers (disregard the circles for the moment). The two most common methodologies used to produce perceptual maps are multidimensional scaling and factor analysis, but we will not discuss these procedures here.

Notice first in Figure 1.4 that this consumer uses two attributes to describe beers: heavy/light and bitter/mild. Some people employ more attributes and different ones (for instance, gaseousness, calorie content), but these two are quite common across the population. Notice further that the brands cover much of the map. This indicates that the

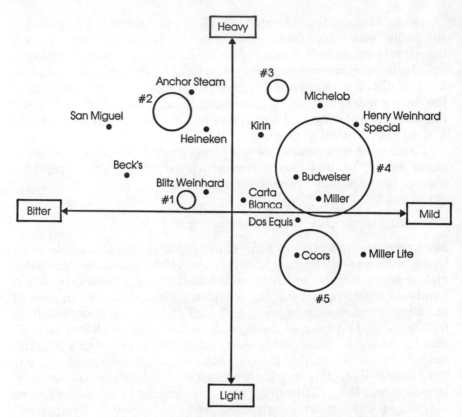

Figure 1.4   Perceptual Map of the Beer Market in Northern California

The dots represent the positions of brands as perceived by one beer drinker. The circles superimposed on this particular map represent centroids of consumer preferences; the size of a circle indicates an estimate of the number of people (or share of the market) preferring that particular combination of the heavy/light and bitter/mild attributes.

consumer believes that brands differ on the two dimensions to a considerable degree. San Miguel is perceived as a rather heavy, bitter beer, for example, whereas Miller Lite is seen as a very mild, moderately light beer.

What can one learn from perceptual maps? First, they indicate the most important attributes in consumer decision-making. These attributes then can become the focal ones in product design and advertising decisions. Second, perceptual maps show where one's own brand and those of the competition score in the minds of consumers on each salient attribute. Management thus discovers where it is strong or weak and who its primary rivals are. Third, perceptual maps suggest possible opportunities in the market. In Figure 1.4, for example, we see that no beer is perceived by this particular consumer to be both bitter and light. This suggests a potential entry point for a new product or an alternative strategy for a beer on the border of the bitter/light quadrant (e.g., Beck's). Of course, whether this unfilled niche is really a viable market or not will depend on (1) the firm's ability to produce and market a light, bitter beer (and/or to convincingly advertise it as such) and — of first importance — (2) the number of people who would prefer such a beer and would be willing to try it.

This brings us to the related and important concept of *product (or brand) positioning*. The goal here is to use perceptual maps to suggest the best competitive tactics to pursue in market selection, product design (or redesign), and communication, pricing, and distribution decisions. Study of a product's position relative to that of its competitors on a perceptual map serves as a starting point for exploring competitive moves and their implications.

To take an example, let us assume the perspective of Carta Blanca. I have replotted the position of Carta Blanca and the other beers in Figure 1.4 and added estimates of preference groups in the market. The circles represent centroids of consumer preferences; the size of the circle indicates the number of people (or percentage of the market) preferring the respective combinations of heavy/light and bitter/mild beer attributes. For purposes of discussion, we will assume that the perceptions of everyone surveyed can be represented as shown. We will further assume that Carta Blanca is losing market share and feels a need to respond accordingly.

Carta Blanca has three options. First, it can compete with Blitz-Weinhard and go after preference group #1. To do this, it might use advertising to stress that it is neither too heavy nor too light, neither too bitter nor too mild. Rather, it is "the best of balanced beers," say. Comparative ads with Blitz-Weinhard might be considered as well. In addition, a reformulation of the brewing process or ingredients might be called for to make Carta Blanca somewhat more bitter. Consumer research would show if this is necessary. Whether pursuit of preference group #1 is viable depends on the number of people in this group, their current brand preferences, the cost of going after these people, and the attractiveness of the remaining two preference group options.

Carta Blanca's second option is to take on Budweiser and Miller, who "own" preference group #4, the largest market segment. This probably is not viable, given that Carta Blanca is an imported beer that appeals to small numbers of beer drinkers, whereas Budweiser and Miller are domestic products with well-entrenched popular images. Budweiser and Miller also have cost advantages and greater marketing resources.

Carta Blanca's third option would be to go after preference group #5. This large segment desires a mild, light beer and currently has only three competitors. Here, Carta Blanca must consider the costs of changing its image, the costs of reformulating its product, and the size and receptivity of the preference group.

Whatever option is chosen, it is important to consider also the likely responses of competitors. For example, Blitz-Weinhard would be likely to counter any threat by Carta Blanca. It could do this by cutting its price (since it has a distribution advantage), by advertising, or by doing both. A long-shot option for Carta Blanca might be to create a new market and pursue a slightly bitter, slightly light position in the hope of changing people's taste preferences or winning new adherents in the empty quadrant. Many other competitive issues are suggested by perceptual maps, but we cannot examine them here.

Before we consider the ongoing management of products, we should mention a recently developed tool that is proving to be especially useful in the design phase. *Conjoint analysis* is an analytical technique that permits management to compare alternative product or service designs on the basis of consumer reactions. The procedure provides measures of consumer utility for attributes of products and enables management to select product versions with maximum appeal.

Managing the Product Through Its Life Cycle

All products pass through life cycles with periods of ups and downs. An ideal sequence of sales might be represented as follows:

> Introduction → Rapid Growth → Slow Growth → Leveling Off → Decline

Of course, some products never make it past introduction, others skip a stage or two, and still others continue on indefinitely as if renewed from time to time. Whatever the pattern of sales, management must orchestrate the application of marketing tactics throughout the life cycle of a product. In this sense, the product life cycle is at least partially controllable by management. Each stage in the life cycle of a product will require a different balance among marketing tactics. Resources must be allocated to advertising, promotion, personal selling, distribution, and pricing in a way that meets the goals of the firm.

During the *product introduction phase,* profits are nonexistent and the objective typically is to increase consumers' product awareness and trial purchases (and stimulation of a healthy repurchase rate in the case of frequently purchased products). Advertising will be heavy in order to inform people. Promotions will be used to motivate dealers and consumers. The sales force will concentrate its efforts on building distribution. The price may be set low to take advantage of experience curve effects and forestall competition. Or it may be set high to reap early rewards (more on this shortly).

During periods of *rapid growth,* adjustments must be made. These should, in turn, be guided by market research, including so-called tracking studies of awareness, attitudes, intentions, trial purchase, and repeat purchase rates. Market share may become a critical barometer too. Fine-tuning and shifts in emphasis from one marketing tactic to another invariably take place. Normative managerial models and simulations may be used to aid in decision-making here also. Advertising will shift from information presentations to persuasion and may be reduced somewhat from the initially high levels during introduction. Promotions, too, will be reduced and shifted from trial-inducing tactics such as sampling to repeat-purchase teasers such as couponing or cents-off deals. The sales force will work to cement dealer relationships and ensure that deliveries, product quality, and so forth will be fulfilled. Prices may be lowered somewhat to meet the competition.

Slow growth and leveling-off periods demand still other responses. Here the firm must assess its own growth in relation to market growth and take into account its market share as well. A change in product design may be required to meet the demanding tastes of people who are slow in trying the product or to compete effectively with a new entrant. Advertising and promotions may have to be changed again to combat wear-out (a decline in ad effectiveness over time) or meet the competition. Prices may have to be lowered still further. Market segmentation takes on a special urgency as a means of survival and furthering the goals of the firm.

As the *decline phase* approaches, difficult decisions must be faced. Should the firm harvest, disinvest, or reinvest? Again, growth and market share must be weighed against goals and capabilities of the firm and the nature of the market and competition. An outcome to avoid is the self-fulfilling prophecy whereby an "apparent" decline is accelerated by a withdrawal of marketing support, and a potentially viable product is brought to a premature end. If the firm decides to harvest, then most expenditures on marketing will be reduced and the product will be left to die on its own. If the firm chooses instead to reinvest, it may have to do so across the board, with major product design innovations, repositioning, and renewed expenditures on advertising, promotions, selling, and distribution.

A final set of product decisions concerns *product-line planning*. The firm must decide whether to have a product line and, if so, what its composition should be. Consumer needs, the location of market segments, competition, market growth, market share, cannibalization, and profitability are important inputs to the decision process. Creating a well-designed product line entails looking not only at the health of each brand but also at the synergy among brands. The image and profitability of brands may be enhanced by careful design of the entire line, since cross-fertilization often occurs. The role of the product line also changes over time with the leveling-off phase of the product life cycle revealing the product line's maximum contribution. The product portfolio and strategic group frameworks are especially useful in product-line decisions. Given the decision to employ product lines, the marketer must view his or her task as allocating marketing expenditures to the support of tactics that will best meet the firm's goals for profitability, market share, and growth.

COMMUNICATION DECISIONS

A Communication Model

Communication tactics are one of the most important and flexible links between an organization and its markets. Unlike product, price, and distribution tactics, which are more difficult to change and which remain relatively stable over time, communication is often the first and most effective lever an organization has to respond to or influence its markets. The range of communication tactics includes advertising, promotion, publicity, and personal selling. The goal of communication is to inform, educate, persuade, and/or influence behavior directly.

In simplified form, the communication process is as follows:

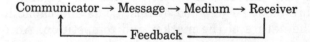

That is, a communicator sends a message through some medium to a receiver who processes the message and responds with feedback. Of course, communicator and receiver often change roles in rapid succession, and instead of a one-way sequence, the process is very much one of mutual exchanges. Nevertheless, in analyzing and designing communication tactics, it is useful to consider the process of communication as being relatively unilateral.

Figure 1.5 outlines the main variables and processes underlying communication in marketing. Let us begin with a description of the processes going on within the consumer (i.e., receiver) after receipt of a message (see bottom of figure). Exposure to an ad, sales pitch, or other marketing communication leads first to perceptual processes. These may or may not occur at the level of awareness or involve conscious allocation of attention. In any case, perceived information may have one or both of two effects (see *a* and *b* in Figure 1.5). One is to influence the consumer's needs or motives and induce affective responses. For example, physiological responses might be stimulated, along with felt positive emotions, and the desire for a product actuated. This, in turn, might lead to thoughts about the brand, how to acquire it, and so forth (*d*). Alternatively, perceived information might lead directly (*b*) to message comprehension and further cognitive responses (for example, generation of support for or counterarguments against, the core selling point). The resulting "information processing" might stimulate feelings about the message, brand, and so on, as well (*c*). Information (*e*) and affective reactions (*f*) then are organized and integrated, and an attitude toward the brand and/or communication is formed (*g*). The output of this stage serves as input to mental decision-making activities in which the consumer activates old preferences or develops new ones. This may lead further (*h*) to intentions to buy and, eventually, to purchase. Postpurchase experiences finally result in satisfaction or dissatisfaction and feedback upon the consumer's needs, motives, and feelings (*i*) and/or knowledge (*j*).

The value of examining how consumers process messages lies in its use in the design of communications. Each stage shown in the bottom of Figure 1.5 will be affected differently by different communication tactics. For instance, humorous ads can be effective in stimulating attention, creating desired emotional responses, and at times inducing yielding to a persuasive appeal. But they are less useful in conveying information and aiding directly in decision making. Rational appeals, in contrast, excel in developing understanding, promoting effective information integration, and generally enhancing decision making. But they are less effective in influencing emotions. One goal in the study of how consumers process messages is to select the most appropriate communication tactic, given the product, consumer characteristics, competition, and stage the product is in in its life cycle. Notice also that the ultimate choice to buy or not will be a differential function of the nature of communications and how they are processed at various stages leading up to choice. Only by considering the differential mental and emotional effects of messages at each stage can managers select the best communication options. This, in turn, requires that consumer

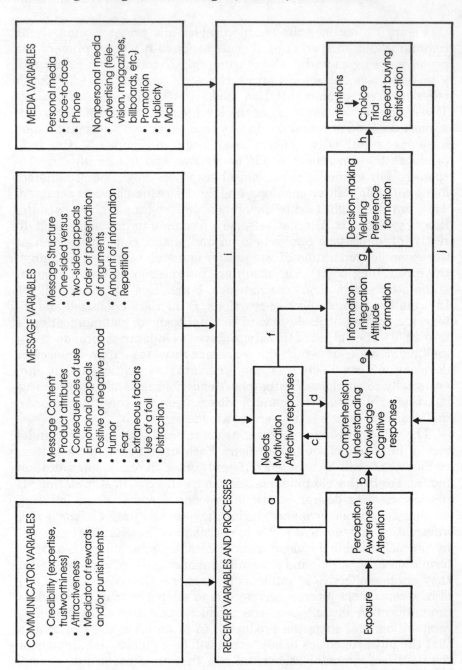

Figure 1.5 Communication Processes in Marketing

research be performed along with the design of communication programs.

The top half of Figure 1.5 presents the three primary levers that managers have to influence the communication process: communicator variables, message variables, and media variables. The options noted for each, individually and in combination, compose the communication mix.

The effect of a message can be augmented through the choice of characteristics of the *communicator*. To the extent that a spokesperson is perceived as being more expert, trustworthy, or attractive, the message will be believed to a stronger degree. Similarly, the more that a communicator is perceived to directly or indirectly provide him or her with rewards (monetary, psychic, or social outcomes), the greater the likelihood that a communication will have its intended effect. Note that communicator variables are separate elements under the control of management and work along with other determinants to influence consumers. Skillful choice of a communicator can lead to the development of a unique brand image (Karl Malden for American Express) and can influence special target markets (Mr. T in antidrug ads).

Perhaps the most effective means of influence lie in the *message* itself (see Figure 1.5). Here managers must give special attention to what is said (message content) and how it is said (message structure).

Two basic choices underlie the *message content* decision. Should rational or emotional appeals be used? A product with distinct attributes and benefits for a consumer or one that has utilitarian overtones lends itself to a rational approach. Ads for drain cleaners, motor oil, and investments generally follow this approach. Products whose appeal lie in psychic or social consequences or brands that differ but slightly from the competition find emotional appeals more effective. We see this in cosmetic, beer, and cigarette advertisements. Of course, sometimes rational arguments and mood or other nonrational stimulants are combined into a single message. Witness Mercedes-Benz ads that stress engineering, yet appeal also to desires for luxury, status, and even excitement. Although difficult to execute, such dual tactics can be quite effective. In addition, seemingly extraneous content will be included occasionally along with the primary message. For example, small levels of distraction will be used to temporarily inhibit counter argumentation by an audience until the focal selling point can seep in. Many ploys common to novels, plays, or the opera are employed: the use of a foil, fantasy, drama, comedy, slice of life, testimonials, satire, suspense, and storytelling, to name a few.

Equally critical is the organization of message content, which we term *message structure* in Figure 1.5. Here decisions must be made as to the use of one-sided versus two-sided appeals (i.e., presentation of only positive or positive and negative information), order of presentation of arguments (whether to place the strongest argument first, in the middle, or at the end), the amount of information to convey in any one message, and the scheduling of messages over time.

A third lever in the communication mix is *media selection*. This is an important problem area, not only because of its obvious role in reaching customers and in market selection, but because some media are more persuasive than others, depending on the needs of consumers and the characteristics of the focal product and the competition. Personal media (i.e., salespeople) are particularly effective for expensive products, prolonged negotiations, custom designing of the product, influencing intermediaries, and closing sales. Nonpersonal media such as advertising, promotion, publicity, or catalog and mail marketing have the advantages of extensive reach capabilities, low cost per prospect reached, and the ability to stimulate trial use or purchase, remind people about availability, and reinforce other modes of selling (for example, advertising can prepare and soften up a prospect before the encounter with a retailer or salesperson).

Advertising and Promotion

Three special concerns of advertising include repetition, message execution, and operations management.

Consider first *repetition*. What is the optimal number of exposures of an ad? One researcher claims that three exposures are all that are needed to achieve the desired effects of advertising.[27] The first exposure to an ad is needed to attract attention. The consumer reacts with a "What is it?" response. A later, second exposure has two effects. One is a recognition reaction ("Aha, I've seen this before!"), whereas the second is an evaluative response ("What of it?"). Beyond this point, no deeper information processing occurs. The third and each succeeding exposure are simply reminder ads calling up from memory what is already known (or believed). According to this argument, more than three exposures is not only wasteful but leads to disengagement of audience interest. This is the so-called *wear-out phenomenon*.

One operational objective of advertising, then, might be to produce as many repetitions as are needed to achieve three exposures for as many people in a target audience as is feasible. Inevitably, some people will become overexposed, and as time passes the message will have less and less effectiveness. This might be indicated by a leveling off in awareness measures or even sales. What can be done to overcome the wear-out phenomenon? One solution is to change the content or structure of the message. New communicators (spokespersons) or new humorous executions might be tried, for instance. Or new media might be explored in an effort to reach previously inaccessible consumers. Still another tactic is to introduce new product attributes not advertised before.

A second important consideration in advertising is *message execution*. How should one design and implement an advertisement? At least three issues must be addressed here. One is *media involvement*. Each medium has its own characteristics, which are more or less interesting to a target customer. For example, television is generally considered a low-involvement medium in that viewers tend to sit passively, let their minds drift, or even tune out commercials. Magazines, on the other hand, are more involving and permit exposure to ads to occur at more active and deeper levels. Obviously, every advertiser attempts to make its ads alluring, whatever the medium chosen. However, product characteristics, consumer media habits, and other considerations suggest that the marketer should carefully match his or her offering to the advertising medium and the target audience. Different media pose different problems and offer different opportunities.

A related issue is *product involvement*. Just as consumers are involved to different degrees with different media, so, too, do they find products to be important in varying degrees. For products of lesser salience to a consumer, information processing may occur in a shallow way, encompass few product attributes, and proceed quickly. Habit and impulse frequently play a role as well. More salient products encourage deeper information processing and over a wider spectrum of attributes, with much comparison among brands. Television ads for Panasonic Video cameras convey about a dozen product attributes, whereas Trident gum ads seldom stress more than one or two. This, too, will affect the choice of media, the type of messages constructed, the scheduling of repetitions, and so on. Note also that *brand involvement* can be a factor.

Finally, message execution should take into account how consumers will react to a message and the processes that they will go through as they react. Marketers have found that the following sequences occur most frequently in real-world decision-making:[28]

1. Learn → Feel → Do
2. Feel → Learn → Do
3. Do → Learn → Feel
4. Do → Feel → Learn

By "learn" is meant the comprehension, information integration, and decision-making activities of Figure 1.5. "Feel" refers to needs, motives, affective responses, attitude, and preference formation. "Do" stands for actual trial or repeat buying activities or other behaviors: shopping, examination of independent reports, talking to a salesperson, making a purchase, and so on.

Sequence 1 applies when products are complex, risky, or expensive, and/or are considered important by the consumer. Here considerable information is first scrutinized and weighed before feelings develop and a decision to act or not is made. The purchase of a home computer would be an example. Sequence 2 also occurs in instances where consumers find the product to be important to them, but where the nature of the product or message is such as to first induce affective reactions. These reactions, in turn, generate thinking processes that lead to action. The purchase of clothing often fits this pattern. Sequence 3 figures in the purchase of everyday items such as dishwashing detergent, coffee, or milk. Either through habit or impulse or because a product is simple or uninvolving, it is purchased with little or no forethought. Its subsequent use or contemplation, however, leads to thoughts about the brand ("For small loads of dishes, I'll try half a capful") and, finally, affective reactions ("I really like brand X detergent"). Sequence 4 is similar to 3, but here feelings follow action directly and then lead to thoughts. For instance, at midmorning, a vaguely perceived hunger pang might stimulate the purchase of a candy bar from a vending machine. Biting into the bar triggers pleasurable feelings and elicits such thoughts as "This is a good buy" and "I think I'll get another."

If advertisers have sound information about how consumers react to messages and the processes they go through in decision-making, they can create more effective ads. For example, products falling within sequence 1 typically require a demonstration of the product's use and benefits and detailed information — which requires considerable ad copy. More involving media, such as magazines or direct mail, may dominate. Products in sequence 2 require emotional appeals to involve an audience and make use of appeals to the ego or to self-esteem. Magazine ads and strong TV executions may be needed here. Those products which elicit sequence 3 demand executions that induce trial purchases or remind consumers of an offering. Radio or TV spots might work well; so might magazine ads with coupons. Sequence 4 products suggest ads that arouse emotions. Magazine or strong TV commercials are a possibility. Point-of-purchase displays are options for products in sequences 3 and 4 as well.

The above considerations are of course only rough guidelines. In the final analysis, any ad will reflect the particular philosophy, history, and style of the ad agency that creates it. Thus a marketer must not only know his or her own product, customers, and competitors well but must also carefully evaluate alternative agencies and ad executions to arrive at a proper fit. These are largely subjective decisions.

Finally, *the advertising effort must be well managed.* Two critical concerns here are copy testing and budgeting. *Copy testing* refers to measurement of the effectiveness of advertising. Although statistical and mathematical modeling can be used to establish the relationship between advertising expenditures and sales (or market share), more frequently the effects of ads are determined by gauging their impact on intermediate variables such as consumers' awareness, knowledge, recall, or recognition of the ad; their beliefs about the product's attributes; their interest in the product; and their intentions to buy or not to buy. Such indirect measurement is employed because it is easier, cheaper, and yet thought to be reasonably valid. Many independent companies offer copy testing services to advertisers.

Advertising budgets are set in a variety of ways. Sometimes a budget is made on the basis of subjective judgments by executives. A second method is simply to peg the budget to that of the competition: to meet the competitor's ad budget, exceed it, or fall below it by some percentage. Usually, however, budgets are set as a percentage of sales (for example, last quarter's or this quarter's expected). Unfortunately, each of the aforementioned tactics tends to be a hit-or-miss affair. A better way is to set ad budgets at levels needed to achieve some desired goal. The *objective and task method* attempts to do just this. The organization first defines a specific goal to be achieved — say "60 percent awareness of our new brand in market Y by next year." Next, the tasks — number of repetitions, media selection, spokesperson, etc. — are designed to reach the goal. The budget is then set on the basis of the tasks needed to reach the goal. Experimentation, statistical modeling, normative models, and market monitoring may be used in trying to meet the goals.

Promotions are incentives directed at consumers or dealers to get them to buy a brand. Whereas advertising is most often designed to induce a psychological response prior to action, promotions are attempts to stimulate actions directly. The most common consumer promotions are coupons, free samples, premiums, cents-off deals, contests, games, and prizes. *Speciality advertising* is really a type of promotion whereby free gifts in the form of a pen, calendar, coffee mug, or other item are given to a consumer. The gift serves as a reward for performing the desired action (trying the coffee, subscribing to the magazine) and usually bears the name and telephone number of the sponsor as a constant reminder. Typical dealer promotions include point-of-purchase (POP) displays, cash allowances, credit, gifts, bonuses, two-for-one deals, contests, prizes, and free advice or information.

An important point to stress is that the communication mix tactics are interdependent and sometimes mutually reinforcing. This is nowhere more evident than with advertising and promotion. One study, for example, showed that advertising and promotion work together to produce a multiplier effect such that sales were much greater when both were used than when either one alone was employed. This study found, for example, that sales of coffee were 0.6 purchases per 100 shoppers when no ads or POP displays were used, 2.5 purchases per 100 when only POP displays were used, 1.9 per 100 with only ads, but 8.1 per 100 when *both* ads and POP displays were used.[29] Note, too, that many promotions only reach consumers through ads.

The question management faces, then, is not so much whether to promote or to advertise but rather what proportion of each to employ. In practice, a wide range of ratios of advertising to promotion budget are used. One consumer product firm sets its ratio at 70 : 30, for example. What factors govern the balance? One is buyer behavior. If, for example, most prospective purchasers of a certain product decide to buy (or not) before they enter the store, then the ratio should be more heavily in favor of advertising. But if most prospects make up their minds at the shelf, then the ratio should favor promotion — specifically, POP promotion. Competition is a second factor. A small competitor cannot hope to emulate a large one, but it may gain a competitive edge by using a vastly different advertising-to-promotion ratio than the competition uses. Still another consideration is the stage a product is in in its life cycle. Introduction, growth, leveling off, and decline require different tactics. Many other considerations, including market share, strategic group position, and firm constraints, may enter the picture.

Personal Selling

Face-to-face communication, while expensive, is the most compelling medium available to a seller. Personal contact permits a dynamic adjustment of needs and offerings on the part of both buyer and seller, and it facilitates the gaining of a commitment. Moreover, salespeople smooth out problems subsequent to the sale (for instance, late delivery), provide feedback about the market, and generate new business. In an age where everything and everyone seems to get lost in the crowd, personal selling lets the firm tailor its offerings, reach the right customer, communicate complex benefits and terms, and push control deeper into the channel of distribution. As a matter of fact, although more expensive on a per-customer basis than advertising, personal selling frequently costs less in absolute terms when the number of customers is small or the items are high-priced, or both.

For decades, researchers and practitioners have searched in vain for the magical profile of the "ideal" salesperson. At one time or another, he or she was thought to need money more than achievement, to have high ego strength, empathy, verbal skills, aggressiveness, an aloof attitude, unusual levels of drive, and so on. Eventually the ideal salesperson could be described by any and all attributes, and no one — or everyone — could fit the bill.

There is no such thing as the ideal salesperson. But within the past few years, research has identified a small number of fundamental attributes or abilities common to most successful outside salespeople. First and foremost, motivation is required. Salespeople must both value the intrinsic and extrinsic rewards associated with selling and believe that working hard will earn them these rewards. Second, leading salespeople tend to have high levels of self-confidence and self-esteem, especially in relation to the specific job at hand. To the extent that attaining high levels of sales is consistent with their task-specific self-image, salespeople are motivated to work hard to achieve at a level in concert with that self-image. Third, the ability to learn from feedback and supervision is crucial, especially as it serves to promote and reinforce job satisfaction. Fourth, successful salespeople generally cope better with ambiguity on the job. (Ambiguity arises from lack of certainty as to what the supervisor, customer, and others expect of one.) Fifth, salespeople must be able to deal with conflict, tension, and strain. These aspects of the job are consequences of organizational boundary spanning activities and differences in interests, points of view, and job pressures. Finally, effective selling requires an ability to analyze customer needs and plan and adjust one's activities and communication tactics to advantage. In personal selling, interpersonal skills reign supreme.

The management of a company's personal selling effort entails several key decisions. After goals for sales and profitability are set, one of the manager's first tasks is to determine the size of the sales force. This might be done by estimating the desired productivity of salespeople and taking into account the number of total customers (actual plus potential) as well as geographic, economic, and other considerations. At the same time, the manager must decide how to organize the sales force (by geographic territory, customer type, product category, brand, or whatever). This done, the manager can determine the size of each territory or the number of accounts and/or products that each salesperson will have. These decisions should, if possible, be based at least partly on target sales or profit figures. A recruitment, selection, and training program must be designed as well. Finally, supervision, compensation, work standards (e.g., call norms), and general planning, management, and control mechanisms must be set in place. Many of these issues can be approached through various normative models that have been proposed by marketers to aid in planning and decision-making. Job design, leadership, and career development principles are important, too.

Just as advertising and promotion are mutually reinforcing activities, so, too, may personal selling combine with other marketing communications to generate sales more effectively. A key decision is whether to pursue a *push,* a *pull,* or a *push-pull* strategy. That is, should the firm place major emphasis on selling to intermediaries (the push strategy), to final customers (the pull strategy), or both? The push strategy requires a vigorous sales force, dealer promotions, and relatively high margin pricing. The pull strategy rests largely on advertising, with perhaps some consumer promotions. Most firms use a push-pull strategy, yet industrial goods sellers rely relatively more on a push mode, whereas the strategies of consumer-goods sellers are more balanced or lean toward a pull mode. The choice of balance between push and pull depends on how and where consumers make decisions, the size of the market, what consumer media habits are, the nature and complexity of the product, the competition, market growth, market share, and so forth.

Price Decisions

Goals and constraints in pricing. Long gone are the days when prices were set haphazardly as an automatic and more or less fixed markup over costs. Today, price is viewed in an active and not merely reactive sense as one way to stimulate demand or compete effectively, or both. As a tactical tool, price offers a number of benefits to the firm. First, unlike most communication, product, or distribution tactics that entail up-front costs as well as involved plans and procedures for their implementation, price moves do not require costly expenditures and can be instituted easily. Second, consumers find appeals based on price easier to understand and respond to than the more indirect and abstract effects of advertising, product attribute, and distribution-based (e.g., location) appeals. Finally, even when other tactics such as personal selling or imagery advertising are the primary concern, price can be a valuable and readily applied adjunct, reinforcing the effects of other marketing tools. On the other hand, price cutting can be perceived as a threat by competitors and lead to price wars in which all companies suffer. Also, price cuts can lead to negative inferences about product quality.

The pricing process begins with the goals of the firm and the objectives for the brand in question. Common options are to view price as a means to achieve or maintain market share, stimulate primary and secondary demand, increase short- or long-run profitability, signal competitors that one means business or alternatively wishes to avoid a price war, discourage new entrants, strengthen and reward intermediaries (e.g., by providing them with healthy margins), communicate value to consumers, stay within the law, or simply act in a socially responsible way. Most of these ends require that the firm do research to determine the relationship between price and sales. This may mean conducting experiments, running statistical analyses of data, performing simulations, or employing normative models based on managerial judgments and other data.[30]

With rare exceptions, prices are constrained to fall within a relatively narrow range. At the bottom end, costs provide a floor below which the firm cannot survive for long. At the top end, prices are constrained by competitive undercutting or by a ceiling on what consumers can afford or what they feel gives them value. In between lies the degree of freedom open to a firm.

Taking an active stance, we can think of the pricing problem as one of maximizing profits or some other goal. For example, we know that profits (z) can be written as a function of price (p), costs (c), and quantity sold (q), $z = (p-c)q$. Our objective is to arrive at the highest level of z through an optimal choice of p. However, p is constrained by consumer preferences, the competition, and government regulations. Further, z can be influenced by keeping c low, which in turn depends on q, experience curve effects, and shared experience and costs with other products (see earlier discussion on overall cost leadership and learning curve effects). Moreover, q itself is at least partially influenceable through p and the remaining marketing mix tools. Thus, z can be increased indirectly by stimulating demand. We find, therefore, that the maximization of z is a complex endeavor. Nevertheless, once we have an idea of the determinants of constraints for p, c, and q, we can use calculus or simulations to arrive at a maximum z. The task thus depends on arriving at realistic functions for p, c, and q. It is beyond the scope of this chapter to cover the many recent developments in this area.[31] I will, however, briefly sketch some of the qualitative considerations.

Consider first the constraints on price and the implications of setting various price levels. To satisfy consumer needs, price should reflect, and be set on the basis of, perceived benefits to consumers. But how can this be done? One way is to use conjoint analysis and treat price as a product attribute along with other attributes. In a survey, the consumer then must choose a product with a bundle of attributes producing his or her highest utility. Conjoint analysis yields the consumer's judged disutility of specific price options and shows the trade-offs between various prices and product attributes. The price suggested by a conjoint analysis is of course constrained further by what competitors are offering and what is legally permissible. Product differentiation and careful market selection can lessen the impact of these constraints, however. A last point to note is that price elasticities — especially those which are a function of product life-cycle stage — must be taken into account in planning.

The determinants of costs must also be scrutinized. Fixed costs that are large relative to variable costs often dictate low pricing in order to increase capacity utilization. On the other hand, large variable costs relative to fixed costs sometimes force up the price. In either case, however, efforts will be made to drive down both fixed and variable costs. Economies of scale, experience curve, shared learning, and product line considerations play a role here. Moreover, overall strategic goals must be taken into account. An overall cost leadership orientation will result in lower prices than will a product differentiation approach, for example.

Pricing must be coordinated with all the tactics used in implementing the marketing mix. This is so not only because the various tactics interact and can thwart or augment each other, but also because profits and other goals are proportional to the magnitude of marketing mix expenditures which stimulate demand, as suggested by the profit formula discussed earlier. Therefore, the effects on demand of *all* the marketing tactics including price must be ascertained when determining price.

Pricing tactics.   Prices come in various forms; they are not limited to a single "purchase price." Quantity discounts, two-for-one deals, promotion allowances, coupons, and other gambits widen the scope of pricing tactics. Let us explore the options open to a marketer.

For new products, either a price skimming or penetration pricing tactic is warranted. With *price skimming,* a high price is set. The hope is that enough customers exist who will be willing to pay a premium for the brand. As this market dries up, prices will be reduced gradually to draw in other customers. Price skimming is used when one wants to create an image of high product quality, when rivals will be slow to enter the market, when buyers value the product highly and demand is inelastic, or when fixed and variable costs either benefit little from experience curve effects or fail to achieve significant economies of scale. Hewlett-Packard, Polaroid, and DuPont have been known to practice price skimming.

Penetration pricing is the tactic of introducing a product at a low price, perhaps in anticipation of future cost declines and a burgeoning market. Over time, the price may or may not be raised. It is frequently employed as part of a market share strategy, as well as a means to generate primary demand. Unlike skimming, penetration pricing tends to discourage new entrants in that it signals strong price competition and relatively low profits. Penetration pricing works best when production and distribution channels are in place, consumers are price-sensitive, either the adoption process is fast or the product is a frequently purchased good, and sufficient economies of scale and experience curve effects are forthcoming. Texas Instruments, Japanese automakers, and Beaird-Poulan have used this approach.

The prices of industrial goods are especially influenced by costs and competition. Indeed, many such goods are sold through competitive bidding arrangements. Alternatively, contracts are employed that focus on cost-plus or target-incentive considerations. Functionality and value are, of course, central concerns. In the selling of industrial goods, much negotiating of terms and tailoring of the product to the individual customer is done. This tends to make price not so much a decision variable, set independently by the seller and presented to the buyer in a take-it-or-leave-it fashion, as it is a mutually constructed accommodation that is constrained by factors that both seller and buyer face.

By contrast, the pricing of consumer goods necessarily is done much more on the basis of company needs and before presentation to the consumer. Although market research is performed, so many buyers are involved, with all their different tastes and resources, that an "average" price must be set. In addition, the manufacturer must often take wholesalers and retailers into account when setting prices. Intermediaries require incentives and compensation for their efforts. This complicates the price-setting task and introduces an additional set of constraints. Industrial goods sold through distributors or manufacturer's representatives exhibit similar problems.

Pricing decisions must be made throughout the life cycle of a product. Price elasticities typically decline as the product moves from the introduction phase through the growth phase to the leveling-off phase. They increase, however, in the decline phase. Moreover, increases in competition throughout the product life cycle drive prices downward. At the same time, variations in growth, market share, and profitability across brands in a product line interact complexly with price decisions and must be watched carefully.

Distribution Decisions

Designing the channel. The *channel of distribution* is the system of institutions used in delivering goods to the final consumer. The intermediaries who make up a given channel might include brokers, manufacturer's representatives, distributors, wholesalers, and retailers. Some or all might be wholly owned by the manufacturer or even by one of the intermediaries. Alternatively, the system might consist of independent businesses that buy and sell the goods of producers or act as the producers' agents through contractual agreements. Still another possibility is that a manufacturer might sell directly to its customers without going through intermediaries. For instance, direct mail, a sales force coupled with delivery through common carriers, or mobile company stores might be used. No matter what system is employed to bring the goods to market, certain *functions* must be fulfilled: transportation, storage, transfer of title, provision of credit or other special services, assortment, selling, delivery, receipt of funds, and so on.

Channel decisions must be considered carefully, for several reasons. First, and most obviously, the channel of distribution is an essential link, a gatekeeper to the market. Shelf space in the supermarket or an account with an aggressive distributor is not only a necessity but tends to function as a self-fulfilling prophecy. That is, the channel stimulates demand just as advertising, product design, and price cuts do. Second, it is very expensive and time-consuming to set up and maintain a distribution channel. The commitment risks are great, and there is little room for error. Moreover, it is difficult to make changes in a channel once the channel has been set in place. Third, the channel of distribution may provide the competitive edge over rivals. This edge may be a unique location, efficient delivery and inventory practices, special selling skills, market monitoring services, or some other advantage. Finally, the selection of a channel will constrain or facilitate the choice and implementation of other marketing tactics. For example, retailers often require assistance from manufacturers in the form of promotions and business advice and at the same time expect the manufacturer to conduct advertising and other demand-stimulating activities. Different channel options imply different balances of power, influence, and control between manufacturer and intermediary as well.

The design of the channel depends on how consumers make decisions about the particular product, the number and dispersion of consumers, the amount of goods to be sold and their value, the costs of various channel options, the tasks that must be performed (e.g., service, credit provision, market research), and competitive practices. For example, when purchasing clothing, most people like to compare many styles, color, and brands, try on alternatives, receive a certain amount of help from salespeople, and make use of tailoring services. These factors, in turn, make clothing stores or store departments the dominant form of distribution. Nevertheless, for a few people who have neither the time nor the inclination to shop, catalog shopping is attractive, despite the uncertainties of fit and the absence of service.

We can view the *channel design* process as follows. First, the firm must decide whether to *sell directly* or *work through intermediaries*. This, in turn, depends upon (1) how well each channel option can perform the aforementioned distribution functions for the firm, (2) the costs of reaching consumers, and (3) the degree of control the firm desires in managing the distribution of its goods. Selling directly provides the maximum control but is more expensive and less flexible in providing certain functions. Management must therefore weigh the gains against the costs to determine what is best in its own particular situation. Most consumer goods manufacturers find that it is easier and cheaper to go through independent wholesalers or distributors than it is to sell to retailers. But there are exceptions. Gallo Wine, for example, is large enough to do much of its own distribution directly to retailers. Industrial goods firms sometimes sell through distributors, yet in many cases they find direct selling possible.

If management decides to sell through intermediaries, then it must choose the *breadth of coverage* needed to reach consumers. Three possibilities exist. One is an *intensive distribution* system, in which the producer seeks as many outlets for its wares as possible in a market area. This option is most appropriate for selling to the mass market, particularly by producers of convenience consumer goods (e.g., breakfast cereal or paper napkins) or undifferentiated industrial goods (nuts and bolts). Buyers of these goods do little shopping around, purchase with a minimal amount of deliberation, and value convenience more than anything else. Intensive distribution also lends itself to products whose costs per unit to store, display, or sell are low. Pepsi-Cola, Johnson's Wax, and Kellogg's Raisin Bran employ intensive distribution.

A second breadth of coverage option is *exclusive distribution*. This is the polar extreme of intensive distribution in that only a single outlet per market area is utilized. The producer hopes to create a unique image for its product, to obtain more vigorous selling efforts, and to extend its control over certain practices of the distributor or retailer (e.g., in pricing, quality control, or market monitoring). In exchange, the intermediary receives the right to be the sole seller for the producer's goods and thereby gains special services and a competitive advantage in the market area. Most automotive companies, some manufacturers of expensive china, and certain appliance makers use exclusive distribution arrangements.

Selective distribution is the third option for achieving breadth of coverage. Here the firm seeks more than one outlet, but considerably fewer than all outlets in a market, in the hope of obtaining many of the advantages of exclusive distribution while at the same time reaching further into the market. However, as a compromise tactic, it shares some disadvantages of both polar extremes. Selective distribution is especially appropriate for medium-priced to moderately high-priced shopping, specialty, or industrial goods where personal selling is required. For example, Calvin Klein clothes, Hartmann luggage, and Pioneer electronics use what is essentially a selective distribution approach.

In addition to choosing a breadth of coverage option, the user of intermediaries also must decide upon the vertical *length of the channel system*. Here, too, at least three possibilities exist: corporate, contractual, or independent (also termed conventional or administered) systems.

The *corporate marketing channel* is one in which all stages from manufacture through distribution come under single ownership. Leading examples include Goodyear tires, Sherwin-Williams paints, and Shell oil and gas services. The advantages of a corporate system include lower costs (through standardization and other economies of scale) and greater control than with the other options. In particular, a firm can achieve more influence over hiring, pricing, promotion and selling, provision of service, and even product quality with a corporate system than it can with a contractual or an independent system. On the other hand, corporate systems require very large capital investments, are risky both financially and legally (i.e., they may invite antitrust actions), and tend to be less adaptive to changing market and competitive conditions. It should be noted that some firms employ a modified corporate channel system by vertically integrating partway into distribution.

Contractual channel systems consist of collections of more or less independent companies bound by legal agreements akin to exclusive distribution, yet going further. The most common contractual systems are *franchises,* but retail cooperatives and voluntary chains organized by wholesalers are also examples. Here we will focus on franchising which accounts for about one-third of all retail sales in the United States.

Under franchising, the franchisor provides the franchisee with materials, a product, financial know-how, and other services. An exclusive right to sell the franchisor's product or service in a market area is also provided. The franchisee in turn agrees to abide by certain requirements and procedures dealing with selling, product or service quality, and other marketing functions, and perhaps also to pay a fee and/or percentage of revenues. Soft-drink producers such as Coca-Cola, for example, sell the right to use their names and market their products in a market area and provide syrup concentrate to bottlers (i.e., franchised wholesalers) in exchange for finished production and marketing services. Another type of franchise operation is exemplified by Burger King, which provides land, equipment, supplies, technical and managerial advice, marketing plans, advertising support, and other services to a franchisee who pays an up-front investment fee, makes periodic royalty payments, and manages the business.

Franchising has pros and cons for franchisor and franchisee alike. On the plus side, franchisors obtain capital, a highly motivated distributor/retailer, and some economies of scale through purchases of supplies, manufacture, advertising, and promotion. Moreover, although franchising affords less control than does a corporate channel system, a strong degree of influence over marketing practice is still possible. Franchisees benefit in that they receive considerable amounts of money and support to get started in their own business, "instant" brand recognition and reputation, and ongoing managerial advice. On the negative side, however, the franchisor loses some control over the franchisees and is even dependent on them. Uneven quality control by one or a few franchisees can hurt the industrywide image of the franchisor's business, and legal encounters sometimes mar ongoing relationships with franchisees as well. Further, franchisees occasionally find that their freedom is restricted and that they must purchase supplies or services they do not want or which they could procure at less cost elsewhere. The initial investment for a franchise can be heavy, too, reaching into the hundreds of thousands of dollars or more.

Independent channel systems — the third vertical option — consist of loose associations of separate private enterprises that cooperate with one another for mutual gain. Typically, an independent wholesaler or distributor handles the goods for many producers and manufacturers. The services that independent intermediaries provide include such functions as storage and inventory control, delivery to retailers, provision of credit to buyers, a sales force, transfer of title, and information gathering on the marketplace. The intermediary usually buys goods from a manufacturer at a discount and resells them to retailers at a profit. Consignment selling and the right to return unsold merchandise are also frequent practices.

Independent channel systems offer producers the advantage of obtaining marketing services at a cost less than they themselves could provide. Moreover, with an independent system, the producer gains more flexibility and incurs less risk than it would with a corporate or contractual system. One may more easily switch to other independent intermediaries or set up an entirely new system in response to a changing market or competitive threats. Still another benefit is the expertise and market monitoring services provided. Unlike a contractual or franchise system, independents deal with competitors and sometimes are closer to the market. On the negative side, producers lose considerable control and at times pay higher margins. Procter & Gamble and General Electric are two well-known users of independent channels of distribution.

Managing channel relationships. Distribution decisions do not end with the design and establishment of the channel. Rather, choices must be made continuously with regard to channel modifications and ongoing management. Consumer tastes and purchase habits change, competitors invent new products and ways of marketing, and intermediaries' loyalties and levels of performance shift over time. The firm must evaluate the effectiveness of its current channel relations and alter them as necessary. This might mean adding or deleting wholesalers or retailers to change the breadth of coverage. More fundamentally, it might even mean introducing or bypassing a level in the length of the channel or exploring entirely new ways of bringing goods to the market. Which of these options is chosen will depend on the discovery of new markets or evolutions in old ones, competitive moves by rivals, or inadequacies in the existing arrangements.

Ongoing management of channel relationships, which may well constitute the producer's largest commitment in time and energy, can be the key to achieving a competitive edge. A central concern here is motivation. The success of a firm rests, in part, on the productivity of individuals over whom it may have limited control. Healthy margins, attractive compensation, credit, contests, promotional allowances, point-of-sale displays, various services, and other facets of the terms of trade can boost individual efforts to the producer's advantage. In addition, the intangible side of management — leadership and the everyday dealings in human contact — deserve attention. Formal and informal lines of communication facilitate the implementation of influence and accommodations that must be made in both directions if the channel is to compete effectively.

Also important is the management of conflict among members of the channel. Misunderstandings, conflicts of interest, and tension are endemic to interpersonal and interfirm relationships. To cope with these, an attempt must be made to reduce ambiguity in expectations, rights, and responsibilities. A climate of cooperation and fairness must be fostered. These can be accomplished, in part, by establishing clear rules and procedures, making communications explicit, and engaging in joint decisionmaking where appropriate.

Finally, a firm must establish managerial controls over channel operations. This means formulating appropriate goals, monitoring performance, administering rewards or corrective actions, and adjusting the functions of the channel to the other marketing tools.

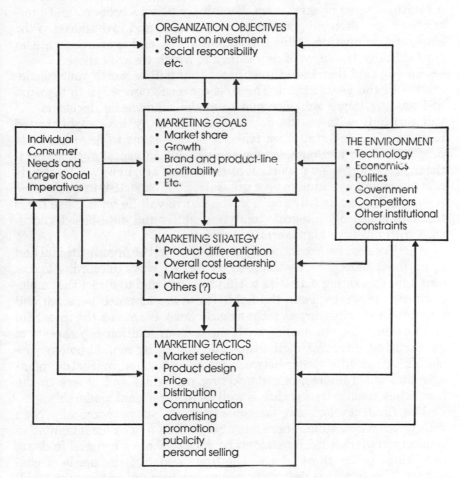

Figure 1.6 Summary of Marketing Management

LOOKING AHEAD

> It is a general human weakness to allow things, uncertain
> and unknown, to set us up in hope, or plunge us into fear.
>
> — Gaius Julius Caesar

As you read the *Wall Street Journal* and other business publications, and as you come into contact with marketing managers, consultants, and academics, you are certain to be told what is new in marketing and be given advice on how to do it. The best counsel I or anyone can give you is this: Consider all such information carefully, but retain a healthy degree of skepticism. Seemingly new techniques and proscriptions are often old goods in new packages, and rare indeed is the emergence of anything truly fundamental. We tend to overestimate, at least initially, the value of new things to which we are exposed.

Having said this, I see three things that will be worth your consideration in the years ahead. The first concerns new ways to measure and analyze buyer behavior and to model managerial decisions. We will certainly witness the development of many new sophisticated mathematical and statistical tools. It is important to have access to people in-house and outside who can use and interpret such state-of-the-art procedures. As important as these tools are, however, it is likely that there will continue to be a great need for expertise in qualitative research. The competitive edge in the future will lie with those firms that can creatively integrate analytical skills and data-based knowledge with intuitive managerial judgments.

Another area for breakthroughs will occur in the organizational and operational sides of marketing. Watch for new ways to coordinate and structure marketing activities within the firm and to direct the implementation of strategies in the field. These are as much personal and interpersonal endeavors as technological ones. We are on the threshold of a new maturity in dealing with the human relationship aspects of coordinating, directing, motivating, and managing conflict among people. These activities occur between buyer and seller, marketing manager and subordinates, and marketing personnel and others in the firm. They require thoughtful as well as inspirational leadership.

The final development for consideration has paradoxically been with us for a long time. There has always been a need for imaginative thinking in marketing, for success belongs to those who excel in doing two things better than others. The first is identifying needs of customers. The second is designing a superior marketing program to fill those needs. As one marketing sage puts it, "No amount of modern marketing science or heavy analysis will work without the protean powers of marketing imagination and high spirits."[32]

We in American business have been much too myopic and ethnocentric in our approach to marketing. We have been myopic in focusing on the surface aspects of buyer behavior. We must learn how to look deeper into the psyches of customers and develop marketing tools that enable us to do a better job of meeting complex needs and influencing choices. We have been myopic, too, in marketing implementation. Success here depends not only on our everyday actions as managers but also on our ability to understand and anticipate interpersonal, inter-firm, and environmental (i.e., economic, competitive, technological, and governmental) forces. In the past, it was sometimes possible to ignore these factors because market growth rates were high and the economic climate and the level of competition were favorable. But today, innovations in strategic management are available to all, product life cycles are shrinking, economic fluctuations are greater and more frequent, and foreign competition is increasing. All these developments call for deeper and speedier responses on the part of the marketing implementer.

Unfortunately, we have been ethnocentric in the sense that domestic marketing has ruled the roost. The consequences are foreboding. Since about 1970, trade deficits have been large and frequent, and our share of world trade has plummeted. Foreign rivals now threaten to overtake us in areas where we once were regarded as invincible. If we are to survive, we must give more weight to international marketing. In the future, global markets will provide opportunities for growth, and a worldwide orientation will permit the fulfillment of organization goals for return on investment, capacity utilization, cash generation, and other objectives. How is your firm meeting the challenges?

NOTES

1. "Marketing: The New Priority," *Business Week*, November 21, 1983, pp. 96–99, 102–4, 106. "To Market, to Market," *Newsweek*, January 9, 1984, pp. 70–72.

2. Some of the facts of this case are drawn from Frederick C. Klein, "How a New Product Was Brought to Market Only to Flop Miserably," *Wall Street Journal*, January 5, 1973, pp. 1, 19.

3. The three approaches are described in Michael E. Porter, *Competitive Strategy: Techniques for Analyzing Industries and Competitors* (New York: Free Press, 1980). See also William K. Hall, "Survival Strategies in a Hostile Environment," *Harvard Business Review* 58 (September-October 1980): 75–85.

4. In later years, after the 1978 acquisition of Seven-Up by Philip Morris and a switch in ad agencies to N. W. Ayer, and into the 1980s, Seven-Up seems to have lost some of its earlier, hard-won successes. It is still far behind the market leaders — Coke and Pepsi — who have over 40 percent of the market, and, with less than 6 percent market share, is being pushed by Dr. Pepper and others. Perhaps Seven-Up has reached a watershed in consumer acceptance, or else the competition is too powerful to overcome.

5. J. Fred Bucy, "Marketing in a Goal-Oriented Organization: The Texas Instruments Approach," in J. Backman and J. Czepiel, eds., *Changing Marketing Strategy in a New Economy* (Indianapolis: Bobbs-Merrill, 1977).

6. "Note on the Use of Experience Curves in Competitive Decision Making," *Harvard Business School,* Intercollegiate Case Clearing House, 9-175-174, 1975.

7. Bucy, 1977.

8. Ibid.

9. Lynn W. Phillips, Dae R. Chang, and Robert D. Buzzell, "Product Quality, Cost Position and Business Performance: A Test of Some Key Hypotheses," *Journal of Marketing,* 47 (Spring 1983): 26–43.

10. The data quoted for the firms in the chain saw industry came from personal communication with Professor Michael E. Porter, as well as two cases he wrote: "The Chain Saw Industry in 1974," No. 9-379-157, and "The Chain Saw Industry in 1978," No. 9-379-176 (Boston: Harvard Business School, 1979).

11. Much of the information presented here on Lipton Herbal Teas is drawn from a presentation by, and subsequent personal communications with, John W. Sullivan, who at the time of the case was president of Kelly, Nason, the ad agency for Lipton Herbal Teas.

12. Porter, 1980.

13. See Ibid.

14. Michael E. Porter, "Notes on the Structural Analysis of Industries," No. 376-054 (Boston: Harvard Business School, 1975).

15. Porter, 1975.

16. Gianni Lorenzoni, "From Vertical Integration to Vertical Disintegration: A Case of Successful Turnaround," unpublished working paper, University of Bologna, Italy, 1984.

17. "A Note on the Boston Consulting Group Concept of Competitive Analysis and Corporate Strategy," No. 9-175-175. Boston: Harvard Business School, Intercollegiate Case Clearing House, 1975. George S. Day, "Diagnosing the Product Portfolio," *Journal of Marketing* 41 (April 1977): 29–38.

18. Charles W. Hofer and Dan Schendel, *Strategy Formulation: Analytical Concepts* (St. Paul, Minn.: West Publishing Co., 1978).

19. S. J. Q. Robinson, R. E. Hichens, and D. P. Wade, "The Directional Policy Matrix — Tool for Strategic Planning," *Long-Range Planning,* June 1978, 8–15; D. E. Hussey, "Portfolio Analysis: Practical Experience with the Directional Policy Matrix," *Long-Range Planning,* August 1978, 2–8.

20. Robert D. Buzzell, Bradley T. Gale, and Ralph G. M. Sultan, "Market Share

— A Key to Profitability," *Harvard Business Review* 53 (January–February 1975): 97–106.

21. "A Note on the Boston Consulting Group . . . ," p. 7.

22. Hall, 1980, pp. 78–79.

23. Porter, 1980, chap. 7.

24. This example is taken from a presentation to one of my MBA classes given by Mr. Elliot B. Ross of McKinsey & Company, Inc.

25. The estimated costs and failure rates are derived from Glen L. Urban and John R. Hauser, *Design and Marketing of New Products* (Englewood Cliffs, N.J.: Prentice-Hall, 1980), chap. 2.

26. Alvin J. Silk and Glen L. Urban, "Pre-test Market Evaluation of New Packaged Goods: A Model and Measurement Methodology," *Journal of Marketing Research* 15 (May 1978): 171–91.

27. Herbert E. Krugman, "Why Three Exposures May Be Enough," *Journal of Advertising Research* 12 (December 1972): 11–14.

28. Richard Vaughn, "How Advertising Works: A Planning Model," *Journal of Advertising Research* 20 (1980): 27–33.

29. Point-of-Purchase Advertising Institute, 1978, quoted in D. I. Hawkins, R. J. Best, and K. A. Coney, *Consumer Behavior: Implications for Marketing Strategy* (Plano, Tex.: Business Publications, 1983), p. 563.

30. Kent B. Monroe and Albert J. Della Bitta, "Models for Pricing Decisions," *Journal of Marketing Research* 15 (August 1978): 413–28.

31. Robert J. Dolan and Abel P. Jeuland, "Experience Curves and Dynamic Demand Models: Implications for Optimal Pricing Strategies," *Journal of Marketing* 18 (Winter 1981): 52–73; C. D. Fogg and K. H. Kohnken, "Price-Cost Planning," *Journal of Marketing* 15 (April 1978): 97–106; Hermann Simon, "Dynamics of Price Elasticity and Brand Life Cycles: An Empirical Study," *Journal of Marketing Research* 16 (November 1979): 439–52; Frank M. Bass and Alain V. Bultez, "A Note on Optimal Strategic Pricing of Technological Innovations," *Marketing Science* 1 (Fall 1982): 371–78; B. Robinson and C. Lakhani, "Dynamic Price Models for New-Product Planning," *Management Science* 21 (1975): 1113–22.

32. Theodore Leavitt, *The Marketing Imagination* (New York: Free Press, 1983).

SUGGESTED READINGS

Strategy

Porter, Michael E. *Competitive Strategy: Techniques for Analyzing Industries and Competitors*. New York: Free Press, 1980.

General Marketing

Richard P. Bagozzi. *Principles of Marketing Management*. Chicago: Science Research Associates, 1986.

Kotler, Philip. *Marketing Management: Analysis, Planning, and Control*, 5th ed. Englewood Cliffs, N.J.: Prentice-Hall, 1984.

Consumer Behavior

Bettman, James R. *An Information Processing Theory of Consumer Choice.* Reading, Mass.: Addison-Wesley, 1979.

Howard, John A. *Consumer Behavior: Application of Theory.* New York: McGraw-Hill, 1977.

Sternthal, Brian, and C. Samuel Craig. *Consumer Behavior: An Information Processing Perspective.* Englewood Cliffs, N.J.: Prentice-Hall, 1981.

Product Decisions

Urban, Glen L., and John R. Hauser. *Design and Marketing of New Products.* Englewood Cliffs, N.J.: Prentice-Hall, 1980.

Wind, Yoram J. *Product Policy: Concepts, Methods, and Strategy.* Reading, Mass.: Addison-Wesley, 1982.

Commmunication Decisions

Aaker, David A., and John G. Myers. *Advertising Management,* 2nd ed. Englewood Cliffs, N.J.: Prentice-Hall, 1982.

Hughes, G. David, and Charles H. Singler. *Strategic Sales Management.* Reading, Mass.: Addison-Wesley, 1983.

Ray, Michael L. *Advertising and Communication Management.* Englewood Cliffs, N.J.: Prentice-Hall, 1982.

Price Decisions

Monroe, Kent B. *Pricing: Making Profitable Decisions.* New York: McGraw-Hill, 1979.

Distribution Decisions

Stern, Louis W., and Adel I. El-Ansary. *Marketing Channels,* 2nd ed. Englewood Cliffs, N.J.: Prentice-Hall, 1981.

Marketing Research and Modeling

Green, Paul E., and Donald S. Tull. *Research for Marketing Decisions,* 4th ed. Englewood Cliffs, N.J.: Prentice-Hall, 1978.

Lilien, Gary L., and Philip Kotler. *Marketing Decision Making: A Model-Building Approach.* New York: Harper & Row, 1983.

CHAPTER 2

Financial Management

James C. Van Horne
Stanford University
Graduate School of Business

With the deregulation of the airline industry, differences in past financial management have a tremendous influence on whether an airline thrives or withers. Braniff, Continental, Eastern, Pan Am, and other airlines heavily financed with debt lacked flexibility in meeting the challenge of a deregulated environment. With rising interest rates in the early 1980s, the debt burden became an albatross around their necks, ever tightening with new entries, rising fuel costs, and competitive price wars. United and Delta, financed with greater portions of equity capital, were able to weather the storm, respond effectively, and, eventually, to prosper. As with numerous other industries, financial policy can determine whether a company flourishes or languishes in the competitive arena. Who is the principal person responsible for such policy?

The chief financial officer (CFO) of a corporation is charged with a number of tasks. Most fall under two broad headings: (1) the allocation of funds among different assets and (2) the raising of funds both externally and internally. The sources of funds are many: trade creditors, bankers, lessors, long-term lenders, and investors in the company's stock. The funds provided from these sources are committed to cash and marketable securities, accounts receivable owed by customers, inventories used to facilitate production and sales, and fixed assets used in the production of a good or the provision of a service. The flow of funds from sources to uses does not happen by chance; the role of financial management is to direct these flows in keeping with some plan or objective.

Although a number of objectives or goals could be advanced, the conceptual foundation of finance is based on the notion that a corporation directs its activities in order to maximize shareholder wealth. The market value of a company's stock reflects investor beliefs about the risk and expected return of that stock in relation to other securities available for investment. If decisions of a company are made in keeping with their likely effect upon share price, the company will be able to attract capital only when its investment opportunities justify the use of this capital on a risk-return basis. If rationality prevails in the capital markets, the savings flows of society will be directed to the most promising investment opportunities, on a risk-adjusted return basis, and society will be well served by this objective function.

This chapter is organized around the principal functions of the chief financial officer. As suggested, these involve the efficient allocation of funds within the corporation and the raising of funds on as favorable terms as possible. Both functions should be pursued with an eye toward maximizing shareholder wealth. We begin with managing the current assets of the corporation — cash, marketable securities, accounts receivable, and inventories. We briefly explore ways of efficiently administrating these assets as well as look at the management of liquidity. Where once the financial manager was concerned only with current assets, he or she now is involved in the allocation of funds among fixed assets. Here we consider capital budgeting under conditions of risk and the required rate of return for a project. Necessarily we will be concerned with valuation issues. The second function involves the raising of funds. Our concern here will be with leverage and capital structure, as well as with actual financing with short-, intermediate-, and long-term financial instruments. In addition, we analyze retained earnings as a source of funds. Because this source represents dividends forgone by stockholders, dividend policy is interrelated with financing policy. Last, we examine acquisitions as a special area of concern to the financial manager. With this road map in mind, we proceed to follow the path described.

CURRENT-ASSET MANAGEMENT

By accounting definition, current assets are normally converted into cash within one year. The most liquid assets, of course, are cash and marketable securities. These constitute the liquidity position of a company. This liquidity position is determined by a trade-off between risk and return. The greater the liquidity of a company, the less the risk, as a liquidity cushion simply permits a good deal of flexibility. However, there is an opportunity cost. Funds must be raised for investment in liquidity, and the return on marketable securities is less than the overall cost of capital of the company.

Cash and Marketable Securities Management

Cash management involves managing the funds of the firm in order to obtain maximum cash availability and maximum interest income on any idle funds. The idea is to accelerate collections, which simply means reducing the delay between the time customers pay bills and the time the checks are collected and become usable funds for the company. Such vehicles as concentration banking, a lock box arrangement, and messenger services for large remittances are all designed to (1) reduce the mailing time of payments from customers, (2) speed the deposit of these funds into the bank, (3) reduce the float during which payments received by the company remain uncollected, and (4) quickly move funds to disbursement banks. With respect to disbursements, efficient control here also results in increased cash availability. Rather than accelerate, the idea is to slow the disbursement of funds. This can be accomplished by paying bills on banks in remote areas or by using drafts. The idea is to increase float. However, this obviously works to the detriment of suppliers. Therefore, it is important to temper any slowing in disbursements to take account of supplier relations. The combination of accelerating collections and slowing disbursements will lead to maximum availability of cash.

The division between cash and marketable securities is usually a function of the compensating balance requirement of the bank. The corporation endeavors to maintain as low a cash balance as possible, but one that is consistent with its transactions requirements. Even without a compensating-balance requirement, a certain level of transaction balances might be necessary. It is important to distinguish between cash shown on the company's books and cash shown on the bank's books. One should be concerned only with the collected balances that are available at the bank. It is possible, and often desirable, to have a negative balance on the company's books and a positive balance at the bank. A good deal of computer sophistication goes into the efficient management of a cash position. Frequently the constraining factor is the balance requirement of a bank, which is designed to compensate it for activity in the account. Oftentimes a company can pay a fee for these services in lieu of maintaining a specific balance. A number of models have been developed to help the financial manager in the split of liquidity between cash and marketable securities. These are beyond the reach of this discussion.

The excess cash above some level needed for transactions or compensating-balance purposes is invested in marketable securities. A number of vehicles are available for investment: treasury securities, agency securities, bankers' acceptances, commercial paper, repurchase agreements, negotiable certificates of deposit, Eurodollar investments, and adjustable-rate preferred stock. The desirability of each security should be judged relative to its duration, default risk, and marketability. The company should seek a portfolio of securities in keeping with its cash-flow needs and the uncertainty associated with these cash flows.

Accounts Receivable Management

The credit and collection policies of a company affect the demand for its product or service. By relaxing credit standards, a shoe company may hope to stimulate revenues. This in turn will lead to larger profits. However, there is a cost to the lower credit standards. As marginal customers are added, they typically are slower in their payment habits, and a larger percentage of bad debt losses occur. The slower collection period results in a higher level of investment in accounts receivable, entailing added costs. Therefore, there is a trade-off between the increased profitability associated with larger sales and the increased cost of carrying additional receivables together with the increased cost of bad debt losses. In addition to credit standards, other policy variables include the credit period, the cash discount given, and the level of collection expenditures.

In each case, a decision may be reached by comparing the possible gains from a change in policy with the cost of the change. To illustrate the trade-offs involved, Figure 2.1 depicts the relationship between the quality of accounts accepted and various factors. The quality of account accepted is along the horizontal axis in all of the panels. Farthest to the left is the best possible account and farthest to the right the worst possible account. As credit standards are relaxed in the upper left-hand panel, sales mount at an increasing rate. This of course is desirable. However, we see in the upper right-hand panel that as credit standards are relaxed, the average collection period increases. The average customer becomes slower in payment, and the receivables must be carried for a longer period of time. In the lower left-hand panel, bad debt losses mount as credit standards are relaxed. Both of these occurrences are bad. Consequently, they must be balanced against the increase in sales in order to determine an optimal credit policy. In the lower right-hand panel, we see that the combination of these influences results in total profits increasing at a diminishing rate. The optimal policy is represented by point X in the figure, depicting the point at which the profits associated with further sales increases are exactly offset by the profitability lost through an increased collection period and bad debt losses.

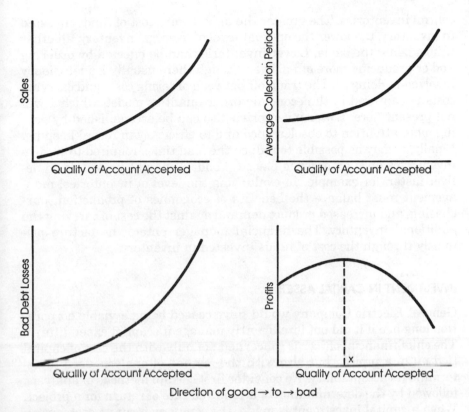

Figure 2.1 Relationship Between Credit Standards and Profitability

The financial manager usually is directly involved in overseeing the credit department of the corporation and in administering credit and collection policies and procedures. Analysts in the credit department evaluate financial information and attempt to categorize the risk of a credit applicant with respect to slow payment or no payment at all. In this regard much use is made of computer technology. In addition to the credit department, the chief financial officer along with the controller oversees the accounts-receivable ledger department, where individual account records are changed every time a customer is invoiced or makes a payment.

Inventory Management

Unlike receivable management, inventory management usually is not the direct responsibility of the chief financial officer. However, the investment of funds in inventory ties up capital. With high interest rates, the financial manager has become increasingly involved in efforts to control inventories. The greater the opportunity cost of funds invested in inventory, the lower the optimal level of average inventory, all other things being the same. Lower inventories can be effected by ordering and/or producing more often, even though there usually is inefficiency involved in doing so. The trade-off between ordering costs and carrying costs is captured in the economic order quantity model, which I will not present here. Lower inventories also can be accomplished by paying more attention to obsolescence and to efficiency in record keeping. Finally, it may be possible to reduce the lead times required to receive inventories once an order is placed. Vendors may be pressured to deliver faster, for example. In evaluating the level of inventories, management must balance the benefits of economies of production, purchasing, and increased product demand against the cost of carrying the additional inventory. The financial manager enters the picture primarily through the cost of funds invested in inventory.

INVESTMENT IN CAPITAL ASSETS

General Electric Company would have ceased being a viable corporation long ago if it did not intelligently manage its capital expenditures. The chief financial officer is concerned not only with the cost of capital tied up in a project, but also with the method of analysis used to determine its acceptability. We consider first certain methods of analysis, followed by the determination of a required rate of return for a project. When a capital investment is made, the company incurs a cash outlay in the expectation of cash inflows in future years. The idea is to compare the likely cash benefits to be received with the cash outflows necessary for the investment.

Most companies use either the net-present value method or the internal-rate-of-return method to make this comparison. The net present value of an investment proposal is

$$NPV = X_0 + \frac{X_1}{(1+k)} + \frac{X_2}{(1+k)^2} + \cdots + \frac{X_n}{(1+k)^n}$$

where X_0 is the initial cash outflow, X_1 is the cash flow, either inflow or outflow, received at the end of period 1, n is the final period in which cash flows are received, and k is the required rate of return. If the sum of these discounted cash flows is zero or more, the project is accepted. If the net present value is negative, the project is rejected. In other words, acceptance occurs if the present value of cash inflows exceeds the present value of cash outflows.

The internal rate of return for an investment project is the discount

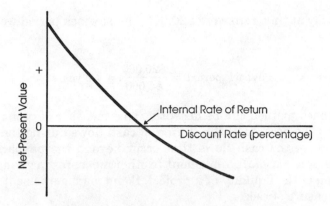

Figure 2.2 Net Present Value and the Discount Rate

rate that equates the present value of expected cash inflows with the present value of the expected cash outflows. If the initial cash outflow occurs at time zero, it is represented by the rate r, such that

$$X_0 = \frac{X_1}{(1+r)} + \frac{X_2}{(1+r)^2} + \ldots + \frac{X_n}{(1+r)^n}$$

The internal rate of return as well as the net present value for a typical project is shown in Figure 2.2. The net present value is on the vertical axis and the discount rate is along the horizontal axis. At a zero rate of discount, the net present value of the project is simply the sum of the expected cash inflows minus the sum of the expected cash outflows. In other words no discounting takes place. As the discount rate is increased from zero to some positive amount, the net present value of the project declines. This is simply to say that the present value of the future cash inflows shrinks relative to the initial cash outlay at time zero. Further increases in the discount rate reduce the net present value until it crosses the zero line. By definition, the internal rate of return is at the point of intersection with the zero line. With further increases in the discount rate, the net present value of the project becomes increasingly negative.

In addition to the discounted cash-flow methods of analysis, frequently a payback period is calculated. The payback period of an investment project tells us the number of years required to recover the initial cash investment. It is simply the ratio of the initial fixed investment over the annual cash inflows during the recovery period. If annual cash inflows were $5,000 a year for ten years, and the initial cash outlay at time zero were $20,000, the payback period would be as follows:

$$\text{Payback period} = \frac{\$20,000}{\$5,000} = 4.0 \text{ years}$$

The payback method can be deceptive as a measure of profitability. It does not take account of the timing of cash flows during the payback period nor of the cash flows that occur beyond the payback period. However, it is a useful supplement to other measures in giving a rough indication of the liquidity of a project. Some managers use it also as a crude measure of risk.

Risk and Capital Budgeting

Risk is better measured by a probability distribution of possible outcomes. The chief financial officer often is involved in determining what information is required in the company's capital request forms. To the extent project risk is a factor of concern, managers requesting a capital project may be asked to provide more than just the expected cash flows. They may be asked for optimistic and pessimistic estimates, to which probabilities can be attached. On the basis of this information, it is possible to formulate a probability distribution of possible net present values associated with the project. (In addition, or instead, one may determine a probability distribution of possible internal rates of return.) I will not go into the mechanics of the calculations, but only indicate that they are not difficult.[1]

Figure 2.3 depicts probability distributions of possible net present values for two hypothetical projects. As we see, Project A has an expected net present value of *A*, on the horizontal axis, and its probability distribution is narrower than that of Project B. Therefore, we would say that Project B has the higher risk. However, it also has the higher expected net present value, as shown by *B* on the horizontal axis. For both projects there is some probability that the net present value will be zero or less. However, this prospect is greater for Project B than it is for Project A. With proper attention to the information requested in the capital expenditure form, probability statements of the sort shown in Figure 2.3 can be portrayed. On the basis of this portrayal, management can determine whether one or the other of the two projects is acceptable, both should be rejected, or both should be accepted. This information is missing in a conventional evaluation where only the expected cash flows are evaluated. The more uncertain the future, the

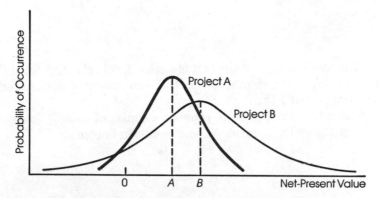

Figure 2.3 Probability Distributions of Possible Net-Present Values for Two Projects

more important it becomes to attach some type of probabilistic assessments to likely outcomes.

REQUIRED RATES OF RETURN AND VALUATION

Perhaps in no other major area is the financial manager's influence more directly felt than in determining a required rate of return for an investment project. In order to determine such a return, the chief financial officer must initiate studies on both the cost of debt and the cost of equity. As equity costs are the more difficult and controversial to measure, we focus initially upon these costs. In this regard, certain valuation concepts are important.

Valuation

The benefits associated with ownership of a common stock consist of dividends paid during a holding period together with the capital gain or loss that occurs upon the sale of the security. For investors as a whole, cash dividends are what give a stock value. These dividends, which may be either regular or liquidating dividends, are all that stockholders as a whole receive from the ownership of the stock. While some stocks pay no dividends, the ultimate expectation is that the company eventually will pay dividends and that future investors will receive a cash return on their investment. Otherwise, it would not be possible to find investors willing to buy the stock. Given these notions, the expected rate of return on a stock can be determined by solving the following equation for r:

$$P_0 = \sum_{t=1}^{\infty} \frac{D_t}{(1+r)^t}$$

where D_t is the dividend at the end of period t, ∞ is the sign for infinity, and the capital Greek sigma reflects the summation of discounted dividends from period 1 through infinity.

If dividends are expected to grow at a constant rate, g, in keeping, say, with the growth in earnings, the equation becomes:

$$P_0 = \frac{D_1}{r-g}$$

For example, if the dividend expected to be paid one year hence were $3, the required rate of return, r, were 15 percent, and the growth rate, g, were 10 percent,

$$P_0 = \frac{\$3}{.15-.10} = \$60$$

Rearranging the above equation, the expected return becomes:

$$r = \frac{D_1}{P_0} + g$$

The critical assumption in this valuation model is that dividends per share are expected to grow perpetually at a compound rate of g. This is not unreasonable for a company that is expected to grow roughly in keeping with the growth rate in the economy. Other patterns of growth can be modeled. For example, it may be that a high rate of growth is expected in the early years, followed by a transition to a slower rate of growth.

The required return on a bond issue by a company also is based upon a present value approach. For a bond that pays interest at the end of the year and has a face value of $1,000, the market value is

$$P_0 = \frac{C}{(1+k)} + \frac{C}{(1+k)^2} + \ldots + \frac{C}{(1+k)^n} + \frac{\$1,000}{(1+k)^n}$$

where P_0 is the present value of the payments stream, C is the annual coupon interest payment, n is the number of years to final maturity, and k is the required rate of return, known as the yield to maturity.

Risk-Return Trade-off in Capital Markets

For both stocks and bonds there is an implied positive relationship between risk and expected return, as measured in the ways described above. Because investors overall dislike risk, they must be offered additional expected return when they take on additional risk. Most investors in the marketplace are not concerned with the risk of an individual security. Because they are invested in a number of securities, they are concerned with the incremental contribution of a security to the risk of their overall portfolio. They are concerned with what we call unavoidable risk, the risk that cannot be avoided by diversification of the securities that are held. Expressed differently, if you invest in a number of securities, some of the individual security risks cancel out. What is left over we call unavoidable risk. It is also known as *systematic* risk.

Assuming as we do that investors overall are averse to risk, there is a relationship between the return they expect from holding a security and its unavoidable or systematic risk. This relationship is known as the *security market line,* and it is fundamental to finance and valuation. The concept is illustrated in Figure 2.4. The expected return is shown on the vertical axis, and unavoidable or systematic risk is shown on the horizontal. At zero risk, the security market line has an intercept on the vertical axis at a positive expected rate of return. This return represents the risk-free rate. It is the rate of return associated with the time value of money. As risk increases, however, the required rate of return increases in the manner shown. Therefore, there is a positive trade-off between risk and expected return that governs the valuation of marketable securities at a moment in time. The slope of the security market line tells us the degree to which investors are averse to risk. The steeper the slope, the more averse they are. However, the slope can change over time, as investors become more or less averse to risk and the line can shift with changes in interest rates.

Building on these concepts, let us outline now the rudiments of the *capital asset pricing model* (CAPM). While this model is a simplification of reality, it allows us to draw certain implications about required rates of return for a stock, assuming the market for stocks overall is in equilibrium.[2]

The unavoidable risk of a stock is described by its beta. A beta simply reflects the comovement of the individual stock with that of the overall market. For example, if a security tended to go up 15 percent

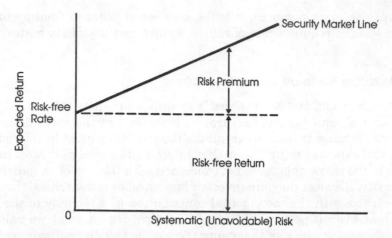

Figure 2.4   Risk-Return Trade-off in the Market

when the market overall increased by 10 percent, and declined by 15 percent when the overall market declined by 10 percent, this stock would have more systematic risk than the typical stock in the market. The beta of the stock would be 1.5. By definition, the beta of the typical stock in the marketplace, or the market portfolio, is 1.0. As a proxy for the market portfolio, most people use a broad stock index, such as Standard & Poor's 500 stock index. If another stock rose by 7 percent when the overall market increased by 10 percent and declined by 7 percent when the overall market declined by 10 percent, this stock would have less systematic risk than the market as a whole. It would be characterized as defensive in nature, and its beta would be 0.7. In summary, the beta of the stock represents its contribution to the risk of a highly diversified portfolio of stocks. It represents the risk of the stock that is unavoidable, in the sense that it cannot be reduced by diversification. The range of betas is roughly 0.3 to 2.5. However, about three-quarters of the betas for stocks fall within the range of 0.7 to 1.3.

The total risk associated with holding an individual stock, or for that matter any security, is composed of two parts:

$$\text{Total risk} = \text{systematic risk} + \text{unsystematic risk}$$
$$\qquad\qquad\quad \text{(unavoidable)} \qquad \text{(diversifiable)}$$

It has been shown that unsystematic risk is reduced at a decreasing rate toward zero as more stocks are added to a portfolio. Thus a substantial portion of the unsystematic risk of a stock can be eliminated with a relative moderate amount of efficient diversification, say fifteen stocks. For the typical stock, unsystematic risk accounts for around two-thirds of its total risk. Through diversification, this type of risk can be reduced or even eliminated. For the well-diversified investor, then, not all of the risk involved in holding a stock is relevant; the unsystematic risk can be diversified away.

Required Rate of Return

If most investors in the marketplace are efficiently diversified, the major risk associated with a stock becomes its systematic or unavoidable risk. The greater the beta of a stock, the greater the risk of that stock and the greater the return required. As a result, the required rate of return for a particular stock, call it j, is

$$R_j = i + (R_m - i) \beta_j$$

where i is the risk free rate, R_m is the expected return for the market portfolio, and β_j is the beta coefficient for the stock as described earlier. In keeping with the presentation of the security market line in Figure 2.4, the required rate of return for a stock is equal to the risk-free rate plus a risk premium.

Suppose that the expected return on short-term treasury securities is 9 percent, the expected return on common stocks overall is 15 percent, and the beta of XYZ Corporation is 1.25. This beta indicates that the company has more systematic risk than the typical stock in the marketplace. Given this information, the required rate of return on the stock would be

$$R_{XYZ} = .09 + (.15 - .09)1.25 = 16.5\%$$

Thus, the estimated required rate of return on equity for XYZ Company is approximately 16.5 percent; this is the rate of return that investors expect the company to earn on its equity. The betas for stocks are published by a number of services, based upon historical stock price movements relative to the overall market. These services allow one to obtain the beta for stock with ease. The treasury security rate is available in the *Wall Street Journal* or other publications. It is more difficult to obtain estimates of the expected rate of return for the overall market. A handful of investment banks as well as commercial banks make these estimates, usually monthly.

Rather than estimate the cost of equity capital using the capital asset pricing model, some use a dividend capitalization model. This model was presented earlier, and it merely states that the market price of the stock is the present value of the stream of expected future dividends. If dividends were expected to grow at a constant rate in the foreseeable future, the perpetual growth model could be used. For example, if dividends of a particular stock were expected to grow at an 8 percent annual rate into the foreseeable future, if the expected dividend in the first year were $2, and if the present market price per share were $25, we would have

$$k = \frac{\$2}{\$25} + .08 = 16\%$$

This rate would then be used as an estimate of the company's required return on equity capital.

The cost of debt of a company usually is expressed simply as the cost of new borrowings times 1 minus the tax rate. For example, if the company could borrow at a 15 percent rate and the tax rate were 40 percent, the after-tax cost would be

$$k_d = 0.15(1 - .40) = 9\%$$

It is important that the after-tax cost represent the marginal, or incremental, cost of additional debt. It does not represent the cost of past debt, but the cost of debt used to finance the new project.

Weighted-Average Cost Capital

Once the costs of the individual components of the capital structure have been measured, one then weights them according to the intended financing and calculates a weighted average cost of capital. Suppose in our previous example that we calculated the after-tax cost of debt as 9 percent and the after-tax cost of equity as 16 percent. Moreover, suppose that the company were planning to use 40 percent debt financing and 60 percent equity financing, either retained earnings or new common stock financing. Therefore, the weighted average cost of capital would be as follows:

Instrument	Proportion	After-Tax Cost	Weighted Costs
Debt	40%	9%	3.6%
Common Stock Equity	60%	16%	9.6%
TOTAL			13.2%

Given the assumptions of this example, 13.2 percent represents the weighted-average cost of capital of the company. The underlying assumption is that the company intends to finance in the proportions indicated, and that the costs of debt and equity have been accurately measured. Certainly the raising of capital is lumpy, and strict proportions cannot be maintained. It is not to say that each project needs to be financed with 40 percent debt and 60 percent equity. It is only that over time the company finances in those proportions. The approach taken so far has aimed at determining a required rate of return for an overall company.

Required Rates of Return for Divisions and Projects

However, if the projects that a company undertakes are not homogeneous with respect to risk, it is inappropriate to use a single required rate of return for all projects. Rather, a required rate of return should be used that varies with the risk of the project being considered. It may be possible to categorize projects into roughly homogeneous groups and then apply the same required return to all projects that are generated from that group. For example, many companies have divisions, and these divisions invest in capital projects in support of the overall activities of the division. Therefore, the risks of individual projects in the division are pretty much the same. However, there may be significant differences in risk across divisions.

One approach to the problem is to establish individual required rates of return for each division and to allocate capital to the division on the basis of its ability to earn a risk-adjusted return. In many cases, a division is similar to a company whose stock is publicly held. When this is the case, it is possible to use the proxy company's beta in deriving the required rate of return on equity for the division. For example, if a company had a paint division, it would search for companies, such as Sherwin Williams, that were primarily engaged in the production of paint. Similarly, other companies can be identified for other divisions of the corporation. On the basis of these surrogates, betas are determined for each division, and from these, divisional required returns on equity capital may be calculated. Assuming debt is employed in overall financing, a weighted-average required return for the division is derived in the same manner as in the previous section. Once divisional required rates of return are computed, capital is allocated on the basis of these required returns. In addition, divisional managers may be judged on the basis of their ability to earn these required rates of return. In other words, managers are held accountable for different return on asset standards in keeping with differences in the risk of the divisions they manage.

Before closing this section, let us consider one major qualification. The illustrations shown, which use the capital asset pricing model, assume that unsystematic risk is unimportant. However, the probability of a company's becoming insolvent depends on its total risk, not just its systematic risk. When insolvency is a real possibility and when bankruptcy costs are significant, investors may be served by the company's paying attention to the impact of a project on the total risk of the firm. As we know, the total risk is composed of both systematic and unsystematic risk. The attention to total risk will depend upon the type of company. For a large company whose stock is publicly traded and which employs little leverage, a strong case can be made for basing required rates of return on systematic risk alone. However, for the closely held company whose stock is inactively traded, and whose debt is high enough to make insolvency an issue, much more attention should be paid to the total risk. The usual procedure is to add a premium for unsystematic risk to the required rate of return that is calculated. For example, it might be that management determines that an unsystematic risk premium of 3 percent should be added to the required rate of return on equity of 16 percent, which was determined using the capital asset pricing model. We will explore this issue in more detail when we take up financing policy in the next section.

In summary, the chief financial officer plays an important role in determining the required rate of return for capital investment projects. This return should change as conditions in both the debt and equity markets change. Only in this way will capital expenditure decisions of the corporation be optimal.

FINANCING POLICY

Having surveyed the allocation of funds among assets, the second major facet of financial management involves raising funds. The raising of funds can be external in the financial markets or internal through forgoing dividends to stockholders. In this section we first consider concepts involving capital structure. This is followed by a discussion of short-, intermediate-, and long-term financing. Later, we take up the retention of earnings through dividend policy.

The incurrence of debt involves the company in paying a fixed cost. The objective, of course, is to increase the return to common stockholders. However, increases in debt also increase the risk of the earnings available to common stockholders. In addition to the variability of their earnings, there also is the risk of insolvency. Both of these risks increase as debt is heightened. We have again the familiar trade-off between risk and expected return. The idea is to strike a happy balance.

Ways to Analyze the Proportion of Debt

One way to study the effect of debt is to analyze the sensitivity of earnings per share (EPS) to changes in earnings before interest and taxes (EBIT) for various financing alternatives. Suppose for simplicity we are considering only two financing alternatives, debt and common stock. If the firm has no debt currently outstanding, any generation of EBIT is reflected entirely in earnings per share after taxes have been paid. If EBIT were zero, earnings per share also would be zero. With debt financing, it is necessary to earn the interest charges before anything is available to common stockholders. If interest on debt were $1 million per annum, for example, it would be necessary to generate $1 million in EBIT simply for earnings per share to be zero.

All of this can be graphed, and Figure 2.5 portrays a typical relationship for the debt versus common stock choice. Earnings per share are on the vertical axis and EBIT is along the horizontal axis. The common stock alternative line starts at the origin, because there is no debt currently outstanding, and traces earnings per share for each level of EBIT. For the debt alternative, the company must earn the interest charges before earnings become available for the common stockholders. As a result, the debt line intercepts the horizontal axis at $1 million, to the right of the common stock line. However, it rises more steeply and crosses the common stock line at what is known as the indifference point. At this level of EBIT, earnings per share are the same for the two financing alternatives. For EBIT above the indifference point, the debt alternative produces higher earnings per share; to the left of the indifference point, common stock produces higher earnings per share.

While this tells us a good deal about return, it tells us nothing about risk. The key here is to assess the likelihood of EBIT falling below the indifference point. Suppose in our example that the probability distribution of possible EBITs were that shown by the bell-shaped distribution in the figure. We see that the most likely level of EBIT is comfortably above the indifference point. The critical thing is the probability that EBIT will fall below the indifference point. If this probability is negligible, a strong case can be made for the use of debt financing, according to this method of analysis. Contrarily, if the expected level of EBIT is close to the indifference point and the prob-

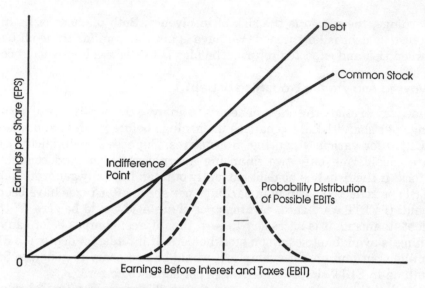

Figure 2.5   EBIT-EPS Analysis of Debt Versus Equity Financing

ability distribution indicates a high probability of EBIT falling below it, the case for common stock financing is persuasive. In our example, we see that there is a low probability that EBIT will fall below the indifference point. According to this method of analysis, a convincing case can be made for the use of debt financing. In summary, then, the higher the level of EBIT and the lower the probability of downside fluctuations, the stronger the case that can be made for the use of debt financing.

In addition to EBIT-EPS analysis, the financial manager should analyze the cash-flow ability of a company to service fixed charges. The greater the amount of debt and other fixed obligations the firm issues and the shorter their maturity, the greater the fixed charges of the company. These charges include principal and interest payments, together with lease payments and preferred stock dividends. All of these charges must be satisfied with cash. Therefore, an assessment of the cash-flow ability of the company to cover them is essential in the comparison of financing alternatives. Inability to meet these charges, with the exception of preferred stock dividends, may result in financial insolvency. It is useful to compute various coverage ratios of cash flow to financial charges. Obviously the greater the probability that the charges will not be met under adverse circumstances such as a recession, the less the case that can be made for nonequity financing.

In addition to EBIT-EPS analysis and the analysis of the cash-flow ability to service debt, the chief financial officer will look at other indicators. The comparison of the debt ratios of the company with those of other companies in the industry is a must. If the firm is contemplating debt significantly out of line with that of similar companies, it is conspicuous in the marketplace. This is not to say that the company is wrong; other companies may be too conservative in the use of debt. However, the company will be conspicuous. In this regard, attention should be paid to the effect that a change in debt will have upon the credit rating of the company by Moody's and Standard & Poor's. Many a financial manager does not want to take on additional debt that will push the company into a lower credit rating category by one or both of these agencies. However, a more fundamental analysis of the advantages of debt may justify accepting a lower rating. All of the methods of analysis suggested are important for the financial officer as well as for certain others in management.

CONCEPTS IN CAPITAL STRUCTURE

These methods of analysis are useful in developing a feel for the effect of a change in financial leverage upon the market price of the stock. A good deal of theory relates to the capital structure decision, well beyond the reaches of this chapter. However, it is useful to review certain fundamentals as they should guide the company in its choice of financing alternative.

In the absence of financial market costs, restrictions, and taxation, it can be shown that the total value of the firm must be the same regardless of its financing mix. In other words, no matter how you divide up the capital structure among debt, equity, and other instruments, the investment value of the overall company stays the same. It is a function only of underlying profitability and risk. Put another way, if the total pie stays the same, it does not matter how it is divided among debt, equity, and other instruments.[3] As a result, the market value per share will be the same regardless of the company's financing mix. The support for this position is simply that investors are able to substitute personal leverage for corporate leverage under assumptions of perfect financial markets (that is, markets free of transaction and other costs and free of taxes). Because they are able to replicate any financial structure the firm might undertake, the company is unable to do something for its stockholders that they cannot do for themselves. Given this notion, capital structure changes would not be a thing of value to stockholders.

Under real-world conditions, most would agree that this proposition does not hold. However, it remains the foundation for building a theory of capital structure. Perhaps the first recognized imperfection was the presence of corporate taxes. Because interest payments are tax-deductible at the corporate level, they constitute a tax shield. The greater the use of debt, the greater the tax shield, and this is a thing of value to the company. This suggests that the value of the firm will increase as more and more debt is added. As companies have considerably less than 100 percent debt financing, this argument is not very satisfying.

The presence of personal taxes on both dividend income and capital gains may reduce the corporate tax advantage associated with debt financing. In the extreme, it could entirely eliminate the corporate tax advantage. This argument is complex, so we will not go through the details of it; it is explained elsewhere.[4] Most scholars contend that the tax advantage associated with leverage is reduced, but not eliminated with the presence of personal taxes. Still, any tax advantage argues for a great deal of debt in the capital structure of the company. Consequently, we must look for other factors influencing valuation.

Offsetting the tax advantage of debt are the presence of possible bankruptcy costs, together with certain agency costs. Bankruptcy costs represent a dead weight loss to security holders and are the combination of legal costs as well as inefficiency costs associated with a company approaching insolvency. Agency costs include the cost of lenders and investors monitoring the behavior of the company. Included are auditor costs, appraiser costs, and other costs of surveillance. As debt is increased, the probability of bankruptcy grows at an increasing rate. As a result, expected bankruptcy costs increase, as do agency costs. Extreme leverage is likely to be penalized by investors. Beyond a point of leverage, many believe that these costs more than offset the value of the tax shield. As a result, the total value of the company turns down. This can be illustrated in Figure 2.6, where value is on the vertical axis and the degree of leverage is on the horizontal axis. As we see, the value of the firm increases with a net tax effect alone, that is, the combination of corporate and personal income taxes. However, with the introduction of bankruptcy and agency costs, the value of the firm turns down after a certain point. As a result, there would be an optimal capital structure. Although this brief discussion does not do justice to the large body of theory on capital structure, it gives the central theme.

It may be possible for a company to increase its share price through a proper degree of leverage. Therefore, the chief financial officer must be guided by the theoretical underpinnings discussed. The methods of analysis taken up earlier give insight into how much debt and other nonequity financing are proper for a company. In practice, it is not

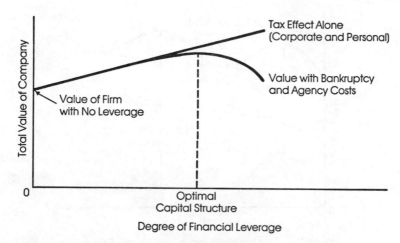

Figure 2.6 Illustration of Capital Structure Theory

possible to identify precisely the optimal capital structure at which share price is maximized. One can only hope to approximate it. In this regard, the financial manager should focus on when additional leverage results in a significant probability of bankruptcy, being mindful of the trade-offs between the tax advantage and bankruptcy-agency costs. This concludes our discussion of the methods of analyzing the use of debt as well as some theoretical notions concerning capital structure. We move now to consideration of various methods of financing.

SHORT- AND INTERMEDIATE-TERM FINANCING

There are a number of types of short- and intermediate-term financing. My purpose is not to describe each in detail, as that information is available elsewhere. Rather it is to point out certain underlying concepts as well as describe the more pertinent uses of certain types of instruments. I assume a familiarity with the types of instruments available.

Temporary Versus More Permanent Financing

A notion has long existed in finance that each asset should be financed with an instrument of the same approximate maturity. This suggests that a company would use short-term debt to finance seasonal variations in current assets and long-term debt or equity to finance the per-

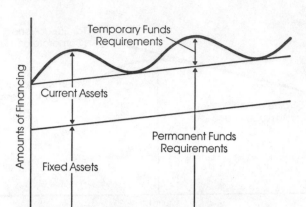

Figure 2.7 Permanent Versus Temporary Financing

manent component of current assets as well as the fixed assets of the corporation. This approach to financing is illustrated in Figure 2.7. The funds requirements of the company are for both fixed assets and current assets. The fixed assets clearly represent permanent funds requirements, but so do part of the current assets of the company. As a company grows, there is an underlying buildup in accounts receivable and inventories. Seasonal fluctuations in current asset requirements are shown by the wavy line at the top. Only the temporary fluctuations would be financed with short-term debt. All other funds requirements would be financed with long-term debt or equity, according to the idea discussed.

As the future is not known with certainty, one cannot project precisely the pattern of future funds requirements. Some companies build in a cushion of long-term financing. As a result, they finance a portion of the expected temporary funds requirements with long-term debt. If expectations are realized, this necessitates their paying interest for the use of funds during times when they are not needed. An aggressive financing posture would be to finance some of the permanent funds requirements of the company on a short-term basis.

In general, the shorter the maturity schedule of a company's liabilities, the greater the risk that it will be unable to meet principal and interest payments. In addition there is uncertainty about interest costs. When interest rates rise sharply, as they did in the late 1970s and early 1980s, a company pays increasing amounts of interest on the rollover of short-term debt. Those companies which had long-term debt in place benefited greatly. While interest rates move both ways, long-term debt costs are known, whereas future short-term interest costs are not. Even though short-term debt often bears a lower interest rate than long-term debt and assures that the company will not pay interest on funds when they are not needed, the risk associated with short-term debt must be assessed. The job of the chief financial officer is to evaluate the trade-off between risk and profitability as it pertains to the maturity structure of debt.

Types of Financing Available

A variety of short- and intermediate-term financial instruments are available to the firm. By varying the maturity composition and conditions of its debt, a company may be able to affect its value. However, the impact is likely to be modest relative to the more fundamental question of the proportion of debt to employ. In what follows, we briefly describe methods of short- and intermediate-term financing.

Trade credit is a significant source of financing for most corporations. When a cash discount is offered but not taken, the cost of trade credit is the cash discount forgone. The longer the period between the end of the discount period and the time the bill is paid, the less this opportunity cost. "Leaning on the trade" involves postponement of payment beyond the credit period. The opportunity cost of "leaning on the trade" is the possible deterioration in the company's credit rating. A major advantage of trade credit is the flexibility it gives the company. It is at the discretion of the company whether a cash discount is taken or not, or whether it stretches accounts payable beyond the credit period. Like accounts payable, *accruals* represent a spontaneous source of financing. However, they typically involve less discretion than trade credit financing. The principal accrual items are wages and taxes, and both are expected to be paid on established dates. Between these dates, the cost of accrual financing is zero, and this financing is more or less continuous.

For large, high-quality companies, money-market instruments may be used as a method of short-term financing. *Commercial paper* is sold either through dealers or directly to investors. One advantage of commercial paper is that the yield typically is less than the rate of interest a company would have to pay on a bank loan. *Bankers' acceptance financing* is another type of money-market credit. The acceptance is highly marketable and can be a desirable source of short-term funds for the company engaged in trade. *Short-term* loans can be obtained from banks as well as finance companies. Unsecured credit is usually confined to bank loans. Interest on business loans is a function of the bank's cost of funds, the existing prime rate, the credit-worthiness of the borrower, and the profitability of the relationship to the bank.

When a company is unable to obtain unsecured credit, it is required to pledge security. To provide a margin of safety, a lender advances less than the market value of the collateral. The advance depends upon the quality of the collateral, the control that it affords the lender, and the clerical costs involved in administration. Accounts receivable and inventory are the principal assets used to secure short-term business loans. Receivables may be either assigned to a lender or sold to a factor. Inventory loans can be under a floating lien, under a trust receipt arrangement, or under terminal warehouse or field warehouse receipt arrangements.

Intermediate-term financing falls in the maturity area of one to five years. The sources of intermediate-term financing are several. Commercial banks, insurance companies, and other institutional investors make *term loans* to corporations. Banks also provide financing under a *revolving-credit arrangement,* which represents a commitment to lend up to a certain amount of money over several years. Such credit usually imposes restrictions on the borrower, known as *protective covenants*. These convenants are contained in the *loan agreement*. If the borrower defaults under any of the provisions of the loan agreement, the lender may initiate immediate corrective action. The covenants usually involve a minimum working capital, limitations on subsequent debt, restrictions on capital expenditures, and limitations on dividends and repurchase of stock. When negotiating intermediate-term financing under a loan agreement, or bond financing under a *bond indenture,* the chief financial officer must make sure that the company can reasonably prosper with the protective covenants imposed. Obviously one would wish to have as lenient a restriction as possible. However, lenders wish protection, so the negotiations involve both parties.

Lease financing is another form of intermediate-term financing and one that has grown in importance during the last two decades. The analysis of lease financing usually is in relation to a debt-financing alternative. The primary reason lease financing sometimes is preferred is the tax benefits. If a company is unable to utilize entirely the tax benefits associated with owning an asset, it may make sense to lease-finance the asset from a party who is able to reap the full tax benefits of ownership. In this way, the lessor can pass on some of the tax benefits in the form of lower lease payments than would otherwise occur. In this way, the lessee enjoys tax benefits that it might not be able to realize on its own through ownership of the asset. In addition, when land is a large factor, the use of lease financing permits the full lease payment to be deducted as an expense, whereas land cannot be depreciated if it is owned. The exact sharing of the tax benefits between the lessor and the lessee depends upon the market conditions in the leasing industry. It is the role of the chief financial officer to focus on the market equilibration process as it relates in particular to the tax benefits associated with leasing.

Long-Term Financing

Long-term financing involves the issuance of long-term bonds, preferred stock, convertible securities, and common stock. If the financing involves a public offering, the company often will use the services of an investment banking firm. The financial officer must interface with the investment banker as well as oversee the registration of the security issue with the Securities and Exchange Commission. Long-term debt issues can be of many types, and have a number of different features. For example the debt may involve collateral, such as a *mortgage;* it may be a *debenture* that is unsecured, or a *debenture subordinated* to other creditors, to name a few types of bond issues. Features such as the maturity, the sinking fund, the call feature, the coupon rate (which may range from zero up to current yield in the marketplace), and the protective covenants in the bond indenture all occupy the financial manager in determining the terms of a long-term debt issue. Rather than offer debt to the general public, a company may place it privately with an institutional investor.

Preferred stock is a hybrid form of security having characteristics of debt and, to a lesser extent, of common stock. The payment of dividends is not a legal but rather a discretionary obligation of the corporation. Here, too, there are a number of features to be negotiated. Almost all preferred stock has a cumulative feature, so that the company is unable to pay common stock dividends unless it is up to date in its preferred stock dividends. Recently a number of companies have issued adjustable-rate preferred stock, where the rate floats in keeping with interest rates on treasury securities. This type of instrument has found greater favor with corporate investors, because 85 percent of the dividend is exempt from taxation to the corporate investor.

Convertible securities represent either debt or preferred stock that is convertible into the common stock of a corporation. A number of interesting valuation questions surround the convertible security. Its value depends primarily on the value of the instrument as a straight bond or preferred stock as well as its conversion value as common stock. For the issuer, convertibles represent delayed-stock financing. The advantage is that there will be less dilution with a convertible

issue than with a common stock issue, assuming the issue eventually
converts. This advantage must be balanced against the uncertainty
associated with being able to force conversion of the instrument into
common stock. The premium at which a convertible security sells
above its conversion value and above its bond value is due to its partial
downside protection as a bond and its upside potential as stock, the
volatility of the common stock, the dividend on the common stock, the
duration of the convertible option, and certain institutional imperfec-
tions. The use of this instrument as a means of financing can be very
exciting, and the chief financial officer becomes involved in a number
of valuation issues bringing such a security to the market.

The *common stockholders* of a corporation are its owners, and they
are entitled to the residual earnings of the company if cash dividends
are paid. They elect a board of directors, typically by proxy; in turn,
these directors choose the management of a company. The chief financial officer of a company is involved in stockholder relations as well as
in keeping abreast of stock price movements, volume of trading, and
the presence of any large accumulation of stock by investor groups. In
today's environment, one is always mindful of the possibility of a take-
over attempt by another company. Usually, the first signs of such an
attempt are unusual activity in the trading of the company's stock. The
financial manager must keep his or her hand on the pulse of stock
movements if early detection is to occur.

When new stock is sold, a company can sell it either to existing
stockholders in a rights offering or to the general public. A right represents an option to buy the new security at the subscription price, and
it takes a specified number of rights to purchase a share. In their early
stages, many high-technology companies rely on *venture capital,*
money invested in a new enterprise. Sometimes a company will issue
different classes of common stock, having different right to dividends,
to asset distribution upon liquidation, and to voting power.

I have presented only a thumbnail sketch of the various financial
instruments available to a company when it raises funds in the external market. The chief financial officer is heavily involved in this responsibility. It is his or her task to raise funds on as favorable terms
as possible, with respect to both interest cost and the features attached
to the security. As conditions in the financial markets are rapidly
changing, this task requires constant vigilance. Not only are the debt
and equity markets volatile with respect to price movements, but there
is continual financial innovation resulting in new instruments, new
features on existing instruments, and new techniques by which to raise
money.

DIVIDEND POLICY

Many corporations rely heavily upon retained earnings as a source of financing. Retained earnings, of course, are simply earnings not paid out as dividends. As a result, the dividend payout ratio of a corporation has a major impact upon its internal financing, the other part coming from those funds provided by operations that are shielded by depreciation. While there are a number of aspects of dividend policy, we focus first upon the dividend payout ratio.

Payout Ratio

If dividend policy were treated solely as a financing decision, the rules for payout would be easy. As long as the company's investment projects had returns that exceeded their required returns, it would use retained earnings, and the amount of debt the increase in equity base would support, to finance these projects. If retained earnings were left over after financing all acceptable investment opportunities, these earnings would be distributed to stockholders in the form of cash dividends. If nothing was left over, there would be no dividends. In this context, dividend policy is a passive residual. That is, the decision is determined by the financing needs of the company and not by any consideration of the effect of dividends upon share price.

Dividend payout is one area of finance that is particularly unsettled. Some factors argue in favor of making the dividend payout ratio an active decision variable, while other factors argue that it should be passive. Most everyone agrees that dividends should be paid if the company does not have need for these funds for acceptable investment projects, either now or in the foreseeable future. The question is whether dividends are more than just a passive residual. Some argue that certain investors have a preference for dividends over capital gains and that this preference is strong enough in the marketplace to dictate dividends being paid. Others argue that investors can manufacture their own dividends simply by selling shares of stock, and that they do not need the company to do it for them. Dividends may have informational content, thereby impacting share price by virtue of the information they communicate to investors about the company's profitability. Presumably dividends speak louder than other forms of communication, if this argument is to be valid. Another factor is the differential taxation of dividends and capital gains. For taxable investors, this creates a powerful bias in favor of retention of earnings, and subsequent capital gains, as opposed to the immediate payment of dividends. However, there are clienteles of investors with respect to taxation. Many investors are tax-free institutions, and certain others are partially exempt from taxation of dividend income. Therefore, the net tax effect is unclear. The presence of flotation costs favors the retention of earnings. Rather than issue common stock and incur flotation costs, the company may be better off retaining earnings and avoiding such costs. Certain institutional restrictions favor the payment of dividends. Some institutional investors are restricted to a prescribed list of eligible securities. Not to pay a dividend may result in an inability of certain investors to invest in the stock. All of these factors may affect share price, but it is their net impact that is important.

Unfortunately, the empirical evidence concerning the effect of dividends on the market price of stock is far from clear. That evidence which suggests that dividends matter is based upon arguments of a preference for dividends by certain investors, the informational content of dividends, and institutional restrictions on investors. These factors are said to more than offset the differential tax effect and flotation costs. Other evidence suggests that dividends are a passive residual and that the dividend payout ratio of a company has no effect upon share price. Finally, additional studies find a net preference in the market for retention, and capital gains, as opposed to dividends. Thus, the evidence is not solid in support of one position; it is all over the map. While a number of companies behave as though dividend payout ratio decisions matter, the empirical support for such action is missing. It is difficult to predict with any accuracy the effect of a dividend payout ratio change upon share price. There seems to be some consensus that dividends have informational content, but whether a change in the dividend paid has a lasting effect upon share price is unclear.

Practical Considerations

The financial manager of a corporation must look at a number of things when evaluating a dividend change. Probably the place to begin is with the funds needs of the company. If funds are left over after financing all acceptable investment projects, this suggests an underlying level of dividends. The liquidity of a company also is a consideration. The greater the liquidity, the more able the company is to pay a dividend and still maintain financial flexibility. Such flexibility also can come from an ability to borrow. If the company has ready lines of credit or other access to financial markets, it may be inclined to pay a higher dividend than otherwise would be the case. Obviously the chief financial officer should attempt to evaluate any valuation information concerning the effect of a dividend on share price. However, as discussed earlier, such information is hazy. Sometimes a protective covenant in a bond indenture or a loan agreement has a binding effect upon the ability of the company to pay a dividend. In determining a dividend payout, a company typically will analyze a number of the factors described above. These factors should suggest the boundaries within which a dividend can be paid. When a company pays a dividend in excess of its residual funds, it implies that the company believes the payment has a favorable effect upon share price. An active dividend policy, then, involves a certain amount of faith because the empirical evidence we have is not supportive.

Other Aspects of Dividend Policy

Although the dividend payout ratio is perhaps the most important factor, *dividend stability* also is an aspect of dividend policy. By stability, I mean maintaining a dividend around a trend line. By using a target dividend payout ratio, a company increases its dividends only when it feels it can maintain the increase in earnings. Companies are reluctant to cut the absolute amount of their cash dividend, owing to the information effect as well as to other things. However, a stable dividend cannot cover up a bad earnings performance in the minds of investors.

Stock dividends and *stock splits* also are a facet of the overall dividend policy of a company. These represent recapitalizations of the company in order to have more shares outstanding at a lower market price. There is no infusion of new capital into the company; stockholders simply receive more shares but have the same proportional ownership in the company as before.

Also a part of dividend policy is a decision to *repurchase stock*. If the firm has excess cash, it can either distribute the cash in the form of dividends or repurchase stock. In particular, the repurchase of stock makes sense when the company wishes to make a one-time distribution. Because of the differential tax on dividends and capital gains, the stockholder is better served by the repurchase of stock. However, the Internal Revenue Service will not allow a steady repurchase-of-stock program as a subterfuge for dividends. In addition to the factors mentioned, the chief financial officer oversees certain procedural aspects involved in the payment of dividends.

MERGERS AND ACQUISITIONS

Of the special topics in finance that come up from time to time, perhaps none involves the chief financial officer more than a prospective merger or acquisition. Of course, a company can be either the acquiring company or the target company. We will focus on the corporation as the

buyer. From the standpoint of acquiring another company, the criterion for acceptance is essentially the same as with a capital investment
decision. Capital should be allocated in order to increase share price.
The incremental cash flows likely to be generated from the merger can
be estimated. These cash flows should take account of any synergy
(that is, operating and other efficiencies) that will occur between the
two companies as well as the necessary ongoing investment to keep
the operation viable. To these cash flows an appropriate discount rate
for the risk involved can be applied. The present value of the stream
of expected incremental cash flows then determines an upper bound
for the price to be paid by the acquiring company.

In addition to a capital budgeting approach to the analysis of an
acquisition, most acquiring companies look at the effect of the merger
upon earnings per share. When the price/earnings ratio of the company
being acquired is lower than the price/earnings ratio of the buying company, there is an initial improvement in earnings per share of the buying company. A dilution occurs when the price/earnings ratio is higher.
Instead of looking only at the immediate effect, most look at the effect
on future earnings per share as well. In competitive financial markets
and in the absence of synergy, we would expect the price/earnings ratio
of the surviving company to be a weighted average of the price/earn-
ings ratios of the two premerger companies.

The empirical evidence on mergers indicates a substantial gain to
the stockholders of the target (acquired) company at the time of the
merger. By gain I mean the premium in price that is paid for the shares
relative to the price that would prevail in the absence of a bidding
situation. The evidence also indicates that there is little or no gain to
the stockholders of the buying company. Certain studies suggest a
modest improvement in share price, while other studies indicate no
effect or even a negative effect upon share price. However, the evidence
pertains to mergers overall and does not reflect the fact that some
mergers may result in significant increases in share price to the acquiring company, whereas others may result in decreases. When we
take account of both the buying and the target companies, it is clear
that wealth overall is increased by virtue of the substantial premium
paid for the target company. In rational financial markets, this suggests that value is created as a result of synergy, tax gains, and perhaps other factors.

The chief financial officer is heavily involved in any merger negotiations and strategy. Perhaps in no other decision is the effect upon
share price so central a focus. Despite this focus, many acquisitions are
simply bad decisions from the standpoint of the acquiring company.
With the wave of merger activities that has occurred in recent years,

it would seem that many a company gets caught up in a bidding war with diminishing reliance upon solid analysis and expectations of what a target company is worth to it. The job of the chief financial officer is to temper excess enthusiasm and try to instill an analytical framework for looking at potential acquisitions.

LOOKING AHEAD

The role of the chief financial officer has changed dramatically in recent years, and we have every reason to believe it will change further. Once these responsibilities were confined mainly to raising funds externally, frequently through bank loans, maintaining the cash position of the company, and looking after relationships with banks and other lenders. Times have changed, because of both external events and conceptual developments within the corporate finance field. For example, with the high cost of external funding, the chief financial officer has become increasingly involved in the overall management of assets of the corporation. It no longer is possible to commit large sums of money to inventories and receivables while giving little or no consideration to the cost of carrying these assets. Similarly, fixed assets have to be justified in terms of earning their ever-increasing economic keep. The financial manager plays a key role in these decisions and must always be alert to the changing interest-rate and equity-cost environment.

We are in the midst of a revolution in the financial services industry. With this revolution have come new types and varieties of securities a company might offer, changes in the ways funds are transferred, and changes in the ways cash, accounts receivable, and accounts payable are managed. Many of the financial innovations that occur are in response to volatile inflation and interest rates, regulatory changes that permit increased competition among financial institutions, technological advances that prompt improved electronic funds transfers, changes in the level of economic activity, and tax law changes. Financial innovation will continue to flourish, as financial markets and the financial services industry become even more competitive. The essential ingredient — change in the factors mentioned above — is all around us.

The challenge to the chief financial officer is to keep abreast of the changing financial market environment. There has been a proliferation of financial instruments and methods, including such things as zero-coupon bonds, options, financial futures markets, floating rate instruments, interest-rate swaps and pass-through securities. When a company can tailor its debt instruments to the unsatisfied needs of the financial markets, it is able to reduce its interest costs relative to what it would have to pay using more conventional types of financing. By staying at the cutting edge of these changes, the chief financial officer can sometimes affect significant interest cost savings and/or flexibility for his or her company.

We can expect also to see further conceptual advances in financial decision-making. Increasingly, the basic decisions of a corporation — investment in assets, capital structure and financing, and dividends — are related to their impact upon the market price of the stock. The notion that a company's debt and equity instruments are traded in financial markets that may be more or less efficient was not fully understood until much of the academic work on portfolio theory and efficient financial markets had been done. This work continues with increasing insights and application to corporate finance. The advent of derivative securities, where instruments having desired features are produced indirectly using options, futures, and other types of special contracts, has particularly benefited from scholarly input. Recently, the heightened interest in acquisitions has triggered further interest in valuation. The chief financial officer simply must be concerned with the valuation of the company's stock and debt instruments in the marketplace. Indeed, the CFO is the principal focal point within the company for this concern, and a proper conceptual framework for approaching financial decisions is essential.

It is hoped that this presentation gives some flavor of the exciting changes that have occurred in finance in recent years. The role of the financial manager is considerably different from what is was twenty or even ten years ago. If there is one thing of which we can be certain, the financial environment will continue to change. The financial manager must accept the changing world in which he or she operates and learn to master its challenge.

NOTES

1. See James C. Van Horne, *Financial Management and Policy,* 7th ed. (Englewood Cliffs, N.J.: Prentice-Hall, 1986), chap. 6, for the details concerning the calculations.

2. The model assumes that the capital markets are efficient, that investors are in general agreement about the likely performance of individual securities, and that their expectations are based on a common holding period, say one year. See William F. Sharpe, *Investments,* 3rd ed. (Englewood Cliffs, N.J.: Prentice-Hall, 1985), for a more detailed discussion of the model.

3. This proposition is associated with Franco Modigliani and Merton H. Miller, "The Cost of Capital, Corporation Finance and the Theory of Investment," *American Economic Review* 48 (June 1958): 261–97.

4. See James V. Van Horne, *Financial Management and Policy,* 7th ed. (Englewood Cliffs, N.J.: Prentice-Hall, 1986), chap. 9. The extreme case for the exact offset of personal taxes against corporate taxes is made by Merton H. Miller, "Debt and Taxes," *Journal of Finance* 32 (May 1977): 261–75.

SUGGESTED READINGS

The following books give a reasonable cross-section of writings involving financial management.

Brealey, Richard, and Stewart Myers. *Principles of Corporate Finance,* 2nd ed. New York: McGraw-Hill, 1984.

Brigham, Eugene F. *Financial Management: Theory and Practice,* 4th ed. Chicago: Dryden, 1985.

Copeland, Thomas E., and J. Fred Weston. *Financial Theory and Corporate Policy,* 2nd ed. Reading, Mass.: Addison-Wesley, 1983.

Higgins, Robert C. *Analysis for Financial Management.* Homewood, Ill.: Richard D. Irwin, 1984. Unlike the other books, this one is narrower in scope. It deals primarily with financial analysis.

Van Horne, James C. *Financial Management and Policy,* 7th ed. Englewood Cliffs, N.J.: Prentice-Hall, 1986.

Journals applicable to the financial executive include the *Journal of Finance, Financial Management,* the *Journal of Financial Economics,* the *Journal of Financial and Quantitative Analysis* and, on occasion, the *Harvard Business Review,* the *Journal of Business,* and the *Financial Analysts Journal.*

CHAPTER 3

Managerial Accounting

Joel S. Demski
*Stanford University
Graduate School of Business*

In broad terms, accounting provides a financial picture of an organization's activities. "Financial accounting" is the side of the coin that deals with reporting to individuals and entities external to the organization. "Managerial accounting" deals with reporting to individuals inside the organization. A common underlying framework serves both reporting activities, but the activities are hardly coextensive. For example, information that is vital to the firm's management may be proprietary or mundane in wider circles. The former is illustrated by proprietary cost information and the latter by the annual cost of cleaning one of the firm's parking lots. Similarly, information that is a centerpiece in financial reporting, such as total revenue for the period, may be uninteresting within the firm, simply because far more detailed information is readily available.

Managerial accounting, the subject of this chapter, occupies an unusual position in the manager's list of important topics: it is thought to be too important to ignore and too mundane to worry about. After all, common sense allows us to speak casually of the "cost of the 1984 Olympic Games," the "cost of the C5A Program," the "cost of patient X's bypass surgery," the "profitability of one of Bank of America's branch offices," the "labor cost at General Motors," the "cost of a community recreation program," and so on. Unfortunately, this is a naive if not dysfunctional view.

In this chapter, I will try to convince you that (1) the organization's

Helpful comments from Rick Antle, Bill Beaver, and Gayton Germane are gratefully acknowledged.

accounting system is an important source of managerial information and (2) this information cannot be gleaned without an appreciation of the subtleties of cost (and revenue) measurement. In short, the answers to numerous questions can be found in the accounting system, but only if you are a clever, informed interrogator of that system.

The chapter proceeds by discussing three questions. What will "it" cost? What will the accounting system report if I do "it"? And how "good" is my accounting system?

The first question focuses on the fact that many managerial tasks, such as deciding whether to entertain an additional customer, to launch a new product line, to lower a product price, and so on, are often framed in a cost and revenue format. Yet this almost universal mode of analysis places a considerable burden on the task of cost measurement. In turn, recognizing this burden is the key to "proper" use of cost measurement information.

The second question dramatizes the point that accounting records are maintained in particular, well-specified ways. This recording system cannot possibly record all the nuances of your various managerial decisions. Thus you must come to recognize that the recording system typically will record results in a manner that is at variance with the analysis you engaged in to produce those results.

The third question deals with the fact that the accounting system is itself the product of managerial choice. It cannot be perfect; after all, accounting is costly and hardly is management's sole source of information. By implication, an important managerial task is the design and maintenance of management's accounting system.

WHAT WILL IT COST?

We begin by asking a seemingly innocuous question: What will it cost? (Equivalently, what did it cost?) The correct answer, it turns out, depends on (1) *why* you want to know, which I will refer to as the decision problem at hand, as well as (2) *how* you have structured or framed that decision problem for purposes of analysis. There is a degree of obviousness in the former. Taxation regulations largely prescribe how the cost of sales is to be calculated for taxation purposes, and the prescribed measurement is typically at odds with what you would like to know when deciding to expand or contract a particular product line. We have a phrase, "different costs for different purposes."[1] But there is much more to the story. The latter, the framing aspect, is even more exasperating. The difficulty is that no unique measure of cost exists.

A Simple Example

Consider a small firm that manufactures a particular line of computer furniture. For simplicity we will assume that the line consists of a single style of desk, called desk A. Also for simplicity, we assume that desks are manufactured only after a customer order is received. This allows us to ignore important (though complicating) questions of how much stock to keep on hand.

A customer has just arrived and inquired about having a desk (desk A, of course) manufactured. The market is competitive, and it is clear that a price of $900 will land the customer, while anything higher will cause the customer to go elsewhere. (Your boss maintains that anything lower will cause you to go elsewhere.) Should the job be accepted? Numerically we ask whether cost is below $900. Cost below $900 will produce a positive profit, while cost above $900 will produce a loss (or negative profit). Thus, presuming a profit motive, the job should be accepted if its cost is below $900. Notice the burden we immediately place on the cost datum. We want it to decide whether to accept the customer's request!

Our mythical firm also has an exemplary internal accounting system that is able to document the follow expenditure categories:

Category	Expenditure
1. Materials (17,500 square feet)	$140000
2. Production labor (10,000 hours)	180000
3. Insurance and taxes on above labor	30000
4. Building lease	12000
5. Production equipment	6000
6. Miscellaneous production materials	10000
7. Office equipment	7000
8. Office supplies	2000
9. General taxes	1500
10. Administrative and clerical personnel (including associated taxes and insurance)	53000
Total expenditures	$441500

These data refer to the firm's total expenditures since it went into business six months ago. No liabilities are present, and 500 desks have been manufactured and sold. (Also assume for convenience that start-up costs were trivial; thus nothing whatsoever is unusual about these expenditures.) So what does a single desk cost?

Cost Behavior

The key to answering our question is to focus on how these various expenditure items vary as a function of the number of desks manufactured. Let's agree to call item 1 *materials,* item 2 *labor,* items 3, 4, 5, and 6 *overhead,* and items 7, 8, 9, and 10 *G&A* (general and administrative). Further suppose that the following equations depict the expenditure pattern, where D denotes the number of desks manufactured and sold:

$$\text{material} = 280 \times (\text{number of desks}) = 280D$$
$$\text{labor} = 360 \times (\text{number of desks}) = 360D$$
$$\text{overhead} = 18{,}000 + 80 \times (\text{number of desks}) = 18{,}000 + 80D$$
$$\text{G\&A} = 58{,}500 + 10 \times (\text{number of desks}) = 58{,}500 + 10D$$

Adding these together we have

$$\text{Total cost} = \text{material} + \text{labor} + \text{overhead} + \text{G\&A}$$
$$= \text{TC} = 76{,}500 + 730D$$

Some specialized though useful terminology arises here. We have expressed total cost as a linear function of output. The constant amount, 76,500, is called the *fixed* cost, while the slope of the function, 730, is called the *variable* cost per unit of output. It is tempting to define the fixed cost as the total cost at an output level of $D = 0$. But it is more useful to regard this overall cost function as an approximation that is reasonably accurate within some range. Viewed in this manner, we regard 76,500 as a cost component that is independent of the output level within some reasonable range (such as 400 to 700 desks in our example). Beyond that range structural changes are likely to significantly alter the firm's cost curve beyond what is depicted in our straightforward expression.

Notice that for $D = 500$ desks we have

$$\text{total cost} = 76{,}500 + 730(500) = 76{,}500 + 365{,}000 = 441{,}500$$

and specific expenditure categories of

$$\text{material} = 280(500) = 140{,}000,$$
$$\text{labor} = 360(500) = 180{,}000,$$
$$\text{overhead} = 18{,}000 + 80(500) = 58{,}000, \text{ and}$$
$$\text{G\&A} = 58{,}500 + 10(500) = 63{,}500$$

Continuing, recall that desks sell for $900 each. This implies a total revenue curve of

$$\text{total revenue} = TR = 900D$$

Combining the total revenue and total cost curves provides a graphical picture of our presumed structure (see Figure 3.1).

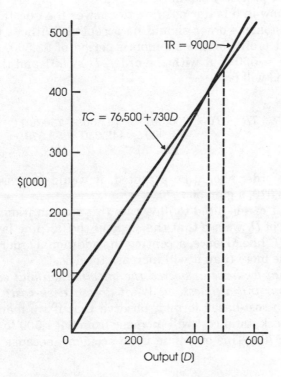

Figure 3.1 Cost and Revenue as Functions of Output

Two points are highlighted here. One is $D = 500$, the presumed level of output in our example. Notice that our firm's profit is total revenue less total cost, or

$$TR - TC = 900(500) - 76,500 - 730(500)$$
$$= 450,000 - 441,500 = \$8,500$$

The other point is $D = 450$. Here the firm's profit is

$$TR - TC = 900(450) - 76,500 - 730(450)$$
$$= 405,000 - 405,000 = \$0$$

This is called the *break-even* point, the output and sales level at which total revenue precisely equals total cost.[2]

We are now in a better position to answer the question of whether the new customer's order should be accepted. Without the order, we have a total profit for the six-month period of \$8,500, as calculated above for $D = 500$. But with the order, $D = 501$ and the total profit for the period will be

$$TR - TC = 900(501) - 76,500 - 730(501)$$
$$= 450,900 - 442,230 = \$8,670$$

That is, the order should be accepted; it would increase profit from \$8,500 to \$8,670, a gain of \$170.

Figure 3.1 can be used to illustrate this computation. At the original position of D, we see that the slope of the TR line is greater than that of the TC line.[3] Hence, accepting the additional order will increase total revenue more than it will increase total cost.

Notice that we have answered the question without ever asking or answering our initial question: What does a desk cost? To place the analysis in a cost-based format, observe that if we manufacture the additional desk, total cost will increase from \$441,500 to \$442,230, an increase of \$730. This of course is no accident, because our model of total cost is

$$TC = 76,500 + 730D$$

Each additional unit adds \$730 to the total cost figure. Recall that 76,500, the intercept of the TC curve in Figure 3.1, is called the firm's *fixed* cost, and 730, the slope of the TC curve in Figure 3.1, is called the firm's *variable* cost per unit of output. Deciding whether to accept the additional order revolves around whether acceptance increases total profit. Reframing this calculation at the level of the single desk in question, this is equivalent to asking whether the *additional* revenue exceeds the *additional* cost. For this particular case, then, a desk costs

$730, the variable cost per unit. And the order should be accepted, with price − cost = 900 − 730 = $170.

From here it is easy to see that any price above $730 would make the additional customer attractive. And remember that our answer to "What does a desk cost?" is derived from our knowledge of the cost structure at hand as well as by framing the order acceptance question in terms of additional revenue versus additional cost.

A Second Example

Suppose our firm expands its line to include desks and chairs. To keep our expanded story uncluttered we will assume that the firm is able to do this without increasing its fixed costs (a nontrivial assumption, to be sure). Its total cost structure is now

$$TC = 76,500 + 730D + 95C$$

where D denotes the number of desks and C the number of chairs. The firm cannot manufacture an unlimited number of desks and chairs, however. It has limited capacity and must confine itself to any number of desks and chairs that satisfy the following capacity constraint:

$$D + \frac{C}{4} \leqslant 600$$

That is, the total of desks plus one fourth the total of chairs cannot exceed a capacity limitation of 600 equivalent "units." In a sense, four chairs require as much space and equipment capacity as does one desk, and 600 "units" of such capacity are available during the (six-month) period in question. The firm might manufacture (1) 600 desks, or (2) 2,400 chairs, or (3) 500 desks and 400 chairs, or (4) 100 desks and 2,000 chairs, or even 1 desk and 2,396 chairs. But 600 desks and 1 chair is an infeasible combination.

We raise the same question as before. A customer arrives and "offers" $900 for one desk. Should the offer be accepted? Suppose that the firm already has orders for 500 desks and 200 chairs, or $D = 500$ and $C = 200$. No other customer is in sight, and it is clearly feasible for the firm to make one additional desk. Let's also assume that chairs sell for $145 per unit. Total profit if the offer is accepted will be

$$TR - TC = 900(501) + 145(200) - 76,500 - 730(501) - 95(200)$$
$$= 479,900 - 461,230 = \$18,670$$

If the offer is rejected, total profit will be

$$TR - TC = 900(500) + 145(200) - 76,500 - 730(500) - 95(200)$$
$$= 479,000 - 460,500 = \$18,500$$

Accepting the offer will increase profit by $170, a familiar datum. Moreover, if we frame the question in terms of revenue versus the cost of a desk, we would again measure the cost of the desk at the variable cost of $730 per unit.

Contrast this with the analysis when the firm's existing plans have $D = 0$ and $C = 2,400$. It is operating at capacity; and the only way to manufacture the desk in question is to cut back on the production of chairs (specifically, four chairs). That is, if the offer is now accepted, chair production will be reduced from 2,400 to 2,396 in order to free up capacity to manufacture the desk in question. Thus, total profit if the offer is accepted will be

$$TR - TC = 900(1) + 145(2,396) - 76,500 - 730(1) - 95(2,396)$$
$$= 348,320 - 304,850 = \$43,470$$

But if the offer is rejected, total profit will be

$$TR - TC = 145(2,400) - 76,500 - 95(2,400)$$
$$= 348,000 - 304,500 = \$43,500$$

Accepting the offer will now lower total profit by $30.

Now what is the cost of the desk? The answer is surely $930, because $900 - 930 = -\$30$. The cost can be derived directly in the following manner. It consists of the $730 expenditure discussed above plus the forgone profit on the four chairs that will be displaced by production of the desk:

$$930 = 730 + 4(145 - 95) = 730 + 200$$

Notice that the 200 datum in this computation does not appear in the itemized breakdown on page 103. It is, in fact, the opportunity cost of diverting scarce capacity from chair to desk production.

The point of all this is to demonstrate that what we mean by "the cost of a desk" is a far from simple question. We are able to deal with the desk decision without ever asking what the cost of a desk is. (This is done by comparing total cost and total revenue for the various alternatives at hand.) Conversely, we are also able to reformulate or reframe the order acceptance question in a manner such that we compare the revenue from that order with the *cost of that order*. In this latter mode of analysis we must, of course, continue to reflect the entire economic structure at hand; and this means that our cost-of-desk measure must carry, if you will, this entire structure. For example, in the case where the firm is already planning to operate at capacity, if we explicitly focus on the entire production schedule, the appropriate cost measure is the 730 slope coefficient in the total cost equation. But if we implicitly focus on the entire production schedule by comparing the desk's revenue with its cost, the appropriate cost measure is the 730 slope coefficient plus the forgone profit from the displaced production.

We could, at this juncture, further complicate the story. To whet your appetite, suppose the firm is not operating at capacity but has decided that it will keep its labor force intact. If additional orders do not materialize, the skilled laborers will be idle. What does this do to our analysis of the problem and cost construction? Similarly, we might introduce issues of customer loyalty. What would this do to our cost construction?

What we mean by the cost of something depends, critically, on what decision problem we are facing and how we have framed that decision problem for purposes of analysis. This simple though difficult-to-grasp observation stems from the fact that not all decision problems are alike and there is no unique method of analyzing any given decision problem. Different "cuts" at the problem exist, and our cost measure must be fine-tuned to the setting and to our method of attack.

WHAT WILL THE ACCOUNTING SYSTEM REPORT IF I DO IT?

The next topic in our overview concerns the contents of the typical cost measurement system. We now agree that what we mean by the cost of something is a specific to the situation. Situations vary, but the accounting system is always there. It must serve a multiplicity of uses, but cannot routinely provide a multiplicity of answers. The key is to understand what answers the accounting system is prepared to give. Enlightened use, then, is a matter of adjusting these answers to the question at hand, as well as knowing when to query other systems.

It is simply impractical to have the formal system designed to produce ready-made answers to every question we might ask. Some of the work, by design, has been delegated to the end user. To do otherwise would be to unduly burden the accounting system with the construction of countless answers, only some of which would be demanded at any given time.

In the original example above, desks were manufactured and sold according to the following total cost function:

$$TC = 76,500 + 730D$$

Recall that this total cost function was actually the summation of

material $= 280D$,
labor $= 360D$,
overhead $= 18,000 + 80D$, and
G&A $= 58,500 + 10D$

We call the summation of the first three categories (material, labor, and manufacturing overhead) the manufacturing cost:

$$\text{manufacturing cost} = 18,000 + 720D$$

Let's now change the story slightly and assume that desks are manufactured in anticipation of customer demand. This way, when a customer arrives, we expect to have a completed desk on hand, ready for sale. In turn, this inventory of completed desks will be recorded in the accounting system.[4]

The typical method of recording this inventory is to "value" each desk at the *average* manufacturing cost. Suppose, to illustrate, that we anticipate the manufacture of 600 desks during the (six-month) period in question. Total manufacturing cost would be

$$18,000 + 720(600) = 450,000$$

and the average cost per desk would then be

$$\frac{450,000}{600} = \$750 \text{ per desk} = \frac{18,000}{600} + 720$$

In particular, notice that with our presumed cost curve this amounts to adding the manufacturing variable cost per desk of $720 to the average fixed cost of $18,000/600 = $30.

Suppose we actually sell 550 desks during this period. Presuming no beginning inventory of completed desks, this means we have 600 − 550 = 50 desks remaining in inventory at the end of the period. Total cost during the period is, of course, the total of manufacturing and G&A:

$$TC = 18,000 + 720(600) + 58,500 + 10(550)$$
$$= 450,000 + 64,000 = 514,000$$

And total revenue is simply

$$TR = 900(550) = 495,000$$

The accounting system will relate the 495,000 revenue datum to the portion of the total cost that is "associated" with that revenue. This is done by treating the average manufacturing cost per desk as the "cost of a desk" that is sold during the period and by treating all G&A as being "associated" with the revenue of the period in question. This leads to the following computation of accounting income for the (six-month) period in question:

Revenue	495,000
Cost of sales	
750(550)	412,500
G&A	64,000
Income	18,500

In effect, we have allocated 412,500 + 64,000 = 476,500 of the total cost of 514,000 to the sale of 550 units. What has become of the remainder, 37,500? The answer is that we have an ending inventory of 50 completed desks, "valued" not at the presumed selling price but at the presumed average manufacturing cost of 750 per unit: 750(50) = 37,500. If, therefore, we produced 600 desks the following period, but sold 650, cost of sales would total 750(650) = 487,500, which exceeds the second-period manufacturing cost by 37,500. Put differently, cost of sales in this second period would be the sum of the manufacturing cost of units produced last period and sold this period plus the manufacturing cost of units produced and sold this period. In this way, the accounting system relates manufacturing cost to revenue.

The point of all this is to alert you to the fact that if you ask this accounting system what the cost of a desk is, it has an answer. In this case the answer is $750. To use this answer in the original additional order example, you must understand how it has been constructed. In particular, the accounting system answers with an average manufacturing cost datum. If variable cost is what you want, you must then remove the average fixed manufacturing component and add the variable G&A component:

$$750 - 30 + 10 = 730$$

This is the cost measure we used in the original example.

In other words, the accounting system will report the "cost of a desk." The reported number is, however, the result of a particular type of calculation. But the meaning of "cost of a desk" depends on the circumstances at hand. And it is these circumstances that determine what type of calculation is used. Thus, we must be prepared to tailor the apparent answer.

To reinforce this observation, suppose a customer arrives and offers to purchase a desk for $740. We are not producing at capacity and, following the analysis in the original example, price = 740 exceeds cost = 730, so we know that accepting the customer's offer is indeed a profitable act. The typical accounting system will, however, compare the price of 740 with a cost of 750. This is not magic (or stupidity). The comparisons are based on incremental cost in the first instance and average manufacturing cost in the second. A cost is not a cost.

An alternative accounting procedure focuses on *variable* manufacturing cost as the cost of a desk in the accounting system. Here we would treat the cost of the desk as $720, and associate the fixed manufacturing cost of the period with the revenue generated during that period. The income calculation would now appear as follows:

Revenue	495,000
Cost of sales	
720(550)	396,000
Fixed manufacturing	18,000
G&A	64,000
Income	17,000

The income difference of 18,500 versus 17,000 is explained by the fact that our end-of-period inventory of 50 completed desks is now "valued" at 720 instead of 750, or 50(750 − 720) = 1,500.

In this system, the cost of the desk is reported at $720. To answer the question posed in the additional customer example, we must now add in the variable G&A component:

$$730 = 720 + 10$$

The important observation is that the accounting system will report something called the "cost of a desk." To understand how to use what is reported, you must know what cost measurement question you are asking *and* what cost measurement question the accounting system is answering.[5]

HOW "GOOD" IS MY ACCOUNTING SYSTEM?

The remaining question in our exploration deals with the quality of the accounting system. In a sense, this is a straightforward issue. If you don't like the accounting system's product, change the system. After all, the system exists to serve its clients, and so it should be designed to fulfill this purpose. Remember, however, that the real issue is one of balancing the system's cost against (1) its ability to produce answers to questions (some of which may be asked only infrequently), (2) its flexibility to answer questions on a demand basis (such as a special cost study), and (3) the disadvantage of having to ignore altogether some kinds of information (for example, it is unusual to find an accounting system that is able to provide meaningful cost statistics on product quality).

One way or another, though, designing the accounting system boils down to deciding what questions you want answered. Accounting theory has no answer to this, and practice varies a great deal. You must decide what is best for you in your circumstance. I cannot tell you what to do. But I can sketch some of the dimensions of the design question that you must consider.

To begin, let's agree that an accounting system is "good" only to the extent that it serves its various clients. Numerous consumers of the accounting product are present in the firm, and we must be careful to acknowledge them when designing the accounting system. We have production, finance, and marketing managers, for example; we have production and service operations within the organization; we have strategic planning and operations planning exercises; and so on. And interwoven throughout are the inseparable activities of planning and control. We have already discussed cost measurement issues in a planning context — namely in deciding whether to manufacture the desk for the new customer. There the only question was whether the customer's order should be accepted, and our search for information (cost measurement in that case) was aimed at helping us resolve that question. But this is only half of the question; the other half deals with control. After the fact, we may want to know what the desk cost simply because that answer will help us in making similar decisions in the future. We may also want to know what the desk cost because that information will provide useful insight in evaluating the performance of the manager who is responsible for desk production. Decisions must be made *and* implemented; and information is in demand in both arenas.

Competing Sources of Managerial Information

A major difficulty in deciding how much of this information is to be provided by the accounting system is to overcome a bias that we appear to have of thinking of the accounting system as a unique source of information. This is, in fact, far from the truth. Any manager has many sources of information, only one of which is the accounting system. The reason is comparative advantage. Do you read more than one newspaper or news magazine? Do you bring legal questions to your physician or health questions to your legal adviser? Do you seek dietary advice from a designer of integrated circuits? Each source of information has particular strengths and weaknesses, and the same is true for your accounting system.

Some strengths and weaknesses will arise because of the particular accounting techniques employed. Others are generic to accounting. In particular, the accounting system has a comparative advantage of dealing with financial information that is both reliable and accurate. Inventory balances, for example, are painstakingly maintained; considerable effort is expended to ensure that every expenditure is accurately recorded; and reliable estimates are required to recognize revenue. Considerable care goes into the running, protection, and feeding of the accounting system. This is its strength, as well as its weakness. It is geared to answer those financial questions that can be answered with relative precision. Learn to recognize and exploit this fact.

It is no accident, then, that numerous nonaccounting sources of information are important to the typical manager. The firm's product market provides one source of information. Here we are able to look at such things as market share, orders booked but not yet produced and delivered, orders booked by competitors, product as well as production method innovations by competitors, and so on.[6] For example, we now see the domestic automobile industry importing production methods as well as engineering and design ideas. We see IBM acquiring Rolm in order to gain access to its expertise. And we see firms sharing cost information through their trade association as well as engaging in joint R&D ventures.

Another familiar source of information is what we call nonfinancial information. In addition to those we would associate with the product market, we see numerous instances of productivity statistics (such as output per labor hour or machine hour), downtime, and employee absenteeism being routinely monitored. A major fast-food chain, for example, routinely audits each of its locations and numerically scores them on the basis of their service, cleanliness, and quality. Other sources are unsystematic. A firm that employs an outside sales force may retain some "house accounts" simply because of what it is able to learn about the marketplace (and, indirectly, about the productivity of its outside sales force) by dealing directly with some of its customers. And we also must mention the proverbial "walk-through." Visiting the troops, whether planned or impromptu, should not be treated as an idle exercise. (Hiring a consultant can also be thought of as acquiring information — the consultant's analysis.)

With some thought, then, we are able to envision a broad range of information alternatives for the manager, some of which will have their roots in the accounting system. But we must also decide which of these items we want to use for some particular purpose. Some are unlikely to be informative for the task at hand, while others are likely to be too expensive to acquire and digest. Indeed, the strengths of accounting measures are particularly important in the control arena because the accounting product is thought to be — in fact is designed to be — an unbiased answer to whatever question is asked. No one enjoys being evaluated with an untrustworthy or biased system.

Performance Evaluation

A question the typical accounting system is designed to answer, then, is, How well (*in accounting terms*) did the manager perform?[7] The major accounting vehicle for approaching the managerial evaluation question is the idea of *responsibility accounting*. Here each accounting event, such as a cost incurrence or revenue receipt, is associated with some manager who is thought to be responsible for that event. Advertising expenditures, for example, would be associated with the marketing manager, just as production cost would be associated with the production manager.

Return to the desk setting discussed earlier and suppose we have a manager in charge of desk production. It seems reasonably clear that we would use the actual labor and material costs (in relation to total production) in helping gauge the manager's performance. Overhead will also more than likely be added to the list; it consists of all production costs that are not in the labor or material categories. At this point, then, we evaluate the manager on output produced in relation to manufacturing cost incurred. It is common to refer to such an evaluation scheme as a *cost center* because the manager's primary financial responsibility is to manage cost (in relation to output).

What about using G&A for this purpose as well? Generally (though not always) this is not associated with the production manager. It bears no discernible relationship to the production manager's activities. The production manager cannot control or significantly influence these cost items; and therefore it would be unfair to use them to gauge the manager's performance. More to the point, though, is whether the G&A expenditures help you gauge the manager's performance. This is, in fact, a subtle question because it is not whether G&A as such is useful for this purpose, but whether, given that you know manufacturing cost, it is useful for this purpose. The question is not whether to use G&A alone, but whether to use it with whatever else we know. Thinking in these terms, I find it difficult to spin a story that would build a convincing case for the G&A expenditures being informative in evaluation of the production manager.

What about also using revenue to evaluate the production manager? The question I am really posing is this: Do we want to treat the production manager as operating a *cost center* or as a *profit center*? In the former case, financial evaluation rests on cost incurred (relative to output), while in the latter it rests on cost and revenue (relative to output). The usual way to approach this is to ask whether the production manager controls or significantly influences revenue. But as with the G&A story, I suggest we ask whether revenue is informative about the production manager, given that we already know the cost. It is in fact easy to spin a story on either side. For example, suppose we know that revenue reflects demand and that in our segment of the desk market demand is directly dependent upon quality. Then, revenue may indirectly tell us something about how well the production manager is performing. On the other hand, we may already have quality assessments in hand (via direct supervision or associated cost overruns necessitated by customer returns), in which case revenue tells us nothing we do not already know about the production manager's performance. An interesting aside here is whether cost alone would tell us all there is to know; after all, higher demand begets higher production and higher cost. But inefficiency also begets higher cost!

To illustrate, the local manager of a fast-food chain outlet is typically evaluated as a profit center, even though the product menu, prices, and advertising are centrally established. And revenue is thought to be an informative datum in this industry. Contrast this with the story of a well-known apparel manufacturer that has numerous plants. Each plant manager was evaluated as a cost center. Finished goods were transferred to a marketing organization. After much debate and soul-searching it was decided to convert the cost centers into profit centers by having them "sell" their output to the firm's marketing division. This was accomplished by crediting each manufacturing facility with an "internal revenue" of the number of items finished and shipped times a predetermined price of P per unit. So in the original system management knew cost and output, and in the new system they knew cost, output, and $P \times$ output. I cannot imagine that the revenue statistic of $P \times$ output would tell them anything they didn't already know.

Finally, we find numerous instances where profit in relation to investment base is the primary focus in the manager's financial evaluation. Here we employ cost, revenue, and investment information in the evaluation process. (Naturally, this is called an *investment center*.) And the motif should be clear. If investment is an informative datum, given we know cost and revenue, then investment is useful in evaluating the manager in question. We see this, for example, in major merchandising outlets, where inventory is an important investment.

In any event, choice among these techniques is a matter of managerial judgment. My advice is to view the accounting system as your system. Managements' demands, not preset recipes, should shape the accounting system.

Substitutes for Accounting Information

In putting this all together we must also remember that numerous information substitutes exist. I mentioned some of these in the above when we discussed competitor comparisons, nonfinancial measures, consultants, and so on. Let's now consider some other substitutes that might be used in evaluating managerial performance. Various kinds of competitions might be used — for example, sales contests or direct comparisons of branch managers on various measures (such as sales). The idea is to use another manager's performance to help gauge that of the manager in question. (What does this tell you about responsibility accounting?)

We might also rely to some extent on "reputation" of the manager. The manager's success in the firm (in terms of continued employment and promotion) as well as employment prospects outside the firm are likely to depend on how well he or she performs. That being so, we might assume that the manager's own career concerns will help motivate him or her to perform well, and we might be able to substitute these career concerns for elaborate measurement of the manager's performance. The classic example here is the professional auditor who cherishes (and trades on) a reputation for independence and thoroughness. In other words, the prospect that deficient performance may one day be discovered may help motivate the manager in question and thereby reduce the demand for direct, financial evaluation of that manager.[8]

The extreme tack in this line of thought is an incentive structure. A performance bonus is, in fact, a substitute for evaluating the manager's performance. A simple sharecropping story illustrates the point. An absentee landowner wants a cornfield well tended until harvest time. He uses the labor services of an employee for this purpose. Crop production is risky: the yield depends on weather and insect patterns as well as the employee's diligence. The employee is a normal sort, however, and enjoys leisure more than long hours of arduous work. So there is some concern that, if left unattended and paid a wage for his services, the employee will be tempted to overconsume leisure at the landowner's expense. If the crop yield is low, the employee will blame the local growing conditions, and the absentee owner will be unable to distinguish a convenient excuse from bad luck.

Of course, the landowner can monitor the employee, say by surprise visits to the site (the "plant walk-through"). But this may be costly and time-consuming. An alternative arrangement is to offer a significant stake in the yield, that is, a sharecropping deal. In this way, the employee is not tempted to shirk, simply because shirking is now personally expensive. If, for example, the employee is to receive 40 percent of the crop production, he will exercise considerable diligence in tending the field.

But this is not an ideal solution either, because we also presume that the landowner is relatively risk-neutral, whereas the employee is relatively risk-averse. This means that the employee takes on a significant share of the production risk when sharing with the landowner in this manner. For example, if the employee receives 40 percent of (risky) production and has no other source of income, nontrivial risk is associated with the employment arrangement. Contrast this with the landowner who presumably is well diversified across many such ventures. If this is so, we presume that the landowner is better able to carry the production risk. And, other things being equal, it is inefficient to have the employee shoulder a major portion of that risk. In other words, the 40 percent deal solves the shirking problem, but at the expense of saddling the employee with nontrivial risk — risk that is personally noxious and that is more willingly borne by the landowner.

The options are clear. One is to invest in some type of costly monitor; the other is to use the crop yield as the only monitor and resort to inefficient risk-sharing between the employee and landowner as a substitute for better monitoring information. In this way, we think of an incentive scheme (such as sharing in the production yield with the landowner) as a substitute for better information. In most situations today, placing an employee's income from labor at risk, via some type of incentive arrangement, does not appear to be an efficient way to arrange the distribution of production risks; after all, we have an elaborate capital market for just this purpose. But placing the employee's income from labor at risk can be thought of as purposely designed inefficient risk-sharing that is used to substitute for costly information.

Put differently, suppose a firm's owner and manager do not have perfectly aligned tastes concerning how the firm should be run. (If their tastes were perfectly aligned, we would never, by definition, have to worry about motivating the manager.) This raises the question of motivating the manager[9] and creates a demand for monitoring information, such as asking how well the manager of the desk production enterprise performed during a recent period. We might decide to generate such information from within the accounting system, we might look to nonaccounting sources of information, or we might go without the information. Understanding, and hence designing, your accounting system can be accomplished only if you have a broad view of the overall information management problem you face. Accounting is an important part of the picture, but it is hardly the entire picture.

LOOKING AHEAD

In trying to convince you of this point, I have sketched a simple production setting and discussed the related accounting story in a static manner. Movement to a realistic setting is best left to your experience and imagination. The static portrayal is, however, worth a closing thought. The web of economic enterprise is hardly constant. This means that the demands for various types of information will change, as will their costs. So we should not only expect to see change, but also concern ourselves with its management.

One important area of change is the nature of production in our economy. Production is hardly an intranational concern. For example, we see significant international dimensions in the location of production facilities. Moreover, international sources of competition, as in steel, automobiles, and electronics, have become quite important. Beyond this movement to a more global definition of production, we see movement toward a service economy as well as increased automation in heavy manufacturing. The implications of these trends cannot be sorted out with any degree of certainty. But they do seem to point toward increased demands for information.

Admitting to this increased demand, we then must ask what role accounting will play in producing the desired information. Sorting this out is one of management's tasks. In dealing with this, you should expect to see changes in the way accounting is practiced. For example, in our simple desk story we identified overhead as a function of the number of desks produced. In a multiproduct setting we often identify overhead in terms of the quantity of labor and then use the relationship between labor quantity and individual units produced to relate overhead to the products in question. But in a heavily automated process we are unlikely to find any meaningful relationship between labor and units of production. Costing techniques, in other words, will have to evolve (as they already have in some process industries) to accommodate the economic characteristics of the production process.

Similarly, in a service setting we often lack highly informative measures of output. The research and development manager, the legal manager, the accountant, the professor, and the fast-food manager are ready examples. As the service sector expands, we should expect to see (and you should expect to produce) innovations in economic analysis and monitoring of such activities.

A second important area of change is in the area of personal computing. The marginal cost of computing has become nearly trivial, the quality of software has dramatically increased, and computer literacy will become commonplace in managerial ranks. In all respects, computing — viewed as a decision aid for the manager — has become inexpensive. This will increase the demand for information, as well as increase the manager's ability to customize approaches to analyzing and accounting for economic activities. And once again I point out that this is part of the managerial task. You must learn to recognize, exploit, and manage change.

In short, economic activity is now framed in a global context. And our particular economy is moving toward a significantly higher proportion of service activities, as well as toward significantly more capital-intensive forms of production in heavy manufacturing. Either trend suggests that yesterday's accounting solutions may not be desirable tomorrow. Moreover, the ever-falling cost of computing and the ongoing development of ever more "friendly" software will lower the cost of customized accounting analyses and answers. From this I conclude that the returns to understanding and exploiting the accounting system's strengths and weaknesses are likely to increase during your professional career.

NOTES

1. This terminology was coined over fifty years ago by J. M. Clark, in what remains to this day one of the most insightful and influential developments in accounting thought. J. M. Clark, *Studies in the Economics of Overhead Costs* (Chicago: University of Chicago Press, 1923).

2. Notice that we are actually working with a simple model in which $TR = PD$ and $TC = F + vD$, where P is the selling price (900 in the example), v is the variable cost per unit of output (730), and F is the fixed cost (76,500). We then have profit $= TR - TC = PD - F - vD = (P - v)D - F$. At such a general level, we have two straight lines, TR and TC. The only general question we can ask such a model is, Where do the lines intersect? This occurs when $D = F/(P - v)$, the so-called break-even point. To me, a much more interesting question is whether additional business should be entertained, whether the firm should be liquidated, whether significant structural changes should be pursued, or whatever. The break-even point gives an indication of how large demand must be to sustain the firm in a profit position. But it is easy to overemphasize such a computation. This is why I think of it as beginning with a simple model that only allows you to ask one question, namely, What's the break-even point?

3. If you have studied economics, you will recognize this as a claim that marginal revenue exceeds marginal cost. Moreover, the cost-based analysis portrayed in the following paragraphs is designed to focus on a comparison of marginal revenue and marginal cost.

4. We now begin a cursory glimpse into the workings of a typical accounting system. I cannot possibly provide here a substitute for detailed exploration. An excellent self-teaching tool is R. Anthony, *Essentials of Accounting* (Reading, Mass.: Addison-Wesley, 1983).

5. I do not mean to imply that it is always easy to figure out what question the accounting system is answering. And by no means do I advocate construction of a stereotypical accounting system that will stand you in good stead. Kaplan reports a simply wonderful illustration of the pitfalls in trying to construct a cost measure from knowledge of what the accounting system is reporting without first understanding what question that accounting system was designed to answer. R. Kaplan, "Management Accounting in Hospitals: A Case Study," in Livingstone and Gunn, eds., *Accounting for Social Goals* (New York: Harper and Row, 1974).

6. I do not mean to imply that this is a straightforward exercise of surveying the market. The term "vaporware" is used to describe a firm's announcement of a pending product introduction that does not materialize. Strategic considerations should not be overlooked.

7. A companion question is, How well are we doing in the desk business?

8. Of course, this is not a one-way street. It is not unknown for a manager to be overzealous in building or maintaining a reputation in the short run, and de facto jeopardize the firm's future in the process.

9. It also raises the question of motivating the owner. The brief sketch here presumes that contractual arrangements can be spelled out and will be honored. The owner is thus presumed to offer a fully specified contract and to not renege on any of its provisions. Both assumptions are at variance

with life, and it is no accident that labor lawyers are in demand in our society.

SUGGESTED READINGS

Arrow, K. *The Limits of Organization.* New York: W. W. Norton, 1974. A superb essay on the economics of organization.

Davidson, S., C. Stickney, and R. Weil. *Accounting: The Language of Business,* 6th ed. Englewood Cliffs, N.J.: Prentice-Hall, 1984. An extremely useful compendium of terminology and illustrations of the power of accounting techniques.

Davidson, S., and R. Weil. *Handbook of Cost Accounting.* New York: McGraw-Hill, 1978. Excellent reference work.

Demski, J. *Information Analysis,* 2nd ed. Reading, Mass.: Addison-Wesley, 1980. Introduction to the economic theory behind accounting thought.

Euske, K. *Management Control: Planning, Control, Measurement, and Evaluation.* Reading, Mass.: Addison-Wesley, 1984. Thoughtful monograph on the elusive topic of management control.

Horngren, C. *Introduction to Management Accounting,* 6th ed. Englewood Cliffs, N.J.: Prentice-Hall, 1984. The classic textbook.

Kaplan, R. "The Evolution of Management Accounting." *Accounting Review,* July 1984. Provocative historical perspective and criticism.

Seed, A. III. "Cost Accounting in the Age of Robotics." *Management Accounting,* October 1984. Insightful description of cost measurement difficulties in a heavily automated production process.

CHAPTER 4

Financial Reporting

William H. Beaver
Stanford University
Graduate School of Business

A major revolution has occurred in financial reporting — that is, in the presentation of financial statements together with such additional financial disclosures as are needed to avoid making the financial statements misleading. The last ten years have witnessed an unprecedented growth in the number and complexity of financial reporting requirements by the Securities and Exchange Commission (SEC) and the Financial Accounting Standards Board (FASB). Moreover, the estimated life of any given standard is growing shorter and shorter, with dramatic effects. A change in standard can turn a reported net income into a reported net loss. It also can increase the volatility of net income and cause factors outside the control of management to dominate net income in a particular quarter or year.

A fundamental change is also occurring in the way financial reporting is viewed. From this new perspective, financial statements based primarily on historical cost accounting are only one part of a larger financial reporting system that includes disclosures about the effects of changing prices, foreign currency translation, and unfunded pension obligations. Financial accounting and financial disclosure, traditionally viewed as distinct and separable items, are now integrated within a single system called financial reporting. As stated by the FASB, the purpose of financial reporting is to provide investors, potential investors, creditors, and others with information about the prospective cash flows of the firm and its securities. Many observers believe that this purpose significantly expands the scope of financial reporting — and think that it may impose an untenable burden upon the reporting responsibilities of management.

Currently, the legal liability of management for financial reporting is at an all-time high. Increased regulation, ambiguous definitions of materiality, and worsening economic conditions have led to a rash of shareholder suits. As firms fail or the price of their securities plummets, security holders seek relief under the Securities Acts, which impose a liability on management for "false and misleading" financial reporting and for failure to disclose "material facts." Nearly 400 such suits were filed in federal courts in 1982–1984. One prominent defendant was Apple Computer, Inc., whose stock price fell from a high of 63 ¼ in June 1983 to 17 percent by November of that same year.[1]

Management is also facing a major change in the nature of the users of financial reporting. Over the last few years, the proportion of shares held and the proportion of shares traded by institutional investors have grown. These professional users demand more complex disclosures, more detailed disclosures, and greater interpretation and analysis of the reported financial data by management.[2]

At the same time that management's responsibility for financial reporting has increased, its control over the financial reporting system has been substantially reduced. These developments have made financial reporting a frustrating and challenging task.

This chapter highlights the major forces influencing the financial reporting responsibility of management. We first examine the major forces in the field of reporting and then consider some current trends in this field. The chapter concludes with a look at what may lie ahead in financial reporting between now and the year 2000.

MAJOR FORCES IN FINANCIAL REPORTING

The most important forces in financial reporting are (1) characteristics of the financial reporting environment, (2) constituencies of financial reporting, (3) current trends in financial reporting, (4) users' attitudes toward financial reporting, and (5) the impact of financial reporting on stock prices.[3]

Characteristics of the Financial Reporting Environment

The major characteristics of financial reporting are summarized in Table 4.1. A key feature of the environment is its complexity and diversity. This means that financial reporting affects individuals in diverse ways; there is no consensus on what is the "best" financial reporting system.

As stated by the FASB, the purpose of financial reporting is to provide information to potential and current investors, among others. As a result, a central part of the financial reporting environment is the investment process. Essentially this process is the giving up of current consumption in exchange for securities, which are claims to future, uncertain cash flows. The investor must decide how to allocate wealth between current consumption and investment and how to allocate

Table 4.1 Major Characteristics of Today's Financial Reporting Environment

1. Larger role of professional investors
2. Larger role of analysts
3. Greater complexity and sophistication of financial markets
4. Greater competition among management for investors' funds
5. Greater regulation of financial reporting
6. Rapidly changing economic environment and increased economic uncertainty

funds set aside for investment among the available securities. The investor, then, needs information that will help him or her assess the future cash flows associated with the securities and the firms that offer those securities.

However, each investor is not acting in isolation but within a larger environment in which the following conditions prevail: (1) Investors can purchase the services of financial intermediaries,[4] such as investment companies, to whom they can defer a portion of the investment process. (2) Investors can use the services of information intermediaries,[5] such as analysts, by delegating to them a portion or all of the information gathering and processing function. (3) Investors can invest in a number of securities and thereby diversify out of some of the risks associated with a single security. (4) Information intermediaries compete with one another in gathering and interpreting financial information. (5) Managements, competing with one another for investors' funds, have incentives to provide financial information to the investment community. (6) Investors and intermediaries have access to financial information[6] that is more comprehensive, and often more timely, than that which is provided in the annual report to shareholders or to the SEC. (7) Security price research suggests that security prices reflect a rich, comprehensive information system. (8) Economic conditions change rapidly and are fraught with ever greater uncertainty.

Constituencies of Financial Reporting

Several groups besides management influence management's financial reporting responsibility. The most important of these are investors, analysts, auditors, and regulators.

Investors. Investors are a heterogeneous group. They differ in their tastes or preferences, wealth, beliefs about the future, attitudes toward risk, access to financial information, and skill in interpreting financial information. These factors affect their demand for financial information. Thus the information demands of professional users (i.e., the financial intermediaries and information intermediaries) often differ from those of the nonprofessional users (for example, individual investors).

Nonprofessional investors can also differ in many respects. Some make their investment decisions unaided; others rely on their brokers for advice. Some rely on a single investment strategy; others employ several strategies. Some read business publications; and employ advisory services; others do neither.

If an individual investor defers a portion of the investment process to a financial intermediary and/or relies upon the analysis and recommendations of an information intermediary, he or she is likely to want or need less financial information. In such a case the individual is substituting the analysis and recommendations (i.e., the information) of the financial or information intermediary for direct financial information (that provided by financial reporting). In this sense, they constitute competing sources of information. Note, however, that the use of a financial intermediary or an information intermediary in itself constitutes an indirect demand for financial information by the individual investor.

Investors also differ in their portfolio strategies. Individual securities are means by which different portfolios can be constructed. Therefore, an individual security is relevant to the investor only insofar as it affects the risk and expected reward associated with his or her portfolios. From this perspective, interactions or correlations among the returns of the portfolio's securities are as important as the expected return and variability of return of the individual security. In well-diversified portfolios, some of the risk of the individual security risk may be relatively unimportant because it can be diversified away. This is the so-called unsystematic risk (see Chapter 3, "Managerial Accounting").

As a consequence, an investor's demand for financial information varies depending on the extent to which he or she chooses to diversify. For the well-diversified investor, factors such as unsystematic risk may be relatively unimportant, and financial information that helps assess such risk may not be of value. But for the less diversified investor, such information may be extremely valuable.

In a similar vein, the investor's demand for financial information can be influenced by whether he or she adopts an "active" or a "passive" trading strategy. Using a passive trading strategy, the investor essentially buys and holds a security and anticipates little trading until it is time to liquidate that security for consumption purposes. In the limit, the investor would simply purchase a well-diversified group of securities (for example, an "index" fund) and would have little or no use for firm-specific financial information. By contrast, an "active" trader — that is, a speculator — needs information about particular securities. In other words, an investor who employs an active policy continually seeks information that will permit the detection of mispriced securities and continually trades on such information. By definition, the turnover of the active portfolio will be greater than that of the passive portfolio. In many cases, an active trading policy takes advantage of short-term aberrations in security prices to open and close the speculative position in a matter of weeks, days, or even hours.

These classifications by no means exhaust the possibilities, and they are not mutually exclusive. They do, however, illustrate a fundamental point: investors are a heterogeneous group, and their demand for financial information is heterogeneous. Moreover, they operate in an environment in which they can rely on financial and information intermediaries and in which they can adopt portfolio strategies that can substantially reduce, or even eliminate, their direct demand for financial information. Thus, many investors have an indirect demand for financial information.

Information intermediaries. Information intermediaries — that is, financial analysts — can be viewed as a group whose factors of production include financial information and other types of data and whose product is analysis and interpretation. The output of the information intermediaries is also a form of information. They take raw data and transform them into another type of information that reflects their ability to understand, synthesize, and interpret the raw data. As indicated earlier, the nonprofessional user who relies upon the information provided by an intermediary typically has less need for the formal financial information provided by financial reporting.

As a result, the relationship between financial reporting and the information intermediary is not simple. Formal financial reporting provides one source of information for the intermediaries. However, to the extent that the intermediary's function is to provide investors with more comprehensive and more timely information, financial reporting competes with the information provided by the information intermediary. Moreover, information intermediaries compete with one another in the gathering and interpretation of financial information.

Information intermediaries engage in "private" or "informal" information search; that is, they seek financial information that is not provided by financial reporting. This information system is large and active: by recent estimates there are over 14,500 financial analysts. Management has incentives to provide information to analysts, and analysts have incentive to seek out and disseminate such information. The informal information network is one of the mechanisms that permit security prices promptly to reflect both formal information (disclosures) and informal information (interpretations of disclosures; information gleaned from other sources besides the disclosing companies).

Financial reporting regulators. A prominent feature of the financial reporting environment is the regulation of the flow of financial information to investors. The primary regulators are the FASB and the SEC, although Congress and the other independent regulatory agencies can also influence financial reporting requirements.

The SEC and the FASB share a concern over the effects of the financial reporting on investors and SEC. This concern appears to be partially motivated by the prevention of perceived adversities and inequities that may befall investors owing to informational deficiencies, such as a failure to disclose material financial information. However, the policy-makers also appear to be concerned with the effects of financial reporting on resource allocation and capital formulation.

A distinctive feature of the regulator system is its dual structure. In principle, the jursidiction of the FASB is the setting of financial accounting standards, whereas the jurisdiction of the SEC is said to be disclosure. Yet the distinction has never been well defined and as a practical matter is not operational. The standards of the FASB typically also include disclosure requirements. The jurisdictional boundaries, then, are unclear. Moreover, no accounting standard of the FASB or of any other private-sector group has ever prevailed without the support of the SEC.

Auditors. Financial reports must be certified by an auditor. Independence from management is a central tenet of the auditor's professional ethics and underscores the responsibility of the auditor to investors and other users of financial statements. This responsibility, like that of management, is reinforced by making the auditor legally liable under the Securities Acts. Auditors are major suppliers of information in the important sense that they express an opinion as to whether financial statements have been prepared in accordance with generally accepted accounting principles (GAAP).

The financial reporting environment primarily consists of management and the constituencies discussed above, although other groups may be involved to some extent. The role and the interest of each of these constituencies differ. Moreover, each constituency is not homogeneous. Thus the various constituencies, and individuals within each constituency, may not be affected in the same way by financial reporting or by its consequences. In this situation, it is natural to expect vigorous disagreement over what constitutes the "best" system of financial reporting.

Current Trends

The major trends are listed in Table 4.2. The increased activism of the SEC and the FASB, aided by a rapidly changing economic environment, has led to the two most prominent trends in financial reporting: rapid growth in financial reporting requirements and a rapid change in existing requirements. The increased role of the professional users has led to three other trends:

1. Financial reports are becoming more complex. This complexity means that, in order to interpret the reported data, users must be more sophisticated and possessed of greater technical skill than had previously been assumed. The FASB's standards on foreign currency translation (FAS No. 52) and accounting for the effects of changing prices (FAS No. 33) are two prominent examples of financial reporting requirements that call for a considerable amount of expertise in interpretation.

2. There is greater emphasis on the reporting of "soft" data, such as forward-looking data (for example, management forecasts) and current cost and market-value data. Financial reporting policy-makers have changed their outlook regarding "soft" data. For example, until the 1970s, the SEC had had a long-standing policy of discouraging such data in SEC filings.

3. There is greater emphasis on disclosure and less emphasis on a single earnings number. Supplemental disclosures are used to report financial aspects of certain events without attempting to prescribe ex-

Table 4.2 Current Trends in Financial Reporting

1. Rapid growth in financial reporting requirements
2. Rapid change in existing requirements
3. Greater complexity of financial reports
4. More emphasis on "soft" data
5. Less emphasis upon financial statements and the determination of net income; more emphasis upon supplemental disclosure
6. Increased debate over economic consequences of financial reporting

actly how those disclosures are to be used to arrive at "the" net income or earnings of the firm. FAS No. 33, on the effects of changing prices, is a prime example of an accounting standard, which requires supplemental disclosure instead of attempting to prescribe the "best" way to report the effects of changing prices. This shift away from a single, "best" measure of earnings helps users to structure financial disclosures in ways they deem most appropriate.

The final trend, increased debate between the regulated and the regulators over the economic impact of financial reporting, is a natural consequence of the increased diversity of users. In this ongoing debate, the emphasis has shifted from the question of what is "good" or "bad" accounting to the more subtle question of whether the economic consequences of a particular financial reporting standard will be "good" or "bad." For example:

1. Opponents of the deferral treatment of the investment tax credit have argued that such treatment acts as a deterrent to capital formation. In the 1970s, Congress passed a law preventing any group (such as the FASB or the SEC) from requiring a corporation to use any particular method of accounting for the investment tax credit; under this law, either the deferral or the flow-through treatment may be used.

2. From 1968 to 1971 the FASB and the SEC considered requiring the inclusion of bad-debt provisions in the net income of commercial banks. Bankers argued that such disclosure would erode the confidence in the banking system and that this erosion would hurt the economy.

3. FAS No. 2 required the expensing of major research and development expenditures. Its opponents argued that it would discourage further research-and-development investment by corporations. The FASB passed FAS No. 2 over these objections.

4. FAS No. 19 required the "successful efforts" method of accounting for intangible drilling costs in the oil and gas industry. Its opponents argued that it favored large corporations and would harm small corporations, and that it therefore would contribute to increased concentration in the industry. In fact, the Antitrust Division of the Department of Justice testified before the SEC against FAS No. 19 that the standard was anticompetitive and would lead to an elimination of smaller corporations. The SEC chose its own form of accounting (Reserve Recognition Accounting) over FAS No. 19. As a result, the FASB suspended the relevant provisions of FAS No. 19 for an indefinite period.

User Attitudes

Some of the impetus for greater regulation of financial reporting stems from users' distrust of the current system. According to an FASB report, financial reporting has lost credibility among users.[7] Moreover, users appear to be placing less emphasis upon reported earnings, in part because they are wary of the emphasis management places on earnings. In their view, this emphasis leads to several practices by preparers of financial statements that reduce the credibility of reported results. These practices include the use of different methods of accounting for the same facts; the use of less conservative accounting methods; the front-ending of net income; the deferral of costs followed by "big-bath" write-offs; and the artificial smoothing of net income.

It is common for two firms within the same industry to use dramatically different methods of estimating the useful lives of depreciable assets and/or very different depreciation methods. Analysts frequently cite airlines as examples. Typically a professional user will adjust for such differences by "backing out" the reported depreciation and calculating pro forma earnings on a uniform depreciation method across firms in a given industry. Research also indicates that stock prices act as if such depreciation adjustments are made by investors. Notwithstanding such adjustments, however, the result is increased distrust of reported earnings and reduced reliance on reported earnings. Both the FASB and the SEC are concerned about the lack of uniformity of accounting methods across firms.

A closely related practice is changing the accounting method to a less conservative one. Two well-known and widely practiced changes are switching from accelerated to straight-line depreciation for reporting purposes and switching from deferral to flow-through for investment tax credits.

It can be argued that there are legitimate business-related reasons for permitting a diversity of accounting methods among firms. "Uniform" accounting, which applies the same accounting method to different economic circumstances, is uniform in form but not substance. Such uniformity may lessen the usefulness of financial reporting — which is why the regulators have been reluctant to impose a uniform set of methods. Major differences are still permitted in accounting for inventory and depreciable assets. But among users of financial reporting it is widely believed that such diversity invites misuse, and that for this reason it seriously impairs the credibility of financial reporting.

The "front-ending" of net income by means of the "premature" recognition of revenue is another disputed practice; so is delaying the recognition of expense by setting up the deferred cost as an asset. Franchising operations, real estate development, and leasing operations commonly front-end their net income; manufacturing firms typically treat their research-and-development expenditures as assets. The effect of both activities is to record higher net income sooner than would a more conservative accounting treatment.

Of course, the criticism of front-ending net income occurs largely with the benefit of wisdom by hindsight. The predominant method of accounting used today is accrual accounting, as opposed to cash-based accounting. Virtually all accruals inherently involve some implicit prediction about the future. Yet the future is fraught with uncertainty.

After the fact, the net incomes of some firms inevitably will be smaller than what had been implied in earlier years by accrual of non-cash assets. When the economy slackens or stagnates, the accrual accounting of many, if not most, of the firms that use this method will appear to have been overly optimistic, as judged by hindsight.

Notwithstanding the unfairness of invoking wisdom by hindsight, it is not uncommon for shareholders to sue companies whose accrual-based earnings forecasts greatly exceed the actual net income that is eventually earned. The publicity received by such suits, some of which lead to settlements in the millions of dollars, impairs the credibility of financial reporting. Cash-basis accounting could remove the judgments (for example, forecasts) implicit in accruals. But a cash-basis accounting system would be of limited usefulness to investors unless it were accompanied by substantial additional disclosure.

Often, costs are deferred rather than immediately expensed in the belief that they will be recovered in future years. In many cases these deferred costs eventually must be written off when it becomes apparent that they might never be recovered. To cite a prominent example, in 1974 the Lockheed Corporation wrote off approximately $475 million in deferred research-and-development costs, with an after-tax effect on retained earnings of approximately $280 million. Lockheed stated that this write-off was necessitated by the firm's need to bring its accounting policy into line with FASB Statement No. 2, issued in 1974. These costs were associated with the giant aerospace firm's ill-fated L-1001 jetliner program, which was discontinued in 1981 (leading to further write-offs).

Artificial smoothing of net income is yet another practice that is perceived by some users as impairing the credibility of financial reporting. A prominent current example is pension accounting, in which amortization of the unfunded pension obligation can be brought into net income over several years. The FASB's objection to "artificial" smoothing is that it may fail to reflect changes in the economic value of the assets, may delay the recording of certain expenses or losses, or may give users a misleading impression of the riskiness of the firm. The FASB has taken the position that financial reporting should provide information on the uncertainty or riskiness of prospective cash flows as well as the timing and magnitude of such cash flows. Such a concern has led the FASB to issue standards that require a form of lower cost or market value accounting for marketable securities, require the reporting of translation gains and losses for multinational firms, require the expensing of research-and-development expenditures, and forbid the use of self-insurance or contingency reserves.

These standards have increased the volatility of net income. Both preparers and some users of financial information have also argued that such increased volatility impairs rather than enhances the usefulness of financial statements.[8] They contend that a volatile net income gives a misleading indication of the long-run or permanent earning process of the firm.

MAJOR ADVANCES IN ACCOUNTING RESEARCH

During the last fifteen years there have been major advances in accounting research having to do with financial reporting and its effect on stock prices. The findings of this research have important implications for the way financial reporting is viewed by management and others.[9]

There are three major aspects of the research: (1) the ability of the financial markets to absorb financial information and to reflect that information in security prices, (2) the relationship between stock prices and earnings, and (3) the behavior of earnings and earnings growth.

Financial Information and Stock Prices

Three types of information affect stock prices: economy-wide information, industry-wide information, and firm-specific information.

It has long been known that economy-wide events are an important cause of changes in stock prices. There are many kinds of economy-wide information, including changes in interest rates, changes in inflation rates, changes in the money supply, and changes in real gross national product. However, research has shown that the effects of this myriad of information can be captured simply by looking at changes in a market-wide index of stock prices, such as the Standard and Poor's Composite Index or the New York Stock Exchange Composite Index. On the average, this market-wide factor accounts for 25 to 30 percent of all stock price movement. Industry information, such as sales, income, and unfilled orders, can also play an important role, although it varies considerably from firm to firm and, on the average, tends to be much less important than economy-wide information. This finding is extremely important. It implies that a major portion of the value of the firm and its securities is determined by factors or information outside of or beyond the firm's financial reporting system.

The research also indicates that, important as economy-wide and industry-wide information is in determining stock price, the major source of information affecting stock price is specific to the firm. Firm-specific information includes dividend announcements, contract awards, litigation, awards of franchises, mineral discoveries, sale or spinoff of divisions, and new product introductions. Rarely, however, is the full impact of such information reflected immediately in net income. Thus net income, or earnings, is only one among many sources of information that affects security prices.

Stock prices typically anticipate information — an earnings announcement, for example. That is, prices at any point in time reflect investors' expectations about the future earning power of the firm. These expectations, in turn, are based upon the total mix of available information. Price changes occur when *unanticipated* information is released that leads investors to alter their expectations. For prices to change, the information released must be "news," not anticipated by the market from the mix of information previously available. The greater the change in the total mix of information, the greater the change in price.

The Relationship Between Security Price and Earnings

Security price at any given moment depends upon investors' expectations regarding the future, long-run (i.e., permanent earning) power of the firm. The importance of current earnings, then, depends upon how much information current earnings convey about permanent earnings.

Permanent earnings. Current earnings do convey some information about permanent earnings, as Table 4.3 dramatically illustrates. This table reports the differential residual price performance of portfolios of firms systematically chosen according to their residual earnings performance during the year.[10] Portfolio 1 represents the largest earnings "losers," which on average over the 1965–1974 span suffered a 154.8 percent decline in earnings per share (EPS). Portfolio 6 represents the largest earnings "winners," which on average had an earnings increase of 185.1 percent.

The residual percentage change in price was also computed for each of the portfolios, for the same time period as the earnings. In other words, the table reports the contemporaneous movements of stock

Table 4.3 The Relationship Between Residual Percentage Changes in Price and Residual Percentage Changes in Earnings

Portfolio	Residual Percentage Change in EPS	Residual Percentage Change in Price[a]
1	−154.8	−17.5
2	− 12.7	− 9.0
3	0.4	− 2.0
4	9.0	2.0
5	23.4	10.4
6	185.1	29.2

[a]*Residual* price changes mean that the effect of economy-wide factors has already been extracted via percentage changes in a market index of stock prices. The procedure used to obtain *residual* earnings changes was based on previous earnings history.

SOURCE: Beaver, Clarke, and Wright (1979), Table 3.

prices and earnings. The relative performance of the portfolios when ranked according to earnings changes is identical with their relative performance when ranked according to price changes. For example, Portfolio 1 has the worst earnings performance and the worst price performance.

Moreover, the magnitude of the difference in stock price performance is enormous. Portfolio 1 suffered a stock price decline of 17.5 percent, whereas portfolio 6 achieved a stock price increase of 29.2 percent.

The significance of this difference is readily apparent. If $10,000 were invested in portfolios 1 and 6 at the beginning of the year, by year end the market price of portfolio 1 would have fallen to $8,250. By contrast, the market price of portfolio 6 would have risen to $12,920. Thus differential earnings performance in one year would have accounted for a market value differential of 57 percent [(12,920 − 8,250)/8,250].

However, the evidence indicates that, while there is a significant positive relationship between price changes and earnings changes, it is not a simple one-to-one relationship. The earnings differential between the two portfolios was much greater than the price differential. For example, the earnings change for portfolio 6 is 185.1 percent, while the price change is only 29.2 percent. In other words, the price change for portfolio 6 is only 16 percent (29.2/185.1) of the earnings change. From various studies including the one whose results are reported in Table 4.3, we know that the average sensitivity coefficient is about 0.12, or 12 percent. In other words, we know that a 100 percent increase in earnings is accompanied by a 12 percent increase in price, on the average.[11]

Transitory earnings. The evidence indicates that earnings, even earnings before special or nonrecurring items, contain a large transitory component. Unexpectedly high (or low) earnings in a given year or quarter are typically due to transitory factors or events. On the average over several hundred firms and over several years, the transitory factor accounts for approximately 88 percent of the unexpected change of earnings.[12] In this sense, earnings contain a large element of "noise" insofar as long-run earning power and stock prices are concerned. The market, then, recognizes both a permanent and a transitory component in earnings, but it considers the predominant portion of the change to be transitory.

Speed of response to earnings. Research indicates that the price reaction to earnings occurs quickly. The evidence is vividly illustrated in Figure 4.1, which plots price changes (ignoring direction of change) in a sample of stocks in the days immediately preceding and following the earnings announcement in the *Wall Street Journal*. The dashed horizontal line shows the average absolute value of the daily residual price change during times outside of the time interval extending from 15 days before to 15 days after the earnings announcements. This value has been scaled to be 1.00. Price changes are 40 percent larger, *on the average*, on the announcement day in the *Wall Street Journal* (day 0) and the day prior (day −1) than at other times. Note that essentially all of the reaction occurs in the day of the announcement and the day *preceding* the announcement. Further investigation revealed that the reaction the day prior to the announcement was due to the market's reaction to the firms' news releases regarding earnings, which are often released one day prior to the *Wall Street Journal* announcement.

Sophistication of response to earnings. Research shows that security prices not only react quickly to earnings announcements, but also react in a remarkably sophisticated manner. In particular, stock prices behave as if they adjust for differences in earnings induced by differences in method of accounting across firms. The evidence also indicates that stock prices act as if they distinguish between changes in earnings that are induced by changes in accounting methods and changes induced in earnings by economy-wide developments.

Certain events may permanently affect the level of accounting earnings, but not in a way that implies a change in the value of the security. A change in the firm's financial accounting system is such an

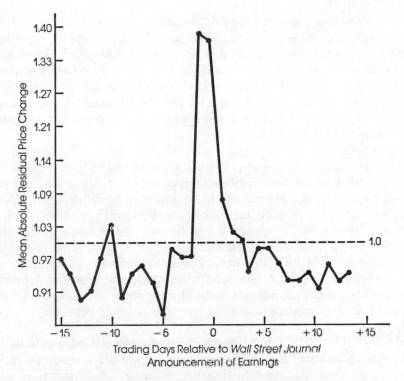

Figure 4.1   Residual Price Changes (Ignoring Sign) in the Thirty Days
Surrounding Earnings Announcements
SOURCE: Morse (1981).

event. For example, if a firm changes its method of accounting for depreciation, this change can produce a change in earnings that is "permanent" in the sense that the level of earnings is expected to be permanently affected; but it may not be an event that alters the firm's
dividend-paying ability; if it is not, then the market price of the firm's
stock will not change.

There are also more subtle effects of the financial accounting system on earnings. Consider the effects of unanticipated inflation. Revenues and many expenses increase with inflation, but some expenses
— for example, depreciation — do not. The result is an increase in net
income that is greater than the rate of inflation, even if nothing has
changed in real terms. Hence, there can be a portion of the change in
earnings that is not associated with a change in dividend-paying
ability.

Firms are permitted to use different accounting methods — for example, some use the method of depreciation, whereas others use the accelerated method — and this difference affects the level of earnings. A given firm may use different depreciation methods for different purposes. However, the discussion and the evidence refers to firms whose *predominant* depreciation method is either straight-line or accelerated depreciation. For example, firms with net growth in asset acquisitions will report higher net income under straight-line depreciation than under accelerated depreciation.

This difference in accounting methods induces a difference in the level of earnings across firms that is unrelated to the future dividend-paying ability of the firm. Price/earnings ratios of firms that use different depreciation methods would be expected to differ, after taking into account other reasons for differing price/earnings ratios. And, in fact, empirical evidence assembled by Beaver and Dukes suggests that price/earnings ratios do systematically differ as a function of the depreciation method used for annual report purposes. The results are summarized in Table 4.4. (All the firms used the accelerated depreciation method for tax purposes; the differences shown stemmed from differences in depreciation methods used for annual reports purposes only.)

In particular, firms that use accelerated depreciation would be expected to have lower earnings and hence higher price/earnings ratios than firms that use straight-line depreciation, assuming that risk, growth, and other things are equal. Table 4.4 indicates that firms using accelerated depreciation, on the average, did in fact have higher price/earnings ratios (16.61 versus 15.08). Moreover, an analysis of other factors indicates that the two groups did not differ with respect to risk or earnings growth.

In fact, on the average, the firms using accelerated depreciation had essentially the same risk and growth as firms using straight-line depreciation. Moreover, when the earnings of the firms using straight-line depreciation were converted to the earnings that would have been reported if accelerated depreciation had been used, the differences in price earnings ratios essentially disappeared. The average price/earnings ratio increased to 16.2 when the earnings of the straight-line group were computed under accelerated depreciation. In other words, when the earnings of the firms using straight-line depreciation were converted to an accounting basis equivalent to that of the firms using accelerated depreciation, the price/earnings ratios of the two groups of firms were essentially the same.

This is consistent with a security price formation process that adjusts for differences in the level of earnings induced by accounting method differences. Even if prices are not dependent upon the method

Table 4.4 Differences in Price/Earnings Ratios, Risk, and Earnings Growth for Firms Using Accelerated Versus Straight-Line Depreciation for Annual Report Purposes

| | Depreciation Group | | | |
| | Accelerated | | Straight-Line | |
Variable	*Mean*	*Standard Deviation*	*Mean*	*Standard Deviation*
Risk (Market beta)[a]	1.003	0.25	1.009	0.33
Average price/earnings ratio[b]	16.61	6.72	15.08	3.82
Earnings growth[c]	0.043	0.11	0.045	0.10

[a]Computed from a time series regression of monthly security return data from January 1950 through December 1967. For a discussion of the concept of "stock beta," see Chapter 2 of this book on Financial Management.
[b]Computed as the median of the ratio of price per share divided by earnings per share at fiscal year end based upon annual data from 1950–1967.
[c]Computed as annual rate of growth in earnings available for common stockholders, assuming continuous compounding over the eighteen-year interval 1950–1967.
SOURCE: Beaver and Dukes (1973), Table 2. (Based on a sample of 123 New York Stock Exchange securities.)

of accounting used but earnings are, the ratio of price to earnings will depend on the method of accounting used. In other words, the prices are independent of which accounting method is used, but accounting earnings are affected by the method chosen. Hence, price/earnings ratios computed under differing accounting methods will also differ, even though price/earnings ratios computed under a consistent, uniform method of accounting would show no difference.

The market-price adjustment process appears to include adjustments for differences in earnings induced by the use of different accounting methods (for example, different methods of depreciation; purchase versus pooling) and for changes in earnings among firms induced by changing methods of accounting (for example, depreciation changes in investment credit methods). As a result, prices act as if they are not a function of the method of accounting used, while the ratio of price to earnings does. Such changes are another reason for a less than one-to-one relationship between price changes and earnings changes.

The Behavior of Earnings and Earnings Growth

As we have seen, the evidence on stock price reaction indicates that the market perceives that yearly earnings changes contain a large transitory component. Another body of evidence, which bears on the behavior of earnings and growth in earnings over time, confirms the market's perception of earnings.

Previous research has shown earnings growth to be notoriously unsustainable. For example, when firms are ranked according to growth in earnings per share over five years, their growth in one five-year period is unrelated to their growth in the next five years. In other words, knowing which were the high-growth firms in the past five-year period is virtually useless in predicting which firms will be the high-growth firms in the next five years. Similarly, a firm's growth rate in any one year is unrelated to its growth rate in the next year.

The lack of consistency in growth rates is not surprising. Abnormal earnings growth (or decline) in a given year may be largely the result of transitory factors, such as economy-wide or worldwide economic conditions (i.e., conditions beyond the control of management), intensified competition that erodes abnormally high earnings, or the difficulty of keeping key employees who are responsible for the growth of a firm.

IMPLICATIONS FOR MANAGERIAL DECISIONS

The major implication for the financial reporting practices of management is that the traditional emphasis upon reported earnings and earnings growth is unjustified, both from the perspective of the shift in emphasis of the regulators and from the perspective of research.

What this means is simple and dramatic. Earnings management is unlikely to have any effect on stock price — and is likely to impose severe legal liability on the firm, the management, and the auditors under one or more provisions of the Securities Acts.

What role does this leave for management in financial reporting? Is management necessarily reduced to being a reluctant partner with the regulators in ensuring compliance with an ever-growing list of financial reporting requirements? There are at least two constructive implications of current financial reporting environment. The first concerns the financial reporting policy of management. The second concerns strategy formulation and decisions other than financial reporting.

With respect to the first issue, management can play an active rather than a passive role in financial reporting. The SEC requirement that management be more responsible for the interpretation and analysis of operations offers a good illustration. This requirement can be viewed as creating an opportunity for management to present its insights to analysts and investors. Management does, after all, have better insights into many aspects of the firm's operations than any outsider has. No earnings number, no matter how well crafted, can ever convey these insights; much less can it ever become a single, all-encompassing indicator of management performance. Any level of financial reporting can be greatly enhanced by management's insights and interpretations of the items disclosed. Thus it follows that financial reporting affords management an opportunity to be innovative and creative in conveying its perceptions and expectations to users.

With respect to the basic financial, operating, and strategic decisions faced by management, the key implication is that *management should focus on adding value to the firm's stock value rather than be misdirected by a myopic, short-run focus on reported earnings.*

There are several areas in which this approach can be readily applied. The first is tax planning. Some managements are reluctant to reduce taxes if doing so would reduce reported income as well. But if the market does focus on economic value added and looks behind reported earnings — and we have seen that it does — then the trade-off between lower taxes and lower reported earnings is simple and straightforward: *adopt the inventory that maximizes value-added and do not worry about the effect on reported earnings.*

A second area of application is financing decisions. Some observers have argued that firms are willing to pay a higher effective interest rate via a lease transaction if the transaction prevents additional debt from showing up on the balance sheet.[13] Yet if the market adjusts for off-balance sheet financing, then such additional financing costs are unnecessary.[14] The optimal decision is to choose the cheapest form of financing (for a given level of financial risk) or, more generally, to choose the financial structure that maximizes value added.

A third type of managerial decision is project selection where the projects affect cash flows for several years. Again, it has been argued that management may reject projects that would add to long-run stock value but reduce short-run earnings.[15] Yet to make short-run earnings the main consideration in the firm's project selection policy is to be unnecessarily restrictive. A project selection policy whose goal is maximization of value added is also the policy that is most likely to maximize share price.

Of course, the ultimate project selection policy is the merger and acquisition policy of the firm. Some people have argued that management's acquisition decision should hinge on whether a particular accounting treatment can be used in reporting the transaction in the annual report to shareholders. Such a treatment does not alter the economic value of the proposed acquisition and is no basis for accepting or rejecting the proposal. The proposal should be evaluated by the criterion of value added, regardless of the accounting treatment used.

Failure to recognize the criterion that will be rewarded by the market can lead to two types of very costly errors: rejecting a proposal that would add value and accepting a proposal that reduces value. In the long run, competitive market forces will give the survival edge to those who avoid such errors.[16]

LOOKING AHEAD

At least three key elements are involved in any forecast of the future of financial reporting: changes in the economic environment, changes in the regulatory climate, and changes in information-communication technology.

Economic Environment

The economic environment will most likely continue to be fraught with rapid change and considerable uncertainty. Ongoing changes in this environment — and management's responses to them — are likely to spawn a series of financial issues that are unforeseen today. Current controversies over accounting for changing prices and accounting for foreign currency translation will probably continue, since it is likely that we will experience further periods of unanticipated inflation and swings in foreign currencies. Moreover, if our economy takes a severe downturn, the concern and skepticism about financial reporting are likely to increase rather than decrease.

Regulatory Climate

Many sectors of our economy have undergone considerable deregulation. Financial services, banking, communication, and transportation are prominent examples. Financial reporting is one of the few areas still untouched by deregulation; in fact, regulation has increased, albeit more slowly in the last three years than in the preceding ten.

Will deregulation occur in financial reporting in the foreseeable future? Ultimately, of course, the answer to that question depends on political considerations. Over the last fifty years, the trend in our economy has been toward increased regulation. It is difficult to know whether the current spirit of deregulation is a temporary aberration or a permanent feature of our economic environment. If deregulation continues to be the economy-wide norm, then ultimately that norm will be felt in financial reporting as well.

However, the political decision to deregulate or not will be influenced by other factors, such as economic conditions and technological changes. As noted, a severe downturn in the economy is likely to spur a demand for additional financial reporting requirements.

Information-Communication Technology

Perhaps the most dramatic potential for changes in financial reporting lies in the field of information processing and communications. From a technological perspective, financial reporting still largely occurs today the way it has for the last fifty years. Annual and quarterly reports are set in type, printed, and mailed to shareholders. Annual and quarterly reports are also mailed to the SEC and filed in its reference room.

Current technology, to say nothing of the technology that will become available between now and the year 2000, has revolutionary implications for the manner in which financial information can be disseminated to and processed by investors, analysts, and other user groups.

A single electronic capital market is a concept to which the SEC is already committed itself. An electronic capital market for some 3,000 unlisted securities has already been created in the form of the NASDAQ (National Association of Securities Dealers Automatic Quotations) system. NASDAQ is the most modern capital market in the world. It is likely that listed securities will be incorporated into a similar system.

A next step is electronic financial reporting. The SEC is currently experimenting with a system that will permit users to access copies of all SEC documents filed via computer terminals.[17] Although such a system is a step toward acknowledging computer technology, it merely scratches the surface of what could be achieved. It substitutes physical mailing or a visit to the SEC reference room with electronic access of the same information via a remote terminal, but it does not alter the information itself.

Information-communication technology could be used to effect a dramatic change in the nature, concept, and content of financial reporting. Current financial reporting represents a highly aggregated set of information regarding the performance of the firm. Such aggregation made sense in a world where it was extremely costly to disseminate and process a large data base of disaggregated elements. The current technology has reduced the costs of data processing and transmission to a tiny fraction of what they were a generation — even a decade — ago.

Technology makes it feasible to construct an electronic financial data base for each firm and then incorporate each firm's data base into a common one that can be accessed by the public. This data base would contain many of the underlying raw, or primitive, data that currently are used to produce financial statements. Such raw data could be accessed by users, making them far less dependent on the firm's particular reported accounting method. With a variety of software packages and the electronic data base, users could compute net income under a variety of acccunting assumptions. If they chose to, they could easily compute 10, 100, or even 10,000 income numbers.

Not only would the users be able to choose the accounting methods they preferred, but the issue of uniformity of accounting methods across firms or over time would disappear. Users would be able to compute net income on a uniform basis, either across firms or over time.

What would the role of accounting standards be if such a system of readily accessible electronic data bases became a reality? Accounting standards as we now know them would be obsolete. The issue would no longer be which inventory or depreciation method to permit. Rather, the standards would deal with more primitive disclosure issues. What should be in the data base? How can we ensure uniformity, across firms and over time, in the data that are placed in a particular location in the data base? These are all important questions, but they are considerably different from the issues the FASB and the SEC now spend time and effort trying to resolve.

Will such a world come to pass? It is already technologically feasible. If it does not come to pass, the reason is more likely to be political than technological.

NOTES

1. Other recent examples are cited in "Shareholders Sue Stock Prices Fall," *San Francisco Chronicle,* April 30, 1984.

2. One example of a more complex disclosure is the reporting of results based on current costs, as required under FASB Statement No. 33, in contrast with the simpler reporting based solely on historical costs. An example of more detailed reporting is the line-of-business reporting as required by FASB Statement No. 14, in contrast with reporting on a consolidated basis with no line-of-business breakdowns. An example of greater interpretation imposed on management is the requirement that the effects of changing prices (for instance, inflation) on the operations of the firm be analyzed.

3. These first three sections draw heavily from Beaver (1981), chap. 1, where these issues are discussed in greater detail.

4. The term "financial intermediary" as used here includes those involved in investing the funds of others. Specifically, it includes mutual funds, closed end investment companies, investment trusts, and pension funds, among others.

5. The term "information intermediary" as used here includes those involved in the gathering, processing, analyzing, and interpreting of financial information. It includes financial analysts, bond rating agencies, stock rating agencies, and brokerage firms, among others.

6. For example, information on interest rates, inflation rates, and unemployment; monthly and quarterly measures of industry sales and unfilled orders; announcements of dividends, new products, contract awards, and mergers.

7. This issue is discussed in greater detail in Financial Accounting Standards Board (1976).

8. A further discussion of this issue appears in Hawkins (1977). ·

9. The issues in this section are discussed in greater detail in Beaver (1981), chaps. 5 and 6.

10. Residual price performance extracts the effect of the market factor through subtracting percentage changes in a market index. Here we have used a procedure to obtain residual earnings changes based on prior earnings history. The decline in EPS can exceed 100 percent by dropping from a positive to a negative amount (a loss).

11. Thus, the *sensitivity coefficient* of a stock is the percentage increase in the market price of a stock that accompanies a 100 percent increase in the earnings of that stock.

12. The research is discussed in detail in Beaver, Lambert, and Morse (1980).

13. The issue is discussed in greater detail in Wyatt (1983).

14. Research indicates the market does adjust for off-balance sheet financing. See Bowman (1980) and Feldstein and Morck (1983).

15. These issues are discussed in greater detail in Rappaport (1978, 1983b).

16. Further discussion of this issue appears in Rappaport (1983a).

17. Details of the plan appear in Nobel (1983).

REFERENCES

Archibald, T., "Stock Market Reaction to Depreciation Switch-Back." *Accounting Review* (January 1972), 22–30.

"Auditing the Auditors: Why Congress May Tighten Up." *Business Week,* December 12, 1983, 130–135.

Ball, R., "Changes in Accounting Techniques and Stock Prices." *Empirical Research in Accounting: Selected Studies,* supplement to the *Journal of Accounting Research* (1972), 1–38.

Beaver, W., "The Information Content of the Magnitude of Unexpected Earnings." Unpublished working paper, Stanford University, 1974.

———. *Financial Reporting: An Accounting Revolution.* Englewood Cliffs, N.J.: Prentice-Hall, 1981.

———, R. Clarke, and W. Wright. "The Association Between Unsystematic Security Returns and the Magnitude of the Earnings Forecast Error." *Journal of Accounting Research* (Autumn 1979), 316–340.

———, and R. Duckes. "Interperiod Tax Allocation and Depreciation Methods: Some Empirical Results." *Accounting Review* (July 1973).

———, R. Lambert, and D. Morse. "The Information Content of Security Prices." *Journal of Accounting and Economics* (June 1980), 3–28.

Bowman, R., "The Debt Equivalence of Leases: An Empirical Investigation." *Accounting Review* (April 1980), 237–253.

Cassidy, D., "Investor Evaluation of Accounting Information: Some Additional Evidence." *Journal of Accounting Research* (Autumn 1976), 212–229.

Dukes, R., "An Investigation of the Effects of Expensing Research and Development Costs on Security Prices." *Proceedings of the Conference on Topical Research in Accounting,* ed. M. Schiff and G. Sorter. New York University, 1976.

Feldstein, M., and R. Morck. "Pension Funds and the Value of Equities." *Financial Analysts Journal* (September–October 1983), 29–39.

Financial Accounting Standards Board. *Scope and Implications of the Conceptual Framework Project.* Stamford, Conn.: FASB, December 2, 1976.

Foster, G., "Accounting Earnings and Stock Prices of Insurance Companies." *Accounting Review* (October 1975), 686–698.

———. "Valuation Parameters of Property-Liability Companies." *Journal Finance* (June 1977), 823–836.

———. *Financial Statement Analysis.* Englewood Cliffs, N.J.: Prentice-Hall, 1978.

Hawkins, D., "Toward an Old Theory of Equity Valuation." *Financial Analysts Journal* (November–December 1977), 49–52.

Hong, H., R. Kaplan, and G. Mandelker. "Pooling vs. Purchase: The Effects of Accounting for Mergers on Stock Prices." *Accounting Review* (January 1978), 31–47.

Morse, D., "Price and Trading Volume Reaction Surrounding Earnings Announcements: A Closer Examination." *Journal of Accounting Research* (Autumn 1981), 374–383.

Noble, K., "S.E.C. Planning to Test Electronic Registration." *New York Times,* November 5, 1983.

Rappaport, A., "Executive Incentives vs. Corporate Growth." *Harvard Business Review* (July–August 1978), 81–88.

———. "Don't Sell Stock Market Horizons Short." *Wall Street Journal,* June 27, 1983a.

———. "New Measures of Executive Performance." *Business Week,* July 18, 1983b.

Wyatt, A., "Efficient Market Theory: Its Import on Accounting." *Journal of Accountancy* (February 1983), 56–65.

SUGGESTED READINGS

Beaver, W. *Financial Reporting: An Accounting Revolution.* Englewood Cliffs, N.J.: Prentice-Hall, 1981. Provides a perspective on the major changes in financial reporting and their implications for the future.

Burton, J. "Emerging Trends in Financial Reporting." *Journal of Accounting* (July 1981), 54–66. A brief summary of current trends written by a former chief accountant of the Securities and Exchange Commission and current dean of the Columbia Graduate School of Business.

Horngren, C. *Introduction to Financial Accounting.* Englewood Cliffs, N.J.: Prentice-Hall, 1981. An excellent introductory text in the field of financial accounting, written by a former member of the Accounting Principles Board.

Foster, G. *Financial Statement Analysis.* Englewood Cliffs, N.J.: Prentice-Hall, 1978. An excellent review of the major developments in and uses of financial statement analysis. It presumes a basic understanding of financial accounting.

Wyatt, A. "Efficient Market Theory: Its Impact on Accounting." *Journal of Accountancy* (February 1983), 56–65. A good statement of one auditor's view of the impact of stock price research on accounting, written by a current FASB member.

CHAPTER 5

Production Operations: Liability or Asset?

Steven C. Wheelwright
Stanford University
Graduate School of Business

Accountants have long followed the practice of showing the assets and liabilities of a firm by means of a balance sheet. For the vast majority of manufacturing firms, the asset side of the balance sheet indicates that a significant portion of the firm's financial investment — fixed plant, equipment, and inventories — is tied up in the production and operations function. In spite of what the financial statements say, in recent years a serious question in many U.S. firms has been whether production operations are indeed an asset or whether they might well be a major liability.

Nowhere has the evidence been stronger for the case that manufacturing is a liability than in the U.S. auto industry. Although U.S. auto companies account for almost 10 percent of the U.S. manufacturing output, employ nearly fifteen million people (directly or indirectly), use a significant share of several major raw materials, and account for as much as 20 percent of U.S. retail sales, statistics on the health of these firms have been anything but encouraging.

In labor productivity, the U.S. auto firms have not fared nearly as well as their Japanese counterparts. In fact, as Table 5.1A shows, in 1981 the cost difference between Japanese and American cars delivered to the West Coast of the United States ranged from $1,300 to $1,500 — and almost half of this difference can be attributed to the greater productivity of the Japanese auto industry's labor force. The capital productivity of the U.S. auto industry was even more unfavorable (see Table 5.1B). While the traditional view of the trade-off between cost and quality would have suggested that lower cost would mean lower quality, this was not the case in the auto industry. In terms of both workmanship and reliability (as measured by frequency of re-

149

Table 5.1 Comparison of U.S. and Japanese Automobile Companies

A. *Comparative Costs and Labor Productivity in Selected United States and Japanese Automobile Companies (1981)*

Productivity/Cost Category	Ford	GM	Toyo Kogyo	Nissan
Labor Productivity				
Employee Hours per Small Car	84	83	53	51
Cost per Small Car				
Labor	$1,848	$1,826	$ 620	$ 593
Purchased Components and Material	3,650	3,405	2,858	2,858
Other Manufacturing Costs	650	730	350	350
Nonmanufacturing Costs	350	325	1,100	1,200
Total	$6,498	$6,286	$4,928	$5,001

SOURCE: Abernathy et al. (1983).
NOTE: Nonmanufacturing costs include the costs of ocean freight (for the Japanese producers), selling, and administrative expenses. Other manufacturing costs include costs of warranty, capital costs, energy costs, and miscellaneous items like insurance.

B. *Productivity of Capital in Automobile Production in Selected U.S. and Japanese Companies (1979)*

	Ford	GM	Toyo Kogyo	Nissan
Capital per Vehicle				
Reported book value (historical cost)	$3,048	$2,123	$1,351	$1,484
Replacement value	$5,052	$4,394	$2,161	$2,344

SOURCE: Abernathy et al. (1983).
NOTE: Capital is defined as the value of plant, equipment, and inventories. Reported book value is the value of the plant, equipment, and inventories as originally purchased. Replacement value is what the plant, equipment, and inventory would cost if it had to be replaced today.

pair), the Japanese auto manufacturers were performing considerably better than their U.S. counterparts.

Such comparative data on the auto industry and a number of other basic manufacturing industries have called into serious question the future of the U.S. in the field of production operations. Furthermore, a broader look at other industries has revealed that the problems confronting the manufacturing segment of the economy are not limited to traditional "smokestack" businesses. In the important area of consumer electronics, most of the color televisions sold in the United States in the early 1980s were made by foreign manufacturers; even the TV plants within the United States were predominantly owned and managed by Japanese firms. Consumer video recorders were first developed by U.S. companies, yet none of the home video systems sold in this country in 1983 were manufactured here; all of them were imported from foreign manufacturers. Even in computers and other "high-tech" industrial products, U.S. dominance was being seriously challenged by European and Japanese high-tech firms.

The type of evidence, as well as the sluggish state of the U.S. economic environment in the early eighties, led several writers to propose various explanations of this decline in U.S. manufacturing and discuss the prospects for manufacturing operations in this country. Most agreed in the early 1980s that the United States was at a basic decision point with regard to its manufacturing base. Two scenarios were widely discussed. One of these suggested that U.S. manufacturing would continue to decline as more and more production operations were transferred to lower-cost, more efficient producers offshore. In the other scenario, much of this country's traditional industry would be regenerated and transformed in order to secure a long-term competitive position for major segments of the U.S. economy. Which scenario each observer favored depended on what each thought was responsible for the decline of U.S. manufacturing and also on how each viewed the nature of the production operations management task in a manufacturing firm.

The next section outlines the traditional view of this function. The subsequent section organizes a range of related issues and integrates the traditional view of the production operations function with two alternative current views. In the next section, three major subclasses of production tasks are described and approaches are outlined for addressing those tasks. The following section considers, in some detail, how one organization transformed its production operations management function into a major contributor to the overall success of the business. Also in this section a simple but useful diagnostic for determining where an organization is at present and prospects for its future with regard to production operations is outlined. The final section provides a look ahead regarding the future of production operations and its management challenges and opportunities.

TRADITIONAL PERSPECTIVES ON PRODUCTION OPERATIONS

Much of the U.S. view of production operations during the 1960s and 1970s can be traced back to the scientific management era in the early 1900s. Popularized by Frederick Taylor and others, this view held that in manufacturing the best results were obtained by removing as much independence as possible from the control of the hourly work force and investing that control in management, who then prescribed in great detail exactly how each operator was to perform every step, indeed every motion, of his or her work activity.

Over time, that basic approach evolved into an organizational structure that was very hierarchical. By the 1980s, most U.S. manufacturing organizations were organized into three levels: at the top was a corporate entity; that was supported in turn by divisions each of which consisted of one or more individual businesses; and within each business, tasks were split up functionally within each of those divisions. Within the production function itself, two very distinct levels were identifiable in most organizations: operations managers and technical specialists. The relationship of these levels is outlined in Figure 5.1.

The direct interface with the divisional general manager was usually assigned to a production operations manager who directed operations and saw to it that the organization's expectations for that function were met. As a practical matter, this generally involved providing the production quantities (volumes) requested on the dates specified by customers through the marketing and sales function. In most cases the operations manager and his or her entire group were told by other parts of the organization what to produce, in what quantities, and at what times. As long as the production operations function met those requirements, it was considered well managed.

Those managers directly responsible for production operations worked with various technical specialists who handled the subfunctions required to produce the product. As outlined in Figure 5.1, these technical specialists included the process engineering group (those responsible for the equipment and the way in which it converted materials into the desired component or product) and industrial engineering (those responsible for matching up the direct labor input with the equipment in order to produce the component or product in a timely and cost-effective manner). Many large firms had separate groups of technical specialists to deal with labor relations, materials management, and information/systems management. Where these latter three subfunctions were not separated out, they generally (often implicitly) were considered within the scope of the operations manager and his or her immediate staff.

The job of operations management was largely one of coordinating and directing subgroups of technical specialists who managed tremendous amounts of day-to-day detail. Operations management was also responsible for integrating the activities of the technical specialties with the other functions of the organization so that products would be produced in a timely and cost-effective fashion.

One consequence of this traditional view of the production opera-

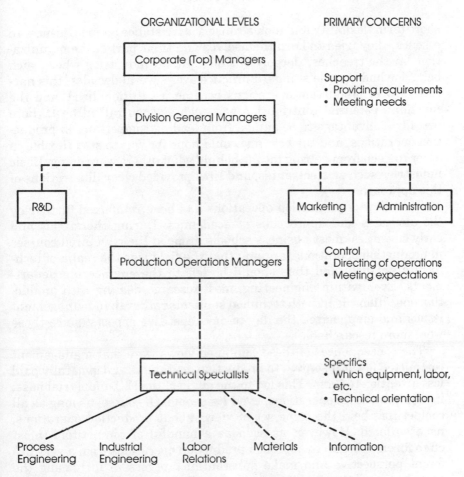

ORGANIZATIONAL LEVELS   PRIMARY CONCERNS

Corporate (Top) Managers

Division General Managers

Support
• Providing requirements
• Meeting needs

R&D

Marketing   Administration

Production Operations Managers

Control
• Directing of operations
• Meeting expectations

Technical Specialists

Specifics
• Which equipment, labor, etc.
• Technical orientation

Process Engineering   Industrial Engineering   Labor Relations   Materials   Information

Figure 5.1 The Organizational-Level View of Production Operations

tions function was that most operations managers saw their entire career as being tied up in directing those technical specialties. Unlike their counterparts in finance and marketing, who often saw themselves as candidates for a general management job, those in the production function in U.S. manufacturing firms seldom found career paths that led them out of it and into another function or into general management. Not surprisingly, this led to a narrow outlook on the part of those within the function and a secondary status in the company.

Most production operations managers responded to their lower-level, "reactor" status in very predictable ways: they strove to maintain short-term flexibility and took a conservative stance on most issues. In essence, they tried to keep themselves and their part of the organization "in the trenches," largely out of sight. In industries where such behavior had become standard practice over several decades, this narrow view of production operations became institutionalized, and the function's potential contribution was seen as "neutral" at best: there was little advantage to be gained from leading competitors in production operations, and the best one could hope for was to stay flexible in order to keep from getting too far behind what others were doing. Basic industries such as steel, autos, and tires provided clear illustrations of this approach.

This view of production operations had been reinforced further by the attitudes and approaches of academics. During the sixties and early seventies, most business schools dropped their required courses in production operations, arguing that the field was the realm of technical specialists and thus should be left to the engineering departments. Even within engineering, most research dealing with production operations dealt with technical subfields rather than management issues and emphasized the day-to-day repetitive aspects (since those were more researchable).

The consequences of these combined views were that management committed fewer resources to production operations and generally paid less attention to them. This led to the aging of the U.S. industrial base: its equipment, its operations, even its people. Of course, as long as all competitors held the same set of views about production operations, none suffered. However, as soon as a handful of competitors (most often foreign) began to approach production operations from a very different perspective and make substantial progress in increasing the contribution of this function to the overall success of the firm, the traditional U.S. approach was no longer viable. The earlier-cited comparative data on the American and Japanese auto industries show what an aggressive foreign manufacturing-based competitor can do when matched against a U.S. firm that takes the traditional U.S. approach to the management of production operations.

Competition alone, however, did not account for all the pressure being brought to bear on U.S. manufacturing industries in the early 1980s. A changing work force with new attitudes, a severe economic recession, and rapidly changing technology all added to the pressure for change in these firms and industries. As a result, by the early 1980s a small but growing number of firms were radically rethinking their approach to production operations. These firms had concluded that either they must become significantly more aggressive and progressive in their management of production operations or they would witness the eventual demise of their manufacturing base. The stage was set for a radical transformation.

A FRAMEWORK FOR UNDERSTANDING PRODUCTION OPERATIONS

As the general public began to recognize the plight of U.S. manufacturers in the early eighties, it became clear that there was much at stake not only for those within the production operations function and for manufacturing firms, but also for those who supplied such firms, for the financial institutions that loaned money to them, for consumers who sought better values, and for the government itself. While no single framework of production operations could capture every aspect of these various perspectives, one general structure proposed by Abernathy et al. (1983) and refined by Hayes and Wheelwright (1984) did provide a useful starting point.

As outlined in Figure 5.2, the Hayes and Wheelwright framework has two dimensions, one relating to organizational scope, the other to the type of task or issue. The framework's first quadrant includes those aspects that are "macro" (country-wide) and structural. Most observers consider these aspects to be the focal point of industrial policy. The major emphasis is on those institutional laws or policies that can be employed to encourage and support various objectives in the manufacturing sector. Through their government's Ministry of International

	Structure ("Hardware")	Infrastructure ("Software")
Macro (Country)	1. Fiscal/Tax Policies Monetary Policies Trade Policies Industrial Policies	2. Culture Traditions Religion Values Social Behavior
Micro (Company)	3. Plant and Equipment Decisions • Size • Location • Technology Vertical Integration	4. Measurement and Control Systems Workforce Policies Management Selection and Development Organization Structure

Figure 5.2 Perspectives on the Competitiveness of Product Operations
SOURCE: Hayes and Wheelwright (1984).

Trade and Industry (MITI), the Japanese have gained a reputation for effectively using this quadrant to support long-term economic objectives.

The second quadrant, also macro in nature, deals with infrastructure, or "software" aspects, and includes such things as culture, traditions, and social behaviors. Focus on the work ethic and the willingness of workers to submit to and adopt group objectives have often been cited as important elements of this quadrant. While much of the popular business writing on the rise of Japanese industry has focused on elements of this quadrant, most observers agree that in the short run little could be done by the individual firm or even by an entire country to change them.

Quadrants 3 and 4 represent the more traditional "micro," or company-level, views. Quadrant 3 contains the structural aspects of production operations — such things as plant and equipment, technology, and vertical integration. Traditionally these areas have been viewed as offering substantial leverage to the firm, and as ones that coincidentally involve substantial investment and thus need to be scrutinized by means of some type of capital-investment analysis.

Quadrant 4 consists of infrastructure elements of production operations within the individual firm. These are what most managers consider tactical, or detailed day-to-day, aspects of producing the product and running the factories. During 1983 and 1984 this fourth quadrant received much attention, owing largely to the book by Peters and Waterman, *In Search of Excellence.* Unlike the supporters of the industrial policy perspective of Quadrant 1 who saw government policy as the means of restoring competitiveness in U.S. production operations, and unlike the management consultants and corporate strategists who saw quadrant 3 as the key to manufacturing competitiveness, Peters and Waterman (as well as a number of others) suggest that measurement and control systems, work-force policies, management selection and training, and attention to detail are keys to long-term competitive advantage.

In the early 1980s, then, many writers focused on only a single quadrant and the opportunities it offered for regaining U.S. competitiveness in production operations. But careful consideration of the potential contribution of all the segments is essential if the major mistakes of the past are to be avoided in the future. Moreover, since most managers cannot change the macro aspects of their environment, it is most useful to concentrate on the micro, or company, level, in considering improvements in production operations. Thus the remainder of this chapter concentrates on those elements that make up quadrants 3 and 4 of Figure 5-2.

MANAGING PRODUCTION OPERATIONS FOR COMPETITIVE ADVANTAGE

Combining the perspectives of Figures 5-1 and 5-2, there are three major problems of managing production operations that an organization must address. One of these is deciding upon the set of production operation resources that the firm needs to accomplish its overall objectives and purposes. The types of decisions that are generally involved in structuring this set of resources are listed in quadrant 3 of Figure 5-2. The second major problem is that of providing the day-to-day systems and procedures that will make the most effective use of that set of production operations resources. These systems and procedures make up quadrant 4 in Figure 5-2. The third major problem is that of coordinating the production operations function with other functions in the firm. On a number of important tasks, such as new product development and quality control, the horizontal integration of various layers of two or more functions' hierarchical structures is essential. Let us look at an example from each of these problem areas.

Structuring the Production Operations Resources

Typically, three main driving forces have led firms to modify their set of production resources. The first of these forces is the need for greater capacity (volume). Traditional responses to this felt need have been to add capacity at existing plants, build new facilities, and change production technologies when higher volumes allow the use of more efficient processes. Since no firm likes to forgo the opportunity for increased sales, increased product demand historically has been the single most important motivating force for change.

A second impetus for change in the set of production operations resources is new products. Since these are the engine of growth in most organizations, and since they generally involve new features, new material, and new specifications, they tend to dictate changes in capacity, production technologies, and the scope of the production operation (vertical integration).

The third major driver for changing a firm's production operations resources is an unprofitable or insufficiently profitable product. Such a product could be one that has yet to meet its original expectations, which competes with a lower-priced or higher-featured product, or one that is made in a manufacturing facility that has so deteriorated that it can no longer provide the cost and quality required. Firms generally respond to such problems by reconfiguring the structural elements of their production operations.

In all three of these settings, it is the explicit need of the product that drives the restructuring of the production resources. In what is perhaps the simplest form of response (and the one used by a surprisingly large number of firms), the set of production resources is altered only after one of these three driving forces has become so strong that it is obvious to the entire organization that changes are required. At that point, the firm usually is under severe time pressure and tends to react with a series of short-term solutions to what is basically a long-term problem. During the 1960s and 1970s, increasing competition, shorter product life cycles, and higher interest costs (and thus higher penalties for carrying excess resources) prompted many firms to seek improved techniques for solving the various problems they encountered in restructuring their production resources. Four structural subareas in which these problems typically arise — capacity, facilities, process technologies, and vertical integration — can be used to illustrate the progress that has been made in finding better long-term solutions.

Capacity. The first of these structural subareas is capacity. When addressed as a structural element, capacity generally refers to long-term (usually one to ten years) capacity needs in planning both the size of the increments to be added and the timing of those increments. Two ideas that have proved valuable here are the notion of a capacity cushion and the concept of scale. A *capacity cushion* is the expected excess or short-fall in capacity that the organization will provide, depending on whether the firm wants to lead demand for capacity, match its supply of capacity as precisely as possible with that demand, or lag demand for that capacity.

From a financial perspective, determining the optimal capacity cushion involves balancing the costs of providing too much capacity (that is, the cost of idle capacity) against the costs of providing insufficient capacity (that is, the cost of lost contribution when sales demand exceeds supply). In the steel industry, for example, excess capacity is extremely expensive, but insufficient capacity forgoes very little in profits because profit margins are low in that industry. Firms in low-profit industries often maintain a very small capacity cushion or even maintain slightly less capacity (on average) than is required. By contrast, in the personal computer industry during a period like the early 1980s, when that market was expanding rapidly, firms' profit margins were extremely high and the cost of capacity was generally quite low (since they were largely circuit-board assembly operations). In such a circumstance, a firm would probably want a very large capacity cushion and would, if possible, add capacity well in advance of demand.

The concept of *scale* recognizes the fact that as the volume of production increases, the cost per unit produced decreases. This outcome is due in part to those costs that are fixed, that is, do not vary with volume. As volume increases, the fixed costs are spread over more and more units. This is, however, only one of several forms of scale economies. An even more important form occurs when increased volume allows production technology to change. One need only compare a small company and a very large company in the same industry to see that, in the small firm, production entails a less automated, more labor-intensive, more customized process than it does in the large firm. The large firm's production process tends to be less flexible, but generally it turns out goods at a lower cost per unit.

Many industries possess minimum-scale requirements: that is, in those industries firms cannot operate on a smaller scale and remain viable. The notion of *optimal scale* recognizes that, while some costs continue to decline as volume increases, other costs may increase. Those costs that increase with added size and volume combine to form *diseconomies of scale*. For example, the cost of coordinating thousands of employees at a single plant, or the transportation costs incurred in shipping longer and longer distances in order to fully utilize a very large plant, would be of this type. Identifying the economies and diseconomies of scale and analyzing them in conjunction with the concept of a capacity cushion are two important steps for dealing with capacity issues.

Facilities. A second structural subarea of production operations is facilities. In this area a firm must decide the scope of activity — the products to be made, the customers to be served, the materials to be handled, and the production technologies to be provided — for each facility, and also decide how that scope will grow and change over time. Today most firms recognize that facilities are not inanimate objects. That is, they understand that they cannot simply put the facility in place and then leave it unchanged for a decade or two. Facilities must be continually renovated and modified to fit ongoing product needs.

The concept of *facilities focus* is analogous to focus in any aspect of a business. It involves limiting the kinds of demand that are made of a given facility. Facilities can't be all things to all people and be fully effective. A good example of very focused facilities in the fast foods business is provided by McDonald's, which has defined a very narrow and specific set of tasks (which results in a very limited menu) for each of its restaurants. Recent evidence (see Hayes and Wheelwright, 1984) suggests that the benefits of focus — improved productivity, quality, and service — can be substantial. Perhaps focus has been undervalued in its trade-off with larger-scale facilities.

Process technology. A third structural subarea is production process technology. Here firms must deal with questions such as the degree of automation to be pursued in the technologies utilized, the flexibility provided by those technologies, and the rate at which the firm should change its process technologies. Issues of this type that gained widespread attention in the eighties include the use of computer integrated manufacturing, robots, and other advanced manufacturing processes.

A concept that is useful in gauging the impact of evolving improvements in production technology is that of the *learning curve*. Learning curves were originally developed to explain why the amount of labor required per unit produced declined as the *cumulative* volume of production increased. This concept explains why, for example, the hundredth unit of the 747 aircraft produced by Boeing took much less labor than the tenth unit, and why the thousandth unit took proportionately less than the hundredth unit. Although a learning curve plots the relationship between labor hours per unit produced and cumulative units produced, the concept often is broadened and referred to as an *experience curve* when it shows the relationship between cost per unit produced (including inputs in addition to labor) and cumulative volume produced. In rapidly growing markets like electronics, where the time it takes to double cumulative volume is relatively short, this concept can be extremely important.

Vertical integration. A fourth structural subarea is *vertical integration*. This has to do with the scope of activities that a firm chooses to incorporate in its own production operations. In its simplest form, the decision is one of "make" versus "buy." When a new component, subassembly, or product is to be incorporated into what the firm offers to its customers, the firm must decide whether to make the item itself or buy it from someone else. Such a decision quickly grows in complexity as a firm considers the sets of things it wants to make rather than buy, recognizes that it doesn't need to make 100 percent or buy 100 percent but can make some and buy the balance, and understands that it can change the make/buy mix as conditions change.

Today there is a trend away from vertical integration toward more dependence on outside suppliers. For example, some electronics firms offer computer terminals and other components while actually doing no manufacturing themselves. They have concluded that their highest value added is in product design and development and delivery of the product to the market. Their production function is simply that of managing the outside suppliers who handle the individual production tasks.

Combining structural elements of production operations with structural elements of marketing. It should be apparent from a review of the four structural subareas above that a number of major structural decisions affect the potential competitive advantage to be gained in the production operations function. Although the traditional approach has been to subdivide these structural elements into such subareas as capacity, facilities, technology, and vertical integration, firms are recognizing the need for a more integrative approach. The need is to *anticipate* future product requirements rather than wait until those requirements are upon the organization in the form of a need for added volume, the need to produce new types of products, or the need to overcome profitability problems.

A particularly useful concept for integrating the tasks in these various subareas is that of the *product and process matrix* (see Hayes and Wheelwright, 1979a and 1979b), which employs the notion of life cycles. Underlying this concept are the premises that (1) there is a set of requirements that are imposed by the markets the company chooses to serve and the products with which it chooses to serve those markets, and (2) these requirements must be matched with the capabilities of the company's production operations.

Four stages normally are identified in the life cycle of a product: low volume–low standardization (startup), multiple products–low volume, few major products–higher volume (rapid growth), and high volume–high standardization (commodities). These four stages are shown across the top of Figure 5-3. The stages of the production operations life cycle can be best characterized in terms of the type of process technology used. As shown down the left-hand side of Figure 5-3, this life cycle starts with a jumbled flow (job shop) process, shifts to a disconnected line flow (batch) process, then becomes a connected line flow, and finally shifts to a continuous flow process.

Various industries can be used to show how these two life cycles tend to match up over time. For example, an industry largely positioned in stage 1 of both life cycles is commercial printing. Each job is custom-designed and then individually produced in a job shop. An industry in which volumes are somewhat higher and products somewhat less customized is heavy equipment, as represented by firms using batch processes, such as Caterpillar. A good example of an industry in which the third stages of both life cycles come together is the U.S. auto industry. Finally, a continuous flow process used to make a commodity product is illustrated by a sugar refinery or a chemical plant.

The product/process matrix reflects a rational matching of what the customer and markets require (through the products and services delivered) with what the production resources (through available tech-

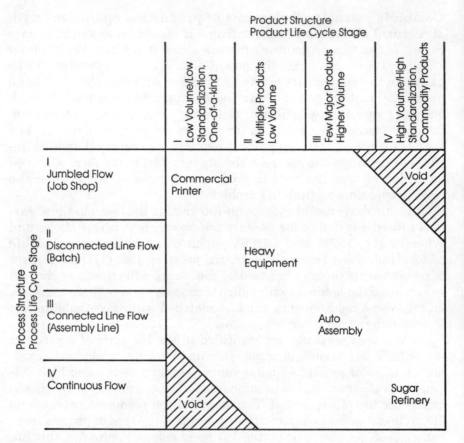

Figure 5.3 Matching Major Stages of Product and Process Life Cycles — The Product/Process Matrix

SOURCE: Hayes and Wheelwright (1979).

nology) can provide. It can also be noted that the upper right-hand and lower left-hand corners of this matrix tend not to be viable positions. The upper right corner would represent the use of a job shop process to produce a standardized product. Although the job shop process is extremely flexible, it cannot compete with more automated processes that have lower variable costs. The lower left corner would represent the use of a continuous flow process to produce a customized product. That match is infeasible because of the inflexibility and high setup costs of most continuous processes and the market requirements for substantial variety.

It is important to note, however, that several of the "new" production technologies — such as computer-aided design/computer-aided manufacturing (CAD/CAM) and flexible machining centers — are sufficiently automated and flexible to enable firms to move further down the vertical scale (toward more efficient production processes) without having to move to the right (toward more standardized high-volume products) on the product market scale.

The product/process matrix can help a firm integrate some of its planning for capacity, facilities, technology, and vertical integration. That is, a firm can decide where it wants to position itself in the matrix, where its competitors are positioned, and how it sees that positioning evolving on both the production resource dimension and the product market requirements dimension.

Individual facilities and subparts of the organization can also be analyzed and planned with the help of the product/process matrix. This type of matching for individual facilities has proved to have substantial strategic leverage in the food service industry. The traditional French or Continental European restaurant, with its tremendous variety and customized preparation of every diner's order, clearly is positioned in Group I (upper left corner). The short-order café looks much more like a Group II positioning, offering as it does a somewhat narrower menu (fewer options for the customer) and employing a more standardized food-preparation process. Burger King and McDonald's have chosen to develop a whole new segment of the market — fast food. Their very limited menus, standardized production processes, and high volume are an effective match between the Group III process and product structures.

Even in dealing with vertical integration issues, the product-process matrix is useful. Often certain types of expansion can be viewed as moving into an entirely new matrix where there is a different set of competitors and product/process dimensions.

Systems for Utilizing Production Resources

As Figure 5.2 suggests, there is conceptual appeal to separating the structural activities of production operations from the infrastructural aspects. Within individual firms this separation has tended to occur not only because of the differences in the decisions in both categories, but also because of the level of the organization most likely to deal with each. Decisions and plans related to the structural quadrants tend to involve a few major decisions and substantial capital investment, and to take many months, even years, to implement fully. The structural quadrants have traditionally been thought of as the areas requiring review by top management and thus have been separated from the infrastructure elements in terms of the decision processes used to handle them and the levels of management involved.

Those areas referred to as "infrastructure" have generally been thought of as involving tactical or ongoing "operating" matters, such as production planning, inventory control, materials management, labor relations, personnel, quality assurance and reliability, and plant supervision. In this section of the chapter we address infrastructure, or the systems used to utilize production operations resources on an ongoing basis.

Production planning. Undoubtedly the most important driving force in the development and application of such infrastructure systems is the shipment schedule for the firm's products. Every production operations manager knows that there is no faster way to gain the attention and wrath of the organization (particularly the sales and marketing people, but the finance people as well) than to miss ship schedules (quantity, mix, or delivery dates). In approaching the task of meeting ship schedules, most production operations do their planning using a system built around a two-dimensional framework like that illustrated in Table 5.2. One dimension decomposes the time horizon into four major categories. The first, long-range capacity planning, is generally included in the structural sets of plans and decisions described in the previous section and covers a time horizon of one to ten years. Whereas long-range capacity planning deals with general capabilities and overall policy issues, the second category, aggregate planning, focuses more on decisions that can be altered within a three- to eighteen-month time horizon. Aggregate levels of each key resource would be planned as part of this category.

Using the aggregate capacity plan as a guide, production operations managers generally set up a schedule to deal with a time horizon of one week to six months. That "master" schedule begins to decompose the aggregate capacity plan in terms of specific equipment, specific products, specific materials, and individual workers. Dispatching is then used to respond to short-term uncertainties and unexpected situations that require rapid adjustment in order to keep production resources fully utilized. Dispatching generally covers a time horizon of an hour to perhaps a month.

On the other dimension of Table 5.2 are the types of resource involved. Generally, firms divide those resources up into the physical assets (physical space and equipment), the human resources (both direct and indirect employees), and the materials to be used in producing the products. With the ship schedule as a driver, the structure shown in

Table 5.2 Planning for Resources Required by Time Horizon

	Types of Decisions — By Time Horizon			
Types of Resources Required	*Long-range Capacity Planning (1–10 years)*	*Aggregate Capacity Planning (3–18 months)*	*Scheduling (1 week–6 months)*	*Dispatching (hourly–monthly)*
Acquiring and deploying *physical space and capital equipment*	Selection of capabilities Location decisions Timing decisions Quantity Capital spending	Minor additions Subcontracting Product mix	Allocation of facilities to products in specific time periods	
Acquiring and deploying *human resources*	Hiring and layoff policies Skill requirements Timing Quantity Training and development	Number of shifts Overtime Hire-fire Line balancing	Overtime — allocation of manpower to products (jobs) in specific time periods	Rescheduling, expediting, and detailed coordination of all three factors of production
Acquiring and deploying *materials*	Material requirements Long-term contracts Vendor selection Warehouse requirements Timing Quantity	Short-term purchase commitments Shipping schedules Inventory planning	Ordering materials Marshalling materials Inventory control Allocation of materials	

SOURCE: Adapted from "Note on Capacity Management" (9-674-081), Harvard Case Services, Boston, MA, 1974.

Table 5.2 facilitates the assignment of responsibility for selected resources and time horizons in such a way that, as increased detail becomes available and as the need for more specific plans develops with the arrival of a given ship date, the requisite set of tasks can be performed.

If a firm produced only one product and had stable demand, the set of tasks required to meet a ship schedule would be trivial. Unfortunately, few firms have it that easy. Even in the absence of uncertainty, planning for the use of production resources is a complex task. For most firms, the mix of products and the seasonality of demand patterns is such that a tremendous number of combinations are possible. It is not unusual for a single plant to deal with 10,000 to 20,000 different component numbers in producing as many as several thousand finished products. Seasonal swings in demand and the expense of carrying inventory complicate matters further and make planning near-term operations a major challenge. The uncertainty that arises when actual orders exceed or fall short of demand forecasts and when business cycles and seasonal patterns do not develop as anticipated complicates this task even more, adding the need for flexibility in both resources and inventories. Generally these operating realities are handled by dividing day-to-day operations management into four subcategories — production planning/materials control (the materials function), labor relations/personnel (the human resource function), quality assurance and reliability (the inspection and test function), and plant operations (the direct labor supervisions function). These functions are coordinated through numerous meetings and daily exchanges.

In the remainder of this section we will use the first of these, production planning and materials control, as an illustration of how U.S. thinking has evolved in the past two decades and how it is likely to continue to develop in the future.

Before the advent of computers that could handle tremendous amounts of information, the only feasible way to deal with the variety and uncertainty associated with most production facilities was to subdivide them into departments, to have each department develop its own forecasts and schedules, and then to buffer (separate) those departments with work-in-process (WIP) inventory. Each department would respond as though it had its own independent demand and was producing for inventory (which would subsequently become input to a downstream department). Thus upstream departments would manufacture components and fabricate parts, intermediate-level departments would produce subassemblies, and downstream departments would do final assembly and testing. The concept of a *batch* was central to managing such an operating structure. A department would seek to balance the economics of carrying inventory against the economics of setting up for another production run in determining the optimal batch size, or what is generally referred to as the *economic order quantity* (EOQ). This is the quantity of product produced in a single batch that minimizes the total annual costs of carrying inventory and setup costs. If batch sizes larger than the EOQ are produced, annual setup costs decline, but those declines are more than offset by increases in the cost of larger inventory carried. (Inventory costs include the physical costs of storage as well as the financial costs associated with the investment in that inventory.) If batch sizes smaller than the EOQ are produced, annual inventory carrying costs decline, but those declines are more than offset by increases in the annual setup costs, since more setups would be required to produce the smaller batches.

The material requirements planning (MRP) system. The increasing breadth and variety of product lines, together with increasingly expensive inventory, spurred management to adopt computers in the late 1960s and employ them to manage the huge amounts of production-related information in an entirely new way. Using the concept of *materials requirements planning* (MRP), it became possible to link together individual departments in the production flow from a planning and scheduling point of view.

The basic idea of MRP is that one develops a production schedule based on anticipated shipments of finished goods and then uses that finished unit schedule to derive subassembly schedules and component schedules. To develop these derived schedules for individual departments requires a thorough understanding of how components feed into subassemblies, and how subassemblies in turn feed into the finished products. This information is referred to as a *bill of materials* for a finished end item.

When planning material requirements it is also necessary to know the timing relationships between various departments and the production cycle times within each department. For example, in a simple plant operation involving components, subassemblies, and final assembly, one would need to know how long it takes to produce the components and how long it takes to produce the subassemblies that go into the final assembly. Knowing the bill of materials for that final assembled item and those timing relationships, one could use the schedule for final assembly to derive (often the word "explode" is used) the schedules by which subassemblies would have to be produced in preceding time periods, and by which components would have to be produced in even earlier time periods, to ensure that the components and subassemblies would come together according to the final assembly schedule. This is the essence of an MRP system. Literally hundreds of MRP systems were installed in U.S. manufacturing firms during the 1970s; by the mid-1980s the 1,000 largest manufacturing firms had such systems in place and the majority of smaller firms were quickly moving in that direction.

The advantage of an MRP system is that when it is effectively coordinated and executed, resources (materials, people, and equipment) can be scheduled much more effectively. As a result, resource utilization can be increased significantly, service levels can be improved (because the right product will be available at the right time), and inventory levels (particularly WIP inventories) can be reduced substantially. Although the concept of an MRP system has tremendous logical appeal, most firms that have adopted such systems have found that their effective use is no simple matter. With an MRP system the need for discipline and coordination is much greater than it is when departments are largely decoupled and insulated by buffer inventories. Also, it quickly becomes apparent that accurate information in the system is essential if it is to work correctly.

The Just-in-Time (kanban) system. By the early 1980s, a system very different from MRP was being employed for handling day-to-day operation scheduling. This approach had been developed during the seventies by the Toyota Motor Company of Japan. Known as Just-in-Time or *kanban,* it had a number of very different assumptions and operating characteristics than most U.S. MRP systems. Whereas MRP had been developed as an information system for use by production planning and purchasing staff people, Just-in-Time originated as a production improvement project whose goal was to enhance the productivity of production operations.

The basic purpose of the Just-in-Time system is to develop and operate a specialized, tightly honed manufacturing system that reinforces the desired operating practices. Such a system seeks to combine, *on the shop floor,* information control and physical control of production rather than separate the two and give information control to a staff group with a large computer and make physical control the responsibility of supervisors and hourly workers.

As stated by Toyota, the objective of its Just-in-Time production system is the elimination of four types of waste — extra operations (tasks that do not add value to the final product), overproduction (producing something before it is needed and thus tying up resources that are not yet required), defective products (producing something that will subsequently need to be reworked or discarded), and stagnation (idle resources). A good example of how Just-in-Time reduces waste and increases the overall effectiveness of production operations is its use in eliminating WIP inventory.

A simple analogy is often used to depict the advantages of eliminating WIP inventories (that is, reducing the waste associated with idle products sitting in inventory). The analogy goes as follows. Inventory can be thought of as the water in a lake or stream that covers the rocks (problems) that exist beneath the surface of the water. If large amounts of inventory are allowed to exist, it becomes very difficult to identify which rocks are the biggest problem, and it's also difficult to work on them underwater.

In the Just-in-Time approach, inventory is systematically eliminated from the production process. As the water level drops, rocks protrude above the surface. These rocks are the problems that hinder production. The intent, then, is not to have some complex scheme to identify problems and determine which of them are most important, but rather to work on the most apparent problem, since without enough water to cover it, that is the one that is impeding progress. Once that rock is eliminated — which can be done much more easily when the entire organization is focused on it and when it is apparent that it is hindering everybody's production efforts — the water level can be lowered further and additional rocks can be identified.

There are, of course, a number of important requirements that must be met if the Just-in-Time approach is to work effectively. These include smooth production rates (stable over an extended period of time), high-quality output, highly reliable processes (minimal unexpected downtime), low setup costs (so that very small batches can be run economically), strict discipline, and rapid information flows. Some who have looked closely at the Just-in-Time system in Japan have often concluded that perhaps the Japanese emphasize quality because the system requires it, and not simply because they discovered that quality will sell with customers.

The types of improvements that are possible with the Just-in-Time system can be illustrated by some of the performance gains achieved by the Toyo Kogyo Motor Company, the maker of Mazda cars, between the mid-1970s and 1980. This company's number of vehicles per employee (number of units produced annually divided by number of employees) went from 19.3 to 43.8, with accompanying improvements in productivity, setup times, work-in-process levels, and quality (of both product and process).

MRP, Just-in-Time, or both? To those who have examined MRP systems and Just-in-Time systems in some detail, it's apparent that the two systems approach the problem of operations from very different perspectives. Whereas both systems have as goals the reduction of production cycle times, the lowering of inventories, the increased utilization of resources, and the overall improvement in production operations effectiveness, they go at it in very different ways. Perhaps the best way to summarize these differences is to say that in a Just-in-Time system the incentive for each subfunction is the continual improvement of production operations, whereas in an MRP system the incentive — unfortunately — is often one thing for the staff group that runs that system and something else for the other line management subfunctions. This does not mean that effective combinations of Just-in-Time and MRP are not possible, but it does mean that it may be easier to complement Just-in-Time with MRP than it is to do the reverse. It is likely that in the decade of the eighties more and more firms will begin to use both systems and that those who succeed at making production operations a competitive advantage will be the ones who best integrate the strengths of both approaches in their efforts to control their production operations.

One final point regarding this infrastructure category of activity in a manufacturing firm is that whether one is looking at production planning and materials control, human resource management, quality management, or plant supervision, the critical tasks for the future are all very similar. These functions cannot be segmented and isolated, but must be integrated. Moreover, while these functions involve many small, seemingly minor day-to-day decisions, the cumulative effect of these decisions can indeed be substantial, as shown by the results at Toyo Kogyo, the Japanese auto manufacturer. Finally, it appears that when competitive advantage is based on such infrastructural arrangements in production operations, it becomes extremely difficult for competitors to imitate, because there are no shortcuts to putting in place the infrastructures needed to realize these results.

Integrating Horizontal Tasks of Strategy: The New Product Case

In the two preceding sections, the focus was on what have traditionally been the two major subsegments of production operations activity — structural and infrastructural decisions. In this section we focus on a type of activity that does not fit naturally into either of these traditional categories. Hayes and Wheelwright (1984) have referred to such activities as *horizontal tasks*. These are tasks that require coordination across functions at fairly low levels of the organization: they cannot be handled effectively by giving a major piece to each of several different managers with different functional responsibilities. Two of the most important horizontal tasks for manufacturing firms in the 1980s are quality management and product development.

The traditional approach to quality management has been to treat it as a *vertical task,* that is, one for which major responsibility can be assigned to a single function. Depending on the nature of the firm and its perception of its quality task, that assignment might be made within the production operations organization by setting up a separate quality subfunction reporting to the operations manager, or it might be separated as a primary function reporting to a general manager as an equal with marketing, R&D, and production. In either case, the intention was to treat it as an area for which primary responsibility and authority could be assigned to a separate part of the organization, with the expectation that it would deliver what was required.

A little reflection on the factors that determine quality makes it quickly apparent that a vertical task approach to quality is fatally flawed. Each of the functions in an organization has a significant impact on quality. It simply is not possible to make a separate function totally responsible for it. For example, the design of the product and the selection of the materials going into the product generally have much greater leverage on the resulting quality than does the way in which the assembly and other production-related tasks are performed by the hourly workers. Similarly, the equipment used to produce the product and the way in which the product is supported by the field service organization can often have a major impact on the customer's perception of the product's quality.

While most quality managers would admit to these cross-functional impacts on their area of responsibility, they continue to operate as though either they really do control what determines quality or they act simply as a police force, making sure that the other parts of the organization don't let "below-standard quality" slip through. In such a setting there is clearly a trade-off between cost and quality. As an increasing number of organizations are learning, this trade-off need not exist if quality is treated as a horizontal task and if various parts of the organization work in an integrated fashion to deal with it on an ongoing basis at fairly low levels.

Another horizontal task involving production operations and of increasing importance to U.S. manufacturing firms as the decade progresses is new product development and the transfer of new products out of the R&D lab into production. The traditional model in this area has been for R&D or the product development folks to call the shots. That is, they would develop the product and *then* pass it on to manufacturing to be produced. It has not been uncommon for production operations managers to refer to the "wall" between themselves and product development and to describe the hand-off procedure as one of R&D "throwing the product over the wall." The result of this sequential procedure tends to be products that are more expensive than planned and late. Substantial amounts of product development resources continue to be needed long after the product is supposedly finished, making them unavailable for other projects.

New Product Development: Lessons from IBM

Before looking at the appropriate management approach for long-term solution, it is useful to examine the problem from a somewhat different perspective. This perspective is prompted by identifying firms that perceive new product development as a major strategic task and then ascertaining what kinds of problems most concern them regarding that task. For example, IBM in the early eighties made a critical examination of the problems and challenges it faced that were tied directly to the new product task. The company identified four such problems. The first was manufacturing overhead. Given the nature of its production processes and product technologies, its major manufacturing cost component, unlike that of many smokestack industries, is not labor. In fact, direct labor tends to be less than 5 percent of IBM's manufactured cost. Materials are a substantial cost category, but even more important from the standpoint of control is manufacturing overhead. It is not uncommon for IBM and other high-technology firms to have manufacturing overheads that are four to eight times the magnitude of the direct labor cost.

A second problem area is that of quality. Here, IBM's analysis suggests that the greatest leverage on quality is in the design of the product. That is, designing products that can be manufactured with the processes available at the time the products are ready for production is the key to good quality. A third problem is cost. Again, in a high-technology business such as computers and communications equipment, cost can also be tied directly to the design of the product. In this regard, once the design is completed, the impact on costs that production operations can have is small compared with the impact that was possible in R&D.

A fourth problem of major import to a firm like IBM is timeliness. This has to do with both the timing of a new product's introduction and the rate at which volume production can be added for a new product. It doesn't do any good — as many firms have found — to have a great new product out on the market before anyone else if you can't meet the demand for it.

These four problems combined all point to the same conclusion: a major element of product design must be the manufacturability of the product. This requires that the designers understand the process capabilities available and — equally important — that production operations provide the most appropriate set of process capabilities for the products that will be developed in the future. IBM's approach is to become much more sophisticated and thorough in planning long-term product development and long-term process development, and in matching the two through effective organizational mechanisms.

As reported by Hayes and Wheelwright (1984), some of the steps pursued by IBM have included parts simplification, the earlier involvement of production operations in the design process, early cross-training in the career paths for both R&D and production engineers, and design review processes that effectively integrate the R&D and the production functions at a fairly low level in the organization. The result is a series of parallel activities in manufacturing and R&D. Even for industries that grow more slowly and employ less advanced technology, such parallel tracking of the inputs to the new product development task makes possible lower overall resource requirements, more timely introduction of new products, and more cost-effective, higher-quality products.

New Product Development: Lessons from GE Dishwasher

An excellent example of a manufacturing operation that has moved aggressively from the traditional view of production operations (albeit the best of that traditional view) to a much more integrated view seeking to achieve an even stronger competitive advantage is General Electric's dishwasher operation. As a business unit, GE Dishwasher is one of several major consumer appliance businesses that the company has participated in for decades. In the late 1970s GE's Dishwasher strategic business unit (SBU) reassessed its position and its future prospects and concluded that its product design, essentially twenty years old, its production processes, also from ten to twenty years old, and its aging work force (with an average seniority of fifteen to sixteen years) were not going to change dramatically unless management took the initiative. An added complication was the fact that there was a strong union in all six plants at the GE Louisville site, all covered by a single labor relations contract.

In spite of some of these operating factors, the company had been very successful in the past; it had long held the leading position in the U.S. market, accounting for approximately one-third of domestic dishwasher sales. In 1977–78, as part of its normal product redesign planning cycle, the division proposed an $18 million investment to incrementally improve its product and manufacturing process. While senior management would normally have approved such an investment and had the division carry on with its traditional approach to production operations, the combination of factors described above led it to rethink that view. Part of the impetus for this reevaluation came from the top managers involved, who felt that there must be a better way — but that if there wasn't, then perhaps the present way was not as attractive as taking the money and putting it into some other high-growth businesses. There was also a group of key middle managers who saw that major opportunities might be created if the division could break out of its traditional mode of thinking.

GE product designers had previously developed a top-of-the-line product with a plastic tub and plastic door liner that was much more expensive than the standard steel product but offered significantly better operating performance. In addition it appeared possible to make a substantial increase in the level of dishwasher standardization if the design and marketing functions exercised some self-discipline and coordination. Finally, since only 55 percent of U.S. households owned electric dishwashers, the business still had considerable long-term growth potential as well as a large ongoing replacement market. When these factors were combined with GE's strong competitive position, management concluded that if the "right product" were introduced at the "right price" and "right quality," GE could actually lower unit costs and significantly expand its market share. Thus encouraged, top management challenged Dishwasher management not just to "fix" its current problems but to "do it right."

As a result, the modest incremental proposal for product and process improvement was abandoned and a much broader proposal put forward. It required an investment of $38 million and, more important, major changes in three elements — attitudes about the work force, product design, and manufacturing processes. On the first element, a major commitment was made to improve the working environment through better communication, feedback, and worker involvement in the design of the process. It required almost two years to lay the groundwork in this infrastructure area, but once in place, the new worker-manager relationships would significantly enhance the contribution of production operations to the overall business.

The second aspect of the proposal was a complete rethinking of the product, which would be called the Permatuff dishwasher. It was redesigned around a central core consisting of a one-piece plastic tub and a one-piece plastic door. To ensure that the product would meet the desired quality standards, extremely tight specifications were established, both for GE and its vendors. In fact, both internal and external suppliers were required to reduce the incidence of defects to one-twentieth of their former levels. Suppliers who could not or would not meet the new standards were dropped. To meet the new product's cost targets as well as its higher-quality specifications, it was necessary to coordinate product and process development rather than separate them as had been the traditional practice.

The third major aspect of this proposal involved the design of the process. Automation was pursued aggressively, not just to reduce costs but to improve quality. The product design was modified in accordance with the capabilities and constraints of the new process in order to meet these objectives. In addition, more worker control and shorter production cycle times were built into the process. Finally, product testing was integrated more completely with manufacturing, rather than assigned to a separate quality-control organization.

By late 1980, the basic building blocks of this new strategy had been defined and agreed to. Each of the functions — product design, manufacturing, and marketing — was expected to pursue a role that would lead to a major competitive advantage for the overall business. Production operations was also asked to help in developing performance measures, to be tracked over subsequent years, that would indicate how well the manufacturing organization was carrying out its responsibilities.

By 1984, significant improvement had been made in such important areas as warranty service call rates, unit costs, materials handling, inventory turns, reject rates, and productivity (see Table 5.3). Other gains were made, including a 70 percent reduction in part numbers, a twenty-pound reduction in the weight of the finished product (which cut freight costs), and significantly more positive worker attitudes. Perhaps most important was the significant jump in market share that occurred during the first twelve months of the new product's introduction. Finally, during 1983 and again in 1984, *Consumer Reports* rated GE's new Permatuff dishwasher as the best value among all U.S. dishwashers.

FOUR STAGES IN THE ROLE OF PRODUCTION OPERATIONS

GE is just one example of a firm that has been successful in making this transition. Other companies that had long been strong in manufacturing's contribution to their competitive advantage include S. C. Johnson (Johnson Wax), Black and Decker, and IBM. As one way to begin calibrating the status of production operations in any particular firm and to provide a general map of how such a transition might be managed and pursued, Hayes and Wheelwright (1984) have developed

Table 5.3   GE Dishwasher: Results

Performance Measure	1980/81 (actual)	1983 (actual)	1984 (estimates)
Service call rate (index)	100	70	65
Unit cost reduction (index)	100	90	88
Number of times handled (tub/door)	27/27	1/3	1/3
Inventory turns	13	17	28
Reject rates (mech/elec test)	10%	3%	2.5%
Productivity (labor/unit index)	100	133	142

Other: 70% fewer part numbers, 20 pounds lighter, worker attitudes (positive 2×, negative 0.5×)

SOURCE: Published GE data, see Robert H. Hayes and Steven C. Wheelwright, *Restoring Our Competitive Edge — Competing Through Manufacturing* (New York, N.Y.: John Wiley & Sons, 1984).

a four-stage model of the evolution of management thinking regarding production operations. In the first stage of that model, the function is considered *internally neutral.* Here the emphasis is simply on minimizing any problems that stem from production operations and keeping the function in a flexible and reactive mode.

In stage 2, referred to as *externally neutral,* management tries to achieve parity with competitors. The following of "industry practice" and the use of capital investment alone to keep up with competing firms are typical of this stage. Here, as in stage 1, the role of production operations is essentially neutral.

In stage 3, referred to as *internally supportive,* production operations are put in the role of providing credible support to the business strategy. This support activity entails screening manufacturing decisions to be sure that they are consistent with the business strategy and seeking to translate the business strategy into its implications for manufacturing. Thus the role of production operations is viewed as one to be "derived," after the other functions have developed their strategies and determined the appropriate direction for the business.

In all three of these stages, it is the responsibility of production operations management to improve itself in its attempts to move toward the next higher stage. Thus, moving from stage 1 to 2 or 2 to 3 does not require any change in the other functions or in how general management views production operations or conducts its own affairs.

In stage 4, referred to as *externally supportive,* the intent is to pursue a manufacturing-based competitive advantage. This stage is different in kind from the first three stages in that it requires the other functions and general management to interact with production operations in an effective, ongoing manner. Actions by production operations, such as anticipating the potential of new manufacturing technologies before they are required, providing input to and influence on marketing and R&D, and developing long-range plans to acquire capabilities in advance of their obvious need, are all parts of this stage.

In the previous sections of this chapter, the distinction between the traditional approach and the progressive or competitive advantage approach is primarily a distinction between stage 2 and stage 4. However, the intermediate stage 3 is an essential building block and evolutionary stage as an organization moves toward stage 4. The challenges are substantial in making a transition to stage 4. However, the prospects for competitive advantage and, ultimately, reward in the marketplace are also substantial. Thus, whether one is selecting an organization to go to work for, trying to define and establish a direction for one's own management activities in an organization, or simply choosing manufacturing firms in which to invest, the implication is clear: firms actively progressing into stage 4 are much more attractive than those not doing so.

LOOKING AHEAD

During the first half of the current decade, the field of production operations has undergone a veritable renaissance. Literally dozens of new ideas, technologies, and management approaches have emerged and begun to be applied, ranging from the focused factory to vendor base management, from Just-in-Time to quality control circles, from Flexible Manufacturing Systems (FMS) to computer-aided design/computer-aided manufacturing (CAD/CAM), and from group technology to robotics.

Much progress can be made by organizations that identify and pursue the two or three of these areas of most leverage to their situation. However, those organizations that want to realize the full competitive potential of production operations will need to apply several of these in an integrated, systematic fashion. That is what is required to become a stage 4 organization in this important function. Perhaps nowhere are the management challenges to accomplish such an objective as clearly discernible as in new product development/manufacturing startup activities.

While a number of specific organizational developments and technical procedures will be refined in the next few years for dealing with the important horizontal task of new product development, some common themes will be pursued by firms that seek a competitive advantage in this important area. One of these themes is the notion that many of the costs associated with product development are period costs (indirect and overhead costs) and that shortening cycle times can reduce substantially the total costs of new product development. That is, a product developed in two years rather than four years may in fact take only slightly more than half as many resources for its development.

A second theme is that shortening cycle times for new product development will have many of the same impacts as shortening the cycle time through use of Just-in-Time procedures. That is, waste will be eliminated. This includes waste of producing the wrong design, producing the design at the wrong time, letting the design sit idle for extended periods of time, and using too many steps to produce the design.

A third theme is that organizations must develop additional procedures and mechanisms for handling new product development tasks in advance of specific new product projects rather than simply trying to do everything on the fly while the new product is under way. That is, it's not simply a matter of managing a specific project more effectively; it requires putting procedures in place so that a stream of new product development projects can be managed more effectively. This suggests the need for consistent incremental improvement in the procedures themselves.

A final theme that is apparent is that improving the production operations inputs to new product development is not simply a task for production operations managers. It requires change on the part of others, both in how they operate their own functions in connection with that task and how they interact with production operations. Thus, unlike many aspects of structural and infrastructural tasks where production operations can be given primary responsibility for improvement, in new product development the improvement process itself requires substantial coordination among the functions.

The notion of horizontal tasks of strategic importance presents both a challenge and an opportunity to manufacturing firms in the United States. For more traditional manufacturers, it may simply be an expansion of the set of things that management must deal with, adapt to, and utilize if production operations are to become a competitive advantage in the future. For high-growth, high-technology areas, such horizontal tasks may be the single most important aspect of their production operations management. Their very success or failure may be directly tied to the effectiveness with which they handle production and operations involvement in these tasks.

REFERENCES

William J. Abernathy, Kim B. Clark, and Alan M. Kantrow. *Industrial Renaissance.* New York: Basic Books, 1983.

Kim B. Clark. "Toyo-Kogyo Co. Ltd. (A) and (B)," Harvard Case Services, Boston, 9-682-092, 9-682-093 (1982).

Philip B. Crosby. *Quality Is Free.* New York: Mentor Books, 1979.

Fred K. Foulkes. *Personnel Policies in Large Non-Union Companies.* Englewood Cliffs, N.J.: Prentice-Hall, 1980.

Andrew S. Grove. *High Output Management.* New York: Random House, 1983.

Robert H. Hayes and Steven C. Wheelwright. *Restoring Our Competitive Edge: Competing Through Manufacturing.* New York: John Wiley & Sons, 1984.

———. "Link Manufacturing Process and Product Life Cycles." *Harvard Business Review* (January–February 1979a), 133–140.

———. "The Dynamics of Process-Product Life Cycles." *Harvard Business Review* (March–April 1979b), 127–136.

Daniel Nelson. *Frederick W. Taylor and the Rise of Scientific Management.* Madison: University of Wisconsin Press, 1980.

Thomas J. Peters and Robert H. Waterman, Jr. *In Search of Excellence.* New York: Harper and Row, 1982.

Richard J. Schonberger. *Japanese Manufacturing Practices.* New York: Free Press, 1982.

Shigeo Shingo. *Study of Toyota Production System.* Tokyo: Japan Management Association, 1981.

Steven C. Wheelwright. "Restoring the Competitive Edge in U.S. Manufacturing." *California Management Review* (Spring 1985), 26–42.

———, and Robert H. Hayes. "Competing Through Manufacturing." *Harvard Business Review* (January–February 1985), 99–109.

SUGGESTED READINGS

Abernathy, William J., Kim B. Clark, and Alan M. Kantrow. *Industrial Renaissance.* New York: Basic Books, 1983. "Using the auto industry as a primary example, this book examines the way in which technology and innovative management approaches can lead to the dematurity of an industry and thus present a whole new array of opportunities and challenges for both countries and individual organizations."

Vollman, Thomas E., William L. Berry, and D. Clay Whybark. *Manufacturing Planning and Control Systems.* Homewood, Ill.: Richard D. Irwin, 1984. "Although written as a reference text for business school students interested in the topics of production planning and control, this is an extremely readable book that covers the basics of material requirements planning, shop floor control, capacity planning, and purchasing procurement and logistics."

Grove, Andrew S. *High Output Management.* New York: Random House, 1983. "This is written by the president of Intel, one of the nation's semiconductor manufacturing firms. Its focus is on how managers can increase their productivity and that of their organizations."

Hayes, Robert H., and Kim B. Clark (editors). *The Uneasy Alliance: Managing the Productivity-Technology Dilemma.* Boston: Harvard Business School Press, 1985. "This book provides a series of papers taken from a colloquium dealing with productivity and technology in the decade of the eighties. Several leading practitioners and academics present their views and supporting evidence as to the problems, challenges, and opportunities relating to technology and productivity."

Hayes, Robert H., and Steven C. Wheelwright. *Restoring Our Competitive Edge: Competing Through Manufacturing.* New York: John Wiley & Sons, 1984. "This book provides an overall philosophy for the role of manufacturing operations in achieving a competitive advantage. Particular emphasis is given to the role of capacity and facilities, vertical integration, and manufacturing technologies. In addition, leading Japanese and German approaches to manufacturing competitiveness are contrasted with traditional U.S. approaches and views."

Schmenner, Roger W. *Production and Operations Management: Concepts and Situations,* 2nd ed. Chicago: SRA, 1984. "Although written as an introductory text for business students, this is an extremely readable book that starts by analyzing the types of production processes encountered in a variety of industries and includes numerous illustrations of the issues and concepts applicable in managing that variety of processes."

Schonberger, Richard J. *Japanese Manufacturing Techniques: Nine Hidden Lessons in Simplicity.* New York: Free Press, 1982. "This book describes the essence of just-in-time or kanban manufacturing techniques as developed by Toyota but practiced by Kawasaki in their plant located in Lincoln, Nebraska. The book describes both the philosophy and some of the specifics of this uniquely effective Japanese approach to manufacturing operations management."

Skinner, Wickham. *Manufacturing — The Formidable Competitive Weapon.* New York: John Wiley & Sons, 1985. "This book outlines the potential role that the manufacturing function can play in the overall direction of a business organization. Particular emphasis is placed not only on the types of decisions through which manufacturing can have its greatest leverage but also on the role of individual managers in making that leverage become a reality."

CHAPTER 6

Logistics

Gayton Germane
Stanford University
Graduate School of Business

Logistics is basically a support activity. Business has borrowed the term from the military, where it refers to the supply and movement of personnel, equipment, and stores. In business management the term "logistics" is applied sometimes to a broad range of activities and sometimes to a relatively limited group of functions. Generally, it covers at least transportation and distribution activities. In this chapter, logistics will be discussed in its broad sense.

The chapter begins with an overview that points up the importance of coordination in the firm's logistics activities, notes several key opportunities that improved logistics offers, and relates logistics to other management functions. Next, we consider "Inventories and Customer Service." This describes various inventory systems and service patterns used to meet different costs and customer needs. The section "Location Analysis and Planning" reviews basic concepts, gives industry relocation examples, and describes some methods for selection of plant locations and distribution area boundaries. Several logistics planning computer applications are discussed, and questions are suggested for review of logistics plans and opportunities. The section "Purchasing, Transportation, and Warehousing" considers — from a manager's viewpoint — the role and some of the features of these three logistics function. "Integrated Logistics Systems" describes the possibilities of increased efficiency that coordination can provide, and discusses the collection and analysis of the necessary information and the step-by-step development of an integrated system. The final section outlines some future changes that will affect logistics and the opportunities for management they present.

OVERVIEW

Logistics can be defined as the *sum of physical supply and physical distribution*. Physical supply includes raw material and supply   181 sources, their planning, development, movement, storage and management. Physical distribution deals with a processed or manufactured product and encompasses the planning, control, and sometimes operation of handling storage, transportation, and delivery to the customers.

Corporate officers, representing one or more logistics activities, are generally found in firms whose delivered costs for their products include a substantial portion of transportation and warehousing expense. Thus, a title such as Vice President for Logistics, or Traffic, Transportation, Distribution, Purchasing, Materials Management, or Raw Materials, is common in the steel, grain and milling, cement, forest products, basic chemical, energy, and similar industries.

In many firms, "logistics area" titles seem to be related to functions that were identified early in the company's existence as opportunities for saving money that required specialized knowledge and experience. This could explain the large number of titles: Vice President for Transportation, or for Traffic, or for Distribution, or some combination of two of those terms. Business titles including the word "logistics" are unusual and probably represent the recognition of a need for coordination not identified in earlier years.

Coordination

Coordination is a fundamental element in logistics for two major reasons: (1) logistics decisions often involve trade-offs among conflicting objectives within or among the organizations's parts, and (2) logistics considerations can have an important influence on the strategic planning of acquisitions, relocation, expansion, diversification, the introduction of new products, and so forth.

Conflicting objectives: International Harvester (IH). A number of years ago, IH's design group gave new emphasis to designing the best possible equipment. This resulted in many new or redesigned parts for the new models of many trucks and types of farm equipment introduced each year. The consequences included a skyrocketing increase in the number of different parts to be stocked in the distribution centers, greatly increased requirements for warehouse space, and a spectacular rise in dollars invested in spare parts. The resulting costs were unsupportable for the product lines concerned.

Strategic plans: Raytheon Corporation. Some years ago, Raytheon was plagued with slow customer service and high inventory costs on its high-value electronic products sold through about 700 franchised distributors across the United States. Nearly 90 percent of these products were manufactured in the state of Massachusetts, and 60 to

70 percent of the shipments weighed less than fifty pounds. All needed fast and accurate handling. Field warehouses were maintained at six different locations in the country to speed service to customers. Under a new operating plan, a single warehouse for distributor products was established in Massachusetts, and the other Raytheon distributor products warehouses in the United States were closed. Electronic order transmission and processing were adopted, and all shipments were made by air. As a result, service was greatly speeded up, total inventories dropped impressively, and cost-of-service per order was sharply reduced. The new system was called Unimarket, and the distribution point was called Unicenter. The innovation was a great success.

As the Raytheon Corporation continued to grow, an expansion strategy based on acquisition was adopted. Plants were acquired on the West Coast and elsewhere in the United States. All of these sources shipped by air to the Unicenter for distribution. In the meantime, the founder of the Unicenter had been replaced by an executive with no prior logistics experience. The new man inherited a high-volume distribution system with a spectacular record of performance. But costs began to rise rapidly and customer service slowed dramatically. The new head of the Unicenter did not recognize the underlying cause of his problems — a conflict of strategies. Centralized distribution worked wonders when nearly all manufacturing facilities were nearby. When the strategy of expansion by acquisition was adopted, it resulted in manufacturing operations scattered across the nation. As a result, the Unicenter distribution system became very expensive in both cost and time.

The failure to anticipate this need for coordination of expansion strategy and distribution strategy led to serious profit problems. Adjustment of the distribution system was necessary to fit the new pattern of manufacturing locations and the continued diversification of sources by the Raytheon Corporation.

Opportunities

In many organizations, logistics system improvements can offer great opportunities. These include the following.

Tremendous leverage on profits.   For example, at a major grocery chain, the profit margin was less than 1 percent on sales. Thus, a dollar saved in logistics (purchasing, transportation, warehousing, etc.) contributed more to profits than $100 in extra sales. What's the leverage in your company?

A "system" point of view.   Many companies are organized on functional or departmental lines, and therefore improvements or trade-offs that cut across these lines frequently have not been identified. It often takes a "system" point of view, as in logistics, to recognize interdepartmental trade-offs.

Long-lived advantage. A logistics innovation takes months of development. It can't be matched by a rival overnight, like a price cut. Once the improved logistics system is in place, a company can obtain a big lead over rivals and, if it continues to improve, can stay ahead.

Increased market share. Logistics improvements resulting in cost and/or service advantage can often produce a larger and very profitable market share. A further substantial market expansion can also be realized *after* the service improvement, or cost-based price reduction, is introduced. The economies of scale resulting from the increased volume add to the initial advantage. Learning curve productivity gains may enhance the cost or productivity advantage and make it difficult for rivals to catch up — even if they ultimately adopt the innovation.

Customer loyalty. When a logistics system is built into a customer's supply operation, there is more resistance to competition. The customer is reluctant to change suppliers when it involves replacing the computerized inventory management, special warehousing, faster service, or order processing, and the like, that the innovation provides. In such cases, a customer can't afford to switch suppliers because some other company is offering special price reductions from time to time.

Relation of Logistics to Other Management Functions

Because logistics is a coordinating activity, it is important to consider its interface with production, marketing, finance, and accounting. This will help identify opportunities for system improvements in the enterprise.

Production. Here logistics is on both sides of the manufacturing activity. Logistics purchases, stores, manages, and delivers the raw materials or parts for production. Getting the right items for production to the right places at the right times, at minimum overall cost is a logistics role. On the other hand, establishing the requirements and the timing for those services is generally considered part of production planning and scheduling. After the production process is completed, logistics handles the movement and storage of the finished goods until they are ready for shipment to the initial customers — and then plans, controls, or operates the delivery services. Thus, production is like the meat in a sandwich, between two slices of bread, called logistics. In relation to production, logistics is clearly a support and coordinating activity.

Marketing. In this case, logistics is a supplier or distributor of Finished Goods to points of sale or to the customers. It is in this connection that many people think of logistics as physical distribution. Marketing creates or stimulates demand and generates the customer orders. Logistics provides the management and physical services required to deliver the product. This may include inventory planning, warehousing and control of Finished Goods, as well as the physical movement or arrangements for transport of the products.

Finance. If we think of Finance as providing and managing the money and credit resources required by the firm, we can see an analogy in the role of logistics, which provides the physical materials and manages product deliveries for the firm.

Accounting. This management function measures, records, and interprets the activities of the firm in numerical terms, often expressed in dollars and cents. Thus, there is an accounting activity in connection with virtually every business activity — including logistics. In this case, logistics is among the users of accounting services to measure, record, and interpret the various activities being undertaken or considered in the logistics phases of the enterprise.

INVENTORIES AND CUSTOMER SERVICE

Varied Patterns

Large firms often have many thousands of items in their inventories. Typically, these items vary widely in unit cost and in the numbers used per year. Thus, different inventory policies are needed for these various categories of items if the firm is to provide reasonable service at reasonable cost. Both unit cost and frequency of need can have a dramatic impact on inventory policy. Below are three examples of contrasting inventory policies, each designed to fit the particular needs of the organization concerned.

AMDAHL computers. AMDAHL is famous for its large-capacity, high-speed computers. These computers employ very large logic chips that increase processing speed. These superchips are mounted on multichip carriers. As an element of service, in its competition with IBM and others, AMDAHL guarantees that none of its computers will be down for lack of parts for more than two hours. Since AMDAHL computers are in use in many major cities, this guarantee requires fast service at any hour of the day or night. Each service representative's carrying case of plug-in chip carriers is valued at over $200,000. Thus, to keep the total chip inventory investment within reasonable limits, a delivery system for service men has been developed involving around-the-clock response, chartered aircraft, hotline international communication links, and records of locations of every plug-in chip carrier. The cost of the system is justified by the reduction in the investment that would otherwise be needed for additional super chips to meet customer service requirements.

A large truck manufacturer. This firm maintains at least three levels of inventory availability for its motorized equipment products. Many commonly used parts are stocked by both dealers and service centers. Less frequently used parts, particularly if they are high cost, are carried at regional parts depots, but not by dealers and service centers. Finally, some parts that are rarely needed are stocked only at the central parts depot.

An electronic repair shop. This enterprise is at the other end of the spectrum from the AMDAHL inventory policy example. Expensive or low usage items are ordered from local distributors as needed. Immediate service is almost never required. The repair shop stores many small, frequently used items in drawers or bins. These parts are the working inventory. In addition to the loose items in each bin, there is normally a supply of the item — the reserve stock — in a plastic bag in the bin. The bag also contains an already completed order form. The instructions are to use the loose items first, and, when the plastic bag must be opened, turn in the order form for mailing to the supplier. The cost of the items is so low and the usage is so limited and irregular that more elaborate means of inventory control and resupply are just not worth the expense.

The 80/20 Curve

This curve, observed in various surveys, reflects the fact that if inventory items are arrayed by frequency of use and also by unit cost, about 20 percent of the items represent about 80 percent of the total inventory value, and 80 percent of the items collectively represent about 20 percent of that value. While there is no magic in these particular proportions, they do indicate that any cost-effective inventory policy must direct most of the inventory management attention to a small proportion of the stock and give much less attention (probably using different control systems) to other categories of the inventory stocks. It is important for any company to consider whether one, two, three, or more categories of inventory should be established to provide the most cost-effective results, or the lowest overall cost for inventory that will meet the stated availability requirements. This classification of inventory items or stock keeping units (SKUs) into cost and activity categories is also referred to as "ABC Analysis," indicating three or more groups justifying separate treatment.

Inventory Dynamics

To describe the interrelations among some of the factors affecting inventory decisions, we will look at some diagrams. Proceeding from the simple to the more complex, they provide a foundation for later discussion of different inventory policies.

Points 1A and 1B in Figure 6.1 are the Reorder Points on their respective graphs. They are the inventory levels at which an order for more inventory items should be placed in order to have the new supply on hand by (or before) the time the present supply is used up. Note that the Reorder Point is a signal for action and does not necessarily determine the quantity to be ordered. In these two examples, we assume the same reorder quantities.

Points 2A and 2B show the inventory levels remaining just as the new supply arrives. In Example A, the remaining inventory is zero, a perfect match as inventory is replenished by the end of the day. The end of the day/start of the day inventory status is shown by the inventory quantity measured from the base to the top of line 3A. This is the inventory level just after the stock has been replenished.

In Example B, there was a reduced rate of inventory usage compared with Example A. As a result, the diagonal line showing the rate of inventory consumption (or for any point on the line, the remaining inventory on hand) is different in Example A and Example B. The steeper slope (faster usage rate) of the line in Example A resulted in

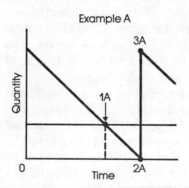
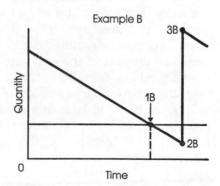

Figure 6.1

all of the inventory being consumed just as the new shipment arrived. In Example B, the lower slope of the inventory line (slower usage) resulted in some inventory remaining when the new shipment arrived. As a consequence, the total inventory on hand after the new shipment arrived (see 3A and 3B) is greater in Example B than in Example A, and by just the amount of the "leftover" inventory in Example B.

Note that in examples A and B the *different* rates of inventory consumption are indicated by the different slopes of the inventory-on-hand lines in the two diagrams. In both examples the constant rates of consumption are shown by the fact that the sloping lines are straight. This constant rate assumption is not always realistic. For example, if there is a significant "learning curve" effect, as in the construction of a newly designed airplane, the inventory usage rate may be much lower per day early in the production period than it is later on, as worker expertise and production process coordination improve. These improvements could produce a convex line for inventory on hand, as illustrated in Example C. Obviously, the latest or the forecast rate of consumption should then be used in determining the reorder point date and/or the reorder quantity to prepare for the ensuing period.

A similar inventory usage effect may occur in some organizations because of customer ordering practices, or internal production quotas. These factors may contribute to a surge in production near the end of a month. This could result in a usage curve that was somewhat flatter than that in Example C (Figure 6.2), near the midperiod, and which fell even more steeply near the end of the period — as the production rate was increased to reach the "bonus pay" output for the month.

In Example C (Figure 6.2), the diagram also illustrates an out-of-stock situation (2C) at the end of the period. Although the new order was placed when inventory reached the regular reorder point (1C), the higher-than-expected rate of consumption would use all of the remaining inventory before the end of the period. Thus, no finished goods would be produced during the time interval marked 4C if the item(s) out of stock were required for completion of the finished goods. The projected amount of the shortage would be indicated by the length of the vertical line from 2C to the zero base line of the diagram.

A changeover to a new model of a product, or slackening of customer orders, could result in a slower rate of production and a reduced rate of inventory consumption near the end of a period. This is illustrated in Example D (Figure 6.3). The normal reorder point is indicated by 1D and the inventory remaining at the end of the period is marked by 2D. The replenished supply adds the ordered quantity to the amount marked 2D and is shown on the line from the base to 3D.

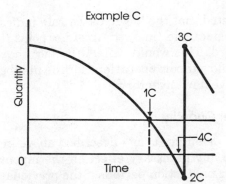

Figure 6.2

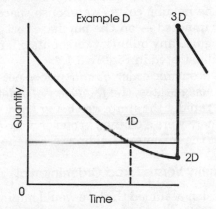

Figure 6.3

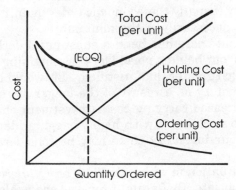

Figure 6.4

If it is expected that the lower usage rate indicated at 2D will continue for a considerable time, the reorder point (level) might be adjusted downward. This would reflect the fact that now a smaller reserve stock would support operations for the number of days needed to order and receive new inventory.

Economic Order Quantity

The changes in inventory usage described above in examples C and D would not have any necessary effect on the inventory quantity to be ordered for later production periods if the previous level of usage were expected to be restored. This appropriate order quantity, called the economic order quantity (EOQ), should be determined by considering the effect of the cost of ordering (paperwork, transportation and handling) compared with the holding costs (warehouse space expenses, plus interest — paid or imputed — on the purchase cost). The purchase cost used should recognize any quantity discounts offered on the products. The trade-off is illustrated in Figure 6.4.

Although the economic order *quantity* does not change with different but constant usage rates, the *frequency* of ordering would vary depending on how rapidly the item was being used. However, the EOQ could change if there were a change in one or more of the factors, noted above, that affect the inventory holding cost or the ordering cost.

Fixed Order Quantity Versus Fixed Order Interval

The above discussion assumed that we would minimize inventory costs by ordering the EOQ as often as necessary. However, to cover large, unexpected increases in consumption on particular items, we may wish to increase our reorder point inventory level by some percentage to serve as a safety stock. Under any of the above circumstances, a fixed reorder quantity (usually the economic order quantity) system should be safe, but not necessarily at the minimum.

If we find that there has been a substantial decline in the usage rate for an item, our holding period for the remaining inventory of that item may be much greater than justified. This would increase our costs per unit of inventory as a result of the longer storage period (space charge) and increased carrying costs (investment charge). If we have many expensive stock items with highly irregular demand (usage), we may find that our inventory costs may be considerably higher than necessary.

This is the situation in which the *fixed order interval* inventory policy seems appropriate. By frequent reviews one is alerted to *overstock* problems that might have gone unnoticed for weeks or months waiting for a reorder point cue from a fixed order quantity system. The possible earlier notice from a fixed order interval system gives us a chance to consider inventory sell-off, or return to vendor, at an early date, with the consequent elimination of potential unnecessary holding costs. Similarly, if the fixed order interval review shows rapid *depletion* of inventory for some items, we can increase the order quantity to avoid a stock out.

As a general rule, the fixed order quantity system works best with "steady state" or "no big surprises" inventory usage for particular items. Fixed order interval inventory systems provide better protection, in some ways, against large and unforeseen swings in item usage.

Smooth-Flow Inventory Scheduling

The patterns of inventory supply and usage which we have discussed thus far all concern *batch flow*. In this process, there is a separate order and a separate shipment for each "batch." Obviously, this one-order, one-shipment pattern is not the only way inventory can be scheduled.

Another pattern is called *smooth flow*. When an item is used regularly, it may be desirable to have multiple deliveries, over time, to fulfill a single order. This procedure can reduce ordering costs (one order instead of several), and multiple shipments of smaller lots can reduce inventory investment and space requirements of both the supplier and the user. There is a further advantage that with smooth flow inventory scheduling, delivery frequency or shipment quantities may be changed to meet shifts in user requirements as volume changes. These advantages are not available with large, individual-order shipments of perhaps once a month or less often.

The contrast in inventory between batch flow and smooth flow patterns can be illustrated by a production operation consuming a truckload of a particular item every working day. With batch flow, six truckloads might be delivered early every Monday morning, or perhaps it would be twenty-four loads, once every fourth week. Of course, each delivery would be on a separate order. Using smooth flow, a load might be delivered every working day on an order covering a two- or three-month supply. The potential results for a weekly batch flow and a daily smooth flow are shown in Figure 6.5. The warehouse space for inventory would need to be sized to the maximum total inventory, marked in the figure with an asterisk (*).

In recent years, the Japanese supply system called Just-in-Time, or *kanban,* has received a great deal of attention. It includes frequent (at least daily) deliveries of parts or supplies. This reduces working

		Mon.	Tues.	Wed.	Thurs.	Fri.	Sat.	Average
BATCH FLOW	Working Inventory	6	5	4	3	2	1	3.5
	Safety Stock[a]	2	2	2	2	2	2	2
	Total Inventory	8*	7	6	5	4	3	5.5
SMOOTH FLOW	Working Inventory	1	1	1	1	1	1	1
	Safety Stock[b]	1	1	1	1	1	1	1
	Total Inventory	2*	2	2	2	2	2	2

[a]Safety Stock of one-third of an order, or two days, on individual weekly orders.
[b]Safety of one full day's supply, with daily delivery.

Figure 6.5

inventories, as illustrated in the smooth flow example shown above. However, the Just-in-Time system also places responsibility on the supplier for "no defects," as well as responsibility for scheduled delivery of exactly the right quantity with "no excuses." Thus, safety stock, and production-line-float,[1] can be eliminated. To make near-perfect coordination feasible, suppliers are encouraged or even required to locate plants very close to the customer's production line. These and other coordination activities in planning and production dramatically reduce in-process inventory, improve product quality, reduce need for inspection, and increase salable output per day.

At least some elements of Just-in-Time management have also been used in U.S. enterprises for many years. For example, in 1952, the Somerville, Massachusetts, plant of the Ford Motor Company was relying on the Boston & Maine Railroad to deliver, early each morning, nearly all of the parts to be used that day on the automobile assembly line.

Customer Service

When suppliers and users are not coordinated by a smooth flow or a Just-in-Time service arrangement, the appropriate customer service level can be a generalized problem for the supplier. A review involves consideration of the available options, the costs, and the benefits associated with various levels of customer service. The options include changes in inventory safety stock and other methods of improving customer service. Some other methods of customer service were illustrated earlier with examples about AMDAHL computer superchips and the truck manufacturer's regional parts depots. Here the discussion will be limited to inventory adjustments as a means of providing the appropriate level of customer service.

Since a variation in demand (sales) creates much of the problem, it is important to consider the possible causes of that variation. For example, variation in demand might result from one or more of the following:

1. Random pattern in orders — suggesting no particular cause

2. Seasonal variation — as in sales of winter or summer sports equipment

3. Business cycle phase — as it affects machinery for manufacturing

4. Long-run trend — as in sales of food items generally.

5. Specific events or dates — as in camera film sales and major holidays

Variations resulting from items 2 through 5 can be dealt with using the techniques of business cycle analysis, company data, and a calendar. A good text on business cycles or economic forecasting will describe the techniques to be applied. Item 1, random pattern, may be affected by items 2 through 5, but the basic element is the chance nature of the variation. Thus, for item 1 the principal reliance will be on application of probability normal distribution concepts to deal with the random aspect of the variation.

The *normal distribution* is a bell-shaped curve representing the frequency and dispersion of numerous random cases of the same kind of activity or event. For example, a graph of the probabilities of rolling values of from 2 through 12, with a pair of true dice, would be a "stair step" approximation of a normal distribution curve. Figure 6.6 is a dia-

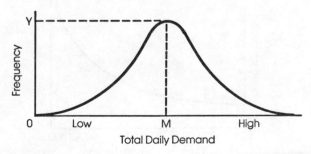

Figure 6.6

gram of a smoothed normal distribution. To provide reliability and a smooth curve, assume that this distribution represents the experience over a considerable period of time. Unless there are specific reasons to object, this set of data will be considered a reliable indicator of the chance distribution of total daily demand that can be expected in the near future. The distance O to M along the base represents the total demand for the average (mean) day. The distance O to Y, on the vertical axis, shows the frequency, or number of times, the mean total daily demand was encountered.

Note how rapidly the curve slopes down from the highest point. This shows that very small and very large total daily demands are rare events. If the firm carried inventory to provide a 50 percent customer service level, it would have enough stock in inventory to cover the total daily demand represented by the middle value (the mean) in the distribution. And, if there were a series of days each with a total demand greater than average, there would be a stock-out and some customers could be disappointed. However, if inventory were increased to cover larger than average total daily demand, the number of additional orders filled (read frequency scale) would drop rapidly, but the inventory requirements would increase steadily. It becomes a real diminishing-returns problem. This increase in inventory requirements, as customer service level is increased,[2] is shown in Figure 6.7.

If we think of inventory levels as cost and of customer service levels as benefit, it is clear that the cost/benefit ratio changes dramatically. In higher inventory levels, increased holding costs could completely eliminate profit. As a result, many organizations find that they cannot afford to rely on inventory size alone to meet competitive customer service levels. Thus, they seek other methods of improving customer service at lower cost.

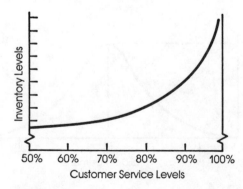

Figure 6.7

Stock-out costs vary with the customer's options and attitudes. Evaluation is very subjective, but particular situations can be modeled to estimate the high, low, and, most likely, cost of the inventory needed to maintain particular customer service levels. (See Coyle and Bardi, *The Management of Business Logistics,* chap. 4.)

LOCATION ANALYSIS AND PLANNING

The location of various kinds of economic activity was explained by J. H. von Thunen in his book *Der isolierte Staat* (The Isolated State) published in the 1840s. He assumed a level, uniform area of equal fertility throughout and reasoned that transportation costs would force the production of low-value items near the center (market) of the area, and that items of higher value per pound could be produced or grown at further distances from the market center. This was an early recognition of the concept that production cost plus transport cost cannot exceed market value (price), or the production of that item will be unprofitable.

Much later, another German author, Alfred Weber, extended von Thunen's ideas by considering the effect of localized availability of some materials versus ubiquitous materials, and of pure materials versus weight-losing (during processing) materials. With these more realistic conditions he concluded that pure materials available everywhere would have no special production point, while products made from localized, weight-losing materials could be produced most cheaply at their various material origin points. As you can see, various combinations of material availability and weight loss would provide a variety of answers to the economic location of an enterprise. Weber then extended the analysis to consider two different materials from separate origins, both used in making a product that was sold at a still different point. A physical model of this analysis is easily imagined. Three cords are tied together at a central knot. Two cords lead to raw materials, and the third cord leads to a market. The production point is at the knot. The three cords form a figure resembling a capital *Y,* and the weighted cords overhang the rim of a smooth, round table. As the relative weights on each cord change, the location of the knot (the most economical product point) is shifted on the table (the land surface).

The most famous work on location analysis in recent years is *The Location of Economic Activity* by Edgar M. Hoover. This comprehensive study expands the theoretical analysis to deal with the modern world by (for example) including *tapered rates* (rates that increase by declining amounts as the distance increases) and *transit privileges* (treatment of a stopover for storage or processing as if there were a continuous trip from origin, through the processing point, to the market).

Important Location Factors

Obviously, the list of factors will be different for different industries, but transportation, labor, materials, and utilities traditionally have been employed. A more extensive set of industrial site selection factors is as follows:[3]

1. Environmental factors
   a. Water supply
   b. Ecological considerations
   c. Air pollution control considerations
   d. Waste water disposal
   e. Solid waste disposal

2. Proximity to good transportation network system

3. Abundant labor supply

4. Availability of suitable land

5. Proximity to market

6. Favorable local and state tax structure

7. Favorable leasing and/or financing

8. Proximity to related industry

9. Community profile

10. Existence of buildings on site

11. Approvals and reviews required

While nearly all the headings above include several subheadings (omitted here), it is interesting to note that "environmental factors," with five *major* categories listed, was not even mentioned among the "traditional" location factors. This is an indication of changing public concerns about plant locations.

Two examples of major corporate moves illustrate that, like links in a chain, any factor in a move can be critical if it is not properly handled.

Jell-O: Replacing four plants with one.   The Jell-O division of the General Foods Corporation planned to construct a new plant in Dover, Delaware, to replace four older plants in nearby states and cities. To shorten the changeover time, the planning and construction process was expedited. This included starting new plant construction before some of the new production machinery had been selected. Three product-supply possibilities were studied: (1) Produce sufficient products of each type to meet market requirements until the new plant comes on line. When this reserve stock is on hand, close the old plants. (2) Continue production at the four old plants until the new plant is running smoothly. (3) Where possible, move one product production line at a time to the new plant while keeping the rest of the particular old plant in operation. Each of these options had special problems and advantages. Because of the wide variety of products, market supply, and production equipment problems, management used each of the options at least once during the construction and startup of the new plant and its diversified product lines. It was a risky operation no matter what choices were made, and the multimethod "cut-to-fit" logistics strategy was successful.

Nabisco: The weekend headquarters move. When Nabisco, Inc., the giant bakery products company, moved its corporate headquarters from a downtown New York skyscraper to a New Jersey office park, the vice president for traffic was put in charge of the operation. He installed sample office modules in the cafeteria at the New York headquarters so that everyone could see and try the various layouts proposed. Then he distributed comment sheets as ballots for voting on the different models and making suggestions for improvement. The comment sheets provided several surprises, so the plans for modules were modified to fit the preferences and ideas expressed. The physical move was planned in great detail. On a Friday afternoon, all of the headquarters staff not involved in the "logistics exercise" left as usual, and on Monday morning they all arrived for work at the new building. Each person received written instructions on his or her location in the new headquarters and found everything in place: files, books, pictures, throw rugs, lamps, and so forth. Desk and file cabinet contents were as left on Friday. Over the weekend, the vice-president for traffic and his staff had supervised a carefully planned and scheduled move — floor by floor — from the old building to the new headquarters. This move involved convoys of moving vans (so no vans would get lost), detailed timetables, and close supervision. The advance planning, briefings, and the moving-day communications and control systems resembled that of a large-scale military operation: it had to be done fast, on schedule, and right the first time. The operation was a complete success.

Methods of Logistics Analysis

In this section, we will consider several examples of logistics analysis ranging from simple arithmetic or graphic methods to some computerized approaches.

Boundary line calculation. The dividing line between the delivery territories of rival firms is normally at the points where their delivered costs are equal. As an example, imagine two firms with factories 100 miles apart. The firms' production and transportation costs are the same. In these circumstances, the boundary line is likely to fall halfway between the two factories — 50 miles from each — because if either advances farther his costs will be increased, and his competitor's costs reduced, by the changes in transport distance. Assume further that transport cost was originally 10 cents a mile from each plant, but later Firm A is able to negotiate a rate of only 8 cents a mile. Now, where will the boundary line be? At the midpoint (50 miles) Firm A will have saved 2 cents a mile for each of the 50 miles, or $1.00 in total transport costs. This saving can be "invested" in market penetration of Firm B market territory. However, every mile that A penetrates into former B territory costs A 8 cents *and* also saves B 10 cents. Thus, the effective cost to A is 18 cents a mile to go beyond the former boundary. Since A now has a margin of advantage of $1.00, or 100 cents, at the old boundary, the effective cost of 18 cents a mile beyond that point would use up the margin of advantage in 5.56 miles ($100/18 = 5.56$). Thus the new equal delivered cost boundary line would be 55.56 miles from A and 44.44 miles from B. The basic concept is that the "invader" can use his accumulated advantage, up to the old boundary, to pay his own per-mile costs and match his rival's per-mile savings for every mile of new market territory acquired. Although competition is rarely so simple, this analysis illustrates some of the important considerations in market boundary determination.

Graphic boundary determination. This method assumes that transportation costs per mile are the same, or close to it, from each of the shipping points. The method is particularly useful when considering the delivery boundaries for warehouses or distribution centers of the same organization. The boundary would fall at the halfway point between the two centers concerned. This can be determined by measuring along a straight line between the points — call them *A* and *B*. Draw arcs from *A* and *B* of more than half the distance toward the other point. A line drawn through the intersections of the two arcs will be at a right angle to the line joining *A* and *B* and halfway between them. Extensions of these right-angle lines can be used to estimate quickly territorial boundaries for several proposed warehouses, or changes in distribution areas if a warehouse is added or deleted from a system. In Figure 6.8, the method has been used to indicate the approximate market or distribution boundaries among five points: Seattle (SEA), San Francisco (SFO), Los Angeles (LAX), Denver (DEN), and Chicago (CHI). The heavy, short bars mark the halfway points on the warehouse-to-warehouse lines. The dotted lines show the approximate boundaries of distribution territories that would be generated by this method.

On examination, if you think the Denver territory may be too large, try adding another distribution point to the pattern or deleting Denver and substituting two new distribution points.

Center-of-gravity location method. This method takes its name from the process of weighting the quantities and distances for various inbound and outbound items so that the aggregate of the transportation ton/miles, or dollars for transport, is at a minimum. To accomplish this, an arbitrary location is selected from which weight/distance, or transport cost, values are calculated. The results from north, south, east, and west provide the basis for adjusting the arbitrary location to a balance point location. There are some serious theoretical problems that should be understood before applying the center-of-gravity method. Consult a good text on logistics for a discussion.

Computerized analysis and planning. Several examples of logistics analysis using computers are described below. They are computer simulation for distribution planning, linear programming and a new plant location, three methods of routing, and two project scheduling systems.

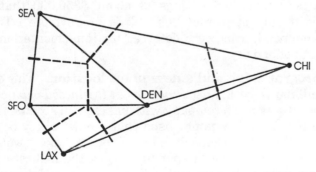

Figure 6.8

Computer simulation for distribution planning. William R. Foltz, the new senior vice-president for distribution for Tri-Valley Growers, was facing the first harvest season since he had joined the organization. Tri-Valley was a growers' cooperative on the West Coast with annual sales of about $700 million, and is currently the largest fruit and vegetable canner in California. The firm used about thirty public warehouses to hold its regional inventories throughout the country. This permitted prompt delivery of customer orders, and with public warehouses, Tri-Valley could change warehouse space or locations on short notice. Foltz believed that distribution efficiency could be improved. A team of students at the Stanford Graduate School of Business proposed to develop a computer program and make an analysis of the warehouse inventory and location problems.

After considerable discussion, the students chose to develop a simulation program rather than an optimizing program. There were several reasons for this choice: (1) With a simulation program, the user understood what change produced a particular result. (2) A simulation program required less computer capacity and produced answers more quickly than linear programming. (3) Easily explained recommendations (the how and why for particular cases) would be valuable in discussing suggested changes with the board of directors. Prompt answers could be given for "What if . . . ?" questions by taking a portable computer terminal to the board meeting room.

The results of the student team's efforts were impressive. For the three major sales areas — Midwest, Metropolitan (Eastern Central), and Northeast — the anticipated savings were over $1.5 million a year, or about 18 percent of the current distribution costs. Management reviewed and accepted these calculations, but the end of the canning period was near. Distribution would soon be necessary, and the firm had neither the time nor the trained personnel available to carry out all of the changes recommended. However, Mr. Foltz quickly went through the plans and identified savings of about $350,000 that could be achieved with only "stop orders" ("Don't do . . . anymore"). The balance of the recommendations were deferred for implementation after the annual peak of activity.

Linear programming and a new plant location. This example is from a well-known book, *Case Problems in Business Logistics*,[4] and describes the situation of a company with bakeries in six cities in the San Francisco Bay area. It was proposed that a new bakery be located in San Jose, near the south end of the bay. This new bakery would provide more than enough capacity to permit closing the highest-cost bakery in the chain, located farther south, in Santa Cruz. How would distribution costs, as well as total costs, be affected by the proposed changes? A computerized linear programming analysis indicated that production costs, delivery costs, and total operating costs would all be reduced by the proposed change.

However, this case also illustrates the importance of asking a variety of questions. Further analysis showed that the company's existing bakery capacity was adequate to meet the expected needs for the next several years — even if the Santa Cruz bakery were closed. The increase in distribution costs produced by this closing would be less than the net added costs (annual financing costs not offset by various savings) of the proposed new bakery in San Jose. Thus, an even better solution than that offered by the new bakery appeared to be to close the Santa Cruz plant, revise production and delivery patterns for the remaining five bakeries, and postpone action on a San Jose plant until its *additional capacity* was required.

Three methods of optimum routing.   This can be calculated using any appropriate variable, such as time, distance, or cost. The Simplex Linear programming technique[5] provides a specific, provable, optimum solution. A difficulty is that, as the number of points to be served increases, the number of possible routes to link all of those points increases. The increase in possible routes is expressed by n factorial (*n!*) of the number of points to be connected. Thus, for five points there would be $1 \times 2 \times 3 \times 4 \times 5 = 120$ possible routes. For six, the total is $6 \times 120 = 720$ possible routes; for ten it is 3,628,800. Clearly, this progression makes the solution of large routing problems expensive in terms of computer time.

Another approach to the routing problem is called LOCKSET. It has received major impetus in this country from the work of Professor Leonard W. Schruben.[6] Using this approach, a logical-feasible solution is obtained with relatively few calculations. At present, it cannot be demonstrated to be an optimum solution except by comparing the LOCKSET answer to the one arrived at by linear programming. However, Professor Schruben has not encountered any case in which the LOCKSET solution was not an optimum.

The method takes its name from the fact that a particular route segment option is tested only once and is either "*locked* into, or out of, the route *set*." The underlying assumption is that, in building a route, if the points are connected in the order of the distance saved, the most efficient total route will be developed. The distance (or time, cost, etc.) saved is measured by making triangles of pairs of points and the origin. The total distance (or time, cost, etc.) around the triangle is compared with that involved if each of the two points is connected to the origin by a shuttle route. The difference between the triangle route and the sum of the two shuttle routes is called the distance-saved coefficient (DSC), and the triangle-route pairs of points are listed in order of their DSC. These pairs of points are then examined in order of decreasing DSC, and, using logical rules, some are selected to build a route that efficiently serves all of the points from a given origin.

The process is easily programmed for computer use and runs very quickly. As an illustration of the calculation advantage, in a particular problem the route involved seventeen separate points to be served. Using the array of pairs of points in DSC order, and the selection rules, only eleven pairs of points were examined before the full route was complete. A linear programming solution would generally take a great many more steps. Professor Charles Bonini has estimated that LOCK-SET is likely to be more efficient than linear programming when there are more than five points to be served on a route.

An important advance in mathematical optimizing methods was announced in late 1984. It is called the *Karmarkar technique,* after its inventor, Dr. Narendra Karmarkar of Bell Laboratories. Major firms, such as Exxon, AT&T, and American Airlines, are interested in the Karmarkar technique because it makes a potentially spectacular reduction in the time and steps required to find an optimum solution to huge problems of 15,000 variables or more. The method can be described in terms of a giant mathematical surface with a vast number of geometrical panels. Imagine this as an immense soccer ball. At some corner of some panel on that surface there is a "best answer." The linear programming solution would check every angle of every panel and select a path (a seam on the soccer ball) to a better solution. Many, many trials later, moving across the surface, the linear programming method would reach the "best" solution. In the Karmarkar technique, the initial position would be from a point inside the soccer ball. Obviously, many locations on the surface panel are close and only one move away. After each move, the surface of the soccer ball would be warped (as if partly deflated and shaped) to reflect the intermediate answer and effectively bring the "best" answer closer.

Two project scheduling systems. For managing complex operations, two different scheduling techniques have been developed. They are the critical path method (CPM) and the program evaluation and review technique (PERT). CPM is widely used in the construction industry, and PERT has found many applications in manufacturing and assembly projects. Both CPM and PERT use the basic concept of a diagram of various events and activities arranged in time-sequence order. The start or completion events are usually shown as nodes or points.

They are connected by lines representing the processes involved in progressing from one event to the next. The great advantage of CPM and PERT lies in providing quick computer update of changing conditions or estimates, and in selecting — again, by computer — the current best "path" in time or cost through the maze of events and activities to the project completion. This is particularly important since in complex projects many schedule changes in elements of the project take place every day. Thousands of different parts or operations may be involved, and thousands of suppliers and subcontractors may be participating in the project. The mass of detail can be too great for speedy analysis by people. In the last decade differences between CPM and PERT have been reduced as each system was made more versatile. However, an important distinction remains. CPM concentrates on evaluating the time/cost needed to perform *processes* or activities, and PERT focuses on the time/cost to reach start or completion *events* in a project.

Conclusions and suggestions. In the preceding sections, several different techniques have been discussed, all aimed at determining best answers or optimum solutions. Before reaching into the "tool kit" of techniques for solutions, however, it is extremely important to review the problem and situation carefully and ask a good many questions. This can avoid wasted effort or right answers to the wrong problems. The steps below are suggested as guides for this review process.

1.*Review the problems or questions. Are the right questions being asked? Are the proper comparisons being made?* Recall the omissions in the bakery location case mentioned earlier as an example. *Are the real causes or effects identified?* Some years ago, Ideal Standard (France) was planning a new automated warehouse for bathroom fixtures. The new warehouse was to be very space-efficient and would store and retrieve toilet fixtures from several levels in the building — all at the push of a few buttons. The new facility was considered necessary because the existing warehouse was almost completely filled and was still not able to meet the market demands for products. Further inquiry led to the recognition that the market demand had not increased. The current high inventory was primarily due to the fact that the foundry was turning out colored fixtures almost exclusively. Because of the internal corporate accounting, the colored fixtures earned more profit for the foundry than white units. In the meantime, white washstands and toilets were in great demand and out of stock. The real problem was the corporate internal pricing system and not the existing warehouse. Unfortunately, many people had become so enthusiastic about the automated warehouse that the real problem had gone almost unnoticed. *Are the problems linked to other functions or activities?* The International Harvester design improvement program, mentioned earlier, was a case in point. The new designs for parts created very serious problems in space requirements and financing. The problems overwhelmed the expected advantages.

2. *What are the simplest methods that are suitable?* Added complexity, speed in performance, quality, accuracy, and capacity all cost money. Make sure that any added features pay their way.

3. *Are the assumptions and requirements:*

Realistic? Are the resources required at hand?

Necessary? How were the assumptions justified? How were the requirements established?

Cost/Effective? Is this the cheapest method for obtaining the benefit needed? What other options were considered?

Complete? Are all of the necessary data available? What are the critical elements (make-or-break features) of the plan?

4. *What are the potential results or conclusions on:*

Best/worse cases? Are their significance and probabilities understood? Are they clearly explained?

Sensitivity? What control do we have over the factors to which the results are most sensitive? Are these sensitive factors reasonably stable? Is their importance or stability changing?

A good example of this group of considerations was the investment of Sea/Land in a set of the world's largest and fastest container ships. They cruised at thirty-three knots and were powered by oil-fired steam boilers driving giant turbines. Soon after a fleet of six was in service, oil prices rose dramatically. The operators could no longer afford to run the ships at planned speeds, and the power systems were inefficient at low speeds. The ships had to be replaced.

PURCHASING, TRANSPORTATION, AND WAREHOUSING

Purchasing, transportation, and warehousing are closely related in terms of both their physical relationship and the management coordination they require. The logistics executive must consider the timing and quantity of items bought or supplied and is therefore often placed in charge of purchasing. Transportation to or from the warehouses, or directly from suppliers to plants, and delivery to customers are also part of the physical flow and require coordination with the other elements. Obviously, warehousing or storage must be planned and managed with consideration of purchasing, transportation, production, and sales. Thus, coordination of purchasing, transportation, and warehousing is vital to the enterprise.

Purchasing

Among the many functions performed in connection with purchasing, several stand out as particularly important. These are determining specifications, price and quantity possibilities, source selection, and monitoring vendor performance. Some of the basic price and quantity considerations were discussed earlier in connection with inventories and customer service. Therefore, the comments here will deal with the other three topics.

Determining specifications. Usually research and development, engineering, the design group, or some similar unit in the enterprise develops an item to be produced. The materials requirements and lists of parts or assemblies to be purchased are identified by the unit handling the design or product proposal. It is typically the responsibility of the purchasing department to see that the needed products are obtained and delivered in timely quantities to the proper locations. This involves considerable coordination with other groups in the firm. For example, should Purchasing buy the tubing already plated, or will that be done at the buyer's plant, or by a subcontractor? Within what temperature range must the switch work perfectly? Does the location of the item in the finished product make it so difficult to replace that a "long service life" component is worth a substantial premium in cost? The correct answers to these, and many related questions, are important if the right product is to be bought at the best price. Note that these price considerations are quite separate from quantity discounts.

Failure of the purchasing activity to perform properly can cost the buying firm a great deal of money in over-specification (and hence unduly costly items) or in failure of parts and components because of poor quality (but bargain price) through inadequate specifications. Sometimes it is difficult to be sure that the price and specifications are properly related.

I recall a staff meeting in the office of the Assistant Secretary of Defense for Supply and Logistics. The Director of Procurement was asked, "Did you explain to Senator _____ (who was running for re-election) about those eight items he was using as 'horrible examples' of procurement waste?" The director replied that he had explained things and that the senator understood that seven of the "ten-cent store" items he had purchased as comparisons wouldn't do the job even though they performed the same functions as the DOD-purchased items. The items in question were going into equipment for a fighter airplane and had to operate reliably in a low-temperature, high-altitude, high-gravity stress environment. The eighth item bought by DOD was too expensive because of the unnecessarily restrictive specifications applied to it.

On the other hand, purchasing can often assist the design group or manufacturing team by offering suggestions for alternate specifications or substitute components. This may take considerable technical expertise, but specialized purchasing staffs often have or can obtain such expertise. For example, some specialty metals salespeople have found their advice as "consultants" to be a major sales tool. Their technical expertise provides a realistic basis for choosing among suppliers when price, quality, and delivery are all substantially the same.

Some questions to keep in mind about specifications are these: *What are the absolutely essential features, qualities, and performance?* Anything else should meet some cost-effectiveness test. *How much detail is enough?* The more complex the specifications, the fewer bidders are likely to be interested, and the more the item is likely to cost. *What is already available in the market?* Unusual specifications can result in higher costs of production, longer lead time for delivery, and so on. It may be worthwhile to inquire about the problems involved in using standard sizes, qualities, or electrical characteristics to avoid delays and higher costs for the finished product.

Selecting sources.   Source selection is a critical decision in procurement because failure by a source of supply is difficult to offset by other means.

1.*Do-it-yourself cost.* The purchasing executive should determine whether in-house production is a reasonable option. The cost comparison with outside sources involves a wide range of internal considerations that may change dramatically from time to time, depending on the availability of the buyer's production equipment, skilled personnel, working capital, storage, and so on, and the value of other applications for those resources.

2.*Delivery schedules and storage.* This involves comparison among sources in terms of *quantity and frequency* (flow rate) of delivery options to determine which will best fit the buyer's needs and storage capacity; *flexibility* in delivery rates to meet possible changes in customer demand, changes in available storage, or other changes; and *coordination* with other operations to obtain full-load transportation economies or round-trip loading for vehicles, or to recognize seasonal storage availability at various plant locations.

3.*Just-in-Time aspects.* Note that this production system gives great importance to delivery schedule and storage elements. Delivery schedules are usually fixed for long periods, depending on quantity and frequency. This permits increased efficiency in supply, transport, minimum inventories throughout the system, reduced investment, and substantial cost reductions in total. However, there is very little flexibility in the rate of operations. For example, a prominent maker of personal computers found that adopting Just-in-Time production in a major plant was a wrenching adjustment internally. Still, over a period of months, the new system produced very favorable results. Unfortunately, when the market virtually dried up for the computer model being produced at that plant, the warehouse became jammed with thousands of unsold units because of the extremely high contract penalties for shutting off deliveries from suppliers in less than three months.

4.*Reliability and multiple sources.* These two factors reflect opposite aspects of many purchasing situations. If you have an extremely reliable supplier, then (other things being satisfactory) there is little need for other sources. Conversely, if you are in doubt about the reliability of supply, either because of the source(s) or because of possible great increases in your requirements, then multiple sources become very important. Similarly, if the product needed is relatively cheap and easy to store, you may find a reserve stock an inexpensive way to protect your production schedule against irregular or not always satisfactory performance by suppliers. This avoids the need to use higher-priced alternative sources.

Monitoring vendor performance. As in most management functions, the job is not complete when the arrangements are made: Performance should be measured as a continuing operation. Early notice that purchase agreements are not being adequately met can minimize problems and possible damage for the buyer. This early notice also helps the supplier in maintaining standards. Slightly off-standard components may shut down assembly operations if the parts don't fit properly, or may force recalls of finished items if the components are of poor quality. The sooner supply deficiencies are noted and corrected, the less trouble it causes for the supplier, the buyer, and the ultimate user. For this reason, vendor performance should be monitored as early as practicable in the supply system. In some cases, for expensive items, specifications are checked against products at the vendor's plant.

Where this is not justified, shipments can be tested as they arrive from the supplier. The kinds and frequency of checks depend on the product and its importance to the buyer. These checks are generally related to at least three aspects of vendor performance: product and quantity verification, quality control, and delivery performance.

Transportation

In considering transportation it is important to think in terms of specifics rather than generalizations, because the "best answer" changes with the particular circumstances. These circumstances include the products, the location(s), shipper plans, and the economic environment. Also, the answers, or best plans, may be very different for high-technology companies, grocery chains, basic industry, and service businesses, to cite just a few examples. In reviewing some of the factors to consider, we will discuss service requirements, touch on mode capabilities, and then look at transportation and traffic management.

Service requirements.   A careful review of the firm's transportation needs should start with an examination of the inbound and outbound products and the plans concerning them. This review should analyze the following factors:

1. *Origin/destination traffic flows.* This information should be collected by product to get a detailed picture of problems and opportunities for flow adjustment. Obviously, costs will be reduced if the same carrier equipment can move loaded in both directions. Even a triangle route can be advantageous if the light-load or empty-haul leg of the triangle is short. Mixing loads is another advantage. For example, a large, diversified corporation was able to nearly balance transport loads, east and west, by placing the shipping for several subsidiaries under common control. In addition to cost savings, frequency of service was improved since a truck didn't have to wait for a full load of products from any particular subsidiary of the principal company.

2. *Cost and volume.* If the volume is heavy and steady, unit costs for the carrier will be lowered because the vehicles will be better utilized. This reduces the number of vehicles needed and total costs per mile. Volume may be large enough to justify using larger-capacity or different types of transport equipment.

3. *Speed and flexibility.* The discussion above noted the possible economy of consolidated shipments. However, that may not be acceptable if the product needs to be delivered quickly or if partial shipments are to be dropped off at intermediate points. Surface transport may be un-

satisfactory if speed is crucial and the distance is great. Medical supplies, machine parts, or technical equipment, for example, may have to go by air because of the time value involved.

4. *Competition available.* It is important for a logistics or transportation planner to protect against monopoly pricing of normal services and against the inability of the preferred source(s) to provide the transport equipment or service. Finding and using a few excellent carriers can provide effective competition and protection against one-company disasters.

5. *Capacity factors.* These factors can affect both the carrier and the customer. As with "back-haul" traffic, a firm has an advantage in cost and service if its greatest transport requirements are in the off-season for the carriers it uses. Carrier responsiveness, service flexibility, and rates can all be favorably affected from the shipper/receiver point of view. Examples of capacity opportunities include using household goods carriers during the winter, or refrigerated equipment on the back-haul, or generally westbound equipment, since the eastbound freight volume typically exceeds the westbound volume.

In summary, examine the transportation needs of the enterprise in detail. Look for patterns and possibilities for flexibility. Next, consider the needs of the carriers. Seek trade-offs that are advantageous by examining how your firm as a shipper/receiver can adjust to carrier needs — and gain important price or service advantages as a result.

Mode capabilities. The services offered by transportation modes vary, as do the prices or rates. Within a mode, individual carriers will vary in their performance. There are also some specific factors that go beyond the skill of any particular carrier management. In general, the various modes of freight transportation represent a spectrum of services in terms of speed, flexibility, dependability, and cost. In the ensuing comments, average revenue per ton-mile in 1983 is shown in parentheses after each mode. *Barges* are the slowest, and transit times vary considerably. Bulk commodities are the most common cargoes. Service is limited to waterside points. (0.818¢) *Pipelines* are also slow, virtually fixed, and very limited in points served, but are very dependable. Liquids, gas, or solids in suspension (slurry) are moved. (1.231¢) *Railroads* are more flexible and much faster than barge or pipeline service, are more varied in points served, and carry a wide variety of freight. (3.13¢) *Trucks* are considerably more flexible than railroad service, are usually much faster and more dependable, and handle a wide range of products with little damage. (21.35¢) Air freight is by far the fastest transport service, generally is quite dependable, and handles a wide range of products with little damage. (47.20¢) *Intermodal* is a combination of two or more different modes of transportation that is becoming increasingly popular. Air freight, of course, relies on truck service for pickup and delivery, as does much of the railroad "piggy-back" and container service. An increasing amount of ocean container service is moving to the coasts, or from coast to coast, by rail or truck as a means of providing dependable, expedited service for international shipments. These ocean (or international) containers are 8 feet by 8 feet by 20 or 40 feet in length. A container may be filled with cargo for one or many shippers. Intermodal rates vary but are generally less than rates for truck service.

Transportation and traffic management. In dealing with carriers, remember that there are several legal types as well as the various modes. For example, in air, truck, and water carrier service, there are the legal classifications of common carrier, contract carrier, and private carrier. Railroads are almost all common carriers; a few are private carriers under common control with the mines they serve. In addition, an operator called a freight forwarder is classed as an *indirect carrier.* Deregulation has considerably eroded the distinctions, but basically they were as follows: The *common carrier* was authorized to serve the public generally and was required to publish standard rates and to operate over particular routes, unless otherwise specified. The *contract carrier* was authorized to serve a limited number of customers (once about ten) and to make separate contracts or deals with each customer. The *private carrier* was in the service of its owner and handled little if any for-hire freight. As a result of deregulation, common carriers are no longer required to publish all of their rates or to have them all approved in advance by some regulatory body. Most can also vary their routes without government consent.[7] Today common carriers can make deals very much as contract carriers do. And the contract carriers are no longer restricted to a limited number of customers or to a particular type of freight. The private carrier is now free to haul for hire (like a contract carrier) in many situations. Finally, the *freight forwarder,* or consolidator, continues very much as before deregulation. He consolidates small shipments into air, rail carload, truckload, or ocean shipping quantities and arranges for their transportation. The freight forwarder makes his profit on the differences between the rate he charges and the less-than-carload, less-than-truckload, or other small-shipment rate that would have been charged by the carrier. Freight forwarders continue to be active in air, land, and water transport, but are not a major factor in nationwide service.

With increased competition and rate flexibility, more emphasis is being placed on costs (as a basis for setting transportation prices) and on the negotiating skills of the parties. For the buyer of transportation service, this highlights the importance of having full information on present and prospective traffic flows.

Warehousing

In this section, we will consider physical facilities for warehousing, warehouse operators, and financial considerations. These topics will provide the framework for a discussion of warehousing as a part of the logistics functions. Space limitations preclude a full treatment of the subject here.

Physical facilities.   Two very important aspects are the location and the service capability of a warehouse. A good location is essential for convenience in receiving shipments and in effectively serving customers. Cargo may arrive by air, truck, rail, or water. For many warehouses, truck and rail service are both required. In addition, there should be convenient access to one or two interstate or U.S. highways. If air transport is important, the warehouse should be on the airport property, or within a few minutes' drive by truck via major roads. Similarly, if water carrier service is important, the warehouse should normally be located at or near the waterfront, with convenient access by truck and rail service.

Since a warehouse is a service center, its specific location is influenced by particular business needs. Thus, a grocery warehouse should be centrally located to serve its many supermarket customers and should have quick access to a good road net to make fast and economical deliveries. A high-tech products distribution warehouse should be close to the factory and have easy access by highway to a major airport as well as to important local users or wholesalers.

Warehouse operators.   There are several categories of warehouse operators. *Private operators* run a warehouse in connection with the operation of some other enterprise. Thus, Sears, Roebuck and Company is a private operator of many warehouses, which it owns or leases for its own use in support of its numerous retail stores. *Public warehouses* are those in which space is for rent, usually along with a variety of warehouse services, as a principal business of some person or company. Public warehouses can be a great advantage for organizations with changing space requirements, or with markets that shift geographically, and for firms that simply do not wish to divert specialized management to a function that can be hired as needed. For example, a giant canned-food distribution organization uses public warehouses extensively. They offer flexibility in space during the year (rented by the month) and in locations. The public warehouses provide, on a fee basis, all unloading, storage, inventory control, order filling, and shipping, along with the associated paperwork, and provide the on-site direction of carriers delivering or picking up goods. *Carrier/vendors* are operators of warehouses which function as an adjunct to a related activity. It can be an advantage to the manufacturer or distributor to deal with a carrier which will store the products and deliver them to customers on the shipper's instructions. With this arrangement, a computer memory unit may leave the carrier's warehouse, on a specialized vehicle, en route to the customer hundreds of miles away — within an hour after the telephone or teletype instructions were received from the manufacturer's sales office.

Financial considerations. In operating warehouses there are the usual problems of budgeting, cost control, collections, and cash flow. However, the policy or strategic questions concern major choices in ownership and control. If close coordination is desired between warehousing and other company operations, the question may become, "To achieve this, do we build, buy, rent, or lease?" Building may provide exactly the facility desired, perhaps at a favorable price. Buying, renting, or leasing may secure a superior facility in the *best* location, right away (no construction time), but at somewhat greater cost. The trade-off is in comparing the need, timing, and prices.

INTEGRATED LOGISTICS SYSTEMS

At the beginning of this chapter logistics was described as basically a support and coordinating activity. This is exemplified by the varied activities in which logistics has a role and by the support and coordinating functions it provides in the business enterprise. Some of these items and functions are listed below. Those involving logistics are marked by an asterisk (*).

Items	Functional Activities
Production materials	*Procurement
	*Transportation to plants
	*Inventory management
Goods in process	Production operations
	Work-in-process control
Finished goods	*Inventory management
	*Sales
	*Physical distribution

From the list, it is clear that logistics has a major role in the efficient coordination of the enterprise. As used here, an "integrated logistics system" means a system in which various supply and distribution activities are closely coordinated or under common control.

Looking at the functional activities list as a process sequence illustrates another aspect of logistics. One function of logistics management is to track activities and make adjustments to maintain a smooth flow of materials and products, consistent with the business plan and schedules. Thus, if procurement deliveries are delayed, it may be necessary to expedite transportation to plants, or turn to additional sources, to avoid a "below-plan" level of materials for production. Perhaps the rate of production at the plant is initially slower than expected. In that case, shipments of production materials should be delayed to avoid excessive inventory buildup. On the other side of production, finished-goods physical distribution may be expedited, for a time, to maintain customer goodwill in spite of limited production. The information flow and feedback to permit this coordination runs through the whole enterprise. Logistics, then, has a significant role in the internal adjustments to *maintain planned performance.*

Another use of information that makes an integrated logistics system important is the comparison of plan versus performance. If sales are substantially above or below plan, it may be time to *change the plan.* Making those changes involves logistics to a considerable extent. The adjustment is not easy. It requires establishing a new dynamic balance within the operating system, at a different level of output.

Information Systems

In order to monitor and adjust the performance of the enterprise, an extensive information system is required. All interested groups contribute to that information system and should have access to it. This information system provides a common base for comparisons and decisions. Ideally, it should also provide the most recent and reliable information. To create or modify an information system to this standard is a long-term project. However, pieces of the system can be created as the opportunities arise, and will provide valuable information for monitoring and adjusting plans or making changes. Below are some specific considerations useful in creating parts of an information system for the enterprise.

1. *Get the various items of data from as far "upstream" as you can.* The information needed to anticipate problems is generally found early in the organization's information flows. Get the best information avail-

able, and remember, it doesn't have to be complete or precise — just helpful. This advance information can provide more lead time to plan and carry out adjustments to *avoid* forecast consequences *or minimize* their impact later in the system.

2. *Track key data through the system.* This is like following a dye injection in the blood through the body's circulatory system. The flow rate changes in various places, and sometimes obstructions are encountered. In an enterprise, the progress of various orders, lot numbers, or products can be checked as they move through the system. The significance of changes can be interpreted for schedules, production rates, quality checks, work-in-progress inventories, shipments, and so forth, and management can use the integrated logistics system to avoid potential problems or minimize their "downstream" effect. An example would be an unexpected jump in next month's sales forecast. This forecast could be translated into impact on finished-goods inventories, work-in-progress inventories, production output plans, and production materials inventory needs. This might lead to timely purchase orders or arrangements to accelerate delivery on multishipment orders already outstanding. Used in this way, the sales forecast could be the basis of efficient, planned adjustments. If the sales forecast proved to be too high as actual orders came in, further logistics adjustments could be made.

3. *Get information as a by-product whenever practicable.* This makes data much easier to obtain. When you are collecting information up and down the organization, most of the sources are likely to be in divisions, departments, and offices other than your own. This situation can cause problems because the trouble and expense involved fall on one group, whereas the benefits accrue to another group. There may be a long struggle on cost estimates and interoffice charges before the information begins to flow, and even then the people doing the work may resist because they're not getting anything extra for the added trouble. However, with modern electronic equipment, and even with some old gear, particular data can routinely be obtained with very little trouble. If the information is going into a computer memory, a small program often can be prepared to extract, accumulate, and process the particular data you need. With no trouble for the source offices, logistics and other authorized units can tap the data files for a wide range of planning and control information.

Controls

In the field of logistics, we are dealing with a wide spectrum of goods and services. As a result, the logistics executive must have a good system of controls in order to identify opportunities and problems promptly and to plan adjustments efficiently. This section covers only a few of the considerations relating to logistics controls. They include schedules, availability, quality, reliability, and cost. To the extent practicable, controls should be based on conveniently available information, and the collection and analysis of that information should be automated.

Schedules. If routine work is scheduled well in advance, the number of time-pressure crises can be greatly reduced. Put review and updating of records, follow-up orders, revision of requirements, correction of price data, and directory lists on schedules. Then arrange for a random check pattern to be sure the work is done. Automate the review process to the extent feasible, and use exception tests to identify items for special attention. For example, any item that varies more than x percent from the last quarter is reviewed.

Availability. Availability is a serious consideration when you need a product or service on short notice. Your information system should give you the data on the product suppliers or transportation organizations that can provide various quantities of goods or services on short notice. The computerized information system also should be able to call up the performance record on quality, reliability, and cost.

Quality. Controls for quality are rarely needed for standard items. If products are bought by specification, random sampling and statistical interpretation of the results usually should be sufficient. On "quality-sensitive" items, controls should provide specific standards, tests for verifying them, and penalties for failure to meet those standards.

Reliability. Reliability is an important matter. For products, it is an aspect of quality. In transportation, reliability can be measured in a variety of ways. It may be elapsed time en route, maintenance of schedules, or product loss and damage. Pick the system(s) appropriate for your situation and find some routine way of measuring performance, if feasible. These data can then be stored in a small computer with statistics and graphics programs. This arrangement will allow you to display the mean and variation for measures of performance for a period. Another program can show performance over time to indicate the trend of improvement or deterioration in service.

Cost. A wide range of cost data can be collected. As stated earlier, it is generally wise to concentrate on the high-value items *and* on the high-usage items. With high-value items, the dollars alone may justify special attention. For low-value, high-usage items, the key element is their importance in keeping equipment units or assembly lines running. A cheap item, out of stock, can shut down an expensive operation. In transportation and other services, cost is matched against some measure(s) of service. Cost provides a convenient basis for selection when service is currently, and expected to remain, comparable among carriers. However, the importance of immediately available substitutes must be kept in mind.

Logistics System Development

Earlier we noted the importance of the efficient pickup of existing information and the value of systems for determining best decisions in large operating networks. Both play important roles in integrated logistics systems and in the total enterprise.

The topic to be considered here adds one more consideration: how to put together a large system, one step at a time. This process has important advantages: (1) specific benefits are available with each step, not just after an extensive system has been completed; (2) additions are compatible with earlier elements, so no previous training or equipment need be wasted; (3) operating savings generated by earlier elements of the system help to pay for the installation of later features. Thus, total capital required is reduced, and the investment is spread over the sequence of steps rather than being an up-front cost.

For brevity, the example below is limited to one logistics activity: movement planning and control. It is, however, representative of the possibilities of step-by-step development in many areas of the integrated logistics system. Table 6.1 shows nine different elements of an integrated movement planning and control system. The elements, or steps, are numbered in a suggested order of adoption so that each step builds on the information generated by previous elements.

1. *Traffic statistics.* These data show how much of what was transported from and to various points, and provide a total for the period, with shares of the total handled by different modes and particular carriers.

2. *Shipper routing performance.* This information indicates any unauthorized routings: point to point, when, carrier, products, and shipping organization responsible. This information makes deviations from instructions clear without special studies, and makes it easier for parties involved to resist bribe attempts and to maintain an honest arm's-length relation.

3. *Shipper schedule performance.* The information in this report is arranged to compare actual shipping date/time with that specified on the

Table 6.1 Step-by-Step Development of an Integrated Movement Planning and Control System

Suggested Sequence	1	2	3	4	5	6	7	8	9
Management tools	Traffic statistic & analysis	Shipper routing performance	Shipper schedule performance	Carrier intransit performance	Intransit locations & inventory	Special equipment controls	Automatic routing instructions	Movement program & capabilities	Automatic route/release system
Sources of information	• Electronic bill of lading (B/L)	• Electronic bill of lading (B/L) • Authorized routing list	• Electronic bill of lading (B/L) • Carrier pickup report • Depot/plants shipping schedule	• Electronic bill of lading (B/L) • Carrier pickup report • Carrier intransit report • Customer receiving or carrier delivery report	• Electronic bill of lading (B/L) • Carrier pickup report • Carrier intransit report • Customer receiving or carrier delivery report	• Electronic bill of lading (B/L) • Carrier pickup report • Carrier intransit report • Customer receiving or carrier delivery report • Special equipment data	• Request for routing • Authorized routing list • Traffic allocation instructions	• Request for routing with delivery date • Authorized routing list • Traffic allocation instructions • Port or destination receiving capability • Carrier movement capability • Intransit times between points	• Request for routing with delivery date • Authorized routing list • Traffic allocation instructions • Port or destination receiving capability • Carrier movement capability • Movement program

schedule for the shipping point — the factory or warehouse, etc. This information can aid in determining where delays occur and how often, and can assist in determining how service can be improved.

4.*Carrier intransit performance.* A report of this type provides a measure of the consistency and elapsed time, for particular carriers, by route, date, and mode. These data permit easy identification of particular cases deserving investigation and provide a basis for statistical analysis. The data can also be presented in graphic display summaries, automatically generated by computer. Materials of this type can save a great deal of time in discussions with carrier sales and operating executives about quality of service, and in determining new shipment allocation policies or shares.

5.*Intransit locations and inventory.* Starting with an opening inventory at each point, quantities delivered to and shipped from each point can be used to generate quantities that should be on hand at each location. Like a checkbook balance, this number may sometimes be in error — and then it is important to find out why. Unreported damage or loss, or excessive inventory buildup, can be detected by these data, automatically collected, compiled, and analyzed.

For particular shipments, the bill of lading number, or other shipping document number, permits particular shipments to be tracked through the system. This allows determination of slow points, and of very efficient operations, in the transport and materials handling system. Finally, with intransit reporting by carriers (now done by many for important customers), items in transit can be located at the next carrier terminal and redirected. In some cases, the shipper can even arrange for radio instructions to be delivered to the vehicle operator.

6.*Special equipment controls.* These reports, based primarily on data already being collected, permit the logistics group to locate any particular units or groups of special-purpose equipment. These units might be special-products tank cars, heavy-capacity truck-trailers, high-cube freight cars, airbag-cushioned truck-trailers, heated cargo barges, or extra-wide door cargo aircraft. The location and condition (loaded, empty, in repair, available) can be determined almost instantly. A computer sort of these data, by location or region, can display all the detail on appropriate special equipment in the territory around any point suddenly requiring additional equipment with special capabilities.

7.*Automatic routing instructions.* From a program stored in the logistics computer memory, shipping instructions can be provided automatically for any inquiry on how to ship, by what carrier, from any company or supplier origin, to any company or customer destination. This system avoids the necessity to have routing clerks at most shipping installations and provides a convenient way to distribute traffic flow among selected carriers, in particular shares, as specified in the routing instructions.

8.*Movement program and capabilities.* A movement program is a control and scheduling plan for transportation service, usually made necessary by a shortage of transportation. The limitations may be in total capacity, as well as by mode, or area. These circumstances are just "facts of life" in military operations and in natural-disaster areas. The movement program is developed by comparing shipping requests (quantities, products, origins, delivery dates, destinations, etc.) and their respective priorities with available transport capacities, by date and mode, between points or within areas. When used, movement programs for the U.S. armed forces are often on a weekly cycle, but this time period can be varied to suit the situation. The transport schedule that results from the analysis is normally specified as a series of allocations of transport capacity by mode and route for each day for particular movement requests. A movement program system is not likely to be used in peacetime. However, it may be very convenient for an enterprise to have a commercial planning and control system that can easily be adjusted, in an emergency, to work with transportation allocations that might result from a strike, fuel shortage, or some other economic dislocation.

9.*Automatic route/release system.* This additional step in expanding the system is of special value to the transport control or rationing center in an emergency. The volume of activity and the mass of data involved make a computerized system necessary to deal with the problems efficiently. Again, having a commercial system that can quickly be adapted to the controls gives the user of the "adaptable system" a substantial advantage in getting and effectively using the share of transport to which he is entitled.

LOOKING AHEAD

Anticipating change and preparing for it are important management functions. A pattern that almost always presages major adjustments is a slowdown in the *rate of change* in currently used methods or equipment. This slowdown in improvements is a good predictor because it represents a continuing opportunity for new methods or devices. With a slowdown, the incentive for change is there, and new technical advances, plus imagination, are likely to provide the means for the next step forward.

As in the world around us, change also is reflected in the area of logistics in terms of "faster" or "cheaper," or both. Examples such as giant unit-trains of raw materials, warehouses with specialized materials handling equipment, and tightly coordinated systems such as Just-in-Time are familiar. Technological change is reflected by the stair steps of improvement in aircraft engines. The radial, triple-row piston engine was replaced by the jet engine. The latter, in turn, has grown larger and more complex. Perhaps a simpler, cheaper power plant will replace most of the aircraft jet engines in a few years. The newest designs of turboprop engines with curved, wide-chord blades, for example, permit greater air speeds than do conventional turbo-props, and greater fuel economy than that of most jet engines. Thus, they might well further reduce the cost of airfreight service and passenger operations.

With deregulation, owner-operators in trucking are providing an increasing volume of service and undercutting former cost patterns of unionized trucking companies. Truck efficiency also appears to be at a breakthrough point. In the Far West, some states permit triple trailers, and twin trailers have been authorized on principal highways in most states.

In the case of railroads, will competition and deregulation result in the reduction of train crew size (already cut from five to two in a few cases), an increase in through-train service, or replacement of diesel-electric locomotives (they've been around a long time) with still more economical power units? All of these changes could reduce logistics costs.

Warehousing provides some similar opportunities. For example, hand trucks and cranes were replaced, in many cases, with pallets and forklift trucks. These operations are now highly developed. Will computer-controlled automatic materials handling systems, or other devices, be their successors in general use?

Beyond the basics of "faster" or "cheaper," there are several kinds of *user-oriented changes* that will have an important impact on logistics costs, inventories, service, and flexibility. These market-driven changes include the following:

Changing products, as we have already seen, in processed foods, electronics, and automobiles.

Broader markets, resulting from a rising standard of living, population growth, and more efficient production and transportation.

Economies of scale and experience curves: For numerous high-volume products, such as electronic components, a late start in volume production can mean that an excellent product never becomes competitive in the market; this pressure for accelerated product introduction will increase the emphasis on logistics support.

Service emphasis: As its importance continues to grow, the logistics problems of service support will increase, and inventory and parts distribution problems will become more important.

An additional item in the list of "change agents" is *computerized strategy analysis.* This technique opens a major avenue for strategic initiative rather than simply responding to market demands and competitive pressures. The growing complexity of competitive problems and logistics options will result in additional emphasis on fast analysis of complex "What if . . . ?" strategic questions. The computer equipment now available can provide the analysis swiftly and economically. At the Stanford Graduate School of Business, a project is now under way to develop a computerized distribution strategy analysis for certain "smokestack" industries. The program will permit simulation of market and financial results of various moves and countermoves by rival firms, leading to conclusions by the user team about what strategy appears best, why, and by roughly what margin. Potential market by counties, transportation rates and likely changes, production cost and volume adjustments, plus promotional pricing, freight absorption, and possible first-, second-, and third-round reactions among the rival firms are all considered in the analysis. Of course, a wide range of options for the various parties must be played out to review the range of possible outcomes.

Extensive developments in this area of computer application will take place in many segments of industry in the next decade. Such analyses will result in increased attention to logistics as a factor in developing strategic plans.

NOTES

1. "Float," the small quantities of parts or components at various points in the assembly process that are sometimes needed to keep a production line running when defective parts or short-time line-segment delays are encountered.

2. Mason and Dixon Lines, Inc., "Needed: Credible Measures of Customer Service," modified slightly from James C. Johnson and Donald F. Wood, *Contemporary Physical Distribution and Logistics,* 2nd ed. (Tulsa, OK: PennWell Books, 1982), p. 74.

3. Frank L. Cross and John L. Simons (editors), *Industrial Plant Siting* (Westport, CT: Technomic Publishing Company, 1975), pp. 137–141.

4. James L. Heskett, Lewis M. Schneider, Robert M. Ivie, and Nicholas A.

Glaskowsky, Jr., *Case Problems in Business Logistics* (New York: Ronald Press Co., 1973), pp. 121–124.

5. Professor George B. Dantzig devised this technique. He is currently Professor of Operations Research and Computer Science and C. A. Criley Professor of Transportation Sciences in the School of Engineering at Stanford University.

6. Professor Schruben perfected the LOCKSET method while on the faculty at Kansas State University, where he has taught and led research projects for many years.

7. U.S. flag vessels receiving Operating Differential Subsidy payments from the federal government must have prior approval to vary their routes.

SUGGESTED READINGS

These titles are in addition to the references given in the notes to this chapter. An asterisk (*) preceding a citation indicates that an Instructor's Manual is available to qualified users.

Logistics/Distribution

*Coyle, J. J., and E. G. Bardi. *The Management of Business Logistics,* 3rd ed. St. Paul: West Publishing Company, 1984. An introductory-level college text with fifteen chapters arranged in four parts. Two short cases follow each chapter.

Robeson, J. F., and R. G. House. editors. *The Distribution Handbook.* New York: Free Press, 1985. A valuable reference book arranged in fourteen sections by major topics.

*Shapiro, R. D., and J. L. Heskett. *Logistics Strategy: Cases and Concepts.* St. Paul: West Publishing Company, 1985. A text and casebook of nine chapters plus thirty cases by professors at the Harvard Business School. About 40 percent of the content is text. Related problem cases follow each chapter. Arranged in three parts: Conceptual Underpinnings; Designing an Integrated Logistics System; and Managing for Effective Logistics.

Purchasing/Materials Management

Burt, D. N. *Proactive Procurement: The Key to Increased Profits, Productivity, and Quality.* Englewood Cliffs, N.J.: Prentice-Hall, 1984. A lively howto book by a professor with career experience in USAF and civilian procurement assignments.

Transportation

*Sampson, R. J., M. T. Farris, and D. L. Shrock. *Domestic Transportation: Practice, Theory, and Policy,* 5th ed. Boston: Houghton Mifflin Company, 1985. This edition of a well-known college text includes new chapters, "The Era of Deregulation" and "International Freight Transportation: Domestic Interfaces."

Temple, Barker & Sloane, Inc. *Transportation Strategies for the Eighties.* Oak Brook, IL: National Council of Physical Distribution Management, 1982. This study by a prominent consulting firm was commissioned by the professional society (NCPDM). The book contains an executive summary, seven chapters, and six appendixes. It should be very helpful to anyone seeking a user strategy or a perspective on commercial transportation in the United States.

Warehousing

Ackerman, K. B., R. W. Gardner, and Thomas P. Lee. *Understanding Today's Distribution Center*. Washington, D.C.: Traffic Service Corporation, 1974. This volume was prepared by three executives with experience as consultants and in operating warehouses and distribution centers. The book is divided into two parts. The first eight chapters cover "Considerations for the Distribution Center User," and the remaining twelve chapters focus on the operator. Two useful appendixes are provided.

Mathematics and Economics

Germane, G. E. *Program Evaluation and Review Technique (PERT)*, rev. ed., S-TM 207. Stanford, Calif.: Stanford University Press, 1970. This is a simple self-instruction booklet, with problems and answers, carrying the method through calculations of the probability of completing the project on time.

Horowitz, J. *Critical Path Scheduling: Management Control Through CPM and PERT*. New York: Ronald Press Company, 1967. A clear and thorough discussion of the concepts and methods of the two systems, with a glossary and an extensive bibliography.

Locklin, D. P. *Economics of Transportation*, 7th ed. Homewood, Ill.: Richard D. Irwin, 1972. This volume is a classic in the field. The economic explanations are clear and balanced. The book covers a wide range of topics in thirty-eight chapters. The discussion of transportation regulation is comprehensive, and the case citations provide a useful reference on prior policies, reasoning, and decisions. The book should not be consulted for interpretations of current deregulation.

Porteus, E. L. "Numerical Comparisons of Inventory Policies for Periodic Review Systems." *Operation's Research* 33, no. 1 (1985): 134–152. This article introduces three new methods of computing approximately optimal inventory policies. These and fourteen other methods are evaluated by computer analysis, on a test bed of 1,200 cases. Important differences in average performance and in variation were found among the inventory review systems tested.

CHAPTER 7

Management Decision and Information Systems

Charles P. Bonini
Jeffrey H. Moore
Stanford University
Graduate School of Business

Computer systems in business traditionally have been devoted to the support of the stewardship function, that is, to maintaining the records of financial transactions. In this role, the primary contribution of computer technology has been in filing and retrieving records, in maintaining the general ledger and other accounts, in order processing and tracking, and the like. Not only are these activities all critically important to proper business conduct, but, because of the structured nature of these tasks and the high volume of activity in them, they are ideally suited for implementation on automated data-handling equipment — that is, on computers. The dramatic improvement in the cost-effectiveness of computer hardware and software for this task over the last two decades, coupled with pressure to perform these tasks efficiently, mandates the use of computer systems in all but the very smallest organizations. However, computer-based information systems have always offered the potential of contributing not only to the efficiency of business operations but also to the effectiveness of the management process itself. That is, automation of existing data handling operations has given way to the more challenging goal of improving high-level management activities. Thus the first theme of this chapter is the deployment of computer-based information systems to directly augment managerial decision-making. The tools necessary for these decision

225

support systems will be introduced and management's use of these systems will be discussed.

Management is also responsible for how information technology is used by other parts of the organization. This management task is not an easy one, because several trends are affecting the technology and its use. Especially important is the increasing importance of information systems technology as a strategic weapon, not only to reduce costs, but to add significant value to the firm's product or service. A second theme of this chapter, then, is the trends taking place in the management of information systems and the challenges they entail.

Before turning to these themes, we develop a framework that provides an overview of how computer-based information systems can be employed for other than routine transactions. Building on the nomenclature developed in this framework, we focus on the issues that must be addressed by management in order to exploit the potential of this technology for decision support.

Types of Information Systems

Figure 7.1 presents a simple taxonomy for classifying information systems according to their uses. The first category goes by various names, commonly *electronic data processing* (EDP) or *automated data processing,* and is the largest category of computer-based information systems in current use. EDP systems subsume most of the accounting and other transactional record-keeping systems in business use today. Examples include payroll and order-entry systems.

The second category, *management information system* (MIS), typically focuses on periodic reporting and aggregating (summarizing) information that is meaningful to managers. This often involves the need to compare performance against a base, such as performance in previous time periods, or against a predefined standard, such as standard cost. Examples include budget reports and sales analyses.

Decision support systems (DSS) focus on providing information for specific managerial decisions, primarily planning ones. The information from internal sources is often needed in very aggregate, or highly summarized, form. And since most planning decisions involve factors external to the firm, information must also be included from external sources. Examples include corporate planning and competitive analysis.

The taxonomy in Figure 7.1 is aimed primarily at business applications of computers and leaves aside engineering and/or scientific applications, such as for computer-aided design, stress calculations, and weather forecasting. Moreover, by focusing on common business uses

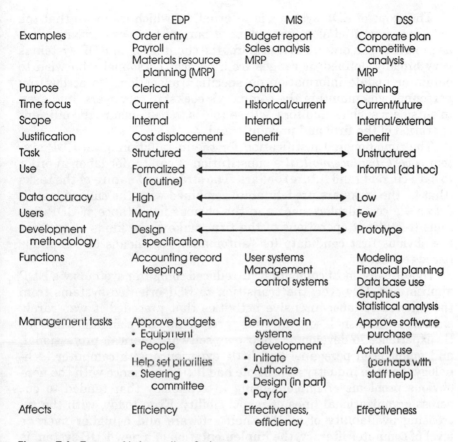

	EDP	MIS	DSS
Examples	Order entry Payroll Materials resource planning (MRP)	Budget report Sales analysis MRP	Corporate plan Competitive analysis MRP
Purpose	Clerical	Control	Planning
Time focus	Current	Historical/current	Current/future
Scope	Internal	Internal	Internal/external
Justification	Cost displacement	Benefit	Benefit
Task	Structured ←—————————————→ Unstructured		
Use	Formalized ←—————————————→ Informal (ad hoc) (routine)		
Data accuracy	High ←—————————————→ Low		
Users	Many ←—————————————→ Few		
Development methodology	Design ←—————————————→ Prototype specification		
Functions	Accounting record keeping	User systems Management control systems	Modeling Financial planning Data base use Graphics Statistical analysis
Management tasks	Approve budgets • Equipment • People Help set priorities • Steering committee	Be involved in systems development • Initiate • Authorize • Design (in part) • Pay for	Approve software purchase Actually use (perhaps with staff help)
Affects	Efficiency	Effectiveness, efficiency	Effectiveness

Figure 7.1 Types of Information Systems

of information systems, this taxonomy ignores state-of-the-art applications, such as artificially intelligent expert systems. While this focus on business applications is somewhat narrow, it does allow us to concentrate upon some of the more common distinctions among information systems that apply across a very wide range of businesses.

Let us examine and contrast each of these information system types in more detail.

EDP systems. Accuracy, timeliness, and currency of information are critical prerequisites for a successful EDP system. Because of its transactions orientation, an EDP system puts a premium on technology that is efficient, reliable, and capable of processing and storing large quantities of raw data.

The scope of EDP systems is internal, by which we mean that the data are generated as a by-product of normal business activity, such as processing an order. Furthermore, the clientele of an EDP system is very broadly defined: it ranges from clerical personnel who wish to obtain or update information on specific transactions, to accounting personnel who maintain the company's books, to managers, and even to outsiders such as auditors, whose role is to help ensure the efficient operation of the firm and prevent fraud.

The time-honored justification for the installation of an EDP system is *cost displacement:* the substitution of capital for labor in order to save current (and future) dollars. The structured nature of the tasks (that is, the tasks are predefinable) combined with the ease of justification via cost displacement and the obvious importance of EDP systems to efficient operations of the firm make these kinds of systems the obvious first candidate for "automation" by means of computer-based technology.

Historically, most companies introduced computer systems via EDP applications. However, the transition to EDP-oriented systems from the inherently labor-intensive activities that preceded it was rarely smooth. Off-the-shelf software was rarely available; companies had little experience in developing their own software; clerical, professional, and managerial personnel had little experience with computer technology; and the industry as a whole had little experience with the non-obvious problems of implementing a technology that tended to cut across organizational lines of responsibility. Even today, with the increasing availability of off-the-shelf software and a higher average level of computer literacy, the implementation of a new EDP system is rarely a straightforward process: implementation difficulty tends to grow geometrically with the number of people who must be involved in the successful operation of the EDP system. Fortunately, the rapid decline in the cost of computer technology, including software, can produce substantial returns to the investment in EDP systems once the implementation turmoil subsides. Nevertheless, it is not uncommon for managers who have experienced unexpected problems in implementing EDP-oriented systems to take a conservative approach when extending the technology into other areas of the corporation.

MIS systems. An MIS system typically involves the aggregation of transaction data collected via an EDP system. Hence, MIS systems are often found on the same hardware and frequently (sometimes mistakenly) use the same software languages as an EDP system. However, a premium is placed on periodic reporting and on the ability to generate aggregations that are meaningful to managers. This typically involves the need to compare performance against a base, such as performance in previous time periods, or against a predefined standard, such as standard cost. The need for interaction via remote processing is increasingly apparent as one goes deeper into the control aspects of MIS systems. As a result, remote access and time-sharing access to a mainframe computer is considered an important requirement for managerial control via an MIS.

Note that the primary thrust of an MIS system is organizational control: using information to answer the question "How is my company doing?" Although much of the data necessary to answer such a question can be found by proper aggregations of the raw data produced by an EDP system, there is a tendency to limit the scope of an MIS to only those data which are internally generated. Hence, an MIS might easily answer the question "Is sales growth rate higher or lower than last year's?" but it might not be able to answer the question "Is my market share higher or lower than previously?" The latter question would require market information not normally captured by an EDP-based MIS. This points to one critical flaw in most companies' approach to MIS: a system designed to efficiently pursue one goal — efficient record keeping and transaction processing — is then pressed into service to pursue the goal of providing management information for managerial control. But such control frequently cannot be achieved from mere aggregations of EDP data alone.

Further, an MIS is difficult to prespecify, because the nature of managerial control is an unstructured task whose benefit is improved managerial control, a concept difficult to quantify in the abstract. Finally, efficient operation of an EDP system requires trade-offs that diminish the effectiveness of the MIS embedded in it. For example, it is more efficient to generate MIS reports periodically as part of the normal EDP cycle for processing transactions. This often results in the more or less automatic production of printed MIS reports that are circulated periodically whether managers want to look at them or not. But effective management control often requires the examination of performance indexes on demand, in an exploratory manner based upon exceptions, a mode of interaction not normally associated with efficient EDP. Confounding matters further, technical specialists charged with the responsibility of developing MIS historically had little understanding of the needs of the managerial clientele demanding MIS support. Attempts to build an MIS with EDP-oriented specialists and with technology optimized for low-cost EDP usually fail to provide what is needed for ongoing managerial control. Fortunately, most managers and technical specialists have come to recognize the importance of MIS to effective organizations. But this recognition requires real cultural and attitudinal shifts on the part of all concerned, and few organizations have made these shifts without considerable effort to develop a general understanding of the role that MIS ought to play in the overall scheme of management within the firm.

DSS system. Although the terms "electronic data processing" and "management information system" have become part of the vernacular, "decision support systems" is a relatively new and potentially very valuable use of computer technology. A good example of a DSS-like system is the use of a spreadsheet package, such as Lotus 1-2-3, to examine the economic consequences of a range of potential alternatives open to a decision-maker. The use of personal computers for this "what-if" application has become widespread. However, some managers have assumed that because a personal computer may be very useful for a DSS application, it is superior for all information processing, including EDP and MIS. This is rarely the case: different types of systems require different blends of technologies, expertise, and operational standards.

The treatment of DSSs here is brief since a subsequent section treats them in detail.

Comparing EDP, MIS, and DSS. Figure 7.1 presents some examples of the kinds of information systems that fall into these three categories and indicates the degree of managerial involvement necessary for the successful operation of each system. In general, more day-to-day involvement by management is a prerequisite to effective use of these systems as one moves from left to right. Furthermore, the managerial models that come into play, and the role of judgment in properly using these models, become increasingly important as one moves to the right. That is, the models for aggregating data in an accounting-oriented EDP system are so standard and well understood that they are rarely thought of as being models. An MIS system, by contrast, may involve several different kinds of aggregations, data collection and storage procedures, blends of internal and external data, and the like, depending upon what particular model a given manager wants to impose on the data.

For their part, DSS applications often are characterized as being abstract in the extreme. That is, there is no generally accepted model for conceptualizing a given class of decision alternatives, and the data to support the assumptions of any given model are rarely available; therefore, subjective estimates must be used. For this reason, DSS use requires care in understanding the underlying assumptions, data, and prejudices of the individual manager who performs the analysis, and for this reason it will be emphasized in the next few sections of this chapter. This is not to imply that EDP and MIS are unimportant. Rather, their development and proper use demand technical skills that are beyond the scope of this chapter.

As can be seen in Figure 7.1, some systems — for example MRP (materials resource planning), used by manufacturers for scheduling, materials planning, inventory control, forecasting, and the like — can span the entire spectrum of information-systems types. Such integration can dramatically decrease the efficiency of any one operation, but it also can produce systems that serve a wide class of managerial uses and users.

In this chapter we focus on major conceptual issues faced by managers who must cope with the increasing pressure to deploy information systems effectively in their organizations. We avoid discussions of specific hardware and software options for achieving the goals we have outlined, because the ongoing rapid evolution in hardware and software would make any such discussion obsolete in short order.

DECISION SUPPORT SYSTEMS

Just what is a decision support system? In the simplest terms it is a way of providing managers with information for making decisions. The word "information" is key here. The system should provide information, not data or numbers. Information means numbers and data that are put in a form relevant and useful to the manager. For example, a twenty-page listing of expenses for all the company's plants is hardly useful. But a short analysis accompanied by graphs, analyzing the cost of key products, could indeed be valuable information.

Managerial Data Base

The first step in providing information for a decision support system is the creation of a data base. As we noted above, this should be a collection of data both from inside the firm and external to the firm. In most managerial problems, the manager probably will not be able to anticipate beforehand exactly what data will be relevant or how those data can be used. However, the general categories of potentially useful data can be known and collected. For example, a marketing manager might need data on customers, sales to these customers, and geographic information, all of which can be provided from internal documents. In addition, the manager would want data on sales of competitive products and demographic data and trends, all of which would come from external sources. From this general data base, the manager could extract information relevant to a particular decision problem.

Tools for Translating Data into Information

It is one thing to have data available and quite another to transform them into useful form — that is, into information. A number of tools are needed. We shall consider the following:

Query languages and report writers

Modeling

Statistical techniques

Graphical techniques

Of these tools, modeling is the most important and least understood by managers, and it will receive the greatest attention here. However, we will look at query and report writers first, since they often accompany the creation of the data base.

Data-Base Query Languages and Report Writers

Above we indicated that the first requirement for a decision support system is a data base of internal and external data. It is equally important that these data be available in a form easily and quickly accessible to the manager. This calls for a computerized data base, with the means available to extract information from it easily and put that information in understandable reports. Query languages are software packages for doing the first task (extraction); report writers are software packages for performing the second. Today's products have features that use a simple language that the manager or an assistant can easily learn. In computer jargon, the systems are "user-friendly."

Today, many such data-base software products can be purchased off the shelf both for large computers and for microcomputers (including personal computers). As an example, the marketing manager mentioned above might be able to type on a terminal or personal computer a command such as

MAKE A LIST OF ALL MARKETS WITH OUR SHARE GREATER THAN BRAND X SHARE

or

MAKE A LIST OF ALL SALESPERSONS WITH SALES OF PRODUCT Y LAST MONTH AT LEAST 25% GREATER THAN THEIR SALES OF PRODUCT Y A YEAR AGO

Queries such as these can provide not data, but information that the manager could use in developing marketing plans.

To imply that information is as easily obtained as shown above is a bit of an oversimplification — but not much. There are data-base and query languages that allow phrasing not drastically different than that indicated. But first the data must be collected and entered into the data base, and they must be maintained and updated if they are to be useful. Furthermore, some training — perhaps only a few hours' worth — is needed for a manager or an assistant to use such software. These systems are only moderately user-friendly, but better ones are on the way — including some that respond to spoken commands.

Modeling

What is a model? In general, it is a simplified representation of some system. For example, architects construct scale models of planned buildings, and engineers construct models of airplanes to test in wind tunnels. These are physical models. Most models in management are not physical models, but symbolic or mathematical models, or representations, of a business system. A marketing manager, for instance, may use a financial model of the projected costs and revenues of a new product to decide whether or not to introduce the product. A production manager may use a model of orders and flows of orders through a factory to schedule production and overtime for the factory. In each of these cases, the situation is represented by simplified equations describing the factors involved. (By "simplified," we mean stripped of variables that are unnecessary to the analysis of the problem at hand. The aeronautical engineer, for example, probably would not put a dummy pilot in the seat of the model airplane; the marketing manager would not put packaging-design graphics in the mathematical cost/revenue model of the new product.)

This is difficult to understand in the abstract, so let us introduce a concrete example. We shall call our company the Pocono Potato Products Company (PPP for short). The company buys potatoes from growers and dehydrates them into potato flakes for sale to two large food processors. In March the company negotiates with the processors the price for potato flakes and the amount to be supplied for the year. Also in March, the company has to decide how much of the needed potatoes to purchase under preseason contracts. These contracts with potato growers guarantee that PPP will purchase the grower's crop at a specified price — in this case $2 per cwt (hundredweight) for process-grade potatoes. Any additional potatoes needed by PPP must be purchased in the open market in the fall at prices that depend on the market price at that time. The major issues facing PPP in March are (1) what agreement to make with the food processors about potato flakes prices and orders and (2) how much, if any, preseason contracting to do.

In preparing for the negotiations with the food processors, PPP management has made some estimates. They feel that if they negotiate a price at last year's level of $33 per cwt for flakes, the processors will order about 800 thousand cwt. They have given some consideration to insisting on a $35/cwt price, but they think the processors would cut their order to 400 thousand cwt in that case. They also think that at the lower price of $31/cwt, the processors might order 1,200 thousand cwt. Finally, they think that intermediate prices and order amounts are also possible; this judgment is represented by the line in Figure 7.2 and resembles what economists call a *demand curve.*

Building the model. As a first step in building a model, the problem must be simplified and important variables must be selected from the set of all variables that might be relevant. For our PPP example, this set of variables is shown in Table 7.1. (Note that this example is over-simplified in order to present the basic idea of a model. A model used by an operating manager would be more detailed and realistic, although still a much simplified — but not, one hopes, oversimplified — version of the real-world situation.)

Note that the variables in Table 7.1 are classified into four categories:

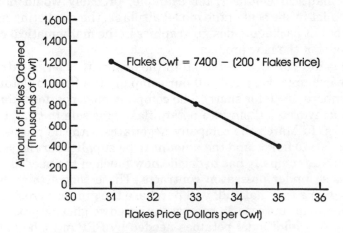

Figure 7.2 Pocono Potato Products
Flakes Price Vs Amount Ordered by Processors

Table 7.1 Pocono Potato Products

Variables

Decision Variables:

FLAKES PRICE — Price ($ per cwt) for potato flakes
CONTRACT POTATOES — Quantity (thousands of cwt) of potatoes (process grade) that are contracted for under preseason contracts

Objective:

PROFIT — Net profit before taxes (thousands of dollars)

Exogenous Variables:

OPEN-MARKET PRICE — Price paid in the open market (after harvest) for process grade potatoes ($ per cwt)
OVERHEAD COST — Overhead cost (thousands) per year

Other Variables:

FLAKES CWT — Amount of potato flakes ordered by food processors (thousands of cwt)
REVENUE — Total revenue from sale of potato flakes (thousands)
TOTAL COST — Total costs for the year (thousands)
PROCESSING COST — Variable cost of processing potatoes into flakes (thousands)
REQUIRED POTATOES — Amount of potatoes (thousands of cwt) required in total to fill the flakes contracts with food processors
OPEN-MARKET POTATOES — Potatoes (thousands of cwt) purchased on the open market (after harvest time)
RAW MATERIAL COST — Total cost (thousands) of potatoes purchased

Additional Factors

1. Six cwt of potatoes are required for each cwt of potato flakes.
2. Variable cost for processing is $13 per cwt of flakes up to 750 thousand cwt and $16 per cwt thereafter.
3. Overhead (fixed) costs are $4 million per year.
4. Preseason contract rate for process grade potatoes is $2 per cwt.

Decision variables: These are the factors under the control of the decision-maker. They represent the decisions that must be made in the situation. In this case, the PPP management must decide how many cwt of potatoes to contract for preseason. The price of potato flakes is not a pure decision variable, since it cannot be set entirely by the PPP management. Rather, it is set by negotiations with the large food processors — so it is partially a decision variable in that PPP participates in setting its value. (This classification of the flakes price is somewhat arbitrary; one might equally well have put it in the "exogenous variables" category.)

Objectives: The objectives are measures of the goals that decision-maker is trying to achieve. There can be several objectives, some of which may be in conflict. For example, a firm may wish to have both high profit and high market share, but may find that it needs to give up some short-term profit in order to attain a higher market share. In this example, we assume that annual profit is the only objective considered by PPP in the model.

Exogenous variables: These are variables that are important to the decision but that are determined externally (exogenously). Typically, general economic conditions, legal and marketing constraints, and other such factors are exogenous variables. The most important factor in our example is the open-market price for process-grade potatoes. This is the price that PPP will have to pay for any potatoes purchased in excess of those contracted for. It is exogenous because it is determined by market factors outside the control of PPP.

Other variables: A number of other variables are used as intermediaries in defining the profit for the firm. In this example, the quantity of potatoes that must be purchased and various cost and revenue categories are included as other variables. The needed amount of potato flakes is also included here, although PPP has some influence over this in the negotiating process.

Defining relationships. After identifying the important variables, the next step in building a model is to determine how the variables are connected to each other — that is, to define the model relationships.

One way to begin is to draw a diagram (sometimes called an *influence diagram*) such as Figure 7.3. Note that our objective, PROFIT, is at the top. PROFIT is derived from two variables, REVENUE and TOTAL COST, which are the boxes on the next level. REVENUE in turn depends upon the FLAKES PRICE and FLAKES CWT (the amount ordered). There are three components to cost — PROCESSING COST, OVERHEAD COST, and RAW MATERIAL COST.

PROCESSING COST depends solely upon FLAKES CWT (amount of flakes ordered). RAW MATERIAL COST depends upon CONTRACT POTATOES (and their price), OPEN-MARKET POTATOES, and OPEN-MARKET PRICE.

In turn, the amount of potatoes purchases on the open market (OPEN-MARKET POTATOES) depends upon the REQUIRED POTATOES and the CONTRACT POTATOES. FLAKES CWT depends on FLAKES PRICE. Finally, REQUIRED POTATOES depends upon the FLAKES CWT.

Note that only the boxes at the very bottom of the figure do not

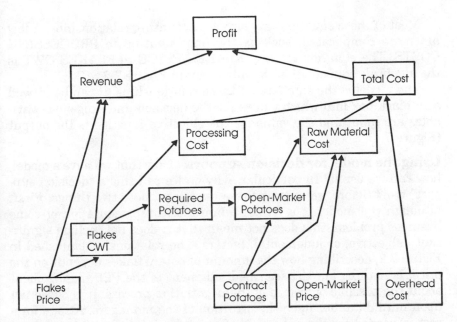

Figure 7.3 Pocono Potato Products — Influence Diagram

depend on other factors (i.e., do not have arrows leading into them). These are either decision variables or exogenous variables.

A diagram such as Figure 7.3 may not be useful in all modeling situations. Here it does give an idea of which variables are connected to which, and which depend on which. The next step is to translate these connections into simple equations.

We start at the top (an asterisk means "multiply by"):

PROFIT = REVENUE − TOTAL COST
REVENUE = FLAKES PRICE * FLAKES CWT
TOTAL COST = PROCESSING COST + RAW MATERIAL COST +
           OVERHEAD COST
FLAKES CWT = 7,400 − (200 * FLAKES PRICE)
If FLAKES CWT < 750 thousand then
  PROCESSING COST = 13 * FLAKES CWT
 Otherwise:
  PROCESSING COST = (13 * 750) + (16 * (FLAKES CWT − 750))
RAW MATERIAL COST = (2 * CONTRACT POTATOES) +
        (OPEN-MARKET PRICE * OPEN-MARKET POTATOES)
OPEN-MARKET POTATOES = REQUIRED POTATOES −
        CONTRACT POTATOES
REQUIRED POTATOES = 6 * FLAKES CWT

Most of these equations are simple accounting relationships. A few are more complicated, such as the ones relating to PROCESSING COSTS. The equation relating FLAKES PRICE to FLAKES CWT is the algebraic equivalent of the line given in Figure 7.2.

The model is the sum total of these relationships. It can be viewed as a black box into which values for the decision and exogenous variables are input and the value for the objective function is the output (Figure 7.4).

Using the model for decision support. Now that we have a model, how can we use it? In particular, why do we call this a "decision support" tool? Before we answer these questions, note two things. First, although the model is a formal quantitative representation of some business problem, this does not mean that it does not include significant subjective, or judgmental, factors. The relationship embodied in Figure 7.2, describing how the amount of potato flakes depends on the price, is nothing but the seasoned judgment of the PPP management about the possible outcomes of the negotiation process. It is based not upon hard data, but upon the intuition of the managers. Also, a forecast is needed for the open-market price for potatoes. While such an estimate might be based partially upon historical data, it includes allowance for judgment of the managers. In building any model, deciding what variables are important for the model is a subjective call. *Hence, although based upon objective data where relevant, a model is largely a subjective creation, reflecting the decision-maker's knowledge of the problem and his or her judgment.*

A second important point to note is that generally there are significant factors relevant to the decision at hand but not incorporated in a model, either because they are not quantifiable or because the manager chooses to exclude them. In our example, PPP's long-term relationships to the food processors, the potato growers, and employees are

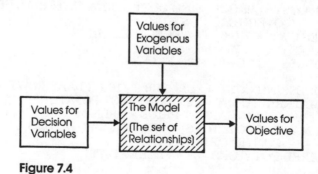

Figure 7.4

certainly important, and management would be unwilling to take actions that would hurt these relationships. Yet these factors are not included in the model. Management's attitude toward taking risk is also not included — although, as we shall see shortly, some decisions involve a significant chance of large losses.

So, if the model is subjective and excludes significant qualitative variables, how can a manager possibly use it to make a decision? The answer is that the manager doesn't use the model to "make a decision" but rather uses it as an aid in understanding the problem better, preliminary to making a decision. *The model is intended as an aid to the manager — as a method of extending insight and understanding of the decision problem.* This will become clearer as we illustrate the use of our model.

Analysis using the model. Let us illustrate how PPP's management might use the model we have just developed. For the past few years PPP has had a policy of preseason contracting for one-half of its requirements for potatoes and purchasing the other half on the open market. Assume for now that this policy is to continue. And consider the negotiations with the food processors. PPP must decide what price to negotiate for potato flakes.

A major unknown is the price that PPP will have to pay for potatoes purchased on the open market (OPEN-MARKET PRICE). Let's examine this unknown using *sensitivity analysis,* that is, by trying out various assumptions. First, let's assume that the OPEN-MARKET PRICE is $2/cwt. Our analysis now looks like the diagram shown in Figure 7.5.

We try our various values for FLAKES PRICE and record the resulting PROFIT. The results are shown in Table 7.2. The optimum price is $32.50 because it results in a profit of $2.3 million.

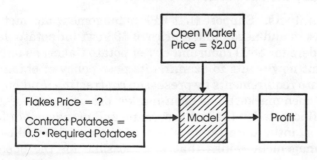

Figure 7.5

Table 7.2 Profit versus Flakes Price (Open-Market Price = $2.00 and Contract Potatoes = 0.5 * Required Potatoes)

Flakes Price (per cwt)	Profit (thousands)
$31.00	$1,850
32.00	2,250
32.50	2,300
33.00	2,250
34.00	1,400
35.00	0

Recall that all this is based on the assumption that the open-market price is $2/cwt. But what if it is $1.50 or $2.50 or some other value? We can repeat the analysis as above, and the results are displayed in Figure 7.6.

From this graph, PPP management can gain some interesting insights about the decision problem. Note that the optimum price for flakes does depend somewhat on what the open-market price for potatoes might be. The curves peak at about $32.00 for an open-market price of $1.50 (the top curve in Figure 7.6), $32.50 for the price of $2.00 (middle curve and Table 7.2), and $33.25 for a potato price of $2.50 (bottom curve). Of course, the profits are quite different in the three cases. But note that the flakes price decision is quite insensitive to the open-market price, as long as FLAKES PRICE is in the $32-to-$33 range. That is, the difference in profit between $32 and $33 (and values in between) is quite small for any value for open-market price (i.e., on any of the curves in Figure 7.6). This implies that management can negotiate the FLAKES PRICE quite independent of expectations of OPEN-MARKET PRICE for potatoes. This is a very important managerial insight, and one not obvious beforehand.

Further analysis. Suppose that PPP management has met with the food processors and negotiated a price of $33/cwt for potato flakes and received orders for $800 thousand cwt of potato flakes, as anticipated. Management now wants to examine its past policy of obtaining one-half its potato requirements by preseason contracting (and buying one-half on the open market). The open-market price for process-grade potatoes has fluctuated in the last few years, and management feels that there is substantial uncertainty about what this price will be. In particular, management thinks that it is possible for the open-market

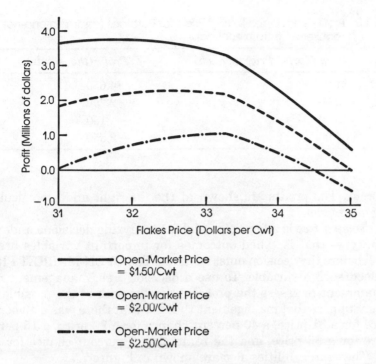

Figure 7.6 Pocono Potato Products Profit Vs Flakes Price

price to be $1, $2, $3, or even $4 per cwt (it could, of course, be any value in between, but to simplify matters, we shall consider only these values). Using the model defined above (with FLAKES PRICE = 33 and FLAKES CWT = 800), the profit can be calculated for PPP's current policy of contracting one-half its potato requirements and for each of the possible prices, and is shown in Table 7.3. Thus the company can make substantial profits ($4.65 million) if the price is low, but could face a loss of $2.55 million if the price goes to $4.

Suppose PPP's management is considering two alternatives to the current policy — namely to contract 100 percent for potatoes (and buy none on the open market) or to contract for 75 percent (and buy 25 percent on the open market). These alternatives, and the past policy (50% contracting, 50% open market), are shown in a diagram, called a *decision tree,* in Figure 7.7. The branches emanating from the decision node (the square on the left) represent decision alternatives. The branches coming from the event nodes (circles) represent events that

Table 7.3 Profit versus Open Market Price for Potatoes (assuming one-half requirements from contracts)

Open-Market Price (per cwt)	Profit (thousands)
$1.00	$4,650
2.00	2,250
3.00	− 150
4.00	−2,550

can occur. The profits are shown at the far right and are calculated using our model.

A *decision tree* is a form of model for analyzing decisions under uncertainty — that is, when outcomes for important variables are not known before the decision must be made. The OPEN-MARKET PRICE is indeed such a variable. To use a decision tree, management must use judgment to assess the probabilities for each of the possible outcomes. Suppose that management thought that there was a 40 percent chance for a $1 price, a 40 percent chance for a $2 price, a 15 percent chance for a $3 price, and the remaining 5 percent chance for a $4 price. These probabilities also are shown in Figure 7.7.

One approach to analysis using a decision tree is to calculate the *expected value* for each event node. The expected value is the weighted average value, using the probabilities as weights. For example, the expected value of profit for the current policy (50 percent contracting) is calculated in Table 7.4, giving an expected value of $2,610 thousand dollars. Thus, expected value takes into account both how likely an event is to occur and the payoff or profit for that event.

Table 7.4 Calculation of Expected Value (policy of contracting 50% for potatoes)

Event — Potato Price (per cwt)	Probability	Profit (thousands)	Probability × Profit
$1.00	.40	$4,650	1,860
2.00	.40	2,250	900
3.00	.15	− 150	− 22.5
4.00	.05	−2,550	− 127.5
		Expected value for profit	2,610.0

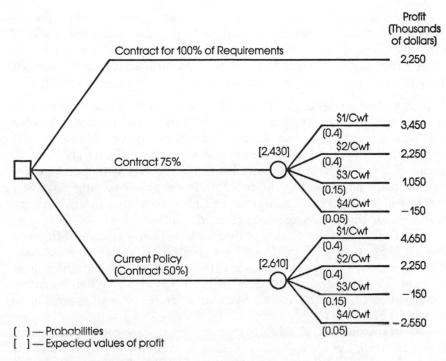

( ) — Probabilities
[ ] — Expected values of profit

Figure 7.7 Pocono Potato Products
Decision Tree for Contracting Decision

A manager who was *not* concerned with the riskiness of a decision could use expected value as the decision criterion when uncertainty is involved. This would lead to choosing the current policy (50 percent contracting), with an expected value of $2,610 thousand, over the other two alternatives (75 percent contracting with expected value of $2,430 thousand and 100 percent contracting with profit of $2,250). Note, however, that substantial amounts (millions of dollars) are at stake and that the alternatives vary considerably in the risk they present. The highest expected value alternative (50 percent contracting) has some chance of a substantial loss of over $2 million. The lowest expected value alternative has no risk related to open-market prices at all (put another way, its probability is 1.0) since 100 percent of potatoes are purchased under contract.

There are formal techniques for aiding management's decision in situations such as this in which risk is a major factor, but they are beyond what can be covered in this expository chapter. In any case, they involve management's judgment about how much expected value to give up to avoid risk. In this example, management may prefer the middle alternative (75 percent contracting) since under the worst of circumstances it involves only a small loss, but has $180 thousand more expected profit than the 100 percent contracting alternative. It may thus be a good compromise between risk and expected profit.

Summary of modeling. It has not been our purpose here to provide an extended treatment of modeling, but rather to illustrate the idea and how managers can use models in decision support. There are several types of models. Figure 7.8 gives a rough classification of these in terms of whether the major variables can be treated as certain (known) or uncertain and whether the problem is simple (involving relatively few variables and relationships) or complex (involving many, perhaps hundreds or thousands, of variables and relationships).

Our first model of Pocono Potato Products is an example of the *case model*. It is relatively simple and we treated all variables as certain (i.e., there were no probabilities involved). The method of analysis is by trial and error and sensitivity ("what if") analysis. When we introduced uncertainty, the model became a *decision tree* approach as shown in Figure 7.7.

When the decision problem is more complex, case models can sometimes be used, but *optimization models* become more valuable. These involve mathematical procedures to search for the "optimum" solution among a set of possibilities. Linear programming is an optimizing technique in common use in business. For example, wood products firms use such models to determine which products to produce and to schedule their production at the firm's various mills. When there is both complexity and uncertainty, a technique called *simulation* is often used. One example is the large simulation model that was built to study the effects of weather and other uncertain causes of flight delays on the operations of O'Hare Airport in Chicago. (Use of this model resulted in one-time savings of over a million dollars for United Airlines.)

Major Factors are Treated as:

Problem is:	Certain	Uncertain
Simple	Case Model	Decision Tree
Complex	Case Model Optimization	Simulation

Figure 7.8 Classification of Models

Management use of models. For the simple models described above, management can actually develop and use the models themselves. Sometimes the models are "back of the envelope" calculations, involving no elaborate analysis. More often, the analysis is done on a computer, especially a personal computer. This build-it-yourself approach offers several advantages. The model truly belongs to the manager — it reflects his or her view of the problem and judgments about key estimates and probabilities. The manager can make the model as simple or as complex as necessary to suit the problem at hand. And he or she can manipulate the model until sufficient insight about the decision problem is obtained. Most important, the manager knows the limitations of the model — what its assumptions are and what has been left out.

For a number of years, computer software has been available to build simple models of the type we have described above.[1] But the big innovation in recent years has been the introduction of personal computers, and particularly the availability of spreadsheet packages, such as VisiCalc and Lotus 1-2-3, for use on them. These spreadsheet packages greatly facilitate model-building, and they are easy to use and inexpensive. Moreover, they enable the manager to build and use models without having to rely on outside groups of computer experts. Software is available for graphic analysis and even for decision trees.[2] More complex packages and optimizing programs are also available for personal computers.[3] All this has opened up a new era in decision support for managers.

For the more complex models described above, the manager would be involved as part of a team in developing such models. The manager would retain the responsibility for ensuring that the model was a reasonable representation of the decision problem, but the actual building and running of the model generally would be done by analysts skilled in such techniques. Models in this class can also be very valuable management tools, but not without substantial care and involvement on the part of the manager.

Statistical and Graphical Techniques

At the beginning of this chapter the tools for decision support were listed as query languages and report writers, modeling, statistical techniques, and graphics. All of these assume the existence of some managerial data base, and all are methods for converting these data into information useful to management. Having considered modeling in some detail, we now turn to the remaining tools.

An old expression states that "a picture is worth a thousand words," and indeed a graph describing how variables are related may be much more effective than a verbal description in helping one understand what is involved. A good example is Figure 7.4, which shows the relationship between profit and the price of potato flakes for different potato prices. The fact that the decision about flakes price is relatively independent of the open-market price for potatoes is more easily understood from this graph. One of the major benefits of microcomputers is graphic capability, and much good software is available to exploit it.

Statistical methodology has been available for many years, but only recently — with the easy accessibility of computers — has it become accessible to managers. One use of this methodology is to estimate from past data the relationships involved in models. In our example of the PPP company, the relationship between the processing cost and the potato flakes volume could indeed have been estimated from cost data in previous years. Marketing managers estimate demand curves such as that shown in Figure 7.2 for data from market research studies.

Forecasting is another application of statistical methodology. For example, a firm may find that its sales are related to basic economic variables such as industrial production or housing starts. These relationships can be exploited for planning purposes. Such models, sometimes called *econometric models,* may involve several interconnected equations. As an example, the *New York Times* built an econometric model to estimate future circulation and advertising volume for its various editions based upon economic variables such as employment, income, and production in various industries.[4]

MANAGEMENT OF INFORMATION TECHNOLOGY

In the introduction to this chapter, we mentioned two themes relating information systems to today's manager. The first theme — the manager's direct use of the technology as support for decisions — has been the focus of the discussion so far. We now turn to the second theme, the management of information technology.

Trends in Information Systems (IS)

Futurists have announced that we have begun the Information Age — that we are riding the crest of a major technological revolution. This revolution is producing a number of trends that are important for the management of information systems.

Information technology continues to change rapidly. One dimension of change is the declining cost of computer hardware — on the order of

20 percent per year, depending upon the type of equipment. This means that equipment with, say, double the capability will be available in three or four years at today's prices. But price is not the only type of change. New technologies appear (for example, laser disk technology and voice input) with great rapidity, and others once thought promising disappear (e.g., bubble memories) with equal speed. In addition, there is a merging of the three formerly separate technologies (and functions) of office automation, telecommunications, and data processing. Computers are now at the core of all these technologies, and a firm may choose to use the same computer or interconnected computers to do one or more of these functions.

Dealing with this rapid change is a first-magnitude challenge. Management's task is to see that the technology is adopted by the organization in an orderly fashion without excessive cost and disruption.

There are equally strong trends in computer software. *As hardware costs decline, software is becoming a more significant part of the computing picture.* Much of the software currently in use is old, badly patched, and in need of replacement or rewriting. Software maintenance costs for most data processing centers are high — as much as half or more of the total budget in some cases. And yet new applications require ever more complex software.

Perhaps the most significant trend in software is the emergence of a strong software market, fed by both the computer vendors and independent software houses. Thus companies increasingly have the option of buying their software off the shelf rather than having to develop and maintain it themselves.

A third trend is a shift in the type of computing going on in most organizations, from sole commitment to EDP toward more effective MIS and, increasingly, decision support (that is, moving to the right in Figure 7.1). The tools and approaches discussed earlier in this chapter are becoming more available and more in demand by managers. This change requires a very different focus and attitude on the part of data processing professionals. In a sense the data processing department is shifting from a production center to a service center.

A fourth trend relates to the tremendous popularity of microcomputers in both the office and the home. People are discovering that computers can do all sorts of things, and they are beginning to demand more of the same from data processing departments in their organizations.

All this results in three overall challenges that face general managers responsible for the direction that information systems in their firms will take:

1. Getting useful computerized systems up and running

2. Organizing IS activities

3. Incorporating IS technology in corporate planning

We shall address each of these in turn.

Getting Useful Systems Running

Some of the trends mentioned above (unbridled enthusiasm of users, high maintenance costs of current systems, merging of office automation and telecommunications, etc.) have resulted in huge backlogs of demand for systems in most organizations. The current staff simply cannot produce software systems fast enough to meet the demand for users of computer systems. Backlogs of two or three years are not uncommon. This has led to substantial friction between users of computer systems and the data processing department. In some organizations, the battle lines are drawn more or less as described in Figure 7.7. The data processing (DP) department worries about interference with its "bread and butter" applications (i.e., the traditional record-keeping operations), and about lack of control of costs and standards for documentation, data integrity (accuracy, timeliness, and proper authorization for access to data in data bases). It also complains that the users don't really know what they want. For their part, users complain about the backlog, about the slowness of DP to respond, about the "can't be done" attitude, and about the priorities that DP has adopted. In response, the users threaten to go outside the organization or to develop systems themselves, becoming competitive data processing departments. DP managers are requesting additional resources, but warn that resources alone cannot solve the problem.

How can enlightened management deal with this conflict? Fortunately, several approaches are being tried, and are succeeding, in some organizations. These are listed in the bottom of Figure 7.9 and will be discussed briefly.

A highly successful approach in many organizations is the creation of *information centers*. The idea of these centers is indeed to let the users "do it themselves" and to provide the tools and support to enable them to do it. The center provides computer resources for the user, sometimes on minicomputers or microcomputers. It provides software for decision support of the type discussed earlier in this chapter. For example, financial modeling, data base, and statistical software are common in almost all information centers. Further, technical help is provided to enable the users to develop their own applications. This

USERS

Urgent problem
Poor (slow) DP response
DP — "Can't be done"
Wrong priorities by DP
Don't understand problem
Too costly

Do it ourselves
Go outside

DP

Poor specification of needs by users
Unrealistic expectations of users
Standardization
• avoid duplication
• compatibility
Our own problems
• shortage of skilled people
• existing systems
• changing technology

More resources?

SOME SUCCESSFUL APPROACHES

Information centers
Fourth-generation software
Purchased software
User's responsibility for developing systems
Prototyping

Figure 7.9 Managing the Interface
DP versus Users

includes training and consultation. Support for personal computers has been a major activity of most information centers, providing help in purchase, training, software, electronic mail, and interface with the corporation's main computer system.

Information centers sometimes also provide a link between the data collected within the corporation in its routine transactions processing activities and the data needed for managerial support. For example, the information center may be responsible for periodically creating and downloading from the main computer a marketing data base containing information about customers, purchases, sales representatives, and so forth. These data can then be accessed by the operating managers using the data base software that we described earlier.

Other approaches to the user/DP interface problem focus on improving the productivity of data processing professionals in order to reduce the backlog. The last few years have seen the development of so-called *fourth-generation software*. Some of this software has been designed for users, to enable them to develop their own applications. As such it fits in the information-center concept discussed above. But much of this new software is intended for the programmer in DP. These new languages are at a higher level: they replace with a few statements what might take a page or more of code in older languages. These packages are called *nonprocedural languages, report writers, applications generators, screen generators,* or *data base languages.*[5]

Another approach is to purchase software from an outside vendor. Such software is available for applications common to many businesses. Thus there is software for general accounting, payables, receivables, and so on; for firms engaged in distribution; for banking, including automatic teller machines; for pharmacies; and even for churches. (Of course, firms must still develop software for applications that are unique.) The advantage of purchasing off-the-shelf software is not only that it is much cheaper than developing one's own software, but also that the vendor undertakes to maintain it in the future. A disadvantage is that sometimes the firm buying such software has to modify its procedures to match the software. An extension of the purchased-software idea is the *turnkey system,* in which a vendor will package hardware and software into a complete system. Such systems are available for hospitals, for manufacturing systems, and for many other applications.

One of the major conflicts in developing useful systems has been in correctly specifying the system requirements. We have already noted that data processing professionals complain that users don't really know what they want, and that they constantly demand changes in system specifications during development. For their part, users feel intimidated or frustrated (or both) in dealing with DP people. Two quite different approaches have met with some success in dealing with this problem. One is to put the system development responsibility on the user: he or she decides what systems are to be developed and what priorities to place on them. The user doesn't actually program the system, but he or she monitors this activity and is charged the development cost. The user then bears direct responsibility if specification is incomplete or if the system doesn't get sufficient management support.

A second approach to dealing with the problem of system specification is that of prototyping. Rather than completely specifying the system beforehand and then developing it, the programmers develop a "quick and dirty" version (a *prototype*) instead and turn it over to the users. The users try it out and suggest modifications, and the prototype goes back for revision. Several revisions may be made before a satisfactory system is developed. Further, the system is developed in "chunks" rather than all at once. The advantage of this approach is that it allows the user to define the requirements after having a better idea of what is needed. Prototyping seems to work well for applications of the decision support type. This approach is usually inappropriate for developing strictly EDP-oriented applications, in which the traditional "systems development life cycle" techniques are preferable.

Organizing IS Activities

In the last few years computers have spread throughout business organizations. This is particularly true of microcomputers, but an observer will find minicomputers and even large computers at many levels in today's businesses. Organizations that would require a careful economic analysis for an expenditure of, say, $250,000 by the centralized data processing department have often allowed managers to purchase personal computers without formal justification. One day, the organization wakes up to realize that it owns 1,000 such units with a total cost of perhaps $5 million. Is this an effective use of computing, or is it out-of-control proliferation? Who should have and manage computers in organizations? This is a major issue for the 1980s.

In the 1970s, many organizations centralized the computing function. The arguments for doing so were the economies of scale available in computing at the time,[6] the avoidance of duplication of systems development, and the need for standardization. The trend is now clearly in the opposite direction. A move toward decentralized and distributed computing is more common.

How should managers decide which approach is best for their organization? First, they must recognize that there are three types of IS activities: operations, systems development, and planning/management (see Figure 7.10). *Operations* involves the actual running of the hardware; *systems development* involves development of software systems; *planning/management* is what the name implies. Each of these activities can be centralized or decentralized. Some companies retain all IS activities in a centralized department; others are completely

OPERATIONS	SYSTEMS DEVELOPMENT	PLANNING/MANAGEMENT
Schedule and run computers	Manage development projects	System priorities
Backup	Hire, train, motivate programmers	Authorize:
Data entry		hardware purchases
Security for facilities	Security for programs and data	software systems
	User interaction/training	Standards for:
		data integrity
		compatibility
		systems development

Figure 7.10 IS Activities

	Pressures Toward Centralization	Pressures Toward Decentralization
Operations (Hardware and Data bases)	Economies of scale Coordinated control Data-base integrity Standardization and compatibility More sophisticated management possible Clear responsibility for planning	Economies for local data entry Local control to meet local needs Reduced cost of telecommunications Possible improvement in service Less sophisticated management needed
Systems Development	Avoidance of duplication (develop common systems) Control of: • standards • documentation • maintenance Better management of DP personnel • career paths • sophistication	Systems and priorities for local needs Availability of purchased software Backlog at central DP Sophisticated personnel closer to client

Figure 7.11 Organization of IS Activities

decentralized in all three functions. Some have a centralized data center (operations) but have systems development and planning/management in their various divisions.

Second, managers should be aware that the three types of computing shown in Figure 7.1 can be handled differently. Because financial records must be audited and controlled, and because information processing is cheaper when done in large volumes, activities of the EDP type may be centralized. On the other hand, DSS activities are easier to decentralize, particularly with microcomputers.

Figure 7.11 lists some of the pressures toward centralization and toward decentralization for operations and systems development. In the planning/management dimension, the factors relate to how the firm is organized in general (i.e., are the divisions or other units relatively autonomous, or under strong control?) and how planning is done for other activities.

There is no clear single answer to the organization of information systems activities. Recent technology developments make decentralization much more feasible, and this is certainly the trend. Whether or not this is the best solution for a particular firm depends upon the mix of pressures noted in Figure 7.9 and on the following factors:

The geographical dispersion of the firm. If the firm is widely dispersed (especially if it is international), decentralized computing is a more likely alternative.

Computing needs of the subunits. If the subunits do similar types of computing (e.g., if all subunits are distributors), then the argument for avoidance of duplicate efforts pushes toward centralization, particularly of the systems development and of the planning/management function.

Management style and corporate culture. The organization of the computing function generally conforms to the organization of the rest of the firm; if it is decentralized, then computing generally is, too.

Strategic importance. The importance of information systems in strategic planning is discussed below. Here we simply note that if information systems are to play a critical role in the corporate strategy, they must be high on corporate management's agenda. This often means centralization, at least for the planning/management function, and often also for the systems development function.

IS Technology and Corporate Strategy

As we noted earlier, information systems technology historically has been aimed at gains in efficiency, particularly in clerical tasks. Although this is a worthy goal, it has not been considered a strategic issue — clerical cost control is usually a middle-management prerogative. Hence, information systems have not been viewed as an important or even necessary part of corporate strategy.

But this view is changing. First of all, there are several industries in which data processing is a significant part of the service being provided and data processing costs are large. Insurance companies and banks are prime examples. In these industries, a corporate strategy calling for low costs dictates mechanization of the paperwork — that is, using information technology to the fullest. Banks are particularly involved because deregulation has removed the barriers to price competition. Banks are introducing automatic teller machines, home banking, and other electronic means to reduce costs. For these institutions, IS plays a critical role in their strategy.

Perhaps even more significant is the belief in many companies that information systems can be a proactive tool in shaping the competitive posture of a company. That is, information systems can be used to add value directly to the products or services that the organization offers. Although, in a way, using information systems as a competitive weapon is nothing more than extending various kinds of efficiency gains into products, services, and their distribution, in the eyes of the ultimate client, such as a customer, it is seen as more than this. The ultimate client rarely distinguishes between the product or service itself and the information related to its delivery or use. It is altogether appropriate, therefore, to view information systems as a component of the products and services that the organization offers to the marketplace.

In order to make these issues more concrete, we shall introduce a few examples. The International Paper Corporation some years ago began to install terminals tied to its own computer systems into the offices of the distributors who purchased paper goods for redistribution to end customers. The terminals were used with accompanying software to facilitate the order entry process, for reordering and resupplying paper goods to these wholesale distributors. Also, the software is capable of assisting inventory management of the warehouse stocks of the *customer* (such as semiautomatic reordering based upon economic lot-size quantities, restocking policies, etc.). From one perspective, this is clearly an improvement in the efficiency of the ordering process and was originally perceived by the management of International Paper to be precisely that — a way of capturing information through point-of-sale technology. However, as seen from the eyes of the customer, what could be conceived of as a commodity item, paper goods, has now been differentiated in the marketplace by means of the delivery system that allows the customer to gain access to it. The end result is a substantial enhancement of International Paper's ability to compete in a market that is otherwise distinguished by little more than price and delivery time.

A similar story comes from Federal-Mogul, a supplier of auto parts. Federal-Mogul spent about $100 million to develop a computer-based warehouse system, with computer terminals in its customers' (parts dealers') premises. This system guarantees delivery of parts within two days, allowing dealers to work from little or no inventory. The dealers, in turn, commit to buy parts only from Federal-Mogul. This system has led to a substantial improvement in earnings for the company.

Another company that has profited from its ability to treat IS as an integral element of its products and services is Foremost-McKesson, a pharmaceutical supply house. Foremost-McKesson put computer terminals in its client pharmacies' premises to expedite their order entries. When it was discovered that the pharmacies often were paid by third parties (for example, health insurance companies) rather than by the pharmacies' retail customers themselves, Foremost-McKesson expanded its IS operation to include billing these third parties directly.

Thus, the company is now actually selling EDP and financial services as well as pharmaceutical products.

A better-known example is that of American Airlines and United Airlines with their reservation systems, SABER and APOLLO. American and United used their expertise in IS technology to develop reservation systems for travel agents, and marketed them aggressively. One of the main advantages of these systems for the developers is that, while they provide information on all airlines, they have subtle biases toward American and United in the way flights are listed and positioned on the screen. Perhaps even more important, they give American and United important information about competitors' bookings. The proof that these systems have been quite successful for the developers is that their use has been challenged in court by other airlines.

Many other instances could be cited of pushing information systems out into the hands of customers who do not have the capital or the expertise to develop such systems themselves. It is easy to see the strategic benefit to the first supplier of such technology. No wholesale distributor is going to install a hundred different terminals from a hundred different suppliers; nor is the distributor going to learn the protocols for more than one or two vendors. Thus there are substantial rewards to the first company that gets its foot in the door. And the ultimate benefit to the supplier of such information systems is that these systems raise the switching cost for the customer, thereby locking in the business.

Since our economy is increasingly services-rich in its activities, any information system use that tends to tie an organization closer to its clientele, to provide feedback for purposes of market research, to provide information for future transactions, or to lock in the customer is a competitive advantage. Thus information systems can be an important element in distinguishing one's product line from what would otherwise be a commodity good in the marketplace.

Allow us one final example to illustrate how profound an effect information technology can have. The CSX Corporation is a holding company that was built around railroading activities (the Chessie system). The company has expanded into other forms of transportation, such as barging and natural gas pipelines. However, in the last few years the Chessie system has been laying optical fiber cable along its right-of-way. The traditional reason for doing something like this would be to facilitate internal communications among the offices of a geographically dispersed organization. But the goal is broader than this and is a part of the CSX strategy of defining its business as transportation in a very broad sense of the word. That is, the CSX management sees the company as a common carrier not only of things but of information, and they are exploiting their unique position in owning right-of-way by laying the "rails of the future," optical cable.

Incorporating IS Technology in Corporate Planning

Granted that IS technology can have a significant impact on corporate strategy, how can it be incorporated in the planning process?

First and foremost its incorporation requires a reorientation of management's thinking to viewing information systems as a potential "value added" resource, rather than as a cost control problem to be dealt with as expeditiously as possible. Unfortunately, the problem mind-set characterizes too many managements. A first step is for management to become better acquainted with potential applications of IS technology. This involves much more than computers themselves, since the company's success in exporting IS technology to various clienteles increasingly depends on the availability of software, the organization of delivery systems, and training in the use of these delivery systems.

A second need is for companies to develop new technological competence in areas where IS may lead to competitive advantages. Knowledge of telecommunications is one example and the ability to develop user-friendly software is another. Companies that have oriented their information systems specialists to traditional mainframe hardware or software systems for traditional kinds of data processing are ill-positioned to exploit the new opportunities.

Related to this is the need for experimentation. No new product would be introduced without extensive research-and-development effort. The same is true for information systems. Management should expect to invest in activities designed to learn, and to develop new approaches. This requires a change in attitude. Many companies, perhaps burned by mistakes, have taken a "trailing edge" philosophy in information technology — that is, they wait until the technology is proven and most of the bugs are out before adopting it. Such a philosophy gives one's competitors the edge. Alternatives include experiments in computer-aided design/computer-aided manufacturing, implementation of the fourth-generation languages for MIS, DSS on personal computers, and pilot tests of office automation. Critical to all this is the development of an attitude and a corporate culture that encourage responsible risk-taking in the IS area — a major senior management challenge.

Finally, *information systems management must be actively involved in the planning process.* This doesn't mean that management develops a plan and then hands it to IS for implementation. Nor does it mean that IS is told to develop the corporate plan. It does mean that people who understand the technology and what it can do should be involved in developing the corporate strategy. This especially means managers.

Perhaps this is a good place to end this section: on a note of management involvement. It has been said that "war is too important to leave to the generals." Because of its value to managers in decision support and its role in helping the corporation stay competitive, IS is becoming much too important to leave to the IS specialists. Managers must become actively engaged in planning and implementing IS activities.

LOOKING AHEAD

What developments can we expect to see in information systems in the years ahead? We can expect a continuation in the trends mentioned earlier in the chapter: rapid change in IS technology, the merging of this technology with that of telecommunications and office automation, a shift in computing toward DSS, and an even wider popularity of personal computers. These trends mean that managers responsible for business firms, and especially managers of information systems, will have to work hard to stay knowledgeable about what is happening and to manage these changes in their organizations.

Much of the spotlight in the next few years will be on the office. More than half of all American workers are now "knowledge workers," and major efforts are under way to supply them with computerized tools. Vendors promise integrated office systems. To date, however, much of this really has been only word processing, an example of clerical or computer processing of the EDP type (see Figure 7.1). The challenge is to provide professionals with knowledge tools that are more of the DSS type of computing, that is, tools that support professional and decisionmaking activities. Beginnings have been made with computer-aided design, with the development of expert systems from the area of artificial intelligence, with electronic mail and teleconferencing, and with various electronic reference systems for professionals such as lawyers and doctors. But this hardly scratches the surface.

We envision the knowledge worker of the future with an "intelligent workstation" (an enhanced personal computer) at his or her desk, connected by a network to various services: to data bases, both personal and corporate; to telecommunications with voice, text, video, and image transmission capability; and to various forms of printers, plotters, and other output devices. The worker will have software available to create his or her work product, whether it is an answer to a customer inquiry, a technical report, drawings for a new product, a financial plan for a division, a medical diagnosis, a legal brief, or a presentation to the board of directors. The interaction with the workstation will be easy and natural. The software will be intelligent (that is, it will guide and help the user through his or her task). This vision will, of course, take time to materialize, and it is early to tell exactly what paths will be taken.

We have mentioned the use of information systems technology as a competitive weapon. This trend is going to continue. The information content in our products and services is continually growing, and companies will be challenged to modify their products in keeping with this trend. We may see major struggles in some industries over who controls and supplies the information in the industry. The current battles over airline reservation systems are precursors of what may happen in other areas.

Indeed we are in an Information Age. Futurists[7] have pointed out the profound impact that this is going to have on our lives and on society. It is going to have equally profound effects on how business firms do their work, on how they are organized, and on how information is processed in them.

NOTES

1. Financial planning and data-base-oriented languages such as IFPS, EXPRESS, EMPIRE, FOCUS, RAMIS, and NOMAD have been available on large computers for several years.

2. A package called Arborist has recently been announced by Texas Instruments.

3. The financial planning language IFPS is now available on microcomputers. The package LINDO, also available on micros, is an easy-to-use optimization program. Programs such as Symphony and Framework are available on micros for integrating spreadsheets, data bases, graphics, and word processing. Javelin will even do influence diagrams.

4. See L. Foreman, "The New York Times Newspaper Planning Model," in Thomas Naylor, *Corporate Planning Models* (Reading, Ma.: Addison-Wesley, 1979).

5. For good discussions of these languages, see James Martin, *An Information Systems Manifesto* (Englewood Cliffs, N.J.: Prentice-Hall, 1984); Werner Frank, *Critical Issues in Software* (New York: John Wiley, 1983).

6. Grosch's law stated that computing power goes up as the square of the cost of the computer. Thus it was more economical to have one large data center than two smaller ones. Grosch's law held pretty well for first- and second-generation computers, and possibly even for the third generation. It has questionable application to the fourth generation, particularly when a mix of different types of computing is involved and software performance increasingly confounds attempts to develop simple performance rules.

7. See, for example, John Nesbit, *Megatrends* (New York: Warner Books, 1982).

SUGGESTED READINGS

Allen, Brandt. "An Unmanaged Computer System Can Stop You Dead." *Harvard Business Review* (November–December 1982). A well-written article on some of the problems facing today's IS management.

Bennett, John L., editor. *Building Decision Support Systems*. Reading, Ma.: Addison-Wesley, 1983. A good discussion of decision support systems and the issues involved in building and using them.

Bierman, Harold Jr., Charles P. Bonini, and Warren H. Hausman. *Quantitative Analysis for Business Decisions,* 6th ed. Homewood, Ill.: Richard Irwin, 1981. This popular text includes a detailed treatment of modeling and various types of models commonly used in business decision problems.

Dixon, Gary W., and James C. Wetherbe. *The Management of Information Systems*. New York: McGraw-Hill, 1985. A recent text by knowledgeable authors discussing in detail issues as viewed by the data processing manager.

Frank, Werner L. *Critical Issues in Software*. New York: John Wiley, 1983. A good discussion of some of the problems of systems development and the use of fourth-generation languages.

Holloway, Charles A. *Decision Making Under Uncertainty: Models and Choices*. Englewood Cliffs, N.J.: Prentice-Hall, 1979. A detailed treatment of decision-making under uncertainty, including the analysis of decision trees.

Martin, James *An Information Systems Manifesto.* Englewood Cliffs, N.J.: Prentice-Hall, 1984. A very readable book for managers, discussing many of the management of information systems issues mentioned in this chapter.

McFarlan, F. Warren. "Information Technology Changes the Way You Compete." *Harvard Business Review* (May–June 1984), pp. 98–103. The article gives some additional examples of companies using IS as a competitive weapon.

————, Warren, and James L. McKenney. *Corporate Information Systems: The Issues Facing Senior Executives*. Homewood, Ill.: Richard Irwin, 1983. An excellent treatment of the issues in information systems management. Much of the material in this book is contained in a series of articles in the *Harvard Business Review* by these authors.

Moore, Jeffrey H., and Michael G. Chang. "Meta-Design Considerations in Building DSS." In John L. Bennett (editor), *Building Decision Support Systems*. Reading, Ma.: Addison-Wesley, 1983. This chapter focuses on the design issues in building a DSS and how they differ from those in building a traditional MIS.

O'Brien, James A. *Computers and Information Processing in Business*. Homewood, Ill.: Richard Irwin, 1985. A good basic text on business information systems, including a discussion of the technology involved (hardware and software).

Strassmann, Paul A. *Information Payoff: The Transformation of Work in the Electronic Age*. New York: Free Press, 1985. An interesting treatment of information technology and its impact on the productivity of professionals and in the office.

CHAPTER 8

Organizational Development

Jerry I. Porras
Stanford University
Graduate School of Business

Managing organizations in this country has become an increasingly complex and demanding task. The impact of foreign competition on our economy, the exponential growth of our technology base, and the changing life-styles of our work force have all served to dramatically increase pressures on American managers to alter both the character and the performance of their organizations. Although the United States continues to be the overall leader in international trade, sharp inroads have been made into our dominant position across almost all industries. We have lost leadership in some and barely hold our own in others as evolving international competition creates new requirements for economic success. We must change our methods of doing business or face long-term degradation of our eminent position in world markets.

No single country has influenced managerial thinking in the United States more than Japan, with its striking accomplishments in automobiles, steel, electronics, ship building, and, perhaps in the very near future, computers. One reaction by U.S. management has been to study Japanese techniques and emulate them as much as possible, consistent with our own beliefs, history, and societal constraints. Whether this strategy has worked for any substantial segment of American industry is not yet clear, but early indications point to some success with activities such as quality control circles (originally a U.S. invention exported to Japan, then imported back to us).

The Japanese example's main contribution to American management is not in the specific techniques it suggests but rather in the fact that it has created a heightened self-awareness of the way we manage our organizations and employees. Increasingly, U.S. managers are

261

focusing on themselves, their styles of management, their values, the organizational cultures they create, the role of the employee in decision-making, the patterns of excellence in U.S. companies, and so on. This self-reflection has become an important stimulus for organizational change.

But given that we do want to change our organizations to make them more responsive to the new demands they face, how do we do it? Fortunately, a field of planned organizational change has been growing and evolving in this country since the early 1960s. This field, called *organizational development,* draws its conceptual roots from social psychology and sociology and its action roots from the work of such applied scholars as McGregor, Likert, Argyris, Beckhard, Bennis, Blake and Mouton, Lippitt, Schein, Seashore, Shephard, and Tannenbaum.

Organizational development (OD), as a field, defies precise definition. In general, it consists of values, assumptions, theories, and techniques all oriented toward the planned change of organizations. Drawn from the behavioral sciences, the conceptual foundations of OD guide actions designed to improve both the long-term performance of the organization and the quality of working life for the individual organizational member. At present, therefore, organizational development is an amorphous collection of substantive ideas and experiences seeking a clearly defined form.

This chapter will acquaint you with the field, its most important underpinnings, its process, its technology, and its potential future. My description of OD will be based on the assumption that the organization's functioning cannot be altered unless the behavior of its members is altered. This perspective limits the set of planned change activities that can be called OD to those which focus on the organization as a system and which also somehow affect the behavior of individual organizational members. A change such as the issuance of corporate stock would not be considered OD because of the very nebulous effect it might have on the behavior of a typical person in the organization. On the other hand, altering the formal reward system as a part of a more comprehensive set of actions would be considered an OD activity (given also that it occurred within a broader scheme of planned change).

This chapter begins with a framework for understanding organizations. This framework, based on systems theory, provides the foundation for understanding the process of management and the leverage points for change available to the manager. Next, I discuss the OD intervention process, which can be used to change these leverage points, and then briefly describe several commonly used change technologies. I conclude with a look at the future of OD and a discussion of several parameters that can be used to judge the effects and usefulness of new change approaches.

AN ORGANIZATIONAL FRAMEWORK

We must somehow conceptualize exactly what an organization is before we can develop techniques and approaches to change it. Yet organizations are complicated entities that constantly change as they adapt to shifting environmental demands. An approach that will help us understand and model organizations is therefore necessary. One such approach, *open systems theory*, is a useful method for representing organizations in a manner that minimizes their complexities.

A system can be defined as a set of objects, each of which possesses certain attributes and certain interconnections with other parts of the system. An open system, a special kind of system, is open to its environment; that is, it has boundaries that are permeable to inputs from its environment such as materials, people, or the information needed to sustain itself. In return for these inputs, an open system exports outputs (products), which in turn generate new inputs and so on.

Since organizations are highly complex open systems, the way we conceptualize them must be relatively simple so that we can subject them to the sort of analyses necessary to change them. Any system can be usefully analyzed by looking at three things: the target system itself, its suprasystem (the larger system in which the target system is embedded), and its major subsystem (one of the key component parts that make up the whole). If we apply these ideas to an organization, the resulting framework looks like Figure 8.1.

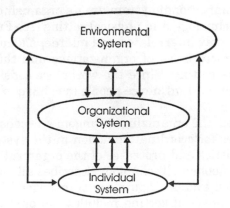

Figure 8.1 A Systems View of an Organization

The target system, the organizational system, consists of all the activities, processes, and components that make up the organization. The suprasystem is the environment in which the organization operates: other companies in its industry, the marketplace, its stockholders, the government, the communities surrounding its facilities, the social culture in which it functions, and so on. The subsystem, or individual system, consists of the people in the organization and their behavior.

As shown in Figure 8.1, all three systems influence each other; however, the dominant effect flows downward. The organization can and does affect its environment (as do individuals), but the impact is far greater in the other direction.

The organizational system provides the context in which the organizational member operates, and to a large degree it determines job behavior. Recent thinking in psychology proposes that a person's environment plays a key role in influencing his or her behavior. The characteristics of the organizational system, then, will play a key role in determining what people do at work. It follows, therefore, that if managers want to change the work-related behavior of their employees, they must in some way alter the environments the employees work in rather than try to change them directly. Managers cannot get inside people's heads and make them behave in any particular way. At best, they can only influence certain characteristics of the organizational system so as to create the internal organizational environments needed to facilitate productive behavior in employees.

We must therefore identify the key characteristics of the internal organizational environment before discussing any concepts of planned organizational change. Four components found to be most useful in describing an organizational system are its organizing arrangements, human factors, technology, and physical setting (see Figure 8.2). These components, all highly interrelated and interdependent, constitute the fundamental characteristics of organizations and the basic building blocks of any work setting. Since the workplace consists of these factors, they are what most influence people to behave in particular ways on the job.

Broadly defined, the organizing arrangements consist of all the formalized guidelines for coordinative action in the system. The people-related characteristics and processes of the organization make up the human factors component. Technology describes all aspects of the process through which system inputs are transformed into system outputs. Finally, the physical setting includes the physical environment people work in. A more detailed listing of the factors that describe each of the four components of the organizational system is shown in Table 8.1.

The four components are coordinated and held together by the purpose of the system. Purpose is the fundamental glue that bonds the organization by providing a definition of the system's reason for being. A clearly defined organizational purpose will result in high levels of integration across the four areas and high levels of coordinated action. An unclear purpose leads to confusion about what each component should look like and how the components should interrelate, and this confusion causes different parts of the organization to pull in different directions, making the overall organization relatively inefficient. Purpose, therefore, is the "star on the horizon" that guides the organization through its various choice points. Without a broadly understood and accepted purpose, an organization cannot effectively survive over the long term.

Some examples of purpose found in the formal documents and informal thinking of several successful organizations should serve to clarify its fundamental role. The stated purpose of a property management company is to "serve the needs of our present and prospective tenants by developing buildings of the highest possible quality and providing superior building management and other services." An association of hospitals declares that its purpose is "to improve the quality of health care delivery by enhancing managerial and organizational effectiveness." A feed company's purpose is the preparation and marketing of products that represent superior values to consumers. A parts manufacturing company states that its purpose is "to earn money for its shareholders and to increase the value of their investment." And finally, a consumer goods manufacturer says that its purpose is "to earn money and enjoy doing so."

The external environment of the organization impacts the organization through the organization's purpose. Shifts in the environment such as a downturn in market demand can affect two organizations in the same industry in very different ways. In one case, a company reacted to a drop in sales by laying off 10 percent of its work force, whereas another company in the same industry reacted to a sales dropoff by cutting the work schedule and the corresponding pay levels by 10 percent so that employees worked one day less every two weeks and were paid 10 percent less. The purposes of the two organizations were different and resulted in different reactions to the same environmental shift.

Figure 8.2 is a graphic representation of the organizational framework that we have been discussing. It indicates the four system

Table 8.1 Organizational Systems Components

Organizing Arrangements	Social Factors	Technology	Physical Setting
1. Formal Structure	1. Culture	1. Tools, Equipment, and Machinery	1. Architectural Design
2. Policies and Procedures	a. Values and beliefs	2. Technical Expertise	2. Space Configuration
3. Goals	b. Norms	3. Job Design	a. Size
4. Strategies	c. Symbols	4. Work Flow Design	b. Shape
5. Administrative Systems	d. Stories	5. Technical Procedures	c. Relative locations
6. Formal Reward Systems	e. Myths	6. Technical Systems	3. Physical Ambiance
a. Evaluation system	f. Rituals		a. Light
b. Pay systems	2. Interaction Processes		b. Heat
c. Benefits packages	a. Interpersonal		c. Noise
	b. Group		d. Air Quality
	c. Intergroup		e. Cleanliness
	3. Individual Attributes		4. Interior Design
	a. Attitudes		a. Decorations
	b. Behavioral skills		b. Furniture
	4. Informal Patterns/Networks		c. Window coverings
	a. Communication		d. Floor coverings
	b. Decision-making		e. Colors
	c. Influence		1. Floors
	d. Status		2. Walls
			3. Ceilings

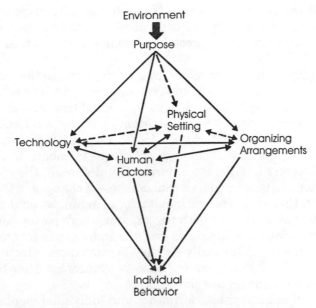

Figure 8.2 A General Model of Organization

components, their interdependent relationship, the coordinative effect of purpose in the organization, the impact of the external environment on the four system components as mediated by the purpose of the system, and the primary effect of the four components on individual behavior.

This, then, is the perspective upon which our understanding of organizations is based. From this comes, first, a view of the management process, followed by a detailed description of the strategies and technologies available for planned change.

THE MANAGEMENT PROCESS

Managers exercise influence and decision-making power over the definition of the organization's purpose and the four components of the organizational system. As noted earlier, they can do little either to directly manage the organization's external environment or directly change subordinates' behavior in the long run. In the short run, managers can, for example, order subordinates to do something and watch over them every minute to make sure that the desired behavior occurs. However, over the long run this is an impossible condition to maintain for all subordinates, who may be responsible for different activities in different locations, at different times, and so on. Consequently, the leverage points for change available to any manager are these five described above, and it is primarily through their alteration that managers influence the behavior of individuals within the organization. Figure 8.3 represents the process of management based on this premise.

On an everyday basis, therefore, managers, through their behavior, affect the four key organizing subsystems. (Purpose is excluded because of its secondary relationship to individual behavior and its relative permanence; that is, an organization's purpose would not be frequently changed.) Their alteration, in turn, constitutes a new work environment for the individual organizational member. Since people respond differently to different environmental stimuli, their work behavior will tend to be altered as a consequence of changes in their work environment. Change in the work behavior of organizational members leads to outcome changes in both the organization's performance (employees work harder and smarter) *and* the individual's mental health (employees grow psychologically as they become more effective in the work setting). Finally, changes in these two outcomes filter back and influence future managerial behavior.

As a set, organizational performance and individual mental health outcome changes constitute one of three sources of influence on managerial behavior. The other two come from the purpose of the organization and the personal purpose of the individual manager. Each of these in turn is influenced by the external environment in which both the manager and organization operate.

Organizational and individual outcomes also affect the external environment, but they do so to a lesser degree than all of the other rela-

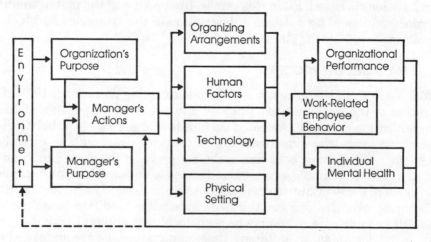

Figure 8.3   A Model of the Managerial Process

tionships depicted in Figure 8.3. For this reason, this effect is represented in the figure by a dotted line to suggest that an impact occurs but that it is not as potent and direct as the others shown.

This view of management highlights the leverage points for planned organizational change, that is, the four areas (organizing arrangements, human factors, technology, and physical settings) that managers can consciously and directly influence to produce changes in employee behavior and in subsequent system behavior. Guided by the organizational purpose as well as his or her own purpose, the manager can make conscious efforts to change the organizing system in planned ways. The methods used to accomplish this constitute the body of organizational development intervention process and technology. These are the foci of the following sections.

THE ORGANIZATIONAL DEVELOPMENT PROCESS

The organizational development (OD) intervention process is rooted in a broader model of change originally formulated in the 1940s by Kurt Lewin, perhaps the most noted figure in social psychology. Lewin proposed that change consisted of three broad phases: (1) an unfreezing stage in which the current behavior, assumptions, attitudes, and so on of a social system are openly questioned and a desire for change is generated; (2) a changing stage, in which these same factors are consciously altered in a planned direction; and finally, (3) a refreezing stage in which the new forms of operating become part of the normal functioning of the system.

This view provides the foundation for the *action research model,* the most common approach to planned change used in organizational development. Figure 8.4 shows the action research process organized in accordance with the Lewinian framework.

Organizational development begins with a decision to change. Implied in this decision is an awareness that problems or opportunities exist in the functioning of the organization and that a need is felt to do something about them.

Following the decision to change, data are gathered to determine the underlying dimensions of the present situation and provide a foundation for action. The generated data are then reported to all relevant organizational members (key managers and employees involved in the change), who analyze the information and decide what actions to take. Implementation of desired actions follows and continues until the new situation is stabilized. Assessments to determine the characteristics of the new organizational state are made and compared with the goals of the change planning, typically triggering a new cycle of change.

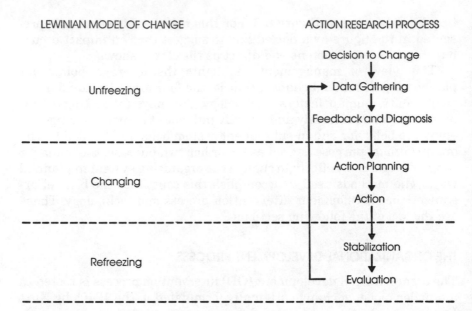

Figure 8.4 The Action Research Process

As represented by the action research process, organizational development is a recurring activity, one that continually cycles through its phases from data gathering through evaluation and back to data gathering again. Problems and opportunities constantly present themselves, and a process of development must, by definition, be continual. Since organizational environments are not static, the process of organizational adaptation and interaction with its environment never ceases. Constant change, for better or worse, is the given condition of any system, and, as such, the organization can, through the action research process, develop its abilities to respond more effectively to the ever-changing demands of its environment.

Using the action research process as a basis, a further description of OD can focus on the methods available for performing two of the key steps in the model: diagnosis and action. The methods used for diagnosing and taking action are commonly called the technology of OD. More precisely, the technology of OD is defined as the particular procedures, techniques, or activities that exist in the field and that have gained relatively wide acceptance as effective tools for precipitating change in organizations. We now turn to a closer examination of this technology.

ORGANIZATIONAL DEVELOPMENT TECHNOLOGY

OD technology falls into two general categories: diagnostic activities and intervention approaches. Although most intervention approaches contain some diagnostic activity as a way of pinpointing the content of an intervention itself, and a diagnosis is often considered an intervention of sorts, for the purposes of this discussion they will be dealt with separately.

"Diagnostic activities," as used here, refers to those approaches for collecting and analyzing information about the broader problems of the target organization. Once problems are clearly understood, an intervention approach consists of a coherent set of activities designed for dealing with them.

Diagnostic Technology

Processes of diagnosis begin with a framework that specifies the more prominent areas to target for scrutiny, ones that provide a basis for assessing key problems and opportunities in the system.

Diagnostic data can be collected from organization members in a variety of ways, ranging from personal interviews to standardized or customized questionnaires. Observation of key organizational activities and the use of archival sources such as annual reports, organizational performance figures, or minutes of key meetings are additional methods of collecting diagnostic data.

Whatever the means for collecting information, it is vitally important to base data collection on an acceptable (to the manager) model of exactly what an organization is and how it functions. If a manager has no clear and comprehensive view of what is central to the effective functioning of the organization, the information collected could relate to secondary factors and, as a consequence, be worthless for the purpose of improving organizational performance. For example, information may be collected about how employees feel about their boss because these are seen as the critical factors in employee relations. In fact, it may well be that other factors such as the designs of the jobs or the timely availability of necessary information are more important determinants of efficient employee behavior. If a manager does not possess a richer view of the organization, the key issues are not assessed and the most appropriate actions are never taken.

The view of organizations presented in the previous section can provide the basis for a systemic diagnostic process.[1] It will be used to present an example of one diagnostic approach developed by me and my colleague Joan Harkness. This approach, part of a broader process for managing change called stream analysis, has been used in a variety of organizations such as an aerospace firm, a high-technology company, a hospital, an electric utility, and a telephone company.

The diagnostic process.   Generally, diagnosis begins with the selection of an organizational model, one that guides the collection of data describing the state of the system. Using one or a combination of the data-gathering techniques mentioned above, information on the key factors specified by the organizational model is first obtained. Once data are collected, they are fed back to key organizational members, who then analyze the information and generate a diagnosis of the situation.

In the stream analysis approach, the model of organization used is the one presented earlier (Figure 8.2). The four organizational factors (organizing arrangements, human factors, technology, and physical setting) are the particular areas about which information is to be collected. These four factors represent "streams" of issues in the organization and, as such, are used to guide data gathering.

Figure 8.5, a stream chart, shows an example of the problems identified in one department of a large aerospace firm. They have been classified into four streams of issues, and arrows have been drawn connecting many of the problems. This chart therefore represents a comprehensive summary of the major issues existing in the organization at a particular point in time.

This chart was developed using a series of steps. After the data were collected from organization members, each problem was first classified according to the stream to which it belonged. For example, the fact that "responsibility for certain decisions was not clear" is a structural issue and therefore part of the organizing activities area of the firm.

The second step consisted of the identification of key interrelationships among the various problems previously specified. Interrelationships were represented with lines connecting boxes and, where appropriate, arrows pointing in causal directions. For cases in which the lines represent mutual effects rather than causal relations, arrows point in both directions. One example of this in Figure 8.5 was the relationship between the cost control system's being ineffective and the fact that many interpersonal conflicts were not resolved. Each could be causing the other and are represented by arrows at both ends of the interconnecting lines.

The identification of connections between issues is critical insofar as any action planned in subsequent steps must deal not only with the target issue but also with the implication of the interdependency of that issue with other issues. Taking actions that solve one prob-

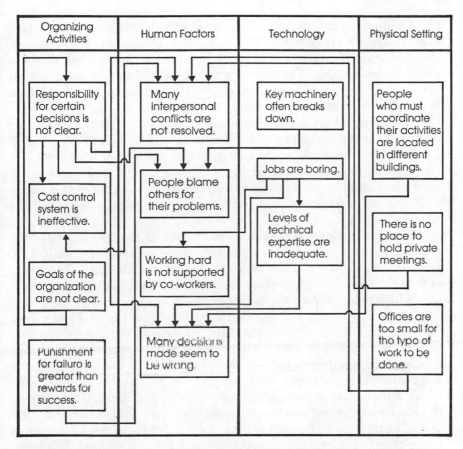

Organizing Activities	Human Factors	Technology	Physical Setting

Figure 8.5 Diagnosis of an Organization Using Stream Analysis

lem may be ineffective if another, interconnected problem remains untouched.

By tracing back from a problem through its interconnections to a deeper problem, then through its interconnections to an even deeper problem, separation of symptoms from more fundamental issues becomes possible. Pictorially, a stream chart can show the difference between symptoms and basic problems. In Figure 8.5, symptoms tend to be represented by boxes in the chart with many arrows flowing into them, while basic problems are located in boxes with many arrows flowing out.

Frequently, action taken on symptoms never seems to improve a situation substantially, whereas action taken on core, or fundamental, issues typically results in wide-ranged improvement. For example, Figure 8.5 shows several arrows coming into the box labeled "Many decisions made seem to be wrong." If one began to attack only that problem, action might take the form of providing training in problem analysis and decision-making. This action would be based on the premise that people don't know how to analyze a problem and make a good decision. But in fact, this may be only partly the case.

The stream chart shows that other factors enter that must also be dealt with if the decision-making problem is to be solved. One factor, for example, has to do with where people are physically located. If those people with whom one must coordinate are not easily accessible, the information needed for top-quality decision-making is less easily available and decisions might tend to get made without using all the necessary data.

From the technology stream comes a second possible source of the decision-making problem. If employees have low levels of technical expertise, they are more apt to make poor decisions about a wide variety of technical problems. Moreover, boring jobs lead to inattention to detail, which can also result in poor decisions.

A fourth potential source of this decision-making problem comes from the organizing activities stream. Cloudy definitions of decision-making responsibility could lead to people making decisions that they shouldn't be making — that is, decisions at odds with the intended structural design of the organization.

This method of laying out diagnostic data can, through the process of identifying deeper issues, focus change interventions on truly important problems and make actions taken more effective. Failures in many change projects are often due to not having identified the correct problems to work on. Any diagnostic model or approach must accomplish the task of picking out basic issues, and these issues must be recognized as such by the model's user.

One final point: the diagnostic process can itself be considered an intervention into a system's functioning. In many cases, data collection activities have never occurred before in the organization. Asking people for their views and opinions on seldom-discussed topics sends a signal to organizational members that something new is happening. *This is a change intervention.*

The second part of the diagnostic process, data feedback and analysis procedures, also signals that things are changing. Typically, in an OD diagnostic process, data are reported to *all* who provided them rather than just to a manager and his or her team. This may not appear to be unique because many organizations collect attitudinal data from their employees and later on publish a report on the findings. The difference in the OD approach is that data fed back are in rawer form and analyses of them are conducted by respondents themselves, not by the staff or consultants who collected the data. Since interpretation of data is performed by organization members, a typical effect of this involvement is broader "ownership" of the problems facing the system and higher levels of commitment to doing something about them.

For large organizations, involving everyone in this type of feedback process is just not possible. In these cases, representatives from various parts and levels of the organization are formed into a working group with responsibility for guiding the intervention process. This group decides how to disseminate information to all organizational members and acts as liaison between those who are managing the change process and the remainder of the system.

Intervention Technology

Once completed, a diagnosis becomes the basis for action — action using any of a wide array of change technologies. Some change approaches are narrowly focused, for example, dealing with a limited problem such as the inability of members in a work team to communicate effectively with each other. Others are broadly focused, for example, dealing with the ineffective flow of information, across an entire organization, or attempting to alter ineffective cultural norms of a system such as one that discourages individuals from working hard and producing more than their peers.

The range of OD change technology can be organized according to which of the four organizational characteristics any particular intervention approach might impact (see Table 8.2).[2] Clearly, over a period of time, any complex change intervention affects more than one of these characteristics. However, typically, one characteristic is the dominant focus of any change activity, and as such it provides a convenient means for classifying the numerous approaches.[3]

We should note that all the OD approaches directly impact human activity in one way or another. Our classification scheme therefore assumes that although an intervention may primarily impact one key organizational characteristic, it does so in light of also having some effect on the human dynamics in the system.

Since space prohibits a thorough discussion of every intervention approach shown in Table 8.2, only a subset of techniques will be described in detail. The more prominent approaches in each column of the table will be described more fully. Readers not interested in these detailed descriptions may briefly skim or skip the sections below; the later discussion can be understood without this information.

Table 8.2 Classification of Organizational Development Interventions by Organizational Characteristic Impacted

Organizing Arrangements	Human Factors	Technology	Physical Setting
1. Autonomous work groups	1. Career planning	1. Autonomous work groups	1. Space design
2. Collateral organizations	2. Confrontation meetings	2. Education and training — technical focus	
3. Contingency organizational design	3. Education and training — behavioral focus	3. Job design	
4. Control systems	4. Grid OD-phase I, II, III	4. Quality circles	
5. Employee ownership	5. Intergroup conflict resolution	5. Sociotechnical systems design	
6. Employee stock ownership plans (ESOP)	6. Job expectations technique/ role analysis technique		
7. Flexible working hours	7. Life planning		
8. Grid OD-phase IV, V	8. Modeling-based skill development		
9. Human resources accounting	9. Organizational mirroring		

10. Human resources administration
11. Information processing organizational design
12. Job expectations technique/ role analysis technique
13. Multivariate analysis participation and structure (MAPS)
14. Matrix organizational design
15. Open systems planning
16. Pay systems design
17. Quality circles
18. Role negotiation
19. Scanlon plan
20. Sociotechnical organizational design

10. Personal consulting and coaching
11. Process consultation
12. Quality circles
13. Responsibility charting
14. Role analysis technique/job expectations technique
15. Role negotiation
16. Survey feedback
17. T-groups
18. Team building
19. Third-party consultation

Organizing arrangements interventions. This set of interventions focuses on altering the formalized coordinating mechanisms of a system, that is, its organizing arrangements. Thus, activities in this group concentrate on changing the structure, policies, and procedures, administrative and reward systems, or goals and strategies of the organization.

A representative organizing-arrangements intervention technique is one that impacts the goals and strategies of the organization, open systems planning (OSP) developed by G. K. Jayaram and his associates. OSP helps management or key planning teams assess the organization and develop plans for its future. It is most appropriate for situations in which the intention is to change the overall organization.

The OSP process, consisting of five unique steps conducted over a three-day period, typically begins with the key management team creating a view of the current organizational situation. This "present scenario" contains a listing of all expectations placed on the organization by (1) its external environment ("What is expected of this organization and who expects it of us?"), (2) its internal environment ("What does each part of the organization expect from every other part?"), (3) transactions, across the boundaries of the organization, between the internal parts and the external domains, and (4) the value system underlying all the expectations identified ("Why does who expect what?").

Next, a "realistic future scenario" is created that assumes that no deliberate activity is taken by the organization to make the world and the organization any different from the direction in which they are both now headed. In other words, "If nothing is done to change our trajectory, what would we look like in the future?" This future scenario contains the same dimensions as those listed above for the present.

Third, an "idealistic future scenario" is developed, one that attempts to depict what the management would like the future to be if it had the power to change things. The question here is: "What alternative futures would you like to create for yourselves as an organization?" A key part of this step is not to be limited by questions of how to achieve this ideal future, but rather to dream uninhibited by any reality.

In the fourth step, the managers compare the idealistic future scenario with both the realistic future scenario and the present scenario and identify broad areas of agreement, uncertainty, and disagreement. In this discussion, views on what is worth trying to change, and why, are clarified.

Finally, the management team takes each discrepancy noted in the fourth step and attempts to define what it intends to do in three time frames: tomorrow, six months from now, and two years from now. For those areas in which there has been broad agreement, concrete plans are made. When broad disagreement exists, plans for how to deal with that disagreement are developed. In some areas there will be uncertainty. For these, more data must be gathered before opinions can be firmed up.

An example of open systems planning in use occurred in a large international chemical plant that had become so inefficient that top management considered closing it. Before making that decision, however, an OSP process was used to assess the broader situation in hopes that it would lead to the eventual change of the ineffective aspects of the plant's functioning rather than its closing. The OSP process left the management team with a clear view of the state it was in, where it wanted to go and why, and how to get there. It was a difficult, tedious process, but one that was found to generate true involvement and support for the goals and strategies developed. The plant wasn't closed and developed into a highly efficient organization.

Human factors interventions.   Organizational development interventions that focus on changing the human factors in the organization are both the most numerous and most frequently used. OD's roots are based on group techniques for changing individual behavior, and consequently many approaches have evolved with a focus on the organization's culture, human process, and informal networks.

Team building or team development, probably the most commonly used intervention in OD, focuses on developing a work team's ability to function more effectively in problem-solving and decision-making situations. Many team development interventions are done over a three- to five-day period away from the work setting, while some take but a few hours and are done during the group's regular meeting time and in the organizational setting.

Typically, team-building processes begin by gathering information from team members about the team's functioning.[4] Information may be collected through interviews of group members by an outside consultant; through open sharing of views by group members at the beginning of a team-building session; or through questionnaires administered prior to a session or, if the questionnaire is relatively brief, completed at the beginning of a session. The information is shared with the team members and a diagnosis is generated by all participants. Actions to deal with identified problems are planned and, to the degree possible, immediately implemented.

A key team-building goal includes creating more effective processes through which the team can carry out its organizational tasks. The discussions therefore are bounded by their relevance to task performance. In other words, team-building activities focus only on those issues that directly affect the accomplishment of the team's work goals.

As Bill Dyer has noted, team-building interventions are most effective when there is a real organizational need for a *team,* that is, when there is formal or informal interdependence between members; when the team manager wants to improve team functioning; when team members feel a strong need for action; when the team is willing to look at itself, its performance, and how it functions; when there is enough time to engage in the process; and when team members are open to accepting new data about themselves and are willing to do something about the information they receive.

Team building tends to work less well if these prescriptions are violated, especially the first one. If there is no real or perceived interdependence among group members, then the motivation to go through the process of jointly solving difficult organizational problems just won't be there. In cases such as this, the team-building process typically falls apart, resulting in a rather sterile experience.

Technology interventions. OD interventions focusing on changes in the organizational technology have their roots in the time-in-motion industrial engineering concepts of job design. However, in the OD tradition, job design concepts have been substantially modified to take into account the human and social needs of the people who must operate the machinery, equipment, and other aspects of the technical system. The techniques included in this category all focus on technology-based interventions that emphasize the human perspective.

One common set of technology-focused OD interventions tries to maximize the match between technological requirements and human needs. As such these interventions have often taken the form of "autonomous" or "self-regulating" work group designs. As Tom Cummings has noted, these designs are characterized by a relatively whole task; members who each possess a variety of skills relevant to the group task; worker discretion over such decisions as methods of work, task schedules, and assignments of members to different tasks; and compensation and feedback about performance for the group as a whole.

Autonomous or self-regulating work groups are most frequently used in technological situations requiring substantial technical interdependence across the tasks performed by different people. If the task performed by one person is heavily dependent on the tasks performed by others and if this is a common circumstance across a group of people, then a very key technical condition for this type of work group design exists. The interdependence can be based on a need to share the same materials or equipment, or it may be the result of technological demands that require that the input to one person's job be the direct and immediate output of another's job.

A second condition for autonomous/self-regulating groups exists if groups of interdependent tasks can be identified and differentiated from each other, creating an opportunity for subproducts to be produced by one independent group. For example, in building an automobile whose important subproducts might be the engine, transmission, chassis, exterior body, and interior, an autonomous self-regulating work team design could assign responsibility for building each of these components to a separate team. The Volvo automobile company has used this type of design in its Kalmar plant, as has the Procter and Gamble Company in several of its U.S. plants.

Autonomous or self-regulating work groups perform many of the functions previously assigned to first-line supervisors, making the role of managing these groups drastically different from a traditional work group situation. In this case, supervisors primarily perform two important tasks: developing group members and assisting the group in managing its exchanges with the larger organizational setting.

Development of group members involves such things as building up their technical expertise, helping them function more effectively interpersonally, and imparting problem-solving and decision-making skills for more effective group functioning. Helping the group to function effectively in the larger context includes such things as assuring that the group always has the raw materials it needs, negotiating schedules for finished products, and developing relationships with other groups so that shared resources can be used collaboratively.

Since the supervisor does not have to spend much of his or her time directing the group's activities, more effort can be focused on understanding the larger organizational context and how the autonomous or self-regulating team fits within it. This frees up supervisor time for greater degrees of planning and dealing with broad organizational demands. It also allows for more effort in helping group members plan their careers and develop the skills necessary to achieve both personal and group goals.

Physical setting interventions. At present, planned change technology focusing on the physical setting in organizations is quite limited in both scope and quantity. However, Fritz Steele, one of the few professionals active in this area, has proposed a series of concepts that are useful in thinking about physical settings and OD.

It is important to recognize that the physical characteristics and configurations of space influence individual behavior in a manner that is either consistent or inconsistent with other organizational factors such as structure, job design, and culture If the culture of an organization, for example, is designed to be very formal and not to allow for easy sharing of information, then a setting with an open layout and no private offices would be inconsistent with the existing or desired culture.

Since the ultimate desire of managers should be to configure all organizational characteristics in such a way as to create more effective employee behavior, then paying attention to how space either supports or detracts from that goal is very important.

A few physical setting concepts should help clarify how key aspects of the organization are affected by space designs and vice versa. According to Steele, people receive four different types of inputs from the physical setting they work in. First, the setting affects the way tasks are performed; this is the *instrumental* effect of space. Second, the setting may communicate information about its user (e.g., status or attitude), reflecting the *symbolic* nature of space. Third, space may bring pleasure to its occupants by being comfortable, beautiful, attractive, and so on. This describes the *pleasure* effects of space. Finally, space may somehow facilitate learning and growth for its users; this is the *growth* function of space.

An example of a situation in which the physical setting strongly influenced the way tasks were performed (instrumental effect) occurred in a poorly functioning engineering design group of a high-technology company. A new manager (the third in four years) was appointed head of a group and told to "straighten it out." As he toured the area in which all the department members were located, he noticed several key physical setting characteristics. First, the manager's and supervisor's offices were all located along the south wall of the large rectangular bull-pen area that contained all the engineers' desks. He also noted that one aisle, running parallel to the south wall, led to the bathroom facilities, while a second aisle, parallel to the west wall, led to the coffee area. These two aisles crossed more or less at the center of the room. The new manager located his office at the intersection of these two aisles and made sure that his door was always open.

After a few months, the department was performing more effectively and within a year was seen as one of the best-functioning areas of the company. The manager believes that locating his office where he did was one of the most important changes he made. The engineers would drop into his office on their way to the bathroom or coffee room, and he would chat with them about their work, the problems they were facing, and so on. He would in return share information that was useful for their getting their own jobs done. The result was a substantial increase in performance.

Since the work space designs should have the effect that its users desire, those organizational members who will use that space must be deeply involved in its design. Through their involvement they can make space serve purposes consistent with both their needs and the organization's requirements.

Physical settings should be designed to allow for a high degree of "spatial research," that is, learning about the effects of space by creating a rather fluid or unfixed physical structure so that it can be changed easily to make it more consistent not only with changing work procedures but also with other organizational factors such as goals, structure, and values.

There is no one correct way to design the physical setting. The best way should be determined by the organizational members and the particular organizational situation. Yet factoring space design into the change equation appears to be a key but often neglected step in effective organizational development.

AN OD INTERVENTION EXAMPLE

An example of a typical OD intervention process should put all the information presented above in clearer perspective. Most often, a change activity begins because an organization has been experiencing difficulties in meeting all of the expectations placed on it. These expectations may come from either inside or outside the organization, but in any case, the result is a need for change perceived by key members of the system. This felt need becomes the key trigger for a planned change process. It is important to note that effective change cannot occur if the system does not feel a strong need for it.

One typical organizational development project conducted in a high-tech firm began when a key manager decided that some planned effort was needed to improve the organization's situation and hired a consultant to aid in the process. The consultant, a business-school professor with a specialty in OD, met with the key change leaders, and after several sessions in which the OD process was thoroughly examined, an agreement was reached to start up a planned change activity. Next, the consultant and client agreed on the degree of openness of the relationship they wished to have with each other, broad methods of work, shared values, time frame, review points, and fees.

One of the first acts of the consultant was to form a change management team with the responsibility for broadly guiding and monitoring all intervention activity. This team was composed of key managers and a cross-section of nonmanagement personnel. The basic goal of this step was to create a group that was both representative and influential and could provide organizational leadership for the change process.

Guided by the consultant, the stream analysis approach for gathering information about the organization (its members, processes, strengths, weaknesses, etc.) was developed and implemented. The data generated were then fed back to the change management team and to various other management and employee groups.

The groups receiving the data analyzed them and developed a diagnosis of key issues and problem areas to begin attacking. The consultant provided technical expertise about the OD approaches available for dealing with various problems. Problems in the production process, for example, were most amenable to sociotechnical systems design. Ineffective management meetings were improved through team-building activities. Conflict across departments required some intergroup conflict resolution activity. And so on.

The role of the consultant was to give the change leaders any needed technical assistance and external objectivity. System members were responsible for providing the energy and interest needed to make things happen. It was not the consultant's job to lead the change process or to push for specific change activity. The consultant acted as a resource to the change management team. It is this team which shouldered the leadership of the change effort.

Periodically, data were gathered again to check on how effective change actions had been and on what new problems had surfaced. Appropriate actions were taken to deal with new issues, and the cycle repeated itself.

At a later point, which was approximately three years after the OD process began, the system had developed the expertise necessary to continue to assess itself and take appropriate action. At this time, the external consultant was needed less often, and his participation in the system became less and less frequent until it ceased entirely. The system was capable of continual self-renewal.

LOOKING AHEAD

Changing organizations to increase effectiveness has been a goal of managers since the invention of the first organization. Within the last two decades, the field of organizational development has evolved as the most commonly employed, broad-scaled approach to planned change. From roots in small-group processes it has grown to encompass a systems view of organizations and a technology that affects a wide array of organizational characteristics. Current intervention techniques and strategies focus on such factors as structure, pay systems, culture, job design, office layout, conflict resolution, and work group processes. But what might we look for in the future? Where is the field headed?

Probably the most important future development will occur when those involved in changing systems possess integrated views of change activities. Richer understandings of interconnections among key factors in the organization will evolve and lead to more complete strategies and interventions for change. In the future, managers will tend to avoid trying to "fix" one problem without, at the same time, making all associated adjustments in other parts of the organization so that solutions are supported rather than hindered by the rest of the system.

A second key trend, which has already begun, is the accelerated increase of employee participation in organizational decisions that relate to their work. This trend has been growing steadily since the middle 1970s and was boosted by the great world market success of the Japanese and by the fact that the Japanese heavily involve their work force in making decisions about work-related problems. The democratic foundations of U.S. society will support this trend in our organizations once managers fully believe that the benefits of employee participation far outweigh any risks they perceive in the process. Organizational development strategies and technologies will hasten this development, and new technologies for facilitating increased participation will be created.

A third trend, but one that has barely begun in this country, is the increase in the number of employee-owned organizations. We can expect this trend to gain momentum in future years. Currently, employee stock ownership plans (ESOPs) have been the primary form of employee ownership. Although these plans will increase in number, a new form of ownership will become more prominent, one in which an *entire* firm is owned by its employees and in which no employee may work for the firm unless he or she is an owner. This change in organizational ownership appears to be the natural outgrowth of the increased level of participation in decision-making that is occurring now. As people become more involved and assume more responsibility, the desire for owning the products of their efforts will also increase.

These organizational forms have gained prominence in some parts of Europe, most notably the Mondragon group in Spain. Currently in the United States there already have been several important employee buy-outs of organizations, including Bates Fabrics, Sea-Pak Corporation, Fibreboard Corporation, and, most recently, Weirton Steel.

Appendix A Organizational Development Interventions Impacting Organizing Arrangements

Organizing Arrangements	Relevant OD Interventions*	
1. Formal structure		
a. Broad structure	1. Collateral organization	(31)
	2. MAPS — Multivariate analysis participation and structure	(33)
	3. Organization design	
	a. Contingency approaches	(38)
	b. Information approaches	(23)
	c. Matrix designs	(15)
	d. Sociotechnical approaches	(14)
b. Interpersonal/group structure	1. Job expectation techniques or role analysis technique	(16, 21)
	2. Role negotiation	(29, 11)
	3. Quality circles	(56)
	4. Autonomous work groups	(13)
2. Policies and procedures		

3. Goals

   1. Grid OD — phase IV, V   (9)
   2. Open systems planning   (32)

4. Strategies

   1. Grid OD — phase IV, V   (9)
   2. Open systems planning   (32)

5. Administrative systems

   1. Control systems   (37)
   2. Flexible working hours   (12)
   3. Human resource accounting   (19)
   4. Human resource administration   (11, 53)
     a. Appraisal   (53)
     b. Manpower planning   (53)
     c. Placement   (53)
     d. Recruitment   (53)
     e. Wage and salary administration   (36, 53)

6. Formal reward systems

   1. ESOPs   (57)
   2. Pay system design   (35)
   3. Scanlon plan   (17)
   4. Employee ownership   (28)

*The numbers in parentheses at right refer to the numbered entries in the "Suggested Readings" section of this chapter.

Appendix B Organizational Development Interventions Impacting Human Factors

Social Factors	*Relevant OD Interventions**	
1. Culture	1. All interventions in this table	(44)
	2. Survey feedback	(2)
2. Interaction processes		
a. Interpersonal	1. T-groups	(54)
	2. Third-party consultation	(9)
b. Group	1. Grid OD — phase II	(48)
	2. Process consultation	(18)
	3. Team building	(6)
	4. Responsibility charting	(16, 21)
	5. Role analysis technique/job expectation technique	(11)
	6. Role negotiation	(9)
c. Intergroup	1. Grid OD — phase III	(10)
	2. Intergroup conflict resolution	(11)
	3. Organization mirroring	(31)
3. Individual attributes		
a. Attitudes and beliefs	1. Education and training	(9)
	2. Grid OD — phase I	(49)
	3. Life planning	(52)
	4. Career planning	(31)
	5. Personal consultation and coaching	(31)
b. Behavioral skills	1. Education and training	(9)
	2. Grid OD — phase I	(47)
	3. Modeling-based skill development	(56)
	4. Quality circles	
4. Informal patterns/networks	1. All interventions in this table	(5)
	2. Confrontation meeting	

*The numbers in parentheses at right refer to the numbered entries in the "Suggested Readings" section of this chapter.

Appendix C Organizational Development Interventions Impacting Technology

Technology	*Relevant OD Intervention**	
1. Tools, equipment, and machinery	1. Sociotechnical systems design	(46)
2. Technical expertise	1. Education and training	(31)
	2. Quality circles	(56)
3. Job design	1. Autonomous work groups	(13)
	2. Job design	(26)
	a. Enlargement	
	b. Enrichment	
	c. Rotation	
	d. Simplification	
	3. Sociotechnical systems design	(46)
4. Work flow design	1. Autonomous work groups	(13)
	2. Sociotechnical systems design	(46)
5. Technical procedures	1. Sociotechnical systems design	(46)
6. Technical systems	1. Sociotechnical systems design	(46)

*The numbers in parentheses at right refer to the numbered entries in the "Suggested Readings" section of this chapter.

Appendix D Organizational Development Interventions Impacting the Physical Setting

Physical Setting	*Relevant OD Interventions**	
1. Architectural design	1. None available	
2. Space configurations	1. Space design	(50)
	a. Instrumental	
	b. Symbolic	
	c. Pleasure	
	d. Growth	
3. Physical ambiance	1. None available	
4. Internal design	1. None available	

*The numbers in parentheses at right refer to the numbered entries in the "Suggested Readings" section of this chapter.

NOTES

1. A variety of diagnostic models exist. Space precludes an in-depth description of each. However, the bibliography contains references to the following eight relatively popular yet different approaches: Blake and Mouton (1968), Hornstein and Tichy (1973), Kotter (1978), Lawrence and Lorsch (1967), Levinson (1972), Likert (1967), Nadler and Tushman (1977), and Weisbord (1978). The interested reader is encouraged to explore this literature more fully to determine the most appealing approach.

2. In Appendixes A through D, the detailed breakdown of each organizational characteristic (shown in Table 8.1) is matched with the particular OD interventions most directly affecting it. Every technique listed is followed by a number that identifies the bibliographic reference describing that technique in detail.

3. Once again, it should be emphasized that these categorizations are not totally precise because of the complex nature of most interventions. However, they will reflect, as noted earlier, the more dominant emphasis of each change approach. In a few cases, a change approach is listed as impacting more than one dimension. In these situations it appeared inappropriate to limit categorization because of the more comprehensive nature of the intervention technique.

4. Examples of diagnostic questions are: What are the things that help us work more/less effectively together? What facilitates/blocks better communication between us? Do we know what our goals are? Are there conflicts between us that remain unresolved? (Dyer, 1977).

5. This brief example provides a small glimmer of what an OD activity might look like. Those readers interested in a much more detailed description should consult Marrow (1967, 1974) and Argyris (1974) for success stories and Mirvis and Berg (1977) for some examples of failures.

SUGGESTED READINGS

The references listed below contain a wealth of in-depth information on the issues discussed in this chapter. However, several of the books are especially important for those wanting more knowledge about the field of OD.

Two textbooks that do a particularly good job of describing the concepts guiding the change field as well as the broad set of technologies in OD are Warner Burke, *Practices and Principles of Organization Development,* and Wendell French and Cecil Bell, *Organization Development: Behavioral Science Interventions for Organizational Improvement* (3rd ed.). French and Bell have teamed with Robert Zawacki to produce perhaps the best collection of readings in the field, *Organization Development: Theory, Practice, and Research.*

The Addison-Wesley Series on Organization Development consists of nineteen short books on the field, each describing a particular OD intervention perspective. It is the single best available collection of writings on how to do organizational development. Two major approaches to intervention not covered by the Addison-Wesley series are very completely discussed in William Pasmore and John Sherwood, *Sociotechnical Systems: A Sourcebook,* which describes the sociotechnical approach, and Daniel Zwerdling, *Workplace Democracy,* which presents a group of excellent articles on employee ownership.

Two books that describe actual successful organizational development projects are Al Marrow, *Making Waves at Foggy Bottom,* describing a long-term change project in the Department of State, and Al Marrow, David Bowers, and Stanley Seashore, *Management by Participation,* describing an OD process in a pajama factory. On the other side of the coin is a book by Phil Mirvis and David Berg, *Failures in Organization Development and Change,* which presents a series of case descriptions of change projects that failed.

1. Ackoff, R. "Conference Presentation." Organizational Development Network Board and Bay Area Planning Congress of the Fall 1980 National OD Conference, January 10, 1980.

2. Argyris, C. *Management and Organizational Development: The Path for XA to YB.* New York: McGraw-Hill, 1971.

3. ———. *Behind the Front Page.* San Francisco: Jossey-Bass, 1974.

4. Bandura, A. *Social Learning Theory.* Englewood Cliffs, N.J.: Prentice-Hall, 1977.

5. Beckhard, R. "The Confrontation Meeting." *Harvard Business Review* 45, no. 2 (1967): 149–155.

6. ———, and R. Harris. *Organizational Transitions: Managing Complex Change.* Reading, Ma.: Addison-Wesley, 1977.

7. Beer, M. *Organization Change and Development: A Systems View.* Santa Monica, Calif.: Goodyear, 1980.

8. Blake, R., and J. Mouton. *Corporate Excellence Diagnosis.* Austin, Tex.: Scientific Methods, 1968.

9. ———. *Corporate Excellence Through Grid Organization Development: A System Approach.* Houston: Gulf Publishing Co., 1968.

10. Burke, W. "Managing Conflict Between Groups." In J. Adams, *New Technologies in Organization Development: 2.* San Diego: University Associates, 1974.

11. ———, *Practices and Principles of Organization Development.* New York: Little, Brown, 1982.

12. Cohen, A., and H. Gadon. *Alternative Work Schedules: Integrating Individual and Organizational Needs.* Reading, Ma.: Addison-Wesley, 1978.

13. Cummings, T. "Self-regulating Work Groups: A Socio-Technical Synthesis." *Academy of Management Review* 3, no. 3 (1978): 625–633.

14. Davis, L. "Organization Design." Source unknown, pp. 2.1.1–2.1.29, 198.

15. Davis, S., and P. Lawrence. *Matrix.* Reading, Ma.: Addison-Wesley, 1972.

16. Dazal, I., and J. Thomas. "Developing a New Organization." *Journal of Applied Behavioral Science* 4, no. 4 (1968): 473–506.

17. Driscoll, J. "Working Creatively with a Union: Lessons from the Scanlon Plan." *Organizational Dynamics* (Summer 1969), pp. 61–80.

18. Dyer, W. *Team Building: Issues and Alternatives.* Reading, Ma.: Addison-Wesley, 1977.

19. Flamholtz, E. *Human Resource Accounting.* Encino, Calif.: Dickinson, 1974.

20. Fordyce, J., and R. Weil. *Managing with People.* Reading, Ma.: Addison-Wesley, 1971.

21. French, W., and C. Bell. *Organization Development.* New York: Prentice-Hall, 1984.

22. French, W., C. Bell, and R. Zawacki. *Organization Development: Theory, Practice and Research.* Rev. ed. Plano, Tex.: Business Publications, 1983.

23. Galbraith, J. *Designing Complex Organizations.* Reading, Ma.: Addison-Wesley, 1973.

24. Gilbreth, F. B. *Motion Study.* New York: Harper, 1911.

25. Gyllenhammar, P. *People at Work.* Reading, Ma.: Addison-Wesley, 1977.

26. Hackman, J. R., and G. Oldham. *Work Redesign.* Reading, Ma.: Addison-Wesley, 1980.

27. Hall, A., and R. Fagen. "Definition of a System." *General Systems* 1 (1956): 18–28.

28. Hammer, T., and R. Stern. "Employee Ownership: Implications for the Organizational Distribution of Power." *Academy of Management Journal* 21, no. 1 (1980): 78–100.

29. Harrison, R. "Role Negotiation: A Tough-Minded Approach to Team Development." In W. Burke and H. Hornstein, *The Social Technology of Organization Development.* La Jolla, Calif.: University Associates, 1972.

30. Hornstein, H., and N. Tichy. *Organization Diagnosis and Improvement Strategies.* New York: Behavioral Science Institute, 1973.

31. Huse, E. *Organization Development and Change.* St. Paul, Minn.: West, 1975.

32. Jayaram, G. K. "Open Systems Planning." In W. Bennis, D. Benne, R. Chin, and K. Corey, *The Planning of Change.* New York: Holt, Rinehart and Winston, 1976.

33. Kilmann, R., and W. McKelvey. "The MAPS Route to Better Organizational Design." *California Management Review* 17, no. 3 (1975): 23–31.

34. J. Kotter. *Organizational Dynamics: Diagnosis and Intervention.* Reading, Ma.: Addison-Wesley, 1978.

35. Lawler, E. "Reward Systems." In J. R. Hackman and J. L. Suttle, *Improving Life at Work: Behavioral Science Approaches to Organizational Change.* Santa Monica, Calif.: Goodyear, 1977.

36. ———. *Pay and Organization Development.* Reading, Ma.: Addison-Wesley, 1981.

37. ———, and J. Rhode. *Information and Control in Organizations.* Santa Monica, Calif.: Goodyear, 1976.

38. Lawrence, P., and J. Lorsch. *Developing Organizations: Diagnosis and Action.* Reading, Ma.: Addison-Wesley, 1967.

39. Levinson, H. *Organizational Diagnosis.* Cambridge: Harvard University Press, 1972.

40. Likert, R. *The Human Organization: Its Management and Value.* New York: McGraw-Hill, 1967.

41. Marrow, A. *Making Waves in Foggy Bottom.* Washington, D.C.: NTL Institute, 1974.

42. ———, D. Bowers, and S. Seashore. *Management by Participation.* New York: Harper and Row, 1967.

43. Mirvis, P., and D. Berg. *Failure in Organization Development and Change.* New York: John Wiley, 1977.

44. Nadler, D. *Feedback and Organization Development.* Reading, Ma.: Addison-Wesley, 1977.

45. ———, and M. Tushman. "A Diagnostic Model for Organization Behavior." In J. R. Hackman, E. Lawler, and L. Porter, *Perspectives on Behavior in Organizations.* New York: McGraw-Hill, 1977.

46. Pasmore, W., and J. Sherwood (editors). *Sociotechnical Systems: A Sourcebook.* La Jolla, Calif.: University Associates, 1978.

47. Porras, J. I., and B. Anderson. "Improving Managerial Effectiveness Through Behavioral Modeling." *Organizational Dynamics* (Spring 1981), pp. 60–78.

48. Schein, E. *Process Consultation: Its Role in Organization Development.* Reading, Ma.: Addison-Wesley, 1969.

49. Shephard, H. "Life Planning." In K. Benne, L. Bradford, J. Gibb, and R. Lippitt, *The Laboratory Method of Changing and Learning: Theory and Applications.* Palo Alto, Calif.: Science and Behavior Books, 1975.

50. Steele, F. *Physical Settings and Organization Development.* Reading, Ma.: Addison-Wesley, 1972, pp. 45–46.

51. Taylor, F. W. *The Principles of Scientific Management.* New York: Harper, 1911.

52. Van Manan, J., and E. Schein. "Career Development." In J. R. Hackman and J. L. Suttle, *Improving Life at Work: Behavioral Science Approaches to Organizational Change.* Santa Monica, Calif.: Goodyear, 1977.

53. Walker, J. *Human Resources Planning.* New York: McGraw-Hill, 1980.

54. Walton, R. *Interpersonal Peacemaking: Confrontation and Third-Party Consultation.* Reading, Ma.: Addison-Wesley, 1969.

55. Weisbord, M. *Organizational Diagnosis: A Workbook of Theory and Practice.* Reading, Ma.: Addison-Wesley, 1978.

56. Yager, E. "The Quality Control Circle Explosion." *Training and Development Journal* (April 1981), pp. 98–105.

57. Zwerdling, D. *Workplace Democracy.* New York: Harper Colophon Books, 1980.

CHAPTER 9

International Business Management

David B. Zenoff
Stanford University
Graduate School of Business

International business now makes up a significant portion of the sales, asset deployment, and/or source of the factors of production of most medium-size and large companies in the non-Communist world. In 1981 the worldwide sales of the top 500 international businesses — or multinationals, as they are often called — were $2,741 billion; the degree of their internationalization was 46 percent; their overseas production and exports from their headquarters countries were $1,254 million.

Some companies, from their inception, have been very internationally oriented: Kodak, IBM, and Nestlé are prominent examples. Others have developed this orientation gradually: Westinghouse, Bank of America, General Motors, and BASF come to mind. Still another group of companies, both large and small, had no apparent intention of being international but were literally forced into offshore activities by such factors as rigorous foreign competition in their domestic markets; production costs that were higher in their home market than abroad; and the opening or closing of home and foreign markets through changes in commercial legislation and regulations, currency exchange rates, or inflation rates.

Many factors suggest that international business will continue to be a vital force in the world economy for almost all countries. The most significant of these factors are nations' inability to function solely on their indigenous resources and production; companies' expansion desires, which cause them to seek foreign markets; companies' desires for asset and/or earnings diversification, which requires geographic diversification; saturated home markets, which propel companies into international business; the need for cheaper or higher-quality factors

295

Table 9.1 Selected List of Giant "Multinational" Manufacturing Companies, 1981

Company	Country	Total Sales (Millions)	Overseas Subsidiaries Sales as % Total Sales
Nestlé	Switzerland	$ 14,120	97
Alusuisse	Switzerland	3,507	91
Seagram	Canada	2,773	93
Massey-Ferguson	Canada	2,646	92
Alcan	Canada	4,978	78
SKF	Sweden	2,680	92
Electrolux	Sweden	5,253	72
Rothmans	U.K.	5,583	81
RTZ	U.K.	6,127	73
Philips	Netherlands	16,998	68
AKZO	Netherlands	5,802	67
Sony	Japan	4,801	71
Sanyo	Japan	4,437	61
Shering	Germany	1,694	70
Henkel	Germany	3,882	62
BASF	Germany	14,056	57
SOLVAY	Belgium	4,239	90
L'Oréal	France	1,781	54
Exxon	U.S.	113,197	74
Mobil	U.S.	68,587	65
CPC	U.S.	4,343	65
Black & Decker	U.S.	1,431	63
Colgate-Palmolive	U.S.	5,261	59

of production, which leads companies to seek foreign resource bases; and slow domestic economic growth, which impels companies to seek faster-growing markets abroad. The efforts of governments and multinational agencies to promote international trade and investment, coupled with countries' historical economic interdependence, also are important factors in maintaining international commerce.

INTERNATIONAL VERSUS DOMESTIC MANAGEMENT

What is the difference between international business management and domestic business management? In some respects, they differ only in degree. For example:

- In international business, commerce normally involves more than one currency. For a firm, this requirement interjects exchange risk, additional costs, frequent impediments to the transfer of capital and goods between nations, and differences in money and capital market conditions.

- Each nation's business environment is different from all others. Firms must learn to understand its peculiarities, assess the opportunities it offers, adapt their business practices accordingly, and remain abreast of trends in that country.

- When goods, technology, capital, or personnel cross national borders, there are usually attendant costs or restrictions on these transactions. For example, in late 1984 the United States and Japan reached an agreement whereby the Japanese consented to "voluntarily" limit their steel exports to the United States. Countries regulate the trade of goods and factors of production for two main reasons. They do so to protect their domestic industries, their domestic culture, and their strategic capabilities, as well as to protect their economies from inflation. They also regulate trade in order to foster trade and investment, with its potentially favorable implications for employment, balance of payments, and living standards.

- Taxation is one of the most important costs of doing business in most countries. A noteworthy difference between domestic and international business is the fact that companies and commercial transactions are taxed differently at home and abroad, and from country to country.

- Companies, products, or employees may experience discrimination because of their foreign origin. Such discrimination can be favorable or unfavorable, strong or subtle.

What, for management, are the key implications of these differences between international and domestic business? First, management must be aware of the differences and understand how they influence business opportunities and operations. Second, management must incorporate these differences into goal-setting, strategy formulation, and the design of organizational structures and management control systems, as well as into daily operations. Third, management must be reasonably capable of anticipating changes in the foreign and international business environment when it sets goals and makes plans.

In this chapter we will examine selected key elements in managing the internationalization of business. We will begin by considering some frequent mistakes that management makes in international business. Then we will make a series of recommendations about the role of general management, goal-setting and strategizing, and selected elements of business strategy and organization. Last, we will look at major trends in international business and future challenges for management.

FREQUENT MANAGEMENT MISTAKES IN INTERNATIONAL BUSINESS

In working with a sizable number of international companies during the past twenty years and in reviewing the findings of other consultants and academicians, several commonly committed mistakes stand out. It is easy to understand *why* these mistakes are made. Forewarning may make it possible for management to avoid them.

1. Senior management's goals for, and commitment to, international business are unclear. Many companies operate internationally for years without international or domestic management's possessing a sufficiently clear picture of the company's longer-range international goals, or how international should fit with domestic business in such areas as product development, production, marketing, and personnel management. An unclear commitment to international business frequently leads to confusion among domestic and international managers, a sense among international personnel that they have "second-class status," inadequate cooperation between the two parts of the business, and inadequate international goals and management control processes.

2. Senior management's goals for international are too ambitious or unrealistic in other ways. For example, as a late entry in international, the CEO might decide to catch up with the firm's traditional domestic competitors, as measured by size of foreign assets or number of foreign installations. Catch-up strategies often include making foreign acquisitions prematurely in order to gain rapid market share and presence, adding too many foreign employees too soon, moving hastily into new markets, expanding without adequately trained personnel, and over-investing in mediocre business opportunities.

3. Some managements are tempted to follow their traditional domestic competitors into international operations without having their own rationale for such activities and without analyzing the considerations that apply to *them* internationally. Frequently, this follow-the-leader behavior burdens the company with such problems as overcapacity in foreign markets, damagingly late entry into a market, a lack of adequate personnel for operations in certain locations, and unclear goals or performance measures.

4. In the early stages of international expansion, many companies become enamored of sales goals or market-share goals. Thus, as they move forward internationally, all efforts are evaluated in terms of sales performance. Imbued with this "go-go" spirit, the company rarely concerns itself sufficiently with the *quality* of international growth — rarely, for example, uses measures of efficiency, or effectiveness of assets use. It does not put in place adequate management control systems to follow, analyze, or guide international operations.

5. Companies in the United States often develop overly ethnocentric assumptions and attitudes about foreign operations. Thus, managements presume that their domestic business success (products, management style, training, R&D activity, marketing strategies and tactics) can be repeated internationally. The risk, of course, is that foreign market and business environments require somewhat different — sometimes altogether different — modes of operations, products, and management styles. Other companies, most notably European, sometimes err by going to the other extreme: They are overly "polycentric" in their management outlook. Senior management presumes that each foreign market/business environment is so unlike every other that a company's domestic and international business experience is unlikely to be relevant elsewhere. The company therefore makes little effort to transfer its existing know-how among foreign operations.

SOME RECOMMENDATIONS FOR THE MANAGEMENT OF INTERNATIONAL BUSINESS

Senior Management

A key starting point is senior management's role: *it cannot be abdicated.*

It is imperative that senior management formulate a clear model or concept of the company's international business presence and its image/role over time and the reaches of geography. For example, "We want 40 percent of our total sales to be offshore North America," or "We want to maintain our position as the fourth most international U.S. bank," or "We want to be a 'world class' manufacturer." In essence, this will provide a "vision" for employees of all levels, to motivate and inspire them as well as to give them a qualitative objective for decision-making, strategizing, and operating. Only senior corporate management possesses the perspective and formal power to develop and mandate the "model/concept."

International operations should be managed with the same professionalism, thoughtfulness, and care that senior management demands in the management of domestic business. Thus, management control systems, personnel development and training, research and development, and performance planning/review/reward must all be instituted and carried out with the greatest possible expertise and diligence.

Strategy: Elements

A company's international business strategy must encompass all of these elements: marketing, production, research and development, finance, ownership of foreign operations, personnel, and the means of expanding internationally (licensing, joint ventures, acquisitions, exporting, importing, turnkeys,[1] minority ownership). An international strategy is incomplete unless it deals with all of these elements. Moreover, the strategy will likely be faulty unless there is congruence and consistency among the foregoing elements.

International business strategy should be *related to domestic business strategy* in such a way that management can build on the respective strengths of both areas, enhance the leverage of assets, and avoid confusion among managers of each side of the business. Although this might seem obvious, it is all too often ignored in practice. To cite just one example, for years many banks' international departments operated quite independently of domestic operations. Domestically oriented officers did not understand Euromarkets, sovereign risks (government borrowers or government-guaranteed borrowing), or foreign exchange risks. When, in the early 1980s, several developing countries and Poland experienced difficulties as borrowers, there were very few bankers who understood the real nature of the problems or could participate meaningfully in the "work-out" process.

A good international strategy will seek *sustainable competitive advantages*. These should make it difficult or expensive for competitors to match, and represent a unique fit of the company's resources with a market's needs.

Diversification is a prudent element of corporate strategy. International business, of course, offers many firms the prospects of geographic dispersion. However, a few words of caution are in order.

Analysis of geographic diversification should take into account all meaningful criteria for defining concentration, that is, factors and circumstances that bind together business opportunities and risks across national borders. For example, if a bank starts off with domestic exposure to large copper mining companies, its expansion into Zambia or Chile (or any country whose fortunes are tied to copper production) is *not* likely to achieve meaningful diversification. In fact, the bank will likely be concentrating its asset portfolio further, increasing its exposure to the performance of copper.

In most businesses, it is difficult to escape the world business cycle. A U.S. company that seeks geographic diversification by establishing operations in Canada or Mexico or Japan may not derive such benefits because those economies are tied closely to the U.S. economy (50 to 70 percent of their foreign trade and a high percentage of their foreign investment flows are with the United States).

Strategy: The Planning Process

The *strategic thinking/planning process* for international operations is likely to differ from that for domestic operations in several respects.

First, information needs are expanded — geometrically — by the need to understand and stay abreast of each foreign business environment. Second, it is frequently the case in small foreign operations that the staff is inadequately trained or too small to produce high-quality strategic thinking. Senior staff support may be required. Third, as changes in relative currency values, exchange controls, and inflation rates will affect foreign affiliates, these environmental forces must be assessed by experts, and management must understand their significance for the design and implementation of strategic plans.

In considering *how* to expand internationally — that is, when planning the so-called linkages between headquarters country operations, and prospective foreign operations — a company has several choices: exporting, importing, wholly owned ventures, jointly owned ventures, licensing, technology transfers through turnkeys, and management contracts. Management should evaluate all of these possibilities when considering an overall international expansion strategy or a particular international move. The optimal choice of linkage is the one which provides the best fit with the following factors:

• The company's international business objectives

- The home government's and host government's attitudes toward, and regulation of, international business

- The company's critical success factors in each foreign business environment, that is, the elements of business on which most of the firm's commercial success is based: for example, low prices, consistent quality, or skilled sales personnel

- The means available to protect the firm's technology, trademarks, and reputation from competitors: for example, copyrights, patents, secrecy, quality control

- The firm's knowledge base, operating experience, and management resources for managing foreign operations

- The perceived riskiness of foreign business opportunities and senior management's willingness to assume different levels of risk

- The extent to which a firm's resources (management, technology, capital) would meet the requirements for success of a new business opportunity and, therefore, the extent to which other principals' resources are required

- The extent to which each foreign venture is integrated into the firm's global operations

If a company is planning to make foreign acquisitions in order to expand internationally, the potential pitfalls of doing so should be recognized. Frequently, foreign companies are available for acquisition because (1) the owner perceives that the company's future prospects are dim, (2) the company is critically deficient in technology, capital, or management to support it through a more competitive era, or (3) the owner seeks to liquify his or her assets by selling the firm. The acquiring firm must consider each of these possible motives as it makes a detailed analysis of its own objectives and resources for managing and supporting the acquired firm. This requires expertise, patience, and adequate data. Too many companies have been burned by moving too quickly, mostly on "gut feel" and with too little analysis.

In considering an acquisition, the firm must also anticipate the process of integrating a newly acquired foreign company into its network. How would the acquisition fit from the point of view of production, marketing, finance, and R&D management? Many companies make acquisitions on the strength of financial analysis and do not consider the subsequent integration process that will be required. The "chase" and the "deal" have a life of their own; almost no one thinks about the organizational fit.

Strategy: Relations with "Publics"

Another area of importance to companies operating internationally is relations with their foreign "publics." The importance of the respective publics will vary, depending on the industry, the extent of the company's international operations, the country in which its headquarters is located, and the particular country or countries in which it has expanded.

In Canada, where at least 45 percent of all manufacturing is owned by foreigners, an important public of foreign investors was the Canadian government's Foreign Investment Review Agency, which approved and reviewed foreign-owned ventures in Canada.

In the case of foreign-owned affiliates of pharmaceutical or food-processing companies, key publics include the home and foreign governmental regulatory agencies whose approval is required before a new product can be marketed.

What are the most frequent and significant concerns that various publics express about the operations of multinational companies? For one, there is concern about the possible *misuse of companies' massive economic power* (see Table 9.2).

How could such power be misused? One possibility is through "absentee landlordism." When the international company's corporate decision-makers are located outside the country, their actions may have little or nothing to do with the needs of the host country's economy or its policies. The international company could choose courses of action that are not favored by the host government or that run counter to its policies or wishes.

Also, by virtue of having a geographically diversified operations base, an international company could shift operations from one geographic jurisdiction to others, thus bypassing restrictive regulation. In this manner, an international company has the potential for bypassing the preferences of the host government. Its action could, for example, reduce employment or value-added production in the host country.

Another concern about international companies is that they may dominate a local marketplace or a local industry. If an industry is deemed of strategic importance or provides a necessity such as pharmaceuticals or a food staple, the host may feel vulnerable to the whims and vicissitudes of international companies and international relations. In such circumstances, the host may seek more self-reliance by fostering indigenously owned companies and/or resisting the foreign-owned company's ability to compete.

A frequent cause of concern among indigenous companies that compete with international companies is that the internationals compete "unfairly." Until the 1960s, many European companies operated as car-

Table 9.2 The 100 Largest Economic Entities in the World in 1980

(Companies ranked by sales, countries by GNP; US $ millions)

United States	$2,377,090
U.S.S.R.	1,082,300
Japan	1,019,480
Germany, Federal Republic of	717,660
France	531,330
United Kingdom	353,630
Italy	298,200
Canada	228,440
Brazil	207,270
Spain	162,330
Netherlands	143,240
Poland	135,450
Australia	130,670
India	125,990
Mexico	107,620
German Democratic Republic	107,610
Belgium	107,320
Sweden	98,580
Switzerland	89,890
Czechoslovakia	80,530
Exxon	79,106
General Motors	66,311
Austria	64,640
Saudi Arabia	62,640
Denmark	60,830
Royal Dutch/Shell Group	59,417
Turkey	58,760
Korea	55,930
Yugoslavia	53,790
Nigeria	53,310
Indonesia	52,200
South Africa	48,980
Mobil	44,720
Norway	43,520
Ford Motor	43,514
Romania	41,830
Hungary	41,270

Table 9.2 (*continued*)

Finland	39,430
British Petroleum	38,713
Texaco	38,350
Greece	36,710
Bulgaria	32,730
Iraq	30,430
Standard Oil	29,948
Algeria	28,940
Philippines	28,110
Thailand	26,920
Gulf Oil	23,910
Libya	23,390
International Business Machines	22,863
General Electric	22,461
Kuwait	21,870
Unilever	21,749
Portugal	21,300
Pakistan	20,990
Korea, Democratic Republic of	19,720
New Zealand	19,190
E.N.I.	18,985
Hong Kong	18,690
Standard Oil (Indiana)	18,610
Egypt	18,600
Fiat	18,300
Malaysia	17,960
Française des Petroles	17,305
Peugeot-Citroën	17,270
International Telephone & Telegraph	17,197
Volkswagenwerk	16,676
Philips' Gloeilampenfabriken	16,576
Atlantic Richfield	16,234
Renault	16,117
Israel	15,710
Siemens	15,070
Daimler-Benz	14,942
Hoechst	14,785
Shell Oil	14,431

Table 9.2　(continued)

Bayer	14,196
BASF	14,139
Petróleos de Venezuela	14,116
Toyota	14,012
Cuba	13,920
Ireland	13,780
Thyssen	13,637
Elf Aquitaine	13,386
Nestlé	13,017
U.S. Steel	12,929
Nissan Motor	12,652
Conoco	12,648
Hitachi	12,633
Nippon Steel	12,595
E. I. duPont de Nemours	12,572
Chrysler	12,002
Mitsubishi Heavy Industries	11,960
Imperial Chemical Industries	11,391
Tenneco	11,209
Matsushita Electrical Industrial	11,128
Western Electric	10,964
Sun	10,666
Petrobas	10,279
Puerto Rico	10,140
Occidental Petroleum	9,555

tels, which enabled them to limit supply and fix prices. Then American companies came in, marketed aggressively in search of market share, and were sometimes accused of competing unfairly. Since the late 1970s, Japanese companies have competed aggressively in the United States and Western Europe by means of superior products and low prices. Now it is the Japanese who are sometimes accused of competing unfairly through "dumping"[2] and "unfair" Japanese government support.

Finally, as a host's concern, international companies can break down a host country's culture by introducing new languages, industrial work-force rules, and values; by competing on different bases for local employees; by altering the rhythm of the country's daily work life, and so on.

What should the management of an international company do about the concerns of these publics?

1. Headquarters and foreign affiliate managements should continually scan the local business environment, be sensitive to existing concerns and any that may be developing, and identify as precisely as possible the source of concerns.

2. They should take great care to avoid making promises that the firm is unable or unwilling to keep about future business operations in a foreign site. The key is to avoid raising false expectations and hopes among the local populace.

3. They should, as part of strategic and operational planning, consider modifications in manufacturing, marketing, employment practices, financial management, etc., that could yield better returns to the local economy — and be perceived as doing so by concerned publics. Normally, international companies negotiate a business franchise with local stakeholders. Management should anticipate that the local stakeholders — and sometimes the local government — at some point will demand that the terms be renegotiated.

4. Throughout the management of an international company, ongoing public affairs training is needed to enhance managers' perspectives, sensitivities to others' concerns, and negotiating skills. Management should examine other international companies' experiences in dealing with the concerns and pressures of local publics. In addition, companies operating internationally should develop a high-quality public affairs function, with capable, experienced executives being continuously responsible for relationships with external parties.

Structure

In thinking about the *organization structure* for international operations, senior management must grapple with three important questions:

What, over time, should the role of headquarters be?

How should international operations be related to domestic operations?

How should the various *functions* of management — finance, marketing, production, and so on — incorporate international operations?

The headquarters role will evolve over time, in keeping with the firm's overall corporate management style, its business objectives, and the extent and nature of its international operations. Thus, one would expect the role of the Swiss headquarters of the Nestlé Company (a mature multinational with approximately 97 percent of total sales outside of Switzerland) to be significantly different from that of an international neophyte from the United States that derives only 5 to 10 percent of its total sales from abroad.

At a minimum, the role of the headquarters of a mature multinational would encompass the following: establishing overall corporate goals and a corporate mission; providing leadership and guidance in strategic thinking and strategic planning; approving foreign affiliates' business plans; ensuring coordination of global R&D, marketing, and production; selecting key officers to manage international business and foreign affiliates; ensuring the systematic scanning of world markets and resource bases for opportunities and threats to the firm; managing the global allocation of resources; approving the acquisition of major assets and liabilities; and overseeing the coordination of the firm's domestic and international activities.

Companies have organized for international operations in different ways. Among companies headquartered in the United States, the most frequently used organizational structure is the *international division*. Figure 9.1 suggests how this might fit a corporation organized along product-division lines. In the 1960s Westinghouse was organized in this way.

An international division focuses a company's skills and resources for international operations in a single unit. The intentions are to (1) maximize the returns from relatively scarce and specialized resources by facilitating collaborative teamwork among those responsible for various facets of international operations, and (2) provide leadership for international operations in conjunction with domestic counterparts.

The international division structure has its attendant shortcomings and pitfalls. By its very design, it is separate from domestic operations. If care is not taken by both international and domestic management, a wide gulf can develop between the two parts of the company, causing mistrust, jealousies, and misunderstanding, and preventing development of liaison, mutual support, common vision, and cooperation. Problems can also arise when a company's international division does not possess its own product R&D or product manufacturing arms, and thus relies on headquarters or domestic divisions for these capabilities. I shall mention three such problems.

First, the international division may not be able to persuade do-

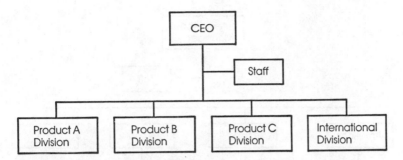

Figure 9.1 Organization by International Division

Typically the international division has responsibility for export sales, administering licensing agreements, and liaison with minority-owned foreign affiliates.

mestic executives to undertake specialized R&D for foreign markets or provide product features to accommodate foreign consumers. As a consequence, the international division's foreign sales efforts may be seriously hampered.

Second, if the company's domestic plants are operating near capacity, the international division may be unable to persuade plant managers to produce for international markets   in which case the international division will be unable to fill its orders. Third, with R&D and manufacturing originated and controlled domestically, companies are unable to ensure that foreign sales and international division personnel in general are *currently knowledgeable* in the company's product line, new technological developments, and so on. Therefore, they have less than optimal capability to represent the company in the market.

These problems can be avoided, or managed as they occur, if senior management makes a clear, strong commitment to international business and fosters international-domestic cooperation.

For however long an international division structure is utilized, it can be elaborated according to the company's management style and the nature and extent of its international operations. Figure 9.2 suggests how an international division can assume a geographic focus, and Figure 9.3 portrays a combination of product and geographic emphases. IBM World Trade is an example of such elaboration.

Companies in the United States, Canada, and Western Europe that utilize a *product division* or *profit center* organizational structure and management style frequently incorporate international operations through *worldwide product responsibility*. Where a company believes that a product's production, R&D, and marketing should be combined under a single responsible manager, a worldwide product organization

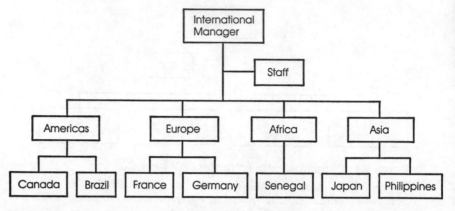

Figure 9.2 International Division: Geographic Focus

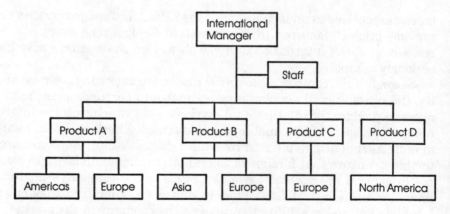

Figure 9.3 Elaborating the International Division: Product Focus

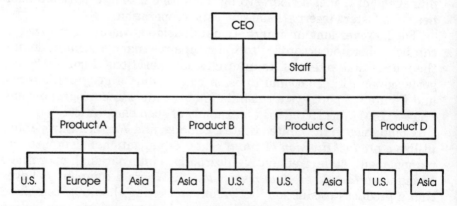

Figure 9.4 The Worldwide Product Organization

can be appropriate. In this scheme, a single manager is responsible for all global operations that affect his or her product's results. This organizational arrangement is shown in Figure 9.4.

Two problems frequently arise within companies that use the worldwide product concept. One is that individual global product managers may, over time, establish redundant sales forces, manufacturing facilities, management offices, and country representatives in the national markets in which they operate. The other problem is that when a company evolves from an international division structure into a worldwide product division structure and delegates global responsibilities to domestic product division managers, these managers — who are presumably well versed in domestic manufacturing, marketing, and R&D — frequently know little or nothing about international business management. Unless the now-global product manager can recruit skilled, experienced internationalists for the division's staff, the division will commit a neophyte's mistakes internationally or slow its international expansion until it is better staffed to proceed.

Companies with a single or limited product line and vertical integration (such as petroleum or mining companies) can use a *global functional management structure* (Figure 9.5). This structure focuses on the global *coordination* requirements of each management function: shipping, exploration, marketing, and so forth. If and as the company elaborates its product offerings, this form of organization cannot readily accommodate the proliferation of specialized product manufacturing, R&D, and marketing knowledge. Therefore, it must be modified. Figure 9.6 depicts a commonly employed variant. Exxon exemplifies such structural elaboration.

A modification of the global functional organization structure occurs when management divides an international company for management control purposes into *geographic* regions. Thus, a company might be structured into four divisions, each having full profit and loss responsibility for manufacturing, R&D, marketing, personnel, and management control within its geographic area (Figure 9.7).

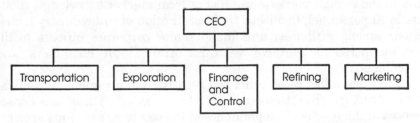

Figure 9.5 Global Functional Organization

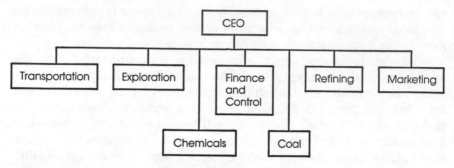

Figure 9.6 Elaboration of Global Function Organization

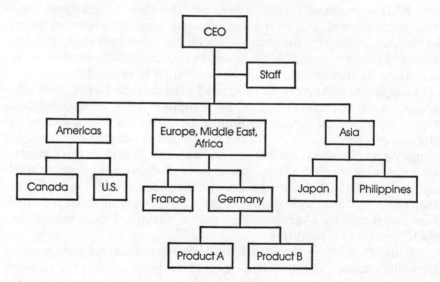

Figure 9.7 Area Organization (One Variation)

Such an organizational structure is intended to reduce the span-of-control[3] burden on headquarters, provide knowledgeable leadership close to the foreign market, emphasize local market knowledge, motivate local personnel, facilitate the coordination of intercountry transactions among affiliates, and make senior corporate officers available for personal contacts with important local customers and governments.

Many companies have benefited greatly from a regional organizational structure. But there are pitfalls to avoid. These are consequences of the relative independence of the company's various area organizations. Rivalries between the areas can develop, sometimes with deleterious effect on the corporate goals. Area general managers may jealously hoard their best officers and slow or block their transfer to another area. Areas may fight for corporate resources without considering the broader, longer-run interests of the corporation as a whole. Individual geographic divisions may develop their own management style, management processes, and employee development, training, and compensation programs without suitable regard for management practices within other divisions.

Thus, the role of corporate headquarters is crucial in ensuring that (1) each division works to achieve the company's *overall* mission, (2) the corporation's total resources are properly allocated among the competing divisions, and (3) wherever necessary, there is coordination and cooperation among divisions.

Defining the Global Mission of Each Management Function

Earlier in this discussion about organizational structures we emphasized that senior management should take care to accommodate both the international and the domestic dimensions of operations in each management function. In companies that are relatively new to international business, or in which senior management has failed to make a strong, clear commitment to international business, there is often an artificial separation between the international and domestic operations of each functional department. In these instances, the domestic marketing managers may not know about or become involved in international marketing. Those responsibilities are then left to junior, less experienced internationalists with inadequate staffs. This state of affairs does not necessarily foreclose all chances of realizing international opportunities, but it is certainly not the best that the company can do to internationally leverage its domestic marketing capabilities.

For the senior management of a company that faces this problem, the following line of analysis is recommended. For each management function, senior management should ask: *What are the four to six most important tasks that the function must fulfill — that is, what is the mission of that function?* Having identified those critically important tasks, management can (1) identify the expertise, skills, and experience levels required of the top few officers within that function and (2) devise goals and performance standards for the senior managers of that function.

In determining the four to six most important tasks that must be done particularly well (i.e., the mission), senior management should consider these factors:

1. The most important *characteristics and qualities of the company as a whole* that should be reflected in the orientation of functional management (for example high price/earnings multiples of the company's stock, capital intensity of the company, degree of maturity of the mature product lines, where geographically the company competes)

2. The most important *international characteristics and qualities* of the company that should be reflected in the orientation of functional management (for example, jointly owned foreign affiliates, operations in eighty countries)

3. The most important *external forces and circumstances* that should be reflected in the orientation of functional management (for example, volatile interest rates, strength of the U.S. dollar, commodity prices)

In the following example of this process, we consider what could be the mission of the finance function of a mature, integrated, multinational, petroleum corporation. (This information was gleaned from publicly available literature about the company during recent years.)

Principal Corporate Characteristics

Huge size

High public profile

Fully integrated

U.S. accounts for 35–40 percent of total revenues, 40–55 percent of earnings, 50 percent of assets, 60 percent of capital outlays

Mature finance-, marketing-, and refining-oriented management

Strong leadership

Top management from the oil industry

Nonoil acquisitions not closely managed by headquarters; relatively unprofitable

Low price/earnings multiple (5–7); stock price at substantial discount from book value

Organization:

Credit rating ranges from AAA/AA for oil company to BB- for subordinated debt of nonoil business

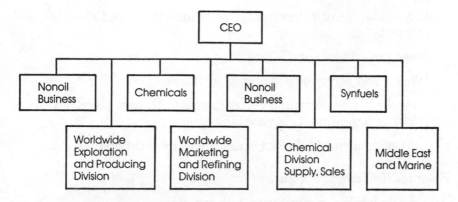

A relatively low-cost operator

High volume of cash flow

Senior management financially conservative

Crude-short, especially in U.S.

Several recent large crude discoveries to be exploited

Strategic Profile

Trying to decrease dependence on Middle East and foreign crude (now 50% of total supply)

Relatively large offshore exploration and drilling operations

Marketing and refining: concentrate sales efforts where possess *good supply logistics;* through *minimum* number of outlets (divesting ineffective marketing assets)

Attempting to maintain/increase margins through cost reduction programs

Corporate International Business Characteristics

Mature as multinational corporation

Global in scope; twenty-four foreign refineries; operations in Europe, Middle East, Japan, Indonesia, Nigeria, with sales one-third each in United States, Europe, Asia/Africa

Foreign earnings a large percentage of total earnings

Integrated; many intercompany transactions

Operates in 105 currencies

U.S. dollar principal currency for transactions and shareholders' interests

Huge projects and operations

Wholly and jointly owned foreign affiliates

Long-term viewpoint and relationships with host countries; have left only Argentina, Lebanon, Libya

Current chairman knowledgeable about international affairs

External Environmental Factors

Volatile foreign exchange and interest rates

Conditions and size of capital/money markets vary

Currency exchange controls in most countries

Commodity and oil price level changes

World business cycle

Government price controls of oil prices

Inflation rates

Interest rates

U.S. government policy regarding domestic acquisitions

Forms and rates of government taxation; foreign tax credits; tax treaties (effective U.S. income tax rates 35–45 percent; rest of world 60 percent)

Credit rating agencies' views

Demand for oil — globally, by region, by product type

Financial accounting follows Financial Accounting Standard No. 52

Various publics' impressions and viewpoints regarding "Big Oil"

From the foregoing considerations, the mission of the company's global corporate finance function might be formulated as follows:

Corporate Finance Mission Elements

Finance implementation of global corporate strategy

Provide global financial planning for senior management

Protect assets against economic foreign exchange risk

Manage liquidity primarily for safety, secondarily for yield

Optimize global tax management

Educate senior management about foreign exchange risk, LDC debt problems, and finance in general as it impacts corporate capabilities and results

LOOKING AHEAD

We can identify several important trends that are likely to characterize international commerce and the environment in which it will take place in the coming decade. This list, while not exhaustive, suggests the nature of the international business management challenge.

The *debt problems and capital requirements of developing countries* will continue to cause disruptions and uncertainties in those countries' economic policies and regulations related to foreign exchange controls, capital flight problems, import restrictions, incentives for exporters, shortage of local credit facilities, and so on.

The *importance of state-owned companies will increase* in most countries. For the internationally involved private-sector company this will mean greater competition for markets and resources. The sizable government resources that can back state-owned companies, as well as their lack of profit motivation, can lead to extreme price competition.

There will be generally *increased competition* for the world's markets and resources, reflecting the growing number of companies operating internationally and the generally increasing commitment of companies to international business.

There will be continued efforts by countries, multilateral organizations, industry trade associations, and individual companies to *clarify and promote compliance with the (largely unwritten) codes of acceptable conduct* for international operations.

There will be continued proliferation of *nontariff barriers* to international trade, despite periodic multilateral efforts to enhance the international flow of goods and services.

There will be *slower economic growth* in most countries than that experienced in the 1960s and 1970s.

For managers of international enterprises, the foregoing forecasts virtually ensure continuation of the *complexity* and risks that characterize international operations. The more a company internationalizes, the more its daily operational management will have to contend with these environmental trends and forces. Managements must therefore be knowledgeable and adaptable in order to fight daily "fires" as well as able to think clearly and comprehensively about basic business objectives, strategies, and contingency plans that would fare acceptably well in the volatile, highly competitive, and unpredictable business environment.

For a complex, diversified multinational corporation, one key management-style issue is the extent to which operations should be *standardized* globally, versus the extent to which *localized* adaptations should be employed. For example, should advertising campaigns be standardized for use in more than one country? Should product features be altered for various markets? Should executive employment policies be altered from country to country? Should manufacturing processes and quality control standards be localized or globally standardized? There is no generally recommendable prescription for management, because the answers to these important questions depend on market characteristics and the nature of the competition as well as on a company's overall management style.

Another important management issue for the future concerns ownership of foreign operations. In the last fifteen years, companies have been forced — or have chosen — to operate with less than 100-percent-owned controlled foreign affiliates (for example, Saudi Arabia's demands on Citicorp, and Mexico's on IBM). Companies' sell down of equity sometimes is to (1) appease local publics who want more of the benefits of foreign-owned operations to be distributed to indigenous stakeholders, (2) lower the company's profile in foreign domains, and (3) share the risks and responsibilities of operating internationally. Whatever the motivations, most companies will have to make further efforts to operate successfully with less and less ownership of foreign operations. The management implications are fourfold:

1. Management must learn how to operate a global network without total control of all parts of the network.

2. Management must learn to identify suitable partners for international operations and to structure partnership agreements for the "new age" in international business.

3. Management must devise control processes suitable for guiding as well as reporting on jointly owned operations abroad.

4. Management must learn to adroitly divest itself of a portion of its equity in foreign ventures, obtain reasonable compensation for the relinquished equity, and reconstitute a manageable affiliate.

Despite all its complexities and problems, international business can be a very rewarding component of a corporation's total operating strategy, and in today's world it is unlikely that many companies can avoid competing with foreigners for markets or resources. Therefore, it is prudent for management to learn well the lessons of how to be a successful world competitor.

NOTES

1. A turnkey is a project that is capable of producing its output upon the owner's assumption of its control — for example, an electric power generating plant or a steel mill.
2. Dumping is the practice of pricing an export lower than the price charged in the country where it is produced.
3. "Span of control" refers to the number of direct reporting relationships an officer has.

SUGGESTED READINGS

Brooke, Michael Z. *International Corporate Planning*. London: Pitman Publishing, 1979. Details the elements, complexities, and useful approaches to planning for international business operations.

Hall, E. "The Silent Language in Overseas Business." *Harvard Business Review* (May–June 1960). Classic description of what constitutes cultural differences among people of different nationalities.

Hout, Thomas, and Michael Porter. "How Global Companies Win Out." *Harvard Business Review* (September–October 1982). Highlights the important differences between a company that operates in many countries with local strategies and companies that have global strategies.

Kapoor, Ashok. *Planning for International Business Negotiations*. Boston: Ballinger, 1982, chap. 1. Highlights the elements that require consideration, expertise, and careful management in conducting international business negotiations.

Keegan, Warren. *Multinational Marketing Management*. Englewood Cliffs, N.J.: Prentice-Hall, 1982. Basic text in international marketing.

Zenoff, David B. *Management Principles for Finance in the Multinational*. London: Euromoney, 1980. Basic pragmatic text for both international business management and international financial management.

CHAPTER 10

Technology Management

William F. Miller
Stanford University
Graduate School of Business

PERSPECTIVES ON TECHNOLOGICAL CHANGE

The recent emphasis on technological progress and intense worldwide competition has created an interest in the fundamental forces and the trends surrounding technological progress. The fundamental forces are not very well understood, whereas trends are easier to identify. It is important for business and industry to recognize and capitalize on the trends while trying to gain a better understanding of the fundamental causal relationships.

With the exception of Joseph Schumpeter, economists have largely treated technology as an exogenous force. In his *Business Cycles* (1939) and *Capitalism, Socialism, and Democracy* (1942), Schumpeter devoted much attention to the central role of technical progress as a means of understanding the dynamics of capitalism.

Today, many states and communities in the United States as well as many nations are experimenting with various means of stimulating technological progress.[1] This chapter provides a framework for examining technological change. We begin by considering several ways of viewing technological change. Next we identify those new technologies which will have the greatest impact on the economy over the next decade or two. This is followed by a discussion of techniques for identifying, monitoring, and incorporating new technologies in a product or process. We close by discussing the roles of government and venture capital in the realm of high technology.

Ways of Viewing Change

Technological change is a many-sided subject. It is possible to look at technology from various angles, make comparisons, and get cross-cutting views of what particular technologies do and the kind of technological change they create.

One way to view technological change is to separate the technologies into those that reduce costs on the one hand and those that enhance capabilities on the other. The cost-reducing technologies are of obvious competitive advantage and provide for classical economic factor substitution. Examples of cost-reducing technologies are new materials such as carbon-fiber-reinforced plastics that can replace metals in aircraft and automobile bodies, sporting equipment, household appliances, gears, and bearings. Other examples are sources of cheaper power and more energy-efficient production processes. A cost-reducing technology of a software type is the employment of operations research methods for scheduling: for example, airline scheduling, production line scheduling, or Just-in-Time delivery systems for inventory control.

On the capability-enhancing side, we can cite as examples the changes in transportation, communications, computing, and health. Air transport may be more costly per unit of weight and per mile than other forms of transportation, but its speed brings about a new quality and a new capability. Rapid communications permits a more rapid feedback and iteration of discussions between business partners or product developers, thereby providing an additional capability. Computing capability provides intellectual power both in the office and the laboratory. Health improvements result in greater productivity.

A second way of approaching technological change is to separate the technologies into physical and social, which is to say hardware and software. Material, or hardware, technologies stem from the sciences of physics, chemistry, biology, and engineering. Herein we use software in its broadest sense; that is, we include not only computer software but also procedures, organizational experience and principles, and service capabilities.

A great deal of current technological change stems from software technologies: social technologies that stem from business theory and practice, industrial engineering, operations research, computer science, artificial intelligence, and the use of mathematics in solving business and industrial problems.

Yet another view of technologies classifies them into those which supply power or replace certain physical capabilities of humans and animals on the one hand, and those which enhance the intellectual capabilities of humans on the other. In the first case, the human operator enhances the capability of the machine by providing direction and control, that is, the intelligence functions. In the second case, the machine enhances the capability of the human in those typically human functions of direction and control.

Areas of activity such as artificial intelligence, operations research, and computer science are generally capability-enhancing, employ both hardware and software, and enhance the intellectual capabilities of society. Areas of activity such as new energy technologies are principally cost-reducing, mostly hardware, and enhance the physical capabilities of society. Of course, some technologies both greatly enhance capabilities and greatly reduce costs. The digital computer, for example, continues to multiply our ability to process and store information while at the same time driving the costs of doing so ever lower.

Current Trends

The rate of introduction of new technologies and the pace of innovation are increasing, not decreasing. Three factors are contributing to what is becoming a virtual explosion of new technologies in the 1980s.

First, the seeds of scientific research planted after World War II are now bearing fruit. Technologies that are being commercialized today are a direct outgrowth of that research. For example, research in solid-state physics has contributed new materials, research in biochemistry and physiology has produced new drugs and the techniques of genetic engineering, and research in computer science has produced techniques for expert systems. Examples of all of these follow.

Not only did the post–World War II impulse produce new scientific ideas; it produced a rapid increase in the supply of scientific and technically trained professionals and managers who are comfortable managing the introduction of new technologies.

Second, industry is making major efforts to capitalize on new scientific ideas. These efforts have been stimulated by global competition, worldwide demand for new products, and growing constraints on the supply of energy and materials. Therefore, the emphasis is on products that permit new levels of performance (for example, ceramic engines) and products that provide new capabilities (such as artificial intelligence). Special emphasis is being given to technologies that conserve energy (such as more fuel-efficient aircraft engines) and technologies that obtain higher performance from new materials.

The most striking recent example of the impact of technology on industry — and, indeed, on society as a whole — is that of the information technologies on the U.S. work force. In the past twenty years, the proportion of the work force involved in information jobs has more than doubled. In 1985, about two-thirds of the U.S. work force was employed in service and information jobs. These changes in composition of the work force, brought about by changes in technology, have been quite painful for some sectors of the population. Nonetheless, the resulting overall growth in GNP has raised the overall standard of living.

The third factor contributing to the explosion of new technologies is the increasing availability of high-risk investment moneys — that is, venture capital — to support and stimulate embryonic, high-technology companies, as well as high-risk research ventures for large, established companies. High-risk venture capital plays a key role in the advance of high technology and its impact on new products and processes.

All three of these factors are part of a ferment and return of eclecticism to American business and American society. The significance of this development can be best appreciated if we observe that historically periods of dynamic growth in societies coincided with periods of high levels of eclecticism.

Europe was very eclectic during and following the Renaissance and into the Industrial Revolution. This long period was an era of experimentation and reaching out in politics, art, religion, and business. The United States was also very eclectic during the nineteenth century and into the twentieth century. In this century, however, American business turned inward and adopted a "not invented here" attitude. In the meantime, the Japanese — following the Meiji Restoration — entered a period of eclecticism and proceeded to select the best worldwide. What we see today in the United States is a return of eclecticism. Companies have dropped the "not invented here" attitude in an effort to search worldwide for new technologies to improve their products and processes.

DRIVING FORCES: THE NEW TECHNOLOGIES

The five technologies that will be driving forces in the next decade are:

Information technology

Factory and office automation

New materials

Biotechnology

Health and medical technologies

There are, of course, other important new areas of scientific and technological progress, but we cannot cover all of them here. We shall address only briefly the entrepreneurial opportunities from space exploration, for example, and we shall omit oceanographic activities entirely.

Of the myriad possibilities that space research may open up within the next five to twenty years, we shall mention two. First, in the zero gravity of outer space, materials of different densities do not separate out from each other, and materials of different temperatures do not meld because heat does not rise. An experiment on electrophoresis aboard the space shuttle found that biological material could be separated at a volume 500 times greater than is possible on Earth, and at greater purity levels. Thus it may be possible to devise new treatments for disease by producing certain cells, enzymes, proteins, and hormones in space laboratories. (On Earth many of these disease-curing substances can be produced only in minute quantities.)

Second, by manufacturing in space, new materials may be created, such as alloys that would separate on Earth during melting and solidification. Glass with an unprecedentedly high index of refraction could be produced by melting and cooling it out of contact with molds. Perfectly spherical ball bearings could be created. Large, pure crystals could be grown for electronic and electro-optical devices.

We must add a strong note of caution, however, about the prospects for manufacturing in space. The cost of large-scale transport and life-support systems will remain prohibitive for many, many years. In the near term, space will be used for manufacturing laboratories — for research, to discover new processes and substances — rather than for factories. Most scientists do not expect true factory manufacturing in space during this century.

Now let us look at the five major technological forces and their impacts.

Information Technology

In 1962, National Educational Television produced a program called "Machines That Think." The concept seemed quite esoteric then — more like science fiction than fact. People were always asking, "Do machines *really* think?" No one asks that question today — nor should anyone, since the world champion backgammon player is a computer.

In the past decade we have witnessed spectacular advances in information technology. The information technologies have had unprecedented impact on the world economy in the past two decades. Moreover, there is no evidence of slowing down. These technologies are creating new products and new business opportunities at an even more rapid pace than in past years.

At the heart of these developments is a tiny device: the microelectronic circuit. Its manufacture makes possible a remarkable cornucopia of information processing and handling possibilities. Already the marginal cost of adding substantial information-processing capability to manufactured products is small. By 1990, that cost will be virtually zero. By then, some experts predict, almost anything that costs more than $20 and plugs into a wall or a battery will contain a microprocessor. A microcomputer is a very small computer made up of a few specialized microelectronic circuits. Already there are in the market microprocessor-controlled calculators that retail for less than $10. The microprocessor in the calculator represents only a small fraction of that $10.

Thanks to microelectronic circuitry, an important change in perspective is occurring that will determine the thrust of technology for the rest of the 1980s. In the broadest sense, this change can be viewed as a shift in emphasis away from optimizing the efficiency of systems and toward optimizing the efficiency of people.

Microelectronics enables us to decentralize our systems to a level at which they can provide support capability to individual workers far from the factory or office. This change may appear in the form of a modular management or office workstation that offers a menu of services on command. Or it may appear in the form of an "intelligent toolbox" in which people carry the resources of their profession or craft wherever they go, just as plumbers or carpenters carry their tools with them today. For example, a financial planner would carry the essential data and a mathematical model of the company's operations in a small portable computer that could be connected by telephone to the company's central data base. A field maintenance engineer could carry a small computer whose memory storage devices contained not only an enormous amount of reference material but also a species of artificial intelligence in the form of a computer program called an *expert system,* which would enable the engineer to diagnose problems in the field equipment and effect a "cure."

Artificial intelligence is a specialty of computer science that deals with reasoning by computers. Within the area of artificial intelligence one of the most exciting developments is the production of expert systems for medical diagnosis, chemical analysis, complex business and military problem-solving, geological prospecting, and other "intelligent" procedures.

An expert system starts with an expert in a given field — say, a psychiatrist — a computer scientist called a knowledge engineer, and a sophisticated interactive computer system. The knowledge engineer, in cooperation with the expert, codifies the judgments of the expert into a specialized problem-solving system. This system, in turn, makes judgments similar to those of the expert. Moreover, it continues to learn from experience. It can actually assist a user in reaching a conclusion — for example, a psychiatric diagnosis — or solving a problem.

SRI International (formerly Stanford Research Institute) has developed a system called PROSPECTOR that can inquire and reason about the location of a particular kind of mineral deposit. PROSPECTOR predicted the existence of a large mineral deposit in the state of Washington — and drilling confirmed that prediction. Stanford University has developed other expert systems that can identify chemical structures, plan experiments in molecular genetics, and assist in diagnosing conditions caused by diseases. A great deal of development work is still needed before such systems become truly widespread, but there is little doubt that we are well on our way.

Another technology that will have great impact is fiber optics. Optical fibers have hair-thin strands of glass that transmit photons of light, rather than wires that transmit electrons. Fiber optics has great potential in the transmission of information, whether over great distances, as in a telephone network, or over very short distances, as within a computer. Photons travel at the speed of light, in contrast to electrons, which travel several orders of magnitude more slowly. Thus, fiber optics and photon technology could enable tomorrow's telephone cables to carry hundreds of times as many messages — and make tomorrow's supercomputers as much as a thousand times faster than the fastest computers that we have today.

Still another use of photon technology is in optical information-storage technologies. If you look at the back of your credit card, you will see a dark strip about one-quarter of an inch wide extending across the width of the card. This magnetic strip can now contain 1,720 bits, or 212 alphabetical and numerical characters of information about the card holder.

Using a photon technology developed at SRI, Drexler Corporation is commercializing an optical recording system that would store five million bits of information on that small strip. This means that literally the entire history of an individual's financial transactions could be stored on a bank card. Or several filing cabinets of information could be reduced into a small optical card. This represents a breakthrough of many orders of magnitude in information storage and retrieval.

For most companies that market devices containing semiconductors, the key determinant of success will be the company's ability to develop these devices and to handle specific software support programs — that is, to develop customized standard microprocessors and do it in the most cost-effective way. Both Intel and Hewlett-Packard have introduced microprocessors that are easily customized.

The significance of these breakthroughs in information technology can best be understood by looking back to 1972, when Intel brought out the first microprocessor, or computer central processing unit on a single silicon (semiconducting) chip. In the thirteen years since that event, the cost of computation in computers has declined essentially to zero. It is likely that ten years from now the cost of computer memory storage will also have dropped almost to nothing. And when the cost of memory is virtually zero, we will see some seemingly incredible new products.

For example, IBM has a voice-actuated typewriter in its lab today. A major problem is that such a typewriter takes an enormous amount of memory. But when the cost of memory is virtually zero — and when today's memory banks shrink to a small, low-cost unit at the back of the typewriter — we will have an entirely new way of interfacing with machines. And, of course, what applies to typewriters also applies to voice interactions with computers, robots, and other mechanical or electrical products. Thus, in ten years we may be able to talk to our machines as we now talk to one another.

Factory and Office Automation

A second promising technology, computer-based automation technology, will soon provide the means of changing our mode of industrial production radically and beneficially. Major batch production industries — for example, earth-moving and construction equipment, aircraft, electrical and electronic equipment, some home appliances — will constitute the greatest market for this technology and will be the most affected by it.

It now appears that the most exciting new applications of robotics will come with advances in artificial vision and machine sensing of touch, force, and torque. For example, vision systems currently employed in manufacturing operations work only in binary (i.e., either the object is there or it isn't), black-and-white environments, in which parts and subassemblies are conveniently separated from one another. Real factory environments tend to have many shadings of gray and brown. Parts and subassemblies tend not to be located and separated precisely. Better vision systems are being developed that can work on gray-scale information and that use better algorithms to discriminate among jumbled parts. These research efforts should result in faster and more powerful vision tools by the end of the decade.

Better sensor input, combined with faster robots in well-conceived work cells, will enable robots to assume significant tasks in assembly operations. These are the most labor-intensive operations in manufacturing. Better productivity — measured against both labor and total inputs — and better-quality products should result from using these sensor-equipped robots. These improvements alone will give a competitive edge to those manufacturers who use them.

No significant technological or scientific breakthroughs appear necessary for the other major technological components of factory automation in batch manufacturing industries. These components include computer-aided design (CAD) and production planning, computer-aided manufacturing (CAM) with numerically controlled (NC) machine tools, machining centers and flexible manufacturing systems, and computer-aided materials control. The performance of these components will continue to improve, as will their accompanying software; and their prices will continue to fall.

To fully exploit automation technology, manufacturers will have to rethink the organization of their processes. Change will be needed not only in plant organization and layout but also in accounting systems; promotional programs and incentives; inventory management manufacturing policies, practices, and organizational structure; and organizational "folklore" (outdated expertise). In short, practically all the ways in which manufacturing is thought about and represented on a day-to-day and practical basis are relics of a mode of industrial production that automation is making impractical and uncompetitive.

This state of affairs is by no means trivial or purely philosophical; it is a real problem facing both sellers and users of automation technology. For example, accounting systems based on labor costs often cannot account for the savings that automation makes possible through higher quality, reduced inventory and scrap, faster turnaround, and so forth. Nor are these systems useful in determining the costs of goods whose labor content is being replaced by machine time, computer time, and other nonlabor factors.[2]

New computer automation is more than simply a new tool. It is part of a radically new way of manufacturing, a new mode of industrial production. In this new mode, information systems and technologies will speed and support the design process. They will transmit manufacturing information directly from design stations to manufacturing operations, on the way to producing and ordering bills of materials. They will control robots, machine tools, and materials-handling devices. They will track, store, and pack finished goods for shipment. They will integrate these functions. And they will tell human operators how well the factory is performing, what needs to be fixed, and even something about how to fix it.

This change in the mode of industrial production means that, to manage a factory and a manufacturing company effectively, manufacturers will above all have to manage the now-dominant information systems effectively.

It is quite likely that the true factory of the future will appear on a significant scale within ten years. Such a factory will employ truly integrated systems of inventory control; Just-in-Time delivery systems; computer-aided design, engineering, and manufacturing; and intelligent, programmable robots. All steps in the manufacturing process will operate as a single integrated yet flexible system.

By 1990, as companies and industries incorporate this technology, the *information and knowledge component* of manufacturing will be the dominant element in industrial production.

I will be very brief in my remarks on office automation. If the true factory of the future is a decade away, the true office of the future is just around the corner. All the necessary technologies are here: the display, information storage, and network and communications systems, as well as the word processing and financial processing software. They require only to be made more user-friendly and integrated into compatible systems. The cost of computing power and memory is dropping so rapidly that the economics of office automation will become extremely attractive within the next two or three years.

The widespread adoption of office automation will lead to breakthroughs in white-collar productivity. We sorely need these breakthroughs because two-thirds of our work force are already employed in information-handling jobs. And this proportion will increase even more as we proceed further into the new Information Age.

New Materials

The third driving technology is new materials. New materials are already making an impact in the transportation, communications, construction, and recreational (sporting goods) industries.

The composite polymers, metallic glasses, new ceramics, and synthetic membranes are especially worthy of note. Both the new composite polymers and the new ceramics soon will be of great importance to the transportation industries. The composite polymers, such as the carbon-fiber-reinforced plastics, are stronger than steel and lighter than aluminum. Body weight is being reduced, and structures are being made stronger through the use of these materials. Their major commercial use to date has been in top-of-the-line recreational products such as ski equipment, fishing poles, golf clubs, and tennis racquets, where high strength and low weight are advantageous and the cost of the material itself is not a deciding factor.

These same properties — lightness and strength — have led to attempts to introduce carbon-fiber-reinforced plastics components into automobiles and aircraft in order to reduce fuel consumption. (They will also reduce corrosion.) Over the years, producers have increased their carbon or graphite fiber manufacturing capacity, but because of costs, consumption always lagged, sometimes being as low as 10 percent of production.

Now, however, the picture is changing. First, Boeing is introducing major quantities of these polymers in its new 757/767 series of widebody airliners. (Lear Avia has already built an "all-composite" aircraft whose fuselage, wings, rudder, and ailerons have developed more sophisticated and automated production processes; they are intermixing glass and carbon fibers to increase strength at a lower cost. Finally, producers of carbon-fiber-reinforced plastics have gambled on greater consumption and have increased their capacity in order to lower costs through economies of scale. All these factors will lead to broader use of these polymers by the end of the decade.

The new ceramics are proving to be very important in high-temperature applications such as engines. Internal combustion engines would be considerably more efficient if they operated at higher temperatures, but metal engines would fail in such heat. Ceramic gas-turbine engines in particular would thrive on higher temperatures; they would operate more efficiently and have lower maintenance costs than steel engines. They would also be lighter in weight. Such turbine engines are now under development. Already ceramic parts are used in the turbochargers of some truck, marine, and industrial engines. We will see more and more ceramic engine components in the next decade as researchers and manufacturers continue to increase the tensile strength and other operating characteristics of ceramic materials.

High technology is even more significant in a second class of materials: metallic glasses. These materials are produced by cooling molten metal so fast that it does not have time to form its customary crystalline structure, but instead remains in its amorphous form. Over the years, researchers have found that these amorphous materials possess a variety of interesting properties, such as low energy losses and mechanical flexibility. However, high production costs have discouraged their use in commercial products. Recently, however, several large corporations have developed continuous processes for making flexible ribbons in a variety of widths from these metallic glasses. Extremely low magnetic losses of these iron-base amorphous alloys make them highly attractive materials for the windings of transformers and electric motors. Prototypes wound from such ribbons have demonstrated that associated energy losses could be three to ten times lower than with conventional materials.

Superplastic alloys — the oxide-dispersion-strengthened metals — have some unusual characteristics. They are creep-resistant and stress-resistant. And because they withstand heat better than almost any other metal, they will be very important where high temperatures are involved, as in combustion engines, heat shields or containers for molten metals, and axles and gears in high-temperature environments. Under other conditions, these remarkable alloys are soft and highly deformable. While many production problems remain to be solved, it seems clear that we are well on the way to a new generation of supermetals.

Another area of materials research — membrane technology — promises to produce some remarkable breakthroughs within the next decade. Synthetic membranes imitate biological membranes, which separate chemicals in living organisms. These new membranes are beginning to replace a whole range of industrial separation processes, from distillation to drum filtration. They are being used on a small scale to filter out pollutants, to purify and concentrate substances, to recover rare minerals, and to produce pure antibiotics. One of their most important applications may be the desalination of sea water by reverse osmosis, a technology that is well advanced in the laboratory.

Biotechnology

It is popular to say that the 1990s will belong to biotechnology, the fourth driving technology. In some areas that may be true, but many — perhaps most — biotechnology applications will come in the twenty-first century. That is not far away.

Eventually, biotechnology's contributions will be truly revolutionary in their impact. The human ability to understand and harness nature's basic life process through technologies such as gene splicing could alter the course of industrial evolution.

Genetic engineering by means of recombinant DNA is an important new technique in biotechnology. Recombinant DNA can be used to change the genetic character (and thus the physical and behavioral characteristics) of simple organisms such as the *E. coli* bacteria, thereby accomplishing in the laboratory in a short time what might take decades or even centuries to evolve naturally — or might not evolve naturally at all.

Recombinant DNA technology excites the imagination because it enables us to direct living organisms to carry out a desired chemical reaction or synthesis. Even the simplest bacterium is a tiny chemical "factory" that continually carries out elegant chemical conversions to make a wide variety of chemical products. If a bacterium or other microorganism can be induced to make a product from common raw materials inexpensively and energy-efficiently, the economic possibilities can be substantial — particularly if the product in demand cannot be made cost-effectively by any other technology.

The driving forces that spur interest in biotechnology include potential process improvements that will reduce energy requirements, increase product yields, and enable researchers to use inexpensive raw materials as energy sources. For example, genetically engineered bacteria have been produced to convert sawdust to alcohol for fuel. Current work is directed toward developing bacteria that carry out this conversion efficiently. Considerable funding, therefore, is flowing into recombinant DNA work from both the public and private sectors in the United States, France, Germany, the United Kingdom, and Japan. The result will be new products that are difficult or impossible to manufacture by conventional technology.

The most promising current applications of biotechnology are in the area of pharmaceuticals. For example, Genentech, a small genetic engineering company, has developed a vaccine for foot-and-mouth disease, long a major destroyer of cattle and other cloven-hoofed livestock. We now know how to make simple drugs from complex protein molecules such as interferon and insulin. These new products permit great new advances in health and medicine. Longer-term prospects lie in industrial chemicals, agriculture, and eventually in metallurgy and electronics — for example, bacteriological extraction of metals and even organic memories for computers.

New "bioprocesses" for chemicals production will be developed, such as enzymatic conversions of specialty chemicals. Biotechnology will provide improvements in food-processing applications and enhancements in energy such as conversion of cellulose waste to fuel.

Some researchers see a virtually unlimited potential for recombinant DNA technology. However, its economic attractiveness varies with each application, and the development time and cost of each application are great.

In the industrial chemicals area, researchers are looking to recombinant DNA technology for new products as well as for more economical processes by which to produce existing products. For example, genetic engineering can produce different bacteria for fermentation that use different feedstocks or are more energy-efficient.

Plant engineering through biotechnology offers exciting possibilities. There is little doubt that researchers will eventually engineer more disease-resistant, more water-efficient, and more energy-efficient plants — as well as plants that can fix their own nitrogen, thus decreasing or eliminating the need for fertilizers.

Despite the economic importance of biotechnology, product commercialization will encounter four major obstacles in the 1980s and 1990s: technological barriers, government regulations, patent disputes, and legal and/or political resistance. Formidable technological barriers will delay some applications until the next century. Indeed, it is already necessary to assemble multidisciplinary teams to overcome the complex scientific and technological hurdles.

Health and Medical Technologies

In the next decade, significant advances in health and medical technologies will greatly enhance our capabilities in both diagnosis and therapy. Deeper understanding of biochemistry and physiology as well as the utilization of the microprocessor in medical instrumentation have made these advances possible.

Space does not permit a fuller exposition of these technologies, but the medical and economic impact will be very large. Medically we shall see more effective drugs for specific diseases through computer-aided drug design and more effective delivery of the drugs to the body through controlled-release techniques. Diagnosis will be vastly improved through use of microprocessors in conjunction with ultrasound and nuclear magnetic resonance (NMR).

ECONOMIC IMPLICATIONS OF NEW TECHNOLOGIES

Let us now turn to the economic implications of the new technologies. First we should discuss the information technologies and how they are misperceived. Many people believe that the new technologies are destroying jobs. Also many governments worldwide have as their basic strategy the protection of the jobs that are being threatened in the maturing industries.

The experience in California suggests that this protection is precisely the wrong course. I believe that it will pay to embrace the new technologies because they will create far more jobs than are destroyed. In general, new technologies are more people-intensive than old ones.

The historical record is quite clear: aggregate employment has always increased after the introduction of new technologies. In looking at such sectors as agriculture, we see that the number of people employed directly in agriculture decreased during the twentieth century because of mechanization. But aggregate farm productivity increased dramatically, and this increase in productivity was so great that it required increased employment in packing, shipping, preserving, distributing, and financing in addition to increased demand for machinery and fertilizers.

We have better data today and can see the effect even more clearly in the case of the information technologies. California may be the best precursor or model of the coming information society. If California were a nation, it would have the seventh largest gross national product in the world — nearly $300 billion. Between 1973 and 1980, the United States created a net of ten million new jobs. (Western Europe, in contrast, lost a net of nine million jobs.) Of the ten million new jobs in the United States, 60 percent were high-technology jobs — and most of these were created in the state of California.

Contrary to what many people might expect, most of these jobs were not created in the electronics industry. As of 1985 California has a population of twenty-three million. Its work force is slightly more than eleven million, or about 45 percent of the total population. (This in itself is an amazing ratio. In most Western European countries, the work force is a lower percentage of the population, about 35 percent.) Yet California's electronics industry employees number only about 400,000 to 500,000 people — less than 5 percent of the eleven million people in the work force.

Where, then, have the jobs been created? The answer lies in the "ripple" effect of the new electronics technologies developed in Silicon Valley and spreading throughout other "user" industries. Let's look at one example: the Pacific Telephone Company, one of the most intensive users of electronic hardware, computer services, and automated communication devices in the entire world. PacTel has automated its services at an almost incredible rate. Yet the effect of introducing these labor-saving systems has not been to decrease the number of jobs, as might be expected. Quite the opposite has happened: between 1973 and 1980, PacTel doubled its size and became the largest employer in the state, with over 100,000 employees.

The reason for this amazing growth is that the new electronics and communications technologies have allowed PacTel to offer new services much faster than it has automated its traditional services. Today, more than half of all of the communications over PacTel's lines involve computers "talking" to computers. And more than half the remaining traffic over PacTel's lines involves people "talking" to computers. Only a small fraction of the telephone business in California involves people talking to people. Although the full effect of the deregulation of AT&T is not clear, it would appear that the operating companies are continuing to introduce new services using their new information technologies.

This spread of new jobs and services from the electronics industry throughout society is creating new wealth. At the core of this wealth-creating revolution are two extraordinary statistics. First, from 1973 to 1978, consumer income in California rose at an average of 12 percent a year. Second, value added in manufacture rose by 18 percent a year. The difference between these two statistics represents the creation of new wealth. Through these processes the new information technologies are creating a wealth-producing machine without precedent in economic history. The ripple effect of this new wealth and growth has benefited many sectors of California. These sectors include diversified light manufacturing enterprises, retail and wholesale stores, financial and other services, and construction and real estate, to mention only a few.

The problem in California is not whether there will be enough jobs to occupy the people. Rather, the problem is whether there will be enough technically trained people to fill the jobs. In short, the problem is the mismatch between a traditional, production-oriented work force and the new information economy that is being created.

If California is the precursor or model of the coming information society, then management practices, educational systems, and public policies should not be directed at protecting mature industries. They should be directed at supporting new information-oriented industries and institutions that educate and retrain the work force of tomorrow. These practices and policies should also be directed toward introducing new technologies into mature industries in order to modernize, or "demature," those industries. This is, in fact, happening today.

Although space does not permit a discussion of every technology, I will cite one more example of economic impacts.

As indicated earlier, flexible manufacturing permits the production of small batches of goods at costs comparable to large-scale batch production. Small batch production of more customized products enables manufacturers to respond to a growing social trend toward individualism and diversity.

Studies at SRI International in values and life-style, and similar studies elsewhere, indicate a growing individualism in the United States. This individualism is not a selfish or narcissistic phenomenon, but rather a trend toward self-development and self-expression. This trend carries with it a desire for more diversity and choice in manufactured products. Flexible manufacturing provides a means of responding to these demands, and so it increases the aggregate demand for products.

TECHNOLOGY STRATEGIES AND TECHNOLOGY MANAGEMENT

Developing a Technology Strategy

What is a technology strategy? It is simply a strategy that employs a technology to give a company a competitive edge with either a new product or service, a more attractive old product, or a lower-priced product. The cost reductions that make possible a lower-priced product include everything from lower cost components to more efficient management processes.

For example, the Ford Motor Company has identified telecommunications as a central technology in its development of a "world car." Given the world-car strategy, which entails product design, engineering, assembly, and marketing on a worldwide basis, how do you hold it all together? Both data telecommunication and teleconferencing make it possible for the geographically diverse team to work together effectively. The design of the telecommunications system must then be made to facilitate those objectives.

Many financial service companies have also identified information handling and communications as central to their growth strategies. Those that have been successful in capitalizing on these new technologies have done so by giving the strategy top management attention. It requires senior-level talent that understands both the strategy and the needs to make the strategy work, as well as the technologies and their capabilities.

Developing a technology strategy has many facets. The most important step is to develop a framework or model within which one can develop the strategy. All too often, companies think that managing R&D or finding new technologies is all that is required. Both of these are important, but they are not enough. The most important elements of a technology strategy are identifying and developing new technologies, deciding when to make the transition to a new technology, and organizing the company for the transition.

How does a company identify new technologies? If they fall within the company's traditional areas of expertise, it is an easier task. The research laboratories of the company are the major source of information and expertise about new developments in these traditional areas. But many companies also acquire other, smaller companies to obtain new technologies.

It is a more difficult task to identify new technologies outside a company's traditional areas — and it is especially difficult for the company to recognize how new technologies from a different area might fit into its overall strategy. For example, a chemical company may have excellent chemists, chemical engineers, and business managers who are expert in chemical processes and chemical products but who have no expertise in biochemistry, molecular biology, or genetics. How does such a company explore areas of biotechnology for incorporation in the company's business? The company has several options open to it: (1) It can hire biotechnology scientists and start a new activity in the company's research laboratories. (2) It can acquire a small biotechnology company. (3) It can form a joint venture with another company engaged in biotechnology. Or (4) it can employ an independent research laboratory to conduct research or searches for new technologies.

The technology-search role is a particularly important one played by the for-profit and the not-for-profit independent research laboratories (Arthur D. Little, SRI International, Battle Memorial Research Institute, Southwest Research Institute, etc.).

The process of helping companies identify appropriate new technologies is particularly interesting. One such process, developed at SRI International, is called Innovation Search. The inputs to the Innovation Search process come from the planning staff, operating staff, and senior management of the client company on the one hand, and the professional staff and management of SRI on the other. Contributions from the company side include a status report on each of its major product lines and new opportunities that the company can identify from within. Inputs from the SRI scientists and SRI industry experts include reports on new technologies and their state of development as well as on changes in other industries that may provide cross-industry competition with the client company. The main event of the Innovation Search process is a highly interactive seminar between the company's staff and managers and the SRI professionals.

The output of the Innovation Search is a short list of new business opportunities for the client company. These opportunities may include, for example, new technologies that would enhance current products, or new or improved manufacturing processes as well as ways to capitalize on the company's distribution system, or new ways to compete in another industry's markets.

As part of their strategy to identify technologies early in the research and development process, many U.S. companies are moving toward long-term institutional relationships with universities and not-for-profit research institutes. Arrangements such as the Monsanto agreement with Harvard and the Exxon agreement with MIT provide the university with support for research in particular areas and give industry access to ideas, and sometimes to patents early in the evolution of the scientific ideas.

Another example is the Center for Integrated Systems at Stanford University, which is supported by some eighteen electronics companies including IBM, Hewlett-Packard, and Intel. This center provides for cooperative research between faculty and the supporting industries. It also provides for the training of both students and industrial personnel. Such programs as this one usually provide advance copies of research reports to participating companies and conferences with faculty, students, and industry representatives to discuss advanced research.

Judgment even more sophisticated than that which is necessary in selecting a new technology is required in deciding when to make the transition to a new technology. Here the overriding question concerns the natural limit of the current technology. Has the company run out of possible improvements, or are there still improvements that can be realized through more R&D? The answer to this question is not easy. The judgments of top management and the R&D managers are the best guides. Beyond that, one can examine trends in the R&D area. Are improvements coming more slowly and with greater investment of time and money? Does the R&D management seem less certain of its ability to maintain the flow of improvement?

Other important questions concern the current state and future prospects of the new technology. Does the R&D management have a judgment about the natural limits of the new technology? Does it have a good sense of where the new technology is on the maturity curve? Does it have a sound understanding of competing technologies and where they are on their maturity curves?

Currently we see a very intense interest, on the part of business and industry, in new technologies and their impact. Much of this interest is due to intense global competition. However, some of it derives from intense domestic competition and the drive for new products.

Some of the intense domestic competition comes from cross-industry competition. New technologies make it possible for one industry to invade another industry's markets. In the United States, for example, electronic funds transfer has made retailers like Sears, Roebuck competitors with bankers. The bankers now have to become retailers to compete with retailers like Sears, Roebuck who are becoming bankers. The electronics industry took over the calculator business from mechanical/electrical companies, and television threatens the printing business.

Industries are being redistributed. In the automotive industry, materials and electronics will be at least as important as automotive and combustion engineering. The role of the traditional automotive company, for example, may become assembly, marketing, and distribution, with much less emphasis on parts manufacturing.

Corporate Venturing

Many companies are once again turning to various forms of internal venturing as a growth and diversification mechanism. The search for new products, loss of complacency about our competitive position both domestically and internationally, learning from the Japanese and Europeans, and the rise of a new entrepreneurial spirit all have led to a lessening of the "not invented here" attitude. There have been many examples of failure or lackluster success of internal ventures in the past, but the recent success of IBM in its rapid development of the personal computer business has spurred other companies to rethink their approach.

A company may initiate a corporate venture into a new, nontraditional product or service by establishing a special unit outside the normal management constraints (as IBM did) or by a joint venture, an R&D limited partnership, or a small acquisition. IBM's acquisition of Rolm Corporation as an entry into the telecommunications industry is a good example, as is GM's purchase of a small fraction of Teknowledge, Inc., in order to become familiar with artificial intelligence. Such a venture permits the company to become familiar with a new technology that may require a different approach to marketing and distribution. It enables the company to test the water before it makes a major commitment or acquisition. And it enables the company to test and integrate a different organizational and operational structure when one is called for.

Air Products and Chemicals, Inc., for example, has turned to a new ventures group to develop and commercialize new products that are related to its current strong base of technologies — industrial gases and chemicals. This is a long-term proposition. The reporting relationship, the compensation packages for the venture unit's managers, and the objectives of the unit are all structured to introduce more entrepreneurship into the process of identifying and moving into new growth markets.

In order to succeed in a corporate venture, the company must make sure that the venture is clearly a part of the company's strategic plan.

PUBLIC POLICY FOR TECHNOLOGICAL DEVELOPMENT

Public Sector Actions and Private Sector Responses

In 1981, for the first time in many decades, U.S. support for R&D from the private sector equaled support for R&D from the public sector. Each contributed about $34 billion. In 1984, the private sector is expected to spend about $49 billion in R&D and the public sector about

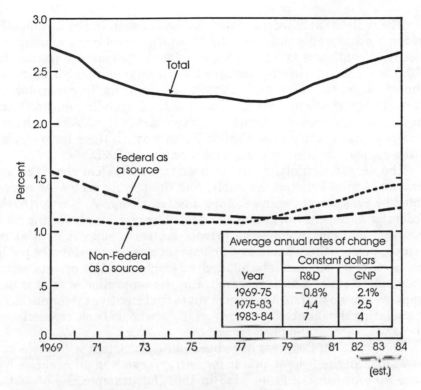

Figure 10.1 U.S. Research and Development as a Percentage of Gross National Product, 1969–1984

SOURCE: National Science Foundation and Department of Commerce

$45 billion. This represents a major shift in public-private policy in the United States. The shift has come about from (1) changing policies and attitudes of the federal government, (2) changing views and policies of the private sector, and (3) changing views of economists.

As Figure 10.1 shows, R&D expenditures as a percentage of GNP declined steadily through the 1960s and 1970s until about 1978. Public debate on government support for research in the years preceding 1978 had emphasized this decline and its negative impact on U.S. industrial competitiveness. This led to a change in the direction of greater public sector financial support for R&D as well as changes in tax laws, antitrust policies, and patent policies that were aimed at encouraging companies to increase their R&D budgets. These changes did lead to more private sector outlays for R&D as well as to the development of new mechanisms and institutional relationships to stimulate R&D and to capitalize on its outputs.

The redirection of federal policy for R&D began in the last months of the Ford administration, extended through the Carter administration, and continued into the Reagan administration. The policies for R&D in these three administrations have been remarkably similar, although there have been some changes of emphasis. In particular, all three administrations have increased federal spending on R&D and have made real efforts to stimulate private sector R&D. Although each has gone about it in a somewhat different way, all three have emphasized support for basic research and for military R&D.

The Reagan administration has been especially clear about the separation of roles between the public and the private sector. As articulated by President Reagan's science adviser, George A. Keyworth, the federal government can gain its greatest leverage by supporting basic research and encouraging the private sector to support applied research. Clearly, these public and private sector roles overlap: the public sector support reaches into applied research, and the private sector does indeed support basic research. But the separation of roles is perhaps greater now. Thus it is important to find creative mechanisms for stimulating the interchange between those who do basic research and those who carry out applied research.

The actions of Congress have been quite consistent with these policies; indeed, the federal budget for basic research in all agencies has gone up considerably. From 1983 to 1984, for example, the budget of the National Science Foundation went up about 14 percent. It is anticipated that basic research will continue to receive strong governmental support.

At the same time, legislative and executive actions have stimulated increased support from the private sector for R&D. For example, changes in the capital gains tax rate, made in 1978 and 1980, have revived interest in venture capital — and, indeed, venture capital is now one of the most creative forms of support for R&D. The reinstitution of the incentive stock option has increased entrepreneurship within established companies as well as in new startups. And the 1981 tax law that increased tax credits for R&D as well as credits for the support of academic institutions and more rapid depreciation schedules has had a favorable impact on R&D spending. Venture capital still amounts to a small fraction of the total outlays for R&D in the United States, but it supports the most innovative (and riskiest) R&D efforts.

A recent survey indicates that four out of five U.S. industrial companies plan to increase their internal research efforts over the next five years. Two-thirds of the companies surveyed say they will substantially increase their investments in laboratories. Competitive pressures, changing technologies, and aging facilities, as well as more favorable tax treatment, are the major factors stimulating these larger investments. A large majority of the companies surveyed intend to increase their level of R&D operating expenditures as well. One-third expect to increase their level by 25 percent over the next five years.

Change in antitrust policies is permitting new forms of technology sharing between competing companies. This is another way of encouraging these companies to become more competitive in the world market. Perhaps the best-known cooperative venture is the Microelectronics and Computer Corporation (MCC), which is supported by ten competing computer companies including Control Data Corporation, Digital Equipment Corporation, and Honeywell, with the explicit purpose of sharing technological developments stemming from the research carried out by MCC. MCC was formed in 1982 with the approval of the Antitrust Division of the Justice Department. The Antitrust Division has published guidelines for joint ventures for the purpose of technology sharing.

The Stevenson-Widler and the Baye-Dole acts of 1980 were specifically aimed at stimulating innovation and R&D. In particular, the Baye-Dole Act has made it possible for universities and not-for-profit research institutes that develop patentable ideas under government contracts to own those patents (with a few exceptions). This legislation gives these organizations a major incentive to foster further research and bring its discoveries into public use by licensing private companies to develop them further and then market them. This incentive is working: today most of the universities and not-for-profit research institutes that receive government funding are working to commercialize ideas that their laboratories developed with the aid of government support.

The Special Role of Venture Capital

Today we are seeing a great burst of entrepreneurship in the United States. This activity is a consequence of three developments: the maturation of science that was supported following World War II and *Sputnik;* the rise of scientists, technicians, professionals, and managers who are comfortable with managing technological developments; and the current availability of venture capital, or risk moneys. The rate of formation of new companies is at an unprecedented high: in 1950 about 93,000 new companies were started in the United States; in 1983 about 600,000 new companies were started. This marriage of the high-technology entrepreneur and venture capitalist will very likely prove to be the seed for a new surge of productivity growth in the United States. It will also shorten the time between the development of new technologies and their applications in the marketplace.

It is important to understand *why* this is so. Traditionally, it has taken twenty years or more for a scientific discovery to reach commercialization; transistors and computers are two classic examples. The interval is now shrinking. It is useful to think of this process as a continuum with science at the left end, technology in the middle, and commercialization at the right end. Science represents the discovery of a new principle (like the transistor). Technology represents the promising applications of the science (computers in the case of transistors). Commercialization represents the significant penetration of the applications in the marketplace.

```
Science              Technology            Commercialization
(Discovery)          (Applications)        (Products)

/-----------------------------/-------------------------------------------------/
Time ---
```

In the past, risk capital became available only at the technology stage — that is, after the prototypes became available. Today, however, risk capital is becoming interested in a discovery before the applications are clear, let alone before the prototypes are developed. Financial resources are thus being applied to the development process far earlier. For example, much of the investment in genetic engineering companies was made after scientific principles had been discovered, but before particular technologies or products had been developed.

We should emphasize that the venture-capital phenomenon is more than just availability of money. Indeed, the change in tax law made the money more readily available, but venture-capital investment should be viewed as a new form of financial service. The venture capitalists have developed the know-how and the skills to identify likely new ideas, the professional and managerial talent necessary to develop the ideas, and the markets into which the resulting products can be sold. These are truly a new set of management skills that have evolved in the last two decades. Banks had the money to engage in these kinds of investments, but they had not developed the managerial and entrepreneurial skills that were required to form and finance successful ventures.

For example, Apple Computer, Inc., and Tandem Computer initially were financed by venture capitalists who recognized that a market niche existed for the ideas behind each company's products. They also recognized that the startup company had the right combination of engineering and management talent to become successful. They did not simply look at the balance sheet of the company as a basis of investment. In fact the balance sheets were virtually nonexistent, so the investors of necessity had to evaluate the other assets of the venture, particularly the strength of the product and the strengths of the people.

Several factors appear to be coming together that suggest an upturn in the fortunes of this country's industries. The increase in support from the public sector and the corresponding responses of the private sector; the availability of dramatic new technologies for improving industrial processes, generating new products, and increasing productivity; changing attitudes of labor and management; and imaginative new relationships in technology sharing among companies and between industry and universities — all these developments, each reinforcing the others, should make U.S. industry competitive once again.

NOTES

1. An excellent summary of the various regional activities in the United States is contained in *Innovations in Industrial Competitiveness at the State Level,* report to the President's Commission on Industrial Competitiveness, prepared by SRI International, December 1984.

2. For a discussion of some of the factors involved in cost measurement, see Chapter 3, "Managerial Accounting."

SUGGESTED READING

Abernathy, William J., Kim B. Clarb and Alan M. Kantrow, *Industrial Renaissance,* Basic Books, Inc., New York, 1983.

Rosenberg, Nathan, *Inside the Black Box: Technology and Economics,* Cambridge University Press, Cambridge, 1982.

Waltz, David, "Artificial Intelligence: Assessment and Recommendations," *The AI Magazine,* Fall 1983.

"Flexible Systems Invade the Factory," *High Technology,* Vol. 3, No. 7, July 1983.

"Advanced Technology Materials," *Science,* Vol. 208, No. 4446, May 23, 1980.

Commercial Biotechnology: An International Analysis, Office of Technology Assessment, OTA-BA 172, Library of Congress Card No. 84-601000, January 1984.

CHAPTER 11

Strategic Management: From Concept to Implementation

L. J. Bourgeois
Stanford University
Graduate School of Business

General Motors arranges a joint venture with the Toyota Motor Company to manufacture a subcompact vehicle in an abandoned automobile assembly plant in Fremont, California. This venture will strengthen General Motors's position in the automotive market and will recover the jobs of many laid-off automobile workers. The Chrysler Corporation challenges the legality of the joint venture in a lawsuit, with the intention of preventing it from ever taking place.

The Calma Corporation, CAD/CAM manufacturing subsidiary of the General Electric Company, spends upward of $20 million a year on R&D for new software. Marketable new products, however, originate not in the lab but in sales engineers' interactions with client user groups. Meanwhile, the R&D budget increases annually.

As the GM example illustrates, corporations are frequently bombarded by external influences that hamper management's ability to execute strategies. Moreover, corporations themselves have become complex organizations with numerous internal conflicts, as in the Calma example. Beleaguered executives, as a result, find themselves "battling" with external and internal forces in order to accomplish the goals and strategies they have set for the corporation. Managers no longer command the total control over their corporations' future as they appeared to at the turn of the century. Instead, many are recognizing their limited roles as influencers of events rather than controllers of certain outcomes. Strategic management, as I use the term, encompasses the activities of senior-level executives in their attempts to influence the overall direction of their corporations. This chapter will cover some of   347 the approaches that are useful in helping executives increase that influence through the development of successful business and corporate strategies.

OVERVIEW

Consider failure. In a survey of over 16,000 business failures in 1981, Dun & Bradstreet reported that 88.4 percent of all failures could be attributed to "poor management," with "managerial incompetence" representing 45.6 percent of the total.

When managers of these businesses were queried about the source of this "incompetence," the causes of failure they most frequently cited included "The world just changed around me," indicating insensitivity to the need for anticipating environmental trends, and "Lack of foresight and planning," a logical corollary of failure to consider the outside world in relation to the firm's capabilities. (The other two most frequently cited causes were financial in nature — cash flow and uncollectable accounts receivable.)

If the lack of planning or looking outside one's firm is a common feature among failures, what distinguishes successful firms? Studies have indicated that firms that engage in some form of strategic management outperform otherwise similar firms that do not. Companies with sound strategies and a clear sense of mission are far more likely to succeed, in terms of growth, financial returns, stock price, and prestige.

Foundations of Strategic Management

The field of strategic management has its intellectual roots in a variety of disciplines. Originally considered to be a "point of view" — specifically the general manager's — it started as a course in "business policy," in which management students practiced integrating their understanding of the various functional fields and business tools in the solution of comprehensive business cases.

Attempts to formalize the thought process involved in setting business policy came with the 1960s' approaches to long-range planning. The "systems approach" from the field of management science found its way into management practice through such techniques as planning-programming-budgeting systems (PPBS) and strategic planning systems. At about the same time, organizational sociologists adopted the systems view and began to consider the strategy problem as one of *coalignment* between the organization and its environment, with the firm continually adapting to external change in order to survive.

In the last decade, economists have contributed to strategic management by bringing perspectives of industrial organization (the structure and behavior of industries) and microeconomics (with the simplifying assumption of profitability as the single corporate goal) to top managers' attempts to chart strategic directions. Thus, issues such as competitive dynamics, market signaling, and the inherent forces that determine industry profitability have been applied to the analysis of business strategy; and consulting firms have developed techniques to assess the potential profitability of individual businesses.

Current Scope of the Field

Despite this intellectual heritage, planning failed to realize its potential in many firms because it became an academic exercise dominated by staff planners or outside consultants. Often the result was plans relegated to bookshelves rather than living corporate strategies implemented by line personnel. Consequently several chief executives, such as Jack Welch at GE, disbanded their planning staffs or cut them back drastically.

One cause of the difficulty of translating strategic plans into action has been the overly analytical and quantitative orientation of some planning methodologies. In their attempts to prescribe ideal strategies — ideal from an analytical, economic perspective — many strategists ignore the human component of the organization. It is not unusual for a proposed strategy to violate the prevailing corporate culture or political system, making implementation virtually impossible. For example, a portfolio analysis of a major multinational American bank indicated that some foreign branches should be "harvested" (milked for cash until dry) to provide growth funds for others. In one case, the branch in question was the only one of that bank in the country and was managed by a local national. Harvesting, in this case, presented a conflict of interest for the local manager (closing the branch, while advantageous to the bank, was deemed a blow to the local economy), as well as the potential alienation of a key manager. The strategy was rejected.

Successful firms have found that good managers are those who transcend the economics of strategy and fully appreciate the organizational realities of what is politically feasible. This has been paralleled in the field of strategic management by two major developments: (1) a sophisticated analytical orientation (usually based on economics, marketing, and finance) has been melded with considerations of implementation (based on behavioral perspectives on corporate culture and corporate politics), and (2) the notion of charting the "perfect" strategy has been subordinated to an emphasis on organizational flexibility and the fostering of entrepreneurial spirit within the firm.

In the sections that follow, we will discuss how these two major thrusts — combining analysis with implementation, and maintaining flexibility — can be applied in today's corporations. First, some basic terminology will be introduced, followed by the main section on application. Finally, some thoughts for the future will be discussed.

THE MAIN AREAS

To set the applied strategic management tools in context, it is important to introduce some basic terminology and conceptual distinctions. First I will describe how managers influence the mission of the firm; then I will delineate the different levels of strategy that this implies.

Dimensions of Strategic Management

Strategic management — what managers do to guide their firms' destinies — consists of two major activities: one involves defining the mission of the enterprise, where the domains of action are defined for the firm; the other is ensuring that the right things happen to execute the mission, that is, that the firm's resources are focused on navigating successfully within the chosen domains. These two activities constitute the two dimensions of strategic management, domain definition and domain navigation.

Domain definition (DD) is the process by which executives (1) choose or expand the scope of the organization's activities (choice of markets, products, production technologies, resources employed), (2) coordinate across activities or businesses and manage synergies between them, and (3) generate new activities by diversifying or fostering internal innovation. For example, in choosing to pursue the "factory of the future," GE expanded its domain to include automated production technologies. By acquiring Calma Corporation in 1981, it brought computer-aided design and computer-aided manufacturing capabilities in-house. GE's initial challenge was to coordinate CALMA's manufacturing design activities with those parts of GE engaged in robotics.

Domain navigation (DN) is the process of rationalizing the stream of activities within each domain, by formulating and implementing business strategies. Current domain navigation activities at Calma, for example, are aimed at ensuring closer coordination between marketing and research (see example at beginning of chapter).

How do domain definition and domain navigation differ in practice? Listen to the different words used in conversation by managers engaged in each. At corporate headquarters of a diversified firm, you might hear executives speaking of major acquisitions in the works that are (or are not) synergystic with current business, how this might affect EPS and the tax picture, and what the cash flow implications are. Finally, they might discuss whether or not the proposed acquisitions will help move them more solidly into the "energy business" or "technology business." These are DD discussions and tend to be somewhat abstract in nature.

Now, at the division level you might hear discussions about working more closely with supplier X, or meeting customer Y at a particular trade show, or planning negotiating strategy for the next labor contract. This might be coupled with speculation about how particular competitors are going to be handling the same issues. These are DN discussions. Note how they reflect a world of tangible events, people, and things, whereas the DD discussion dealt with more abstract concepts.

The classic argument that the railroads might have prospered in the wake of the growth of our highway system if they had defined their business as "transportation" rather than "railroads" was simply a suggestion to think of one's business in more abstract (DD) terms. Saying that your business is "transportation" does not tell you how to compete (DN) — it merely helps to define your scope of activities. This is important to survival in a changing world, but it is clearly not enough. Both DD and DN are necessary strategic management activities.

Levels of Strategy

Domain definition and navigation refer to the process of strategic management — the activities managers engage in. Of equal importance is the resulting substance of their decisions, or the *content* of a company's strategy. Although the word "strategy" has several definitions, the most relevant distinction for business purposes is in reference to the organizational level at which strategic decisions are made. Thus, *corporate strategy* determines what businesses (domains) a corporation will enter or exit and how to allocate resources among the various businesses. For example, through its acquisition of Calma, GE made the corporate strategic decision to enter the CAD/CAM business. In diversified corporations, corporate-level strategy is usually formulated at the headquarters or group level.

Business strategy refers to the competitive decisions made within a particular product-market with an eye to achieving competitive advantage and developing distinctive competences within an industry. For example, Calma's location in Silicon Valley gave it a competitive advantage when it made the business strategy decision to sell "Cadillac" systems to the semiconductor market. Business strategy decisions are generally taken at the division general manager level in diversified firms or at the chief executive level in single business corporations.

Functional strategies in marketing, operations, finance, R&D, and so on, while formulated at the department manager level, should provide support for the business strategy.

Clearly, in a well-run company the domain definition and navigation practices are such that a set of businesses is chosen (corporate strategy) that has internal logic or cohesion (synergy) and that capitalizes on external trends; each business competes effectively in its respective industry (business strategy); and the many departmental activities in advertising, distribution, purchasing, and so on (functional strategies), are coordinated so as to achieve efficient use of resources. The next section will describe how many well-run companies achieve this.

DEVELOPING A STRATEGY

There are a variety of approaches to strategic management, many of which have been derived from the planning techniques mentioned earlier in this chapter. Although the details differ, they all have some fundamental components in common. This section will outline the application of these typical fundamentals of strategic *planning* as well as introduce some new ones critical to strategy *implementation*.

Modern Concepts and Methods

All strategic planning approaches attempt to find an optimal match between the resources and capabilities available within the firm and the external market conditions and environmental trends. In essence, this is the notion of coalignment mentioned earlier; the coalignment results in strategy, whose efficacy translates into some level of corporate performance. The basic dimensions of this fairly straightforward approach are illustrated in Figure 11.1.

A key feature in the basic strategy model shown in Figure 11.1 is the reciprocal influence of all of the variables. For example, in the late 1960s a major science-based consulting firm ("Sigma Consultants") observed that (1) there was an accelerating level of expenditures on health care in the United States, a trend likely to continue unabated, and (2) the firm had several competent professionals on its staff who had carried out health-care-related assignments such as designing

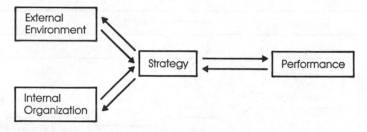

Figure 11.1 The Basic Strategy Model

hospitals and evaluating medical group acquisitions. By responding to the market opportunity and articulating a "health care strategy" or consulting practice, Sigma would be defining a new domain (arrow from strategy to environment) based on existing internal capabilities (arrow from internal organization to strategy). Having chosen the new domain, the firm would now have to respond to the dictates of the marketplace (arrow from environment to strategy) by, for example, designing products and services that were in demand or adapting to whatever governmental regulation might be relevant. To implement the new strategy (domain navigation), Sigma might reorganize its staff so that all health-care-related professionals were grouped together (arrow from strategy to internal organization). Over time, this group might become increasingly proficient though the sharing of experience, knowledge, and the like. The degree of success would be manifested in some level of performance (arrow from strategy to performance); and, in turn, the performance level would serve as feedback, indicating that further adaptations of strategy might be in order (arrow from performance to strategy).

In essence, then, the model represents a system of interacting parts. But the picture painted thus far is not complete. A "perfect" strategy may be found that violates managers' predispositions — this was the case of the foreign branch in the financial institution mentioned earlier. Or, conversely, a management's values may suggest strategies that are not optimal in an economic sense. For example, President Jay Monroe of the Tensor Corporation refused to change his very "functional" high-intensity Tensor lamps when new competitors started introducing style variations. As a result, his company lost 50 percent of the market, which it probably could have retained had Mr. Monroe's values been more economic than aesthetic. So, in formulating any economic strategy, we have to bring management's noneconomic values into the picture.

In our Sigma Consultants example, there was strong support for

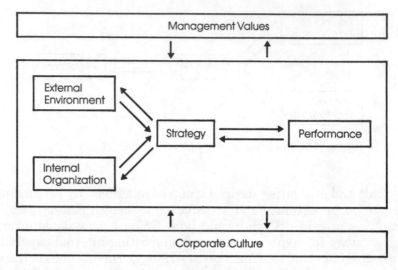

Figure 11.2 The Complete Strategy Model

the health care venture among senior management and some of the professional staff. That is, the venture fit the values of top management. However, Sigma was originally organized on the model of a research lab, in which professionals were unimpeded by bureaucratic hierarchy and were free to choose their projects. Assignment to projects was by invitation, and, assuming the invited person was billing sufficient time to avoid the pressure to join projects indiscriminately, he or she could turn these down. The health care strategy, in contrast, suggested an organizational unit in which consultants would be expected to dedicate themselves to one major type of activity. This ran smack against the prevailing culture. The strategy was abandoned.

So the basic model shown in Figure 11.1 — a very "rational" model of strategy — needs to be amplified if we want to consider the implementability of strategy. We need to include the "soft" sides of strategy, political feasibility, and organizational acceptability. Thus, our full model would include explicit consideration of managerial values and prevailing corporate culture, as shown in Figure 11.2.

The basic model outlined above suggests a sequence of activities in the strategic management process. These activities constitute the fundamental components of strategic management:

Environmental analysis (forecast of trends and industry analysis)

Organizational analysis (resource audit)

Strategy analysis (identification of past strategy)

Table 11.1 Fundamental Components of Strategic Management

	Domain Definition	*Domain Navigation*
Environment Analysis	Forecast of major trends in the general environment — economic, social, political, technological, etc.	Analysis of customers, competitors, suppliers, regulators, technology
Organizational Analysis	Macro structural arrangements and coordinating mechanisms	Resource audit — financial, human, technological, market position and market power, physical
Strategy Analysis	Linkages (synergy analysis) and portfolio planning techniques	Business strategy identification
Coalignment	Evaluation of past performance Evaluation of risk	Tests of consistency with environment and internal resources
Cultural Analysis	Making corporate ideology (management values) explicit	Analysis of corporate culture and subcultures

Coalignment (strategy evaluation)

Cultural analysis

These components are carried out within both the DD and DN processes, and the basic techniques behind them will be spelled out in the remainder of this section. A variety of methods are used in these processes; they are outlined in Table 11.1 (Since the methods of industry and competitor analysis — part of DN environmental analysis — are covered in Chapter 1, they will not be covered here.)

Environmental Analysis and Forecast

> We are not fit to lead an army on the march unless we are familiar with the face of the country — its mountains and forests, its pitfalls.
>
> He who exercises no forethought but makes light of his opponents is sure to be captured by them.
>
> Hence the saying: If you know the enemy and know yourself, you need not fear the result of a hundred battles. If you know yourself but not the enemy, for every victory gained you will also suffer a defeat. If you know neither the enemy nor yourself, you will succumb in every battle.
>
> Sun Tzu, *On the Art of War* (c. 300 B.C.)

Much recent writing on business strategy has incorporated military metaphors likening economic competition to battle. And, as in the waging of war, it is the relative irreversibility and long-time commitment implied in strategic decisions that make environmental analysis so crucial to the effective making of strategy. But our definition of strategy merely as a coalignment is limited in that it is static. Environments, of course, change; they are discontinuous and often complex, volatile, and possibly even hostile. This means that for the coalignment to remain effective, it must also change. As a result, strategy-making is an ongoing managerial process, one that has been likened to shooting at a moving target. The strategist must not only continually reassess the organization's trajectory (as set by prior strategies), but also keep an eye on the constantly moving target through persistent scanning and surveillance and regular and accurate forecasts.

Components of the External Environment. The environment can usefully be thought of as consisting of two parts that overlap. These are termed the *general environment* and the *task environment,* and effective strategy-making by coalignment with the environment requires the analysis of both.

The *general environment* includes those elements which affect all organizations in a particular culture. In any one country it will include the political setting and governmental institutions, the cultural setting and social trends, the state of the economy and financial markets and institutions, the law, taxation, and the state of scientific and technological development.

The *task environment,* on the other hand, consists of those elements directly affected by, and impinging upon, the organization in question. It includes such things as the basic structure of the industry — the number and size of firms, the degree of interaction and interdependence between them, and the nature of the cost structure within the industry. Of vital concern are the nature, type, and characteristics of the markets — actual or potential — to which the organization provides goods or services. These, in turn, will dictate the nature of demand (which may, in some cases, be subjected to sophisticated forecasting techniques).

Using the concepts introduced earlier, we might say that domain definition takes place within the general environment. Once a domain has been chosen, the firm enters the task environment of a particular industry and must focus now on domain navigation. The major components of the environment are listed in Table 11.2.

The Analysis. For domain navigation, a detailed industry and competitor analysis should be undertaken in order to assess the profit po-

Table 11.2 Major Components of the Environment

I. General Environment
  A. Macroeconomics
  B. Demographics
  C. Sociocultural system
  D. Political-legal system
  E. Technology
II. Task Environment
  A. Customers and markets
    1. Distributors
    2. End users
  B. Competitors
    1. Competitors for markets
    2. Competitors for resources
  C. Suppliers
    1. Suppliers of physical resources
    2. Suppliers of human resources
    3. Suppliers of capital
  D. Regulatory groups
    1. Government
    2. Unions
    3. Special interest groups
  E. Technology
    1. Rate of development
    2. Potential substitutes for your product or service
    3. Stage of product or industry life cycle

tential of the industry as well as likely competitor behavior in the near term. (Since Chapter 1, "Marketing Management," outlines an approach to industry and competitor analysis, it will not be covered here.)

For domain definition a broader perspective is required. There are numerous techniques for environmental assessment, such as market research, econometric modeling, or speculations about the future based on trends in news articles (the method described in John Naisbitt's *Megatrends*). The environmental scanning method suggested here, developed by Professor David Jemison at Stanford, yields much the same results as many sophisticated techniques, but much more efficiently. The approach takes as its starting point the assumption that the top management team of a firm is constantly interacting with various components of its environment. Since each member of management tends to interact with components relevant to his or her function — financial managers see bankers, marketing managers see customers, production people see suppliers — the team *as a whole* continually scans *most* of the task environment. Thus, the top management team *collectively* should have a good appreciation of environmental trends. The key task, then, is to collect management's shared perceptions into a consolidated environmental analysis.

The analysis involves three steps: individual analysis, small-group discussion, and team consensus negotiation.

Each *individual* should go through the following thought process. Think of where you were and what you were doing during some major event in the past ten to twenty years or so (say, when Kennedy was assassinated in November 1963). Now examine the developments since then — in terms of your company, your country, the world. Consider the fundamental changes that have occurred. Could you have predicted the world oil shock, simultaneous inflation and recession, test-tube babies, the equivalent of a 1970 mainframe computer reduced to a quarter-inch chip? You probably could not predict all of these developments, but reasonable thought and analysis would allow you to discern some trends in your external environment.

Now consider the general environment in which your firm operates and, thinking ahead ten to twenty years, try to (1) identify the major environmental trends that will affect your firm's ability to survive and prosper, (2) estimate the anticipated date of the trend's impact on your industry and firm, (3) cite evidence to support your contention that this is indeed an important trend, and (4) rank the trends in descending order of importance. Here you might consider such questions as these: Are there recent political or social developments that will affect the industry or the firm? What economic conditions are present or are likely to develop that will affect the firm? What technological innovations or improvements are possible or probable that might affect our raw materials, production processes, products, or customers? How will these affect the way in which we or our competitors do business?

The next step is to have each manager share his or her perceptions with three or four other managers, and for the *group* to arrive at some consensus regarding what the five most significant trends are for the company.

Finally, the group summaries should be compared. Frequently at this stage, it is found that several groups have identified different aspects of a common theme (for example, the changing demographics of the post–baby boom marketplace has implications both for selling services and for finding management talent). These themes form the basis for a consensus forecast.

The usefulness and efficiency of this method can be illustrated by the experience of a major law firm (call it Delta & Delta). Most observers would recognize the increasing competitive nature of the legal profession and the major forces for change. Delta & Delta was initiating strategic management procedures at the same time that one of the professional organizations to which most lawyers belong had formed a "future issues committee," established to identify and explore some of the major issues that would be confronting the profession. Consisting of senior partners from major firms and a leading academic in the field, the committee struggled for more than a year with the need for environmental scanning. During this time, the committee engaged the services of a variety of consultants — facilitators, futurologists, John Naisbitt's group, USC's Center for Future Research. The results of their thirteen-month effort was a list of ten major issues. Delta & Delta, on the other hand, assembled its thirteen top people with a facilitator for four hours and, using the method described here, produced a forecast of five key trends that mirrored the top five issues identified by the future issues committee. These included the increasing computerization of legal practice, the tendency of major clients to expand in-house counsel and rely less on the law firms, the reduced prestige of the profession in the eyes of laypeople, and increasing tax practice competition from CPA firms. These had major implications for the strategic management of law partnerships in the next decade.

The key is that most management teams have most of the information resources needed for good strategic thinking within their own ranks. The major task in strategic planning is to organize this information in a way that facilitates strategic decisions. The following sections will indicate how the other fundamental components of strategic management can build on managers' knowledge of their corporations and how the information from each component should come together to form a cohesive strategy.

Organizational Analysis

There are two aspects of assessing one's organization. One is the *architecture* — how the firm is organized into business or responsibility centers and the systems through which these differentiated pieces are coordinated into a working whole. The other aspect is the *quality* of the organization — its strengths and weaknesses. This section will address the assessment of strengths and weaknesses, or the *resource audit*.

A resource audit can be conducted at two levels, global and specific. At the *global* level, it is important for management to identify its firm's *distinctive competence*. That is, what factor or set of factors distinguishes the firm from its primary competitors and makes its products or services attractive to customers? For example, does the firm have a unique relationship with suppliers (say, proximity) or ability to deliver on time or new product development capabilities? Every firm, no matter how seemingly homogeneous its industry, has *some* characteristic that has allowed it to survive in the marketplace. For example, Delta & Delta delivered close partner-client contact to its medium-size business clients. This contrasted with the typical big law firm practice, where a partner made the initial sale to a large client but most of the ensuing client contact was carried out by midlevel managers. Delta & Delta's distinctive competence was its ability to foster strong personal ties with its clients, resulting in a level of client loyalty unusual in the industry. The importance of articulating a company's distinctive competence is that it forms the foundation for achieving a competitive advantage within an industry and for evaluating the potential for synergies with other businesses in a corporation's portfolio.

At the *specific* level, management should identify the firm's strengths and weaknesses in at least six areas: financial, human, physical, technological, managerial, and market position. A *financial* analysis is probably the easiest to conduct since the tools are well developed and the measures are relatively objective. In addition, there are standards of comparison for each industry; a firm can assess its relative liquidity, for example, as compared with the average and top and bottom quartiles of its industry, using such publications as Robert Morris Associates and Dun & Bradstreet.

Although most managers believe people to be their company's most important asset, *human resources* are probably the most difficult to assess. Embodied in human resources are the more tangible aspects of investments made in people, such as recruiting, training programs, and experience. But management must also assess the more intangible aspects of human resources such as loyalty and commitment, creativity, and willingness to cooperate or to adopt new technologies or work methods.

In contrast, *physical resources* are the most tangible aspects of a corporation's assets. One can examine plant and equipment, buildings, and other facilities, and determine their condition and adequacy for the volume and nature of activity taking place. Equally important are such factors as location and adaptability of physical facilities to more than one kind of production.

In assessing *technological resources,* management must ask whether the technology embodied in the acquisition, production, and delivery of the product or service is state-of-the-art and therefore vulnerable to bugs, standard for the industry, and therefore tried and tested, or relatively old and therefore perhaps approaching obsolescence. Another dimension to examine is the source of new technology and its application within the firm. That is, are technological changes driven by customer requests, indicating managerial adaptivity to the marketplace, or are they driven by creative forces within the firm? Conversely, a firm's technology can be a reflection of a commitment to the past, may be "behind the times," and therefore a real weakness. Finally, the firm should assess the degree of flexibility embodied in its technology. For example, the steel industry has been saddled with assets that are dedicated to the production of steel and do not have adaptability to other uses. By contrast, some electronics companies have a job-shop orientation, so they can adapt their technology to new products.

When assessing *managerial* resources it is essential to cast an unbiased eye on such factors as the skills, level of experience, and company loyalty among management. For example, many new high-technology companies are strong on the engineering side but deficient in marketing. Recognition of this deficiency was reflected in the hiring of CEOs with consumer product and marketing backgrounds by both Apple and Atari in 1983.

In addition to the resource areas mentioned, a company may want to evaluate such intangible resources as market position, brand identification, or patent position.

Having conducted a resource audit and made a preliminary evaluation of the company's strengths and weaknesses, the strategist should set this assessment aside until the strategy evaluation phase of the strategic management process. But, before a strategy can be evaluated, it must be identified in sufficient detail to subject it to scrutiny. It is the identification of strategy to which we now turn.

Strategy Analysis

To many managers, and most strategic planners, the idea of thinking about and influencing the future of their firm is an exciting one. Most managers are eager to set corporate goals and then to start formulating strategies that will help achieve those goals. However, there are two fundamental problems inherent in approaching the strategic management task this way. First, most businesses are ongoing concerns and have set in motion certain activities that are a reflection of decisions made in the past. To think about the future without a thorough understanding of what is actually taking place may lead managers to formulate strategies that are either unrealistic or impossible to implement. Second, managers sometimes are tempted to engage in a strategic redirection of their firm without a thorough understanding of the *healthy* parts of their existing strategy. This tendency to throw the baby out with the bathwater can be thwarted only by making sure that management thoroughly understands the basis and the results of its present strategy.

All firms have a strategy, whether or not management has made that strategy explicit in advance. Often, a firm's actual strategy can be quite different from what management thinks it is or from what it originally was intended to be. Before going through the following procedures to identify your business and corporate strategies, take a moment to write down what you believe to be your firm's strategy (three or four sentences will do).

This section will describe how to identify your corporation's present business and corporate strategies. After this identification process is complete, *then* you can assess the quality of that strategy in order to ascertain which aspects of strategy might be candidates for change and which are certain candidates for retention. (Note that a perfectly acceptable outcome is for management to conclude that no changes are necessary. This process then becomes one of validating an already sound strategy.)

Since the fundamental building block of a corporation is the business, we will proceed in our strategy identification by first identifying the business-level strategy of the corporation, followed by the identification of corporate-level strategy.

Identifying Your Firm's Business Strategy. Strategy identification at the business level is a straightforward process. In essence, a business strategy is built on a set of functional strategies, representing the competitive weapons that a company employs to compete in a given industry. The way to identify a business strategy is simply to go through each of the functional areas and identify what pattern of decisions have been made in each, as follows.

Marketing Strategy. *What* products or services are being sold by the corporation? To *whom* are these being sold, and in what geographic areas? *How* does the company's price compare with that of the rest of the industry? Is the company a price leader, or does it tend to match the prices set by others? What is the company's promotion strategy and distribution strategy? Each of these questions should be pursued in detail. For example, the Sigma Consulting Company described earlier had a marketing strategy of selling *any* set of problem-solving skills to any client, at any time, any place. Its pricing strategy was to charge consultants' time at a multiple of four times the individual's hourly salary rate. In contrast with Sigma Consultants, most strategy consulting firms price their services at a multiple closer to five times the consultant's hourly salary rate. Therefore, Sigma would be considered a standard-rate pricer, whereas some of the specialized strategy consultants would be considered premium-rate consulting firms. Whether it is beneficial for a firm to be premium-priced is not an issue under consideration yet. What is important is that, in order to be able to evaluate the quality of one's strategy, it is first necessary to recognize what, precisely, the strategy is and how it compares with the strategies of other firms in similar circumstances.

Operations Strategy. Here, management should consider the question of how it transforms inputs into outputs for the marketplace. For example, what kinds of facilities does the company use? Are they concentrated in one location, or are they dispersed over a broader area? What is the company's capacity strategy — does it build capacity in anticipation of demand, or does it wait until there is a backlog of orders before adding capacity? For example, Sigma Consultants always hired new professionals in anticipation of increased volume. In contrast, Delta & Delta would staff its tax practice with paralegal part-timers during the peak tax season and maintain a leaner staff during the rest of the year.

Is the firm's product or service made to order, or are inventories expanded to serve demand as it occurs? What is the company's strategy with respect to vertical integration? Does it source most of materials in-house by integrating backward, or does it subcontract much of its production? For example, prior to its introduction of the SX-70 instant camera, the Polaroid Corporation managed with a low investment in plant and equipment by subcontracting most of its component manufacturing. In contrast, the Kodak Company was fully integrated; at one point it even owned a stockyard to provide the raw materials for some of its chemicals. What Kodak gained in bringing operating margins in-house, Polaroid gained in flexibility and the ability to change products quickly.

Financial Strategy. While many firms are fairly explicit about the marketing and production strategies that they follow, some of these same firms are vague when it comes to articulating their financial strategy. Usually, this is because a firm just starting its operations pays attention to cash flow and meeting the payroll, but fails to pay close attention to its balance sheet. The identification of the financial strategy can help to assess how the firm is managing its financial resources.

Here, the company should identify its capital structure, how it uses its cash flow (does it pay dividends?), its strategy toward investment in plant and equipment (owning versus leasing), and how it attempts to enhance its stock price.

Research-and-Development Strategy. Firms vary considerably in the extent to which they include research and development as a salient component of their business strategies. For example, the average percentage of sales spent on research is approximately 10 percent in high-technology companies, whereas it might be as low as 0.5 percent in such basic industries as steel and cement. Nevertheless, each of these companies does have a strategy with respect to its activities which might generate new products or new means of manufacturing their products.

The company should determine whether its research focus is primarily basic or applied. For example, the Polaroid Company was dedicated to the "perfection of photography," which implied a heavy allocation of its research budget to basic research in optics. In contrast, a company such as Crown Cork and Seal, which manufactures steel-plated and aluminum cans, engaged only in a limited amount of applied research and was positioned as a "fast second" in implementing new developments. Crown Cork and Seal's management has felt that, as one of the smaller firms in the industry (in 1978 it was number four in sales and held 8.3 percent market share), it could leave the technological innovation to others.

With the identification process completed, the manager should generate a statement of the firm's domain definition. That is, how would you define your business in terms of product/market scope and overall economic mission? In an attempt to get to the core of the business, the manager should attempt to answer this question in as few sentences as possible. Examples of domain definition statements for a variety of firms are given in Table 11.3.

Having identified the components of the business strategy, the manager now has the raw material with which to evaluate the quality of that strategy. This evaluation process will be covered presently.

Corporate Strategy Identification. When firms expand into a variety of businesses, frequently they transfer the successes in the initial business to the subsequent businesses. For example, when Bic Pen Corporation expanded beyond ballpoint pen production into disposable cigarette lighters, it used the same plastic-injection molding technology and similar distribution channels to sell what was essentially another mass-marketed, disposable consumer item. The additional learning required to design and produce this new product was relatively low,

Table 11.3 Examples of Domain Definition Statements

Tensor Corp.	Tensor Corporation is the leading manufacturer of premium-priced, high-intensity lamps and third leading maker of metal tennis rackets. Tensor also manufactures a disposable flashlight and seeks further diversification of its product lines through applied research and development in electromechanical products.
Bic Pen Corp.	Bic is a cash-rich leader in the low-priced disposable pen, cigarette lighter, and safety razor industries that reached its position through a strategy of expanding primary demand for its product by aggressive promotion, low price, and high quality. All of its products employ high-volume, precision plastic-injection technology and are distributed through mass retail outlets such as drugstore chains.
Boston Symphony Orchestra	The BSO presents traditional programs of high-quality classical, symphonic music to a select, wealthy, and well-educated segment of the public; it finances such programs by high-priced subscriptions and large contributions from patrons. Related components of this strategy are a well-educated, loosely structured administration, a prestigious board of trustees, and a high-quality subsidized music school.

given that the same technology was employed in the factory: plastic was injected into a mold to form a casing, into which dispensable liquid was poured, and metal parts were attached to dispense the fluid.

When firms adopt similar business strategies in different lines of business, they have adopted what we might term a *generic* business strategy across all their businesses. Hewlett-Packard and Texas Instruments are two firms that compete in various segments of the electronics industry, that have both employed generic strategies in many of their product lines, and whose generic strategies are quite distinct (see Table 11.4).

Using generic strategies to build a corporation from a variety of businesses implies some sort of cloning of an original strategy onto new businesses. This, of course, is only one means of extending the boundaries of the corporation into new domains. To the extent that a corpo-

Table 11.4   Examples of Generic Business Strategies

	Hewlett-Packard	*Texas Instruments*
Marketing Strategy	Industrial and some consumer markets	Consumer and industrial markets
	High-tech, custom products	High-volume, low-cost standard products
	Premium price, lag experience curve	Low price, push experience curve
	Promote quality/ reliability/service	Promote availability/price
Production Strategy	Small plants	Large plants for large volume
	Small-batch/job-shop technology	Mass-production technology with automation and robotics
	Build capacity with demand	Build capacity ahead of demand
Financial Strategy	Self-funding ("pay as you go") within divisions	Allocate cash among divisions according to need
	Make profits early on through high margins	Fund ahead of experience curve
R&D Strategy	First to market with new products	Improve existing products in proven markets
	Primarily product R&D	Both product and process R&D
	Features- and quality-driven	Cost-driven
	Design for product performance	Design for cost reduction

ration expands by building upon a core business and the set of skills embodied in that business, we can say that it is realizing synergies across its businesses. At the other extreme are pure conglomerates, which are built through the acquisition of unrelated businesses. It was not unusual during the 1960s for corporations to build conglomerates based on the theory that the acquisition of unrelated businesses in countercyclical industries would smooth out the cash flows for the whole corporation. This led to the development of a variety of portfolio planning techniques for managing corporate strategy by such firms as the Boston Consulting Group and McKinsey and Company. These techniques typically plotted the variety of businesses on a two-dimensional grid, with market position or market share on one dimension and industry growth or attractiveness on the other. The theory was that high-market-share businesses were likely to be lower-cost manufacturers than smaller-share businesses, simply through a volume or scale economies effect, which allowed those businesses to realize higher profit margins and greater cash throw-off per dollar of sales. With a portfolio of businesses, the cash throw-off from the better-positioned firms could be used to fund the growth of more promising — perhaps smaller-market-share — businesses in the portfolio. Essentially, these portfolio techniques were cash management methods for diversified corporations. (For the details of this approach, see Chapter 1, "Marketing Management.")

One of the shortcomings of the portfolio techniques was that it treated each business unit as if it were totally independent of any other unit. That is, recommendations to grow a particular business or to divest another frequently failed to take into account the fact that two businesses might be closely related and have a strong dependence on each other. For example, the two businesses might share manufacturing facilities, raw material sources, or a distribution channel or sales force. To reduce the activity in one business might result in increased costs for the sister business, given that a lower overall volume would be realized in the shared resource. In addition, some academic research completed in the mid-1970s indicated that corporations consisting of closely related businesses had better economic performances than corporations composed of unrelated businesses. This led to the development of some concepts concerning the degree to which businesses in the corporation are linked to each other, forming a basis for synergies. Specifically, the works of Professor Richard Rumelt, and later of Thomas and Co., a strategy-process consulting firm, have introduced one of the more modern theories of corporate strategic management. That theory relies on the concept of direct linkages. The analysis of direct linkages among businesses provides the identification and subsequent evaluation of corporate strategy.

Direct linkages exist to the extent that businesses share a common resource, knowledge, or experience base that is specific to markets, technologies, or product characteristics. The research evidence indicates that companies characterized primarily by direct linkages between their businesses tend to secure a higher degree of economic return. There are three kinds of direct linkages: market, technology, and product linkages.

Market Linkages. A market linkage exists when a company uses its current customer base to sell new products. One example is the expansion of Sears, Roebuck and Co. into such areas as insurance (Allstate) and income tax services (H&R Block). Once consumers are under Sears's roof to purchase merchandise, they can be sold these and other services. Restaurants in hotels and movie theatre concession stands are other examples.

Another type of direct market linkage is using the same distribution channel to distribute different products. For example, McDonald's hamburger outlets were sitting vacant during the early-morning hours, so they introduced breakfast foods: same distribution channel, new products. Similarly, Bic exploited synergies in distributing disposable cigarette lighters and safety razors through the same outlets that it had developed to sell its highly successful disposable ballpoint pens.

A third type of direct market linkage is the use of brand identification to develop and market totally unrelated products. A vivid example in recent times is the broad line of products tied to the immensely popular film *Star Wars:* toys, clothing, comic books, and so on. The success of the Tensor metal tennis racquet can be directly attributed to the successful, high-quality brand image gained by the original Tensor high-intensity lamp.

Technology Linkages. A second kind of direct linkage is through technology. A company experiences direct technology linkages when the same operations technology is used to manufacture a variety of products or render a variety of services. For example, General Motors manufactures not only automobiles, but also trucks and locomotives. The Bic Pen Corporation applied the same plastic-injection molding technology to the manufacture of a variety of products: the same skills, assembly processes, and raw materials were used for each of its disposable pen, cigarette lighter, and safety razor product lines.

Another type of technology linkage occurs when corporations find that they can sell by-products to an external market. For example, the chemicals that were originally a waste by-product from the petroleum refining process formed the foundation for today's petrochemical industry. Exxon Chemicals is a major player in this market and represents a technology linkage to the original Standard Oil Company, which refined gasoline and kerosene products.

Product Linkages. A product linkage occurs as a product line is extended to new markets. This occurs, for example, when a company provides the same products or services to buyers in new geographic locations, as do most franchises and many multinational corporations. Another product linkage occurs when a vertically integrated company

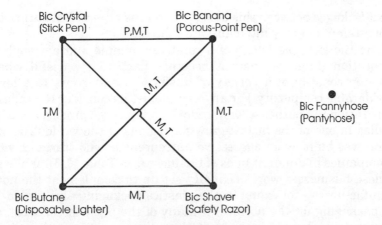

Figure 11.3   Direct and Indirect Linkages: Bic Pen Corporation

experiences excess capacity at different points backward or forward along the product flow chain and can market these products or services externally. For example, General Motors can market its Delco radio products independently of its automobile dealerships. The United Fruit Company, which extrudes plastic bags for use in packaging bananas in Central America, fills excess capacity by supplying local bakeries with printed bread bags.

Why is it important to understand direct linkages in a company? For one, it is a convenient way of identifying the company's corporate strategy and isolating which parts of the corporation are closely, or loosely, related to the rest of the corporation. Second, it can provide clues to high-potential expansion opportunities.

A useful way of conducting a linkage analysis is to diagram the direct linkages within a company. For example, Figure 11.3 illustrates the direct linkages among Bic Pen Corporation's businesses. Where our analysis shows that there are direct linkages between any two businesses, we draw a line. Next to the line we draw a *T, P,* or *M* wherever there is a technology, product, or market linkage, respectively. As illustrated in the diagram, the ballpoint pen, felt-tip pen, disposable cigarette lighter, and disposable safety razor businesses all have some very solid, direct linkages between them. In contrast, the disposable pantyhose business was one where there was no shared sales force or distribution channel (the pantyhose were sold in supermarkets, whereas most Bic pens were sold in drugstores), the production technology was different, and the function of the product was totally different from that of the previous products. Correspondingly, our diagram shows no direct linkages between this business and the others. Not surprisingly, Bic's attempted entry into pantyhose failed.

The Bic example is one of a relatively simple and uncomplicated corporation. Linkage analysis becomes particularly useful where a company consists of a variety of businesses and grows to a level of considerable complexity. For an example, let us consider the Indo Jaya Corporation in Southeast Asia. Indo Jaya is a large producer of instant noodles in one of the fastest-growing regions of the world. The corporation was built by an aggressive entrepreneur who started a variety of companies in different lines of business (see Table 11.5). While some of these businesses were originally set up to complement the noodles manufacturer — for example, the plastics packaging firm provided retail packaging for the noodles — many of the businesses, such as the motorcycle dealership, were started as a means of investing the cash flow from the original business. When the entrepreneur wanted to make greater sense out of the collection of businesses that he had as-

Table 11.5 Indo Jaya Corporation

1. *Distribution Company* (Import/Export)	5. *Plastic Products Manufacturing*
Noodles	Fishing line
Beer	Fishing net
Confectionery	Polyester
Printing inks	Polyethylene sheets
Office supplies	Polyethylene bags
2. *Instant Noodles Manufacture*	6. *IJ Musical and Distribution*
	Pianos
	Band instruments
	Guitars
	Amplifiers and electrical
3. *Wood Products Manufacture*	7. *Motorcycles*
Chopsticks	Yamaha distributorship
Toothpicks	Motorcycle parts and service
Pencils	
Rulers and yardsticks	
4. *Printing and Packaging Co.*	8. *Trading Company*
Offset printing	Cooking oil
Flexible packaging	Spices and condiments
	Toiletries

sembled and to build an integrated corporation, he applied a linkage analysis. At first glance, his businesses seemed to be a rather jumbled collection, as diagramed in Figure 11.4. After going through the logic of linkage analysis, however, the picture of his corporation was clarified and resulted in the diagram shown in Figure 11.5. Notice how Figure 11.5 "cleans up" the depiction of the relationships among the different parts of the Indo Jaya businesses. As a result of this analysis, the firm's executives gained a much clearer understanding of their corporation and could then make some critical strategic decisions about which parts of the business should be emphasized and which might be candidates for divestiture. (The Musical Distribution business was eventually divested through a leveraged buyout to the division general manager.)

These kinds of decisions are facilitated after a management team goes through the process of evaluating the quality of its corporate and business strategies, the subject to which we now turn.

The Coalignment: Evaluating the Environment-Organization-Strategy Link

Disciplining oneself to go through the strategy evaluation process is important: only after gaining a thorough understanding of the

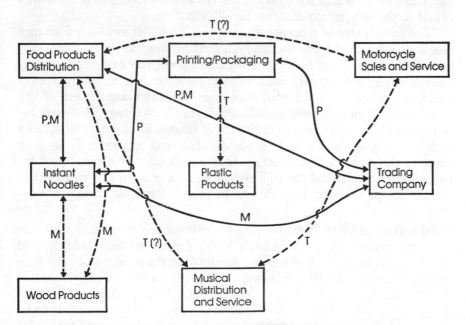

Figure 11.4 Indo Jaya's Jumble of Businesses

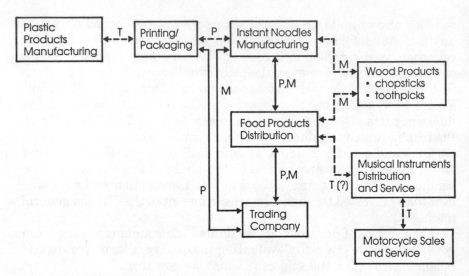

Figure 11.5   Linkage Analysis of PT Indo Jaya

strategy's quality can one know *what elements of strategy should be changed,* and, equally important, *which elements of strategy are sound and should not be altered.* In addition, the evaluation process itself will result in the suggestion of strategic alternatives.

The complexity of a corporation defies its being evaluated on any single dimension. As any security analyst knows, the quality of a corporation's stock must be judged on more than the historical performance of the firm; equally important are the firm's plan for the future and the quality of the internal resources and the management of the corporation. Similarly, one should evaluate the strategy of a corporation by examining it through a variety of lenses. Each lens will give us a different perspective and, possibly, different answers. It is only through the combined perspective that comes from looking at past results, future plans, and the riskiness inherent in a firm's strategy that we can assess the overall quality of the firm's strategic thrust.

Evaluation of Past Results.   Peter Drucker has written that to survive and prosper, firms must both "do things right" (be efficient), and "do the right things" (be effective). Evaluating the past results of a firm tells us whether the firm has been doing things right — it gives us a reading on the quality of past decisions. Looking at the past enables us to be objective about accomplishments, and it also enables us to be precise (since we can see whether specific targets have been met).

To evaluate past performance we can look at the extent to which certain objectives have been attained, and we can look at how well the company has performed in relation to other firms.

In evaluating performance against objectives, we must take a variety of objectives into consideration. We could simply look at management's objectives and see if these have been met. However, if we want to be more rigorous, we will want to look at how well management is meeting the objectives of the corporation's other stakeholders. This is important: not only are the objectives of management sometimes different from those of various other stakeholders, but even the objectives of the various stakeholders can conflict. For example, employees might have a different stake in the business than, say, stockholders or suppliers. Employees might value quality of working life and leisure time, which might reduce the efficiency of the firm, while stockholders might be seeking increased dividends and suppliers might want rapid payment of invoices. In a world of limited resources, satisfying all these demands on the firm's liquidity is clearly a delicate balancing act.

Evaluating performance against objectives is relatively straightforward: one must simply answer the questions "What are your company's major articulated goals?" and "How has your business been performing with respect to these?" The answers to these questions should generate a list of goals and a list of actual results, to which management should attach some score (say, from 0 to 10) that reflects the degree to which that objective has been reached. An example of this has been given in Table 11.6A, which shows the self-evaluation made by the Delta & Delta law firm.

In evaluating performance against stakeholders' objectives one should ask: Who are our major stakeholders? What are their stakes with respect to our business? How well is our strategy meeting these stakes? Some of the stakeholders that might be considered, and some of their possible stakes, are as follows:

Stakeholder	Stake
Stockholders	Dividends, capital appreciation, safety of investment
Customers	Quality of products, variety, reasonable price, reliability, availability, delivery
Employees	Quality of working life, steady employment, decent wages, safety
Management	Career progress, compensation, excitement
Creditors	Timely payment
Suppliers	Timely payment, steady quantity contracts
Community	Clean air, employment, tax base
Government	Same as community (presumably)

Table 11.6   Evaluation of Delta & Delta Strategy

A. What are your company's major articulated goals? (List them.) How has your business been performing with respect to these?

Goal	Results	Score
1. 430,000 billed hours	447,000 hours	10
2. 85% realization rate	83.2%	5
3. 14% net income	15%	10
4. Name recognition	Definitely improved	7
	Summary Evaluation:	⑧

B. Who are your major stakeholders? (List them.) What are their stakes with respect to your business? How well is your strategy meeting these stakes?

Stakeholder	Stakes	Result/Score
Clients	Service satisfaction	8
	Price satisfaction	6
Partners	Compensation	9
	Personal & professional satisfaction	8
	Reputation	6
	Variety of work	4
Employees	Compensation	8
	Development/career/up-mobility QWL	7
Families	Visibility, presence at home (i.e., reasonable work week)	3
	Separate "career" from family	2
Profession	Quality standards	10
	Summary Evaluation:	⑥½

C. Who are your major competitors and potential (growing) competitors? How well is your firm performing compared to them in terms of the criteria listed?

Competitor	D&D Relative Financial Performance	D&D Market Position	D&D Technological Performance	
			People	Products
1. Law firm AB	Lower	Losing position to AB	=	−
2. Big NYC firms	Same	Losing position	=	−
3. 4–5 locals	Better	Gaining	=	+
4. Other locals	Superior	Clobbering		
5.				
Summary:	So-so to OK B	Not so good C −	A	C
Overall:				B/B −

Table 11.6 (continued)

D. How does your strategy "fit" with the major trends and discontinuities
projected for your environment (refer to environmental analysis exercise)?

Trend	Date of Impact	How Does Strategy Match or Mismatch?
1. Increasing computerization	1993	Have portable micros & new mainframe (score = 7)
2. Expanding in-house counsel	1990	Poorly (5)
3. Increased tax practice competition from CPAs		
4.	1993	Badly (3)
5.		

Summary Evaluation: ⑤

E. How well do your company's internal resources or capabilities support
your strategy? Do the following areas represent strengths or weaknesses
with respect to your strategic posture?

Resource Area	Strength or Weakness (Why?)	"Fit" with Strategy

1. Financial	W — Constraint on R&D investment
	W — Less able to subsidize:
	  a. Discounts for new client acquisition
	  b. Overhead (unassigned people)
	  c. Hiring new specialists
		Low

2. Human	S — Strong "care factor" but less loyalty S — Some people willing to do less sophisticated work W — No excess or slack — capacity constraint W — Unwillingness to engage in PD (marketing)	Medium
3. Technological	S — Tax knowledge S — Strong background in banking and automotive industries	High
4. Managerial	W — Lots of worker bees . . . "sole proprietors" . . . not a "team" W — No entrepreneurial skills (e.g., don't read *Inc.* magazine for leads)	Low
5. Other: a. Client base	S — Some prominent firms in area W — Most clients are too small	Medium
a. Reputation	Neither S nor W (has improved to "average")	

Based on the above, generate a statement of your firm's distinctive
competence.

Table 11.6B gives an example of how Delta & Delta evaluated their strategy with respect to their stakeholders' objectives.

The second major way of evaluating performance is one that gauges how well the company has done compared with its direct competitors. In the past, analysts tended to compare a company with its competition by means of a single criterion: financial performance. More recently, research in strategic performance has indicated that other criteria, such as market performance and technological performance, are equally important. The key consideration is, At what stage in an industry's evolution is each criterion most appropriate? In the early stages, many companies attempt to develop their product design to satisfy customer needs and (they hope) set the industry standard. At this stage, technological criteria should dominate the consideration of how well the strategy is performing. In fact, it is quite possible that the overzealous application of financial criteria at this stage will prove to be the death knell for struggling new ventures or new projects.

At the middle stages of an industry's evolution, a company should attempt to grow big enough to establish economies of scale and, subsequently, lower product costs. These lower costs will be important as the industry matures and a shake-out takes place, because those companies which can compete with lower prices are more likely to be survivors than those which are still having difficulty keeping their cost structures in line. After some of the technological questions have been worked out in an industry, competing products start to become very similar and brands begin to compete on price. This shift has become evident, for example, in the home computer industry, where there were a large number of competitors in 1982, each using different operating systems and hardware. By the end of 1983, however, two or three operating systems became standard, and three companies — Apple, IBM, and Commodore — emerged as the industry leaders, while such prominent firms as Texas Instruments and Osborne dropped out when the price competition became more intense than they could handle. So, at the middle stages of industry evolution, criteria such as market share, market penetration, and price leadership become important.

It is not until the final, or mature, stages of an industry's evolution that the more traditional financial criteria become important. At this stage, most products have become fairly standardized and manufacturing technologies have stabilized. Market positions have, by and large, been established, and the surviving firms are competing more along marketing or service dimensions than along technological breakthroughs and product development. At this point it makes sense to evaluate a strategy in terms of return on investment, stock price, return and sales, and other profitability measures.

A straightforward way to evaluate your strategy against those of competitors is to address the following questions: Who are our major competitors and potential competitors? How is our firm performing compared with the others in terms of financial performance, market position, and technological performance? By listing your competitors and comparing your firm along each of the three dimensions, you will produce a picture of how well the firm has been performing against its competition. An example of Delta & Delta's evaluation of its performance compared to relative competitors is given in Table 11.6C.

By evaluating the company's past performance, management will have judged the extent to which a company has been "doing things right," to use Drucker's term. But a look at the past is not sufficient. A firm must also make an assessment of how well the strategy will perform in the future. In this case, we want to look at what Drucker has termed "doing the right things." To make this assessment, we examine the consistency of the strategy along a variety of dimensions.

Tests of Consistency. As we have seen, strategy is a multifaceted set of activities that a company is performing at any given time. In order to assess the degree to which these activities are helping move the company in a healthy and appropriate direction, two tests of consistency must be applied: tests of external consistency, or how well the strategy matches the environment, and tests of internal consistency, or how well the pieces of the strategy are mutually reinforcing. One way to think of the tests of internal and external consistency is to refer to Figure 11.1, where performance was portrayed as the outcome of the firm's "fit" achieved between the firm's strategy, environment, and internal resources.

External consistency is the degree to which the strategy fits the environmental trends that have been identified during the forecasting phase of the strategic management process (upper part of Figure 11.1). In essence, one must ask, "How does our strategy 'fit' with the major environmental trends we have projected? How does the strategy fit with the changing values of the various stakeholders?" (See Table 11.6D for the Delta & Delta example.) When Procter & Gamble assessed the demographic trends indicating a lower birth rate in the United States, it concluded, logically enough, that a continued reliance on the baby market for its Pampers brand disposable diapers was inconsistent with the prevailing trends. However, were we to apply the test of consistency to their present strategy of marketing Pampers to incontinent patients, particularly in rest homes, we would conclude that there is a significant logic to entering a market (basically, the over-sixty-five population) which is expected to grow over the foreseeable future. Similarly, when Sigma Consultants made the assessment that the consulting industry was becoming segmented and that the health care market was emerging as a significant segment, the test of external consistency would have indicated that the present strategy of undifferentiated marketing to all possible client bases was inconsistent with some prevailing trends.

Internal consistency refers to the fit between the strategy and the competences and resources available within the firm, as well as the fit among the functional strategies themselves. At the business level, it is this latter fit among the functional strategies that underlies the concept of synergy.

In order to test the consistency of the strategy with competences and resources, one should return to the resource audit and use it to answer the following questions: How well do our company's resources or capabilities support our strategy? Do they represent strengths or weaknesses with respect to your strategic posture? Here one should list the resources (financial, human, etc.), identify whether and why each resource is a strength or a weakness, and determine whether this resource represents a fit with that company's strategy. An example of Delta & Delta's evaluation of consistency between the business strategy and internal resources is given in Table 11.6E.

To look at the fit of the functional strategies with each other, one should return to the strategy identification procedure and ask, "To what extent do the various functional strategies reinforce each other, or detract from each other?" For example, the case of the Calma Corporation, in which the marketing and R&D strategies were out of synchronization, was cited at the beginning of this chapter. Unfortunately, this example is not unique. As a company increases in complexity, it is not unusual for the various components of the business — their functional departments — to start working at cross-purposes. This is sometimes a result of rewarding different functional managers for different types of behavior. For example, salespeople rewarded according to the volume of sales they generate might strive for sales by making promises to clients that the production department cannot fulfill. Or a production department that is geared toward making standardized products might not be responsive to custom design promises made to customers by salespeople.

Some companies rate high on tests of both internal and external consistency, and these high ratings generally translate into high performance evaluations as well. For example, the Crown Cork and Seal Company thrived financially in what was essentially a commodity industry by managing all of the components of its strategy with precision. By exiting from market segments where decreasing metal can usage was the trend, as in motor oil, and concentrating primarily in the areas where growth was expected (soft drinks and beer), Crown Cork and Seal positioned itself exclusively in the growth part of the market.

Clearly, however, such a shifting of markets is not enough, since the big competitors are free to do the same thing. This is where the internal and external tests of consistency come into play. Traditionally, the only way to differentiate a company in a commodity industry is by price. Crown Cork and Seal, however, differentiated itself from its competition by maintaining excess capacity so that it could meet surges in customer demand, thereby alleviating customers' inventory needs. In addition, the company was alone in providing technical help on customers' production problems, thereby becoming a problem-solver as well as a can-provider. Since it was dealing in such "hard to hold" products as carbonated beverages and aerosols, the problems of packaging these products were considerable. By providing flexibility in delivery as well as technical advice to clients in the growth segment of the can-consuming market, Crown Cork and Seal was able to charge a premium price and avoid the price competition game. The company also followed a "fast second" R&D strategy, in which it would quickly adopt new technological innovations, after allowing other firms to make the initial investment. This made for lower R&D expenditures and, therefore, lower overhead. While Crown Cork and Seal's competitors were using the cash generated by their business to expand into unrelated diversification, Crown Cork and Seal repurchased stock, resulting in steadily increasing earnings-per-share figures.

Note that the marketing strategy of fast delivery and flexibility was consistent with the production strategy of excess capacity; the technical service component of marketing strategy was consistent with the fast-adoption R&D strategy; and the premium price marketing strategy was consistent with the financial strategy of generating sufficient margin to provide the cash for repurchasing stockshares. All of these strategies had a high degree of internal consistency, and all were consistent with the trends in the environment. As a result, Crown Cork and Seal regularly ranked at the top of the industry in financial returns to investors, as well as growth. This company is an example of how (when strategy is uniformly consistent) a firm can become a well-oiled machine that gathers momentum and builds competitive strength. Crown Cork and Seal's position as the leading performer in the metal can industry has been unassailed for the last twenty-six years, an enviable record for any strategic manager.

Evaluation of Strategic Flexibility and Risk. Having addressed the question of how well a company's strategy fits with the external trends of the environment and how well the internal parts of the strategy fit with and reinforce each other, a company should ask where strategy has the most flexibility or inflexibility, and how this translates into a risk profile. For example, a strategy that relies on heavy capital investment and assets that are dedicated to a particular type of product may find itself in a position where it cannot exit from an industry or market if conditions should so warrant. Such has been the case for the American steel industry; the closing of steel mills in many northeastern industrial areas is an indication of this difficulty. In contrast, a company such as Crown Cork and Seal found that it could take its "old" technology for manufacturing tin-plated steel cans and export them to new markets in less developed countries while investing at the same time in the newer aluminum can technology in the United States. Crown Cork and Seal is betting that the market and technological development overseas will lag that of the United States and that whenever domestic conditions warrant, the company will have the flexibility of a "technological rollout" to the overseas locations.

In assessing the flexibility of its strategy, a company should question the degree of risk presented by its strategy. Traditionally, most such discussions have considered whether or not a company is facing financial risk — risk of bankruptcy, illiquidity, or, from the stockholder's standpoint, earnings fluctuations. But this is just one dimension of risk. Other elements that a firm should consider are the degrees to which it is facing business, competitive, and managerial risks.

Business risk refers to the degree to which the company lacks the capability to manufacture and sell a product to present or new markets. It also includes the question of whether there is sufficient customer demand for the product under consideration.

When evaluating a proposed strategy, business risk can also be assessed in terms of the strategy's downside potential and the possible impact of a failing strategy on the firm as a whole. The important dimensions are the strategy's consequentiality, pervasiveness, and revocability. *Consequentiality* refers to the potential negative impact of failure — what is the percentage of corporate funds committed, for example; or how might results affect corporate reputation? IBM's introduction of the personal computer (PC) was a relatively small financial commitment, but failure would certainly have damaged "Big Blue's" corporate image. By contrast, General Motors' decision to downsize its models in the late 1970s had enormous financial consequences because of the extensive retooling required. *Pervasiveness* refers to how much of the firm becomes involved in the strategy. IBM, by relegating the PC effort to a separate organizational unit in Florida, kept pervasiveness low — a failure would be isolated from the firm's core activities. *Revocability* reflects the ability to "back out" if the market for a new business fails to develop as planned. Polaroid's entry into the SX-70 was virtually irreversible, given its large investment in specialized plant and equipment. In contrast, IBM sourced most of its PC components externally and entered the business primarily as an assembler — any single component of the PC strategy was revocable. In sum, one could conclude that the IBM PC strategy had relatively low business risk: IBM had the technical skills, the market was there, and consequentiality, pervasiveness, and irreversibility were all relatively low. IBM's primary risk was to its reputation.

Competitive risk refers to whether the present competition will retaliate against any moves being made or contemplated by the company and, equally important, the likely intensity of this retaliation. For example, when Kodak entered the instant camera market, it had severely underestimated the extent to which Polaroid would retaliate by introducing a barrage of new products at lower prices. Kodak found itself caught in a losing price war, which depressed corporate earnings for a two-year period. The assessment of competitive risk is where strategic planning frequently is deficient. Most companies not only underestimate the extent to which present competitors will move in retaliation against their contemplated strategic moves, but also underestimate the extent to which new entrants from unanticipated corners might crop up.

Managerial risk has two components. First, one must consider whether management has the skills, capability, and longevity to execute a particular strategy. For example, although Crown Cork and Seal was constantly achieving increased earnings per share, its stock price did not show a healthy price/earnings ratio. The primary reason was the age of John Connolly, the company's president. As of 1984, Connolly, at seventy-nine years of age, was still running the firm and had not yet groomed a successor. It is probably this last factor that has heightened analysts' perceptions of managerial risk for the company and has consequently made them leery of Crown Cork and Seal as a long-term investment.

The second aspect of managerial risk relates to management's enthusiasm for a particular strategy, given the values of the top management team. Sometimes an "ideal" strategy can be worked out on paper but, for whatever reason, does not conform to the true predilections of top management and will not be carried out with as much energy as might otherwise be the case. (I will address this aspect of strategy implementation in the next section.)

Having analyzed the quality of a company's strategy, both by looking at past performance against a variety of criteria and applying various tests of consistency, we see that no one technique of strategy evaluation is sufficient, since each approach might yield a different result. For example, a strategy that may have been successful in the past may be ill-equipped to provide healthy returns in the future for any number of reasons. It may be out of sync with the trends in the environment, or management may be approaching retirement age without having groomed successors, or the plant may be aging. The above approaches provide several lenses through which to evaluate a strategy. Management must take all of these evaluations into consideration when making a summary evaluation of the quality of the current strategy. A useful way of summarizing and synthesizing all of these evaluations is to generate a new statement of the firm's distinctive competence and competitive advantage. Having gone through the above analytical steps, management is often able to generate a rich statement of the firm's business definition and its strengths and weaknesses. After completing the strategy evaluation described in this section, Delta & Delta generated the strategy evaluation summary shown in Table 11.7. Notice how the statement encompasses consideration for fit with the external environment, as well as internal resources, and lends some insight into areas that Delta & Delta might wish to address in charting any new strategy.

Cultural Analysis and Corporate Mission

Analysis of Corporate Culture. Anthropologists have long known that the introduction of any new social change can meet with failure if they ignore the culture of the community in which the change is introduced. Managers, however, often think they should formulate a strategy first, and then create the culture and other implementation mechanisms required to implement the strategy. The method introduced here should be used during the strategy formulation process itself in order to allow a firm to assess its own culture and analyze the degree to which that culture will facilitate or hinder the achievement of the proposed strategic alternatives. The ultimate outcome of the analysis is the mutual adjustment of both the strategic alternatives under consideration and some of the management practices and corporate culture elements needed for strategic health.

As in the environmental analysis conducted previously, the analysis of culture involves the various members of the top management team.

Table 11.7 Delta & Delta Strategy Evaluation Summary

Delta & Delta is a profitable firm, but a susceptible one: the loss of one or two key clients could put it in the red. Because of compensation bonus criteria that reward billed time, it often backs off from investing in practice development (marketing). There are talented, marketing-oriented people at all levels who get along, but who are not really "Delta & Delta loyal," although there is a high level of open communication. There is a "run-lean" philosophy that has been a problem and could continue to be one.

It is a tax-oriented office, with above-average skills in the banking, automotive, and manufacturing industries. Client base includes some plums, but not enough to be an asset in getting more. Our reputation has improved; however, it is still sole-proprietor-oriented with few entrepreneurial skills.

The approach engages each manager in a mixture of individual analysis, small-group discussion, and action-planning sessions, allowing both personal and group introspection and critique.

Individual analysis. First, each manager should think about the concept of culture in the context of his organization by listing words or phrases that describe the company's culture. This list could reflect decision-making style, the practices that management follows in transmitting or analyzing information, the social norms of the organization, and the stories told about the company's history that transmit a flavor of "what the company's all about"; or the list might include how managers are compensated and motivated, what kinds of behaviors are encouraged or suppressed, and, generally, the company's values. After preparing this list, the manager should cite evidence that each factor mentioned is indeed an element of his company's culture. This evidence could be in the form of policy statements or simply a description of actual managerial behavior.

Small-group discussion. Next, each manager should share his or her perceptions with other executives, and the group should arrive at some consensus regarding a description of the company's culture. In addition, this step will link the company's culture with the strategic requirements of the environment that have been identified previously. Each group should record its conclusions in two columns. In one column are those elements of their culture that they considered to be out of sync, or a mismatch, with the trends that they had identified in their environment. In the other column are those cultural factors that could be considered supportive or "matched" with the environmental trends and the company's strategy. Essentially, we are here applying tests of external consistency to the corporate culture.

After developing the matches and mismatches, the managers should rank-order the cultural elements within *each* list according to their relative strength. The strongest element — and therefore the one most difficult to change — should receive the rank of 1, the next strongest the rank of 2, and so forth. The purpose of this step is to help management develop an understanding of and appreciation for the difficulties of change. The idea is that a strong corporate culture, like an individual's values, is very difficult to change, whereas relatively weak cultural elements, such as individual attitudes, are more pliable.

Action planning. Once the cultural matches and mismatches have been identified, they must be integrated into an overall program of strategy implementation. This is done through a session on action planning, during which managers should identify those elements of their culture which would be potential candidates for change and which, at a minimum, should be considered potential constraints during the strategy implementation process. This session should also identify those cultural elements which should not be tampered with or which warrant little or no effort in attempts to change them.

As an example of the cultural analysis process, consider the case of Alpha Corporation, an Indonesian subsidiary of a North American basic metals firm. In the Alpha situation, two strong elements of culture were identified in the strategic management process: one a match, the other a mismatch. The executive group had identified a "management education" cultural element as a strong match with their strategic requirements. By this, they meant that the company committed resources to any activity that would improve the knowledge and level of skill of the executive group. For example, the chief financial officer had conducted tutorials in management accounting.

The strongest cultural mismatch that the executives identified was what they termed a "please-the-boss" culture. The executives perceived this to be a strong mismatch with an increasingly competitive environment because they knew from experience that if the executives were shielded from the unvarnished truth, poor decisions would be made.

During the final phase of strategic analysis, Alpha examined the various elements of its corporate culture to determine which could be relied upon to facilitate strategic change and which would inhibit it. This examination included a detailed discussion of each of the cultural elements identified earlier and the need to change some elements, given the overall strategic opportunities that were seen for the firm. This was a critical section of the strategy analysis. As Alpha's executives developed the various strategic alternatives, they repeatedly returned to the cultural elements to see if these elements were consistent with the strategic action being considered. The executives were particularly interested in the "please the boss" cultural element and its impact on several of the strategic alternatives that were presented. But, when asked whether this was an element that they should consider working on in the future, their response was a surprising no. Why would an organization not wish to work on that aspect of culture that it had identified as the severest mismatch with the changing trends in their environment — especially since it was an organization committed to learning new concepts and management skills and techniques?

The answer was quite simple. During the analysis of the environmental trends, a factor that had been highlighted was that Indonesia had been a Dutch colony until 1949, when it became an independent nation. Each of Alpha's Indonesian managers had grown up under Dutch rule. The period of colonialization had engendered an attitude of "tell the persons in charge what they want to hear, even if it's not always the truth." Alpha's managers believed that the next generation of Indonesian managers, who would have grown up under independence, would have considerably different outlooks on life-style and work-related questions, and that they would probably not harbor the "please the boss" attitude. Consequently, the group decided to recognize the implications of "please the boss" in their current attempts to formulate strategy. But, in addition, they felt that the amount of time it would take to change this element of culture was almost equivalent to the amount of time that would pass before the next generation of managers was running the company anyway. Therefore, it was their view that the natural forces at work in the environment made any concerted attempt to change internal culture unnecessary. They concluded that their best strategy was to focus instead on some of the other strategic tasks ahead of them.

Creating a Mission Statement.   Whereas corporate cultures at the division level can reflect the domain navigation activities and strategies of the various businesses in the corporation, and can therefore be quite distinct from each other, corporate management usually tends to hold a prevailing set of values that will reflect the mission of the corporation.

Corporate ideology — or management values — is that set of assumptions and guidelines which influences how management thinks about the future and how it directs the daily activities of the corporation. Often, they are not explicitly articulated, although some firms, such as Hewlett-Packard, have been able to crystallize their values and translate them into a statement of corporate creed. However, many companies publish a so-called corporate creed that reflects an idealized version of what the company should stand for or else states certain platitudes that are not explicit guides to action. For example, many companies make statements about the need to be responsive to the community and to employees while serving the interests of stockholders. These principles are worthy but vague; they do not really indicate what the company's mission is. The procedure described here is designed to reveal the basic ideology of the firm and to state it in operational terms. The outcome serves as a mission statement for management.

The recommended procedure is as follows. First, management should set aside for the moment any existing statement or publication regarding corporate creed or mission. What you want to do is crystallize the corporate ideology and develop a consensus around the bare minimum number of guidelines. In order to do that, you and your top management should produce a list of what you consider to be the "ten commandments" your company uses to guide corporate behavior. Assume that immediately upon issuing these commandments, you (and/or top management) will be isolated on a desert island for two years. You should feel that, once issued, these guidelines will provide sufficient direction for the firm's decisions, such that all decisions made in your absence will be regarded as acceptable, as long as they satisfy the guidelines.

Now, most managers will find that a list of ten is much too short to encompass what they think is basic to corporate behavior. However, as Ian MacMillan of New York University states, "If the God of Moses can condense his set of principles to a list of ten, and if the framers of our constitution were satisfied with a bill of ten rights, then any corporate executive should be able to do the same with his or her firm."

Managers often would prefer to state their commandments in a manner that reflects how they wish their company would behave rather than the actual set of values guiding the firm. To provide a reality check on your initial list of ten commandments, list three to five of the most important decisions made by the corporation in the last five years. Then try to determine which of the listed commandments relate to those actual decisions. If there is any decision that cannot be linked to a commandment, perhaps the list of commandments should be amended to reflect reality better.

As an example of the commandments of one firm we have been following, Table 11.8 shows some of the selected commandments of Sigma Consultants. Notice that the commandments reflect a combination of value statements, managerial style, and strategy statements. For example, marketing strategy is reflected in the commandment that the company will take any business that comes in over the transom, and

Table 11.8 Selected Commandments of Sigma Consultants

1. The consultant is king; he or she is the firm's key resource and shall be treated as a professional.

2. No bureaucratic hierarchy shall be imposed upon the professional staff.

3. Work on projects is by invitation, not by assignment from above. (Consultants are free to decline invitations, subject to commandment 4.)

4. Time is money. (Staff should stay at least 82 percent billable. I.e., up to 18 percent of chargeable time can be devoted to prospecting, personal development, etc.)

5. We will sell anything to anybody. (We will accept any interesting problem-solving assignment that comes in over the transom, as long as a staff member is willing to spearhead it).

                    .

                    .

                    .

                    .

10. Keep work fun as well as profitable.

an administrative value statement is reflected in the commandment that there should be no hierarchy or bureaucracy.

Implementing Strategic Change. Having articulated the company's ideology, the firm is now ready to approach the final stage of strategy analysis. At this point, management will have considered all the important strategic elements and can now begin to pinpoint the areas that need to be changed and the areas that need to be sustained for future strategic advantage. The question often arises, however, of how a strategy should begin to be implemented. Here is where the ten commandments can be of use.

First, consider which of the commandments should be attacked first, if change is in order. Note that the minute one commandment is addressed, another might be affected. For example, if Sigma Consultants were to decide to develop a more focused marketing strategy in order to pursue the health care business, then commandment 5 should be amended to state, "We will accept any assignment that comes in, *and* we will target a sales effort in the health care business." In order to do that effectively, Sigma Consultants might have to establish a separate administrative unit to handle just the health care business. Since this would violate the prevailing corporate culture and ideology, it is possible that the only way to implement this kind of strategic change would be to set up a separate administrative unit to handle this line of business. Clearly, this unit would have to be staffed voluntarily by those professionals in the firm who are already predisposed to pursue health care consulting. Perhaps, in the Sigma case, it is only by isolating a separate administrative unit with its own set of strategies and values, or corporate culture, that this kind of strategic thrust can succeed. Such an arrangement is not unusual. For example, when IBM decided to pursue the personal computer business, it set up an entirely separate administrative unit in Boca Raton, Florida, in order to develop the product and pursue its own marketing strategy. In the words of John Carey, the president of IBM at the time, "We had to set up a bureaucratic mechanism to protect the new venture from the bureaucracy."

In selecting a place to start implementing strategic change, a few principles can serve as useful guidelines:

1. *Initiate those changes which require the least amount of change* from prior behaviors or that require only minor adaptations to the current way of operating. For example, a move from a profit-centered, divisional organizational to investment centers, where performance evaluation is based on return on assets as well as return on sales, would imply a much less dramatic shift than one from functional departments to divisions. In the case of Sigma Consultants, the move from a loosely structured system to, perhaps, a task force with part-time responsibility for health care, would be a smaller step in the direction of a new strategy than would be implied by an entirely new administrative unit.

2. *Choose changes that are the least systemic.* This means that a strategic move that affects a part of the organization is preferable to one that affects the entire organization. For example, many firms have experienced an information system or payroll system disaster when a computerized system is adopted company-wide, rather than pilot-testing it in a small segment of the organization.

3. *Institute changes where there are some clearly identifiable champions.* In this case, one should attempt to initiate strategic change that has already been proposed by committed managers at lower levels of the organization. In such a situation, energy for implementation has already been expended, and the implementation of the strategy can be concluded far more successfully.

4. *Get some early, visible wins.* It is always beneficial to initiate strategic change in parts of the organization that are best equipped to succeed and that are more likely to be seen by the rest of the corporation.

A successful early win by a visible part of the corporation provides what is known as a demonstration effect. If one division sees another division of the corporation earning above-average profits that are the result of some strategic changes, it is far easier to persuade the remaining divisions to adopt whatever change was tried in the pilot attempt.

The modern concepts and methods of strategic management have now been covered. By going through the strategic management steps outlined here, management will secure an understanding of and appreciation for the trends in its external environment, the strengths and weaknesses of its organization, the quality of its current strategy, and the nature of its corporate culture and ideology; in the process, it will identify some potential strategic redirections and evaluate the efficacy of these. It will identify logical places to begin to implement strategic change. And it will evaluate the culture of the corporation early in the process in order to facilitate implementation of the strategy.

LOOKING AHEAD

Strategic planning tools have developed enormously over the past twenty years. Such techniques as the growth/share matrix and the experience curve are in widespread use, and other planning techniques allow the manager to evaluate the impact of alternative strategies on the stock price of the corporation. Management consulting firms offer strategic planning on a commodity basis, and any new M.B.A. comes equipped with at least one method for developing such plans.

Unfortunately, the tools for implementing strategies have not developed as quickly as the tools we use for planning. Recently, however, business writers have begun to pay more attention to the problems of implementation. Corporate culture is now widely acknowledged as an important force in the success or failure of business ventures; studies of Japanese management practices point out the effectiveness of participative methods in securing wholehearted commitment to new strategies at all levels of the organization.

Research shows that managers do not analyze opportunities exhaustively before taking action; rather, they shape strategy through a continuing stream of individual decisions and actions. How can we reconcile the static academic dogma "First formulate strategy, then implement it" with the dynamic reality of managerial work?

This chapter has shed some light on how the planning process can be managed so that the strategies that emerge are realistic, not only in terms of the marketplace, but also in terms of the politics, culture, and competence of the organization. It has also addressed the question of how strategic intentions can be converted into action by taking the implementability of alternatives into account during the strategy formulation process itself. (There is also a fairly large body of literature that addresses the issue of how to initiate large-scale organizational change if present administrative arrangements are not appropriate for the new strategy. See Chapter 8, "Organizational Development.")

A third issue — shaping strategy as it develops within the firm — is the issue of the future.

Strategy Implementation as Internal Corporate Venturing

Although much of the current attention in strategic management is captured by the thorny issues of improving the feasibility or implementability of strategic plans and translating strategy into action, what is beginning to emerge in the consciousness of corporate America is a concern for entrepreneurship and strategic renewal within our major corporations. This has been fostered both by the perceived failures of strategic planning efforts per se and by increasingly successful foreign competition.

In addition, as corporations grow in size and diversity, headquarters executives are increasingly unable to know and understand all of the strategic and operating situations facing their various divisions. Instead, senior executives are recognizing that much of their time is spent responding to strategic initiatives coming up from the divisions, not crafting strategies from above. This, of course, reflects the fact that (1) headquarters cannot perceive all of the opportunities facing the corporation — top management does not interact daily with the many-faceted world of customers, suppliers, manufacturing, and sales — and (2) good managers are naturally inclined to develop opportunities as they encounter them in the course of their day-to-day management.

Recent research indicates that most corporate innovation comes from experimentation on the firing line, not from centralized strategic planning. So the strategic question is becoming not "How do I craft a detailed and economically ideal strategy?" but "How do I encourage managers to come forward as champions of sound strategies?" Note that this entails a shift from what might be termed analytical planning to the development and maintenance of innovative capability in the organization. The latter might be termed *crescive strategic management* since it involves "growing" strategy from within the firm (*crescive* derives from the Latin *crescere,* "to grow").

Given a top management that recognizes the limitations of centralized control and wants to harness and exploit the initiatives taken at lower levels, the job of the strategic manager becomes one of encouraging and fostering a vigorous pace of innovation within the firm. But in order to prevent resource-consuming fiascos, he or she must also devise and successfully employ an effective filter for screening out inappropriate or ill-conceived programs. This is a delicate balancing act between initiative and control. How can the strategic manager of the 1980s accomplish it? The answer to this question is, I believe, the key to the next generation of strategic management.

SUGGESTED READINGS

Andrews, Kenneth R. *The Concept of Corporate Strategy.* Homewood, Ill.: Dow Jones–Irwin, 1971.

Gluck, Frederick W., S. P. Kaufman, and A. S. Walleck. "Strategic Management for Competitive Advantage." *Harvard Business Review* 58, no. 4 (July–August 1980).

Haspeslagh, Philippe. "Portfolio Planning: Uses and Limits." *Harvard Business Review* 60, no. 1 (January–February 1982): 58–73.

Mintzberg, Henry. "Strategy-Making in Three Modes." *California Management Review* 15, no. 2 (Winter 1973): 44–53.

Pearce, John A., and Richard B. Robinson, Jr. *Formulation and Implementation of Competitive Strategy.* Homewood, Ill.: Richard D. Irwin, 1982.

Porter, Michael E. *Competitive Strategy.* New York: Free Press, 1980.

Quinn, James Brian. *Strategies for Change: Logical Incrementalism.* Homewood, Ill.: Richard D. Irwin, 1980.

Schwartz, Howard, and Stanley M. Davis. "Matching Corporate Culture and Business Strategy." *Organization Dynamics,* Summer 1981.

Thomas, Dan R. E. "Evaluating a Business Strategy." Stanford Business School Working Paper, 1979.

Tilles, Seymour. "How to Evaluate Corporate Strategy." *Harvard Business Review* (July–August 1963).

Index